AF793183

The Invisible Hand(out)

CRITICAL FRONTIERS OF THEORY, RESEARCH, AND POLICY IN INTERNATIONAL DEVELOPMENT STUDIES

Series Editors
Andrew Fischer, Naomi Hossain, Briony Jones, Alfredo Saad Filho, Benjamin Selwyn, and Fiona Tregenna
The contemporary world is characterized by massive wealth alongside widespread poverty, inequality, and environmental destruction---all bound up through class, race, and gender dynamics of inequality and oppression.

Critical Frontiers of Theory, Research, and Policy in International Development Studies, the official book series of the Development Studies Association of the UK, was established to contribute to critical thinking about local, national, and global processes of structural transformation. The series publishes cutting-edge monographs that promote critical development studies as an interdisciplinary and applied field and shape the theory, practice, and teaching of international development for a new generation of scholars, students, and practitioners. As the series evolves, we wish to publish a diverse and inclusive range of authors whose work engages in critical, multidisciplinary, decolonial, and methodologically plural development studies.

Recently published in the series

The Rise and Fall of Neoliberal Rentier Capitalism

The Political Economy of the 20th and 21st Centuries
Luiz Carlos Bresser-Pereira

Politics and the Urban Frontier

Transformation and Divergence in Late Urbanizing East Africa
Tom Goodfellow

The Spectre of State Capitalism

Ilias Alami, Adam D. Dixon

Business of the State

Why State Ownership Matters for Resource Governance
Jewellord T. Nem Singh

Disrupted Development in the Congo

The Fragile Foundations of the African Mining Consensus
Ben Radley

Politics and the Urban Frontier

Transformation and Divergence in Late Urbanizing East Africa
Tom Goodfellow

Equity, Evaluation, and International Cooperation

In Pursuit of Proximate Peers in an African City
Gabriella Y. Carolini

They Eat Our Sweat

Transport Labor, Corruption, and Everyday Survival in Urban Nigeria
Daniel E. Agbiboa

The Invisible Hand(out)

Aid, Trade, and Unequal Globalization

Samuel Brazys

OXFORD
UNIVERSITY PRESS

OXFORD
UNIVERSITY PRESS

Great Clarendon Street, Oxford, OX2 6DP,
United Kingdom

Oxford University Press is a department of the University of Oxford.
It furthers the University's objective of excellence in research, scholarship,
and education by publishing worldwide. Oxford is a registered trade mark of
Oxford University Press in the UK and in certain other countries

© Samuel Brazys 2025

The moral rights of the author have been asserted.

All rights reserved. No part of this publication may be reproduced, stored in a retrieval system, transmitted, used for text and data mining, or used for training artificial intelligence, in any form or by any means, without the prior permission in writing of Oxford University Press, or as expressly permitted by law, by licence or under terms agreed with the appropriate reprographics rights organization. Enquiries concerning reproduction outside the scope of the above should be sent to the Rights Department, Oxford University Press, at the address above.

You must not circulate this work in any other form
and you must impose this same condition on any acquirer.

Published in the United States of America by Oxford University Press
198 Madison Avenue, New York, NY 10016, United States of America

British Library Cataloguing in Publication Data
Data available

Library of Congress Control Number: 2025932804

ISBN 9780198970439

DOI: 10.1093/9780198970422.001.0001

Printed and bound by
CPI Group (UK) Ltd, Croydon, CR0 4YY

Links to third party websites are provided by Oxford in good faith and
for information only. Oxford disclaims any responsibility for the materials
contained in any third party website referenced in this work.

MIX
Paper | Supporting
responsible forestry
FSC® C013604
FSC
www.fsc.org

The manufacturer's authorised representative in the EU for product safety is Oxford University Press España S.A. of El Parque Empresarial San Fernando de Henares, Avenida de Castilla, 2 – 28830 Madrid (www.oup.es/en or product.safety@oup.com). OUP España S.A. also acts as importer into Spain of products made by the manufacturer.

Preface

This book's origins can be traced to the seminar room at 513 N. Park Avenue in Bloomington, Indiana and a paper for Y673, "Institutional Analysis and Development," with Elinor Ostrom in the autumn of 2006. "Aid for Trade" seemed an apt topic given my intent to study International Political Economy and the straightforward idea of evaluating if aid could impact exports. Little did I know that innocuous seminar paper would develop into my first peer-reviewed manuscript and ultimately send me on an 18-year journey across five continents first as a student, then a practitioner, then an academic (and back to a practitioner again!). Along the way, my thinking on aid, trade, and development has radically evolved as I've been exposed to new people, ideas, and experiences. I have been lucky to have received an immense reserve of financial, intellectual, and emotional support along the way. At times I wasn't sure if the work would coalesce into a book project, but I think in the end there is a coherent story to tell. In some respects, my thinking has become more cynical as I've observed the waste, obfuscation, and irrationality of aid and trade efforts. But at the same time, I've also been incredibly inspired by the development practitioners, small business owners, and government bureaucrats that have forged successes through determination and ingenuity, even when the deck has seemed stacked against them. More than anything, my journey has taught me how much I have yet to learn and that, as Lin told us all those years ago in the seminar room, there are "no panaceas."

Acknowledgments

Any book that takes 18 years to germinate leaves a vast debt of obligation and gratitude in its wake. To the late Elinor Ostrom, Karen Rasler, Jeff Hart, and all my other supervisors and instructors at Indiana University, I owe an immense intellectual debt. I am forever grateful to the AidData team at the College of William & Mary, without whose vision and efforts the data which underlies so much of my work would not exist. Special acknowledgment must be made to my mentor and friend, Mike Tierney, of whose incredible generosity and enthusiasm I am only but one of many recipients. I could not have been luckier than to have landed at University College Dublin for my academic career, where I have found intellectual and financial backing as well as a brilliant and supportive group of colleagues, many of whom I have been fortunate to write with, especially Alex Dukalskis, Jos Elkink, and Krishna Vadlamannati, who each worked with me on projects directly related to this book. Without the financial support of the Irish Research Council, I would have been unable to conduct many of the studies which add depth to this book, especially my work in Bangladesh where I had the good fortune to collaborate with the always insightful Minhaj Mahmud and in Colombia where I was able to work with the brilliant Carolina Urrego-Sandoval. To my many friends and colleagues in the Federated States of Micronesia, and especially my good friend Kemsky Sigrah, thank you for letting me work with you and for opening my eyes to so many realities of development that I otherwise would not have had the privilege to see. To the countless colleagues, both anonymous and not, who have provided feedback on aspects of this work over the years, I am incredibly grateful for your time and attention in making this work better. I especially want to acknowledge Lindsay Dolan, Axel Dreher, Alice Iannantuoni, Christopher Kilby, Silvia Marchesi, Bernhard Reinsberg, Haley Swedlund, Jen Tobin, Kate Weaver, and Matt Winters who gifted a weekend of their time to workshop an early draft of this book. To the army of research assistants, PhD students, and post-doctoral researchers who have worked with me on this project, especially Doris Aja-Eke and Arya Pillai, this wouldn't have been possible without you. Finally, to my wife Jamie and our children Luisne, Eibhlin, and Seamus, whose support and inspiration made all the difference, thank you.

Contents

List of Figures

List of Tables

List of Boxes

List of Acronyms

ACP	Africa, Caribbean and Pacific
ADB	Asian Development Bank
AfT	Aid for Trade
AGOA	Africa Growth and Opportunity Act
AIMS	Aid Information Management System
AoA	Agreement on Agriculture
AMRATA	Agribusiness Market and Support Activity
APEC	Asia-Pacific Economic Community
ASEAN	Association of Southeast Asia Nations
ATC	Agreement on Textiles and Clothing
BRI	Belt and Road Initiative
BTA	Bilateral Trade Agreement
CAP	Common Agricultural Policy
CBD	China Development Bank
CCP	Chinese Communist Party
CNMI	Commonwealth of the Northern Mariana Islands
Comecon	Council of Mutual Economic Assistance
CPTPP	Comprehensive and Progressive Agreement for Trans-Pacific Partnership
DAC	Development Assistance Committee
DOI	Department of the Interior
DRC	Democratic Republic of the Congo
EAEU	Eurasian Economic Union
EBA	Everything But Arms
EDF	European Development Fund
EFTA	European Free Trade Association
ELG	Export-led Growth
EPA	Economic Partnership Agreement
EPB	Export Promotion Bureau
EU	European Union
FAS	Freely Associated States
FSM	Federated States of Micronesia
FTA	Free Trade Agreement
GAO	General Accounting Office
GATT	General Agreement on Tariffs and Trade
GBS	General Budget Support
GDP	Gross Domestic Product
GNI	Gross National Income
GoV	Government of Vietnam
GSP	Generalized System of Preferences

HS	Harmonized Schedule
HTS	Harmonized Tariff Schedule
HTSUS	Harmonized Tariff Schedule of the United States
IBRD	International Bank for Reconstruction and Development
ICBC	Industrial and Commercial Bank of China
ICBG	International Cooperative Biodiversity Group
IDA	International Development Association
ILO	International Labor Organization
IMF	International Monetary Fund
ISI	Import-Substitution Industrialization
ITO	International Trade Organization
JICA	Japan International Cooperation Agency
JCRP	Joint Committee on Compact Review and Planning
JEMCO	Joint Economic Management Committee
KKN	*Korrupsi, Kollusi, Nepotisme*
LDC	Least Developed Country
LMIC	Lower Middle-Income Country
LNA	Large-N Analysis
MDB	Multilateral Development Bank
METI	Ministry of Economy, Trade and Industry
MFA	Multi-fiber Agreement
MFN	Most Favored Nation
MNC	Multi-National Corporation
MOF	Ministry of Finance
MOFA	Ministry of Foreign Affairs
MPI	Ministry of Planning and Investment
NAFTA	North American Free Trade Agreement
NAM	Non-aligned Movement
NGO	Non-governmental Organization
NICC	Nikkeiren International Cooperation Center
NNTT	New New Trade Theory
NT	National Treatment
NTB	Non-tariff Barrier
NTFC	National Trade Facilitation Committee
NTR	Normal Trade Relations
NTT	New Trade Theory
ODA	Official Development Assistance
ODI	Overseas Development Institute
OECD	Organization for Economic Co-operation and Development
O&M	Operation and Maintenance
PACER	Pacific Agreement on Closer Economic Relations
POW-MIA	Prisoner of War-Missing in Action
PPP	Purchasing Power Parity
PRC	People's Republic of China
PTA	Preferential Trade Agreement
RCT	Randomized Control Trial

RMG	Reade Made Garment
RMI	Republic of the Marshall Islands
ROO	Rules of Origin
RTA	Regional Trade Agreement
SAP	Structural Adjustment Program
SAFTA	South Asian Free Trade Agreement
SAPTA	South Asian Preferential Trade Agreement
SBOC	Statistics, Budget, Overseas Development, and Compact Management
SBS	Sector Budget Support
SME	Small and Medium Enterprises
SNA	Small-N Analysis
SPARTECA	South Pacific Regional Trade and Economic Cooperation Agreement
SPS	Sanitary and Phyto-sanitary Measures
STAR	Support for Trade Acceleration
STEP	Special Terms for Economic Program
TBT	Technical Barriers to Trade
TEA	Trade Effective Aid
TIFA	Trade and Investment Facilitation Agreement
TNC	Trans-national Corporation
TVET	Technical and Vocational Education and Training
TWEA	Trading With the Enemy Act
UNCTAD	United Nations Conference on Trade and Development
UNESCO	United National Educational, Scientific and Cultural Organization
UNGA	United Nations General Assembly
UNSC	United Nations Security Council
UMIC	Upper Middle-Income Country
US	United States
USAID	United States Agency for International Development
USSR	Union of Soviet Socialist Republics
VCP	Vietnamese Communist Party
VER	Voluntary Export Restraint
WASH	Water, Sanitation and Hygiene
WB	World Bank
WCO	World Customs Organization
WTO	World Trade Organization

1

The Invisible Hand(out)

The Great Divergence

The year is 1985. Numerous events have recently rocked the developing world. A decade of financial turmoil brought on by the collapse of the gold standard, the Arab Oil Embargo, sky-high interest rates driven by the Paul Volker-led Federal Reserve, and Structural Adjustment Programs (SAPs) being implemented by the World Bank and International Monetary Fund. Many developing countries are mired in the middle of what will become known as the "lost decade" of little or no growth.

However, the world is about to embark on 35 years of remarkable expansion, driven by the forces of financial and economic globalization. While tempered by financial crises in the late 1990s and 2000s, global living standards for billions of people will reach unprecedented levels by the time of the onset of a global pandemic in early 2020. The intervening 35 years will have seen hundreds of millions of people lifted from abject poverty, and scores of nations will have transitioned from subsistence societies to economies that reap the benefits of global markets. In many ways, this time-period represents a development miracle. The prospect of abolishing extreme poverty across the globe will appear tantalizing close.

But the rising tide of economic globalization has not lifted all boats equally, or at all. This is illustrated through the example of five countries, displayed in Table 1.1. In 1985, they share an average per capita income that hovers near the World Bank's threshold for extreme poverty of $1.90 per person, per day.[1] Yet, 35 years later, only one of these countries (Country "E") has surpassed the cutoff for upper-middle income countries which stands at $5.50 per day. Country "A" has reached lower-middle income status at $3.20 per day, Country "B" falls just shy of this mark and the final two—Countries "C" and "D" have failed to climb out of extreme poverty.

These selected countries do not only illustrate the divergent paths that developing countries have taken since the mid-1980s. These disparities date

[1] In 2011 terms.

The Invisible Hand(out). Samuel Brazys, Oxford University Press. © Samuel Brazys (2025).
DOI: 10.1093/9780198970422.003.0001

Table 1.1 The great divergence of per capita income per day4[a]

Country	Income (1985)	Income (2020)	V-dem Rank	Polity Rank	WGI Rank
A	$1.41	$4.67	65	77	37
B	$0.89	$2.75	69	85	45
C	$1.95	$1.17	47	65	9
D	$0.89	$1.52	63	76	79
E	$1.33	$6.63	71	15	71
World	$14.74	$25.71	182	178	214

[a]World Bank. (2012). *World Development Indicators 2012*. The World Bank; Lindberg, S. I., Coppedge, M., Gerring, J., and Teorell, J. (2014). V-Dem: A new way to measure democracy. *Journal of Democracy*, *25*(3), 159–169; Marshall, M. G., Gurr, T. R., and Jaggers, K. (2020). Center for Systemic Peace. *Polity V Project*; World Bank Group, Kaufmann, D., Kraay, A., and Mastruzzi, M. (2010). *Worldwide Governance Indicators*. World Bank Group.

to the restructuring of the global economic system following the end of World War II. Despite record levels of global growth, and the highest living standards in human history, in 2020 the world remains a deeply unequal place. Some countries have seen spectacular economic growth, jumping from a state of impoverishment to economic prosperity in the space of a generation or two. Others have languished, developing at an anemic pace, or even seeing their material wealth falter and regress. The economic gains of the globalization era are unequal.

What explains this divergence? Two seminal works, the 2000 article "Aid, Policies and Growth" in the *American Economic Review* by Craig Burnside and David Dollar; and the 2013 monograph by Daron Acemoglu and James Robinson, "Why Nations Fail" place much of the answer at the feet of the institutions in the developing country.[2] In short, countries that are well governed succeed, while those that are not fail to achieve sustainable development. Yet, the table above suggests that this explanation cannot account for all of the variation in development outcomes. Each of the countries "A–E" above ranks roughly in the bottom half to bottom third across a range of different metrics of governance averaged over the time periods of each indicator. These metrics include the Varieties of Democracy (V-dem) measure of the quality of democratic institutions and civil society, the Polity V gauge of authoritarian and democratic governance, and the World Governance Indicators (WGIs), which capture features including the control of corruption, the effectiveness

[2] Burnside, C. and Dollar, D. (2000). Aid, policies, and growth. *American Economic Review*, 90(4), 847–868; Acemoglu, D. and Robinson, J. A. (2013). Why Nations Fail: The Origins of Power, Prosperity, and Poverty. Currency.

of government, political stability, regulatory quality, the rule of law, and the degree of voice and accountability.

Take, for example, Country "E," which is ranked 15th worst globally in terms of their average Polity measure of democracy and authoritarianism and ranked in the bottom half of countries for both the V-dem and WGI scores. By 2020, "E" had achieved the highest income and most impressive overall growth of any country in the group. Likewise, country "A," the second highest achiever, ranked second worst (37th) in the WGI scores and, again, in the bottom half of the V-dem and Polity scores. In contrast, neither country "B" nor country "D" lived up to the growth of "E" or "A," and, despite starting from an identical income level, country "B" outstripped the growth of country "D" despite very similar rankings across the governance measures.

While only meant to be illustrative, this sample of countries highlights that governance quality does not appear to be a catch-all for explaining why some countries succeed more so than others. The best performer, Country "E," is Vietnam. Following the end of the Vietnam War in 1975, the country was economically devastated and cut off from Western economies. Yet, in the 35 years since 1985, the country has developed remarkably, despite having one of the most authoritarian regimes on the planet and overall institutional and governance quality which is no better than middle of the pack. Likewise, country "A," Bangladesh, only achieved independence in late 1971 and was still mired in extreme poverty as of 1985. However, Bangladesh also has achieved this strong growth as neither a paragon of democracy nor good governance.

In contrast, and despite average governance that is not markedly worse than Vietnam or Bangladesh, Nepal (country "B"), and Malawi (country "D"), failed to develop to the same level. As of 2020, Malawi was still below the extreme poverty threshold on a daily per capita basis. In comparison to Vietnam and Bangladesh, both of these countries are comparatively smaller and landlocked. However, having a coastline did little for Mozambique, Malawi's larger neighbor. Mozambique is similarly situated in terms of WGI (74th), Polity (75th), and V-dem (59th) but also had Gross Domestic Product (GDP) per capita of only $1.07 in 2020, a decrease from $1.23 in 1991 (the first year of data availability). Likewise, Nepal's mountainous neighbor, Bhutan, had a daily per capita income that jumped from $2.01 in 1985 to $7.15 in 2020 despite being similarly small and landlocked.

In this book, I argue that the focus on the importance of domestic institutions only tells part of the story for the great divergence in outcomes for developing countries in the era of economic globalization. Certainly, the cherry-picked examples above do not and are not intended to disprove the contention that domestic institutions matter for development. Indeed, the poorest performing country in Table 1.1, country "C," has an atrocious ranking (ninth worst) in the WGIs and the worst in V-dem of all the countries in the sample. This country, the Central African Republic, has faced nearly continuous internal conflict and political strife and, in 2023, was ranked as the eighth most fragile state globally, sandwiched between Sudan and Chad.[3] It serves well as a confirmatory case of the domestic institutions' thesis. Indeed, a number of the absolute worst states on the various governance measures—the Democratic Republic of the Congo, Afghanistan, Sudan, North Korea, Turkmenistan—are also those states that have experienced the worst economic performance over the past 35 years. But outside the scope of these extreme cases, how well does the institutional explanation for development hold up?

Accordingly, while recognizing that good governance may be an important catalyst for export-led growth in a globalized world, on its own it is neither a necessary nor sufficient factor. While the lack of solid domestic institutions may go a long way in explaining the experiences of the countries at the very bottom, that thesis loses traction in sorting out the divergent experiences of some of those countries in the middle of the pack. Why does Vietnam succeed where Mozambique fails? Why does Nepal struggle to get its head above the poverty line, while Bhutan or Bangladesh surge ahead? Something else is going on.

This book argues that at least a partial answer lies in the extent to which different countries have been able to take advantage of export-led growth in a globalized economy. As the world economy became increasingly integrated throughout the late 20th and early 21st centuries, the countries that succeeded in achieving growth were those that had the tools and the access to take advantage of an interconnected global economy. Tools include the physical and human infrastructure needed to produce and compete effectively in a global economy. In many instances, those tools can be built using funding provided in the form of foreign aid. Likewise, access entails both the ability to procure production materials and to send goods and services to overseas markets. However, aid and market access do not fall randomly like development manna from heaven. The distribution of the right mixture of aid and market access to fully take advantage of globalization is politically determined.

Developing countries that have successfully pursued export-led growth strategies in an era of increasing globalization have been able to do so because of both political and economic considerations. Export success is driven by

[3] https://fragilestatesindex.org/country-data/ (accessed 24-10-2023).

firms that are able to send their wares to meaningful external markets and whose production is supported by the necessary domestic public goods and physical and human capital. While the capacity to identify and develop those public goods largely rests with domestic government, the financing may often come from external partners. Likewise, external partners are always responsible for the provision of market access. Developing countries' success in securing this aid and market access will depend on the extent that country is economically or strategically important to a developed country partner and the extent to which that importance can overcome any domestic opposition in the developed country.

The book will develop an argument that both *tools* and *access* are needed for export-led growth but will also show that they are, at times, treated more as substitutes than complements by donor countries. Rich countries that have balked at providing broad or deep market access have tended to compensate by offering resources like development assistance. Yet in the absence of meaningful market access, this development assistance will not work. Likewise, market access, without the physical and human capital to exploit it, will be doomed to failure. Finally, the integrated nature of the global economy implies that the development haves may benefit at the expense of the have nots. Thus, the provision of tools and access to some may have spillover effects for others. Growth in one country may come at the expense of another.

This book focuses on building and providing evidence for a theoretical argument to at least partially explain unequal export-led growth in the post-war era. Importantly, this book focuses on economic growth as measured by per capita income. This is an imperfect metric and is not wholly substitutable for broader conceptualizations of "development" which may place more emphasis on freedom, equality, human development, or environmental sustainability.[4] While higher income levels are generally associated with freer and fairer societies which emphasize human and environmental rights, these correlations are not perfect. The core claim of the book is that developing countries need both aid and access to achieve export-led growth and benefit from economic globalization. However, in order for this combination to bear fruit, the aid must be effective, and the market access must be meaningful. The ability to secure these goods is a function of the international and domestic politics of both the developing countries and their developed country partners.

[4] Macekura, S. J. (2020). *The Mismeasure of Progress: Economic Growth and Its Critics*. University of Chicago Press.

Market Access—The Invisible Hand

"Export led growth" has been one mantra trumpeted for development success since the end of World War II. Observing the miraculous development success of the East Asian "Tigers" Taiwan, Singapore, Hong Kong, and South Korea, development specialists the world over saw investment in human and physical capital, at times with state-led interventions, and a sufficiently open and outward-facing growth policy as the key to replicating the efforts that moved these jurisdictions from poverty to riches in less than a generation.[5] In 1997 Anne Krueger used her Presidential Address to the American Economic Association to trumpet the role of export-oriented trade policies in securing economic growth, a commonly held view. In the context of the unipolar, neo-liberal, triumphalist moment of the late 1990s this view was widely upheld and implemented through the policy prescriptions of Washington Consensus. Indeed, it seemed that the prospect of free markets under inevitable and complete economic globalization would make underdevelopment a thing of the past.[6]

Over the past 15 years my research team and I have conducted hundreds of interviews and surveys, across dozens of industries, eight countries, and three continents with exporting firms, development practitioners, and government bureaucrats and policymakers. During those conversations, we have found that market access has been a primary determinant for the success or failure of exporting firms in the developing world. While the interviewed firms have encountered numerous obstacles to their business—demands for bribes, bureaucratic red tape, poor infrastructure, labor and material shortages, and so on—if they have had a market, they have found ways to overcome these challenges. If they did not, or, more often, if the terms of their market access changed, they failed. And, as go firms, so goes the export success of the countries in which they reside.

Yet market access remains significantly constrained, and widely varied, for firms and countries in the developing world. Market access has historically been most distorted in the sectors where it is needed most for development: agriculture and, to a lesser extent, textiles.[7] Agriculture is a vital sector for

[5] Birdsall, N. M, Campos, J., Kim, C. S, Corden, W. M., MacDonald, L., Pack, H., Page, J., Sabor, R., and Stiglitz, J. (1993). *The East Asian Miracle: Economic Growth and Public Policy*. A World Bank Policy Research Report. Oxford University Press.

[6] Frankel, J. A. and Romer, D. (1999). Does trade cause growth? American Economic Review, 89(3), 379–399; Krueger, A. (1997). Trade policy and development: How we learn. *American Economic Review*, 87(1): 1–22.

[7] Anderson, K., Martin, W., and van der Mensbrugghe, D. (2006). Incidence of trade and subsidy policies on developing country welfare, exports and debt sustainability. Washington, DC: The World Bank, 29.

many developing countries, not only for domestic consumption but also as a value-added industry where they can exercise comparative advantage. Or rather, agriculture is where they could exercise comparative advantage, if global agriculture markets weren't both massively distorted through rich world subsidies and closed through both tariff and non-tariff rules.[8] Likewise, the textile sector is the fundamental stepping-stone in moving toward an industrialized economy. With low technology and capital requirements, and high use of low-skilled labor, textiles are the natural first rung on the industrialization ladder.[9] Indeed, a historical progression of mass-market shirt labels reads like a "who's who" of countries that have successfully industrialized since the Second World War. Take a shirt from the 1950s and there's a good chance that, if the tag is from a foreign country, it will be "Japan" or the "Republic of China." Move to the 1960s and 1970s and you're more likely to see "Republic of Korea." The 1980s might see a tag from Hong Kong while the 1990s move on to mainland China. In the new century, you would have been increasingly likely to see a "Vietnam" tag while, in the most recent decade, odds are the tag reads Bangladesh. Head to the shop today and it's not uncommon to see India printed on the label.

But the globalization of market access is an incomplete and unequal project. While nearly all countries have now joined the World Trade Organization (WTO), the globe's biggest trade club, there are still a handful of states that remain on the outside looking in.[10] However, recent years have seen trade rules move away from the global to regional, or preferential, free trade areas (RTAs, PTAs, and FTAs). These smaller and more select clubs have often been "North–South" arrangements wherein rich countries in the global "North" sign more comprehensive trade agreements with selected developing countries in the global "South."[11] Based on the WTO principle of "reciprocity," these agreements have often forced open the markets of the Southern states for Northern wares, but have failed to provide meaningful market access to the Southern states for the goods or services which they are best placed to produce. Even when these agreements do provide meaningful access, such access only accrues to those with sufficient importance

[8] Anderson, K. and Valenzuela, E. (2007). Do global trade distortions still harm developing country farmers? *Review of World Economics*, 143, 108–139.

[9] Kabeer, N. and Mahmud, S. (2004). Rags, riches and women workers: Export-oriented garment manufacturing in Bangladesh. In M. Carr (Ed.), *Chains of Fortune: Linking Women Producers and Workers with Global Markets* (pp. 133–164). Commonwealth Secretariat.

[10] Brazys, S. (2014a). Outside looking in: Non-accession to the WTO. *Cambridge Review of International Affairs*, 27(4), 644–665.

[11] Manger, M. S. and Shadlen, K. C. (2014). Political trade dependence and North–South trade agreements. *International Studies Quarterly*, 58(1), 79–91.

in the international system to be brought to the bargaining table. The network of the global trade regime today manifests as what Jagdish Bhagwati has deemed a "spaghetti bowl" of overlapping rules and agreements.[12] While this entangling web can provide opportunities for firms in those states that are well-placed in the network, it also can create a vastly complex environment in which firms in developing countries can struggle to find or understand market access opportunities.

Yet despite these obstacles, some industries in some countries have been able to achieve outstanding success. In many instances, this is attributable to the presence of *preferential* market access via decades-old schemes under the Generalized System of Preferences (GSP). Market access under these rules has led to some spectacular cases of growth and development. As explored later in the book, the development success of many countries in the Association of South East Asian Nations (ASEAN) might be attributable, in part, to these schemes.[13] However, the bestowal or removal of GSP or other preferences can also create significant unintended consequences by leading to trade diversion, wherein production moves from one developing country to another in order to take advantage of more favorable conditions in the other.[14] This type of "beggar-thy-neighbor" practice reinforces the notion that market access can create both winners *and* losers.

Foreign Aid—the Handout

Since the end of World War II, nearly ten trillion dollars in today's prices have been poured into the Global South to promote growth and development. Since the group of rich donor countries in the OECD formed a club, the "Development Assistance Committee" in the 1960s, most of these resources have come in the form of "Official Development Assistance" or "ODA." By definition, such assistance comes either as outright grants or concessional loans and can manifest in anything ranging from physical projects like roads, schools, or hospitals, to "technical assistance" in the form of external consultants, to outright cash grants. In recent years, and largely because of the rise of non-traditional development-assistance partners like the People's Republic of China (PRC), "aid" has taken on broader connotations, and now is also

[12] Bhagwati, J. (2008). *Termites in the Trading System: How Preferential Agreements Undermine Free Trade*. Oxford University Press.

[13] Cuyvers, L. and Verherstraeten, S. (2005). The EU's Generalized System of Preferences and its ASEAN beneficiaries: A success story. CAS (Centre for ASEAN Studies), (47).

[14] Ornelas, E. and Ritel, M. (2020). The not-so-generalised effects of the Generalized System of Preferences. *The World Economy*, 43(7), 1809–1840.

often used to refer to non-concessional forms of financing as well as flows (both concessional and not) from non-state actors. While these different assistance modalities undoubtedly have consequences for the aid's effectiveness, each at least has the *potential* to build the tools necessary for utilizing market access.

Despite the massive amounts invested in aid there is little academic or policy consensus on if, when, or how aid is "effective." Sixty years of scholarship has produced claims that aid facilitates growth and development, that it does so but only when accompanied by the right types of governance and policy, that it has no effects, or that it can act as a "curse," undermining development efforts.[15] Undoubtedly many of these conflicting results stem from the difficulty in trying to identify a causal effect of a macro input, aid at the country level, to a macro output, economic performance at that same level. Certainly, many countries that have received aid have experienced remarkable growth and development. Botswana, a country whose aid-to-GDP ratio was as high as 25% in late 1960s is today one of the richest countries in sub-Saharan Africa.[16]

Yet, other countries who have received large and sustained amounts of aid have failed to see meaningful growth or development. Since their independence in 1986, the Federated States of Micronesia (FSM) and the Republic of the Marshall Islands (RMI) have seen major inflows of development assistance, averaging some 30–35% of GDP annually.[17] However, despite this assistance, both countries have stagnated in their economic growth and development. While some of this performance may be attributable to the remoteness of these islands and their lack of natural resources, other countries in the region, including their sister-state Palau, have realized markedly better growth paths.

As a result of the inability to identify unambiguous relationships between aid and growth at the country level, more recent work has turned to identifying micro-level effects of particular programs or interventions.[18] While the stand-out work in this area has garnered Nobel recognition, there often

[15] Dalgaard, C. J. and Hansen, H. (2001). On aid, growth and good policies. *Journal of Development Studies*, 37(6), 17–41; Djankov, S., Montalvo, J. G., and Reynal-Querol, M. (2008). The curse of aid. *Journal of Economic Growth*, 13, 169–194; Hansen, H. and Tarp, F. (2001). Aid and growth regressions. *Journal of Development Economics*, 64(2), 547–570; Rajan, R. G. and Subramanian, A. (2011). Aid, Dutch disease, and manufacturing growth. *Journal of Development Economics*, 94(1), 106–118.

[16] While much of this is undoubtedly due to Botswana's rich natural resources, particularly its endowment of diamonds, many other similarly resource-rich countries have been unable to turn those natural endowments into national wealth, instead falling afoul of the "resource curse."

[17] Brazys, S. (2018). Aid dependence as aid persistence? Non-declining aid and growth. *Journal of International Relations and Development*, 21, 717–738.

[18] Banerjee, A. V. and Duflo, E. (2011). Poor Economics: A Radical Rethinking of the Way to Fight Global Poverty. Public Affairs.

remains a gap in explaining micro-success but macro-failure. While rigorous Randomized Control Trial (RCT) studies might show the effectiveness of a particular development program or policy, those interventions may have seemingly little effect on spurring the overall, long-term, economic growth of a country.

Much of the ambiguity on aid's macroeconomic effects also stems from the fact that aid efforts can support a broad range of activities. While investment in human capital, via better education or health, may ultimately translate to economic gains, the linkages are diffuse and long-term. Recognizing the link between trade and growth, donor countries increased the rhetoric surrounding aid for this purpose in the 1990s and 2000s. First coined "Trade Capacity Building Assistance" by the United States in the 1990s, this type of aid was globally branded as "Aid for Trade" (AfT) in the 2005 WTO Hong Kong Ministerial meeting. While still a broad moniker, AfT was intended to capture aid efforts that mitigated supply-side constraints to export-led development. These efforts would encompass not only trade-related infrastructure that could be utilized by firms—roads, ports, utilities—but also aid that upgraded country systems in customs or other border procedures or trained firms in how to better navigate those rules, both at home and abroad. Finally, AfT also ended up encompassing industry-specific development projects, where particular products or sectors would be targeted for export development.

Like the scholarship on aid more generally, investigations of the effectiveness of AfT also yield mixed results. While a handful of studies have found country-level linkages between (some types) of AfT (from some donors) and increased exports, other micro-level work, tying exports from individual firms to AfT projects has found fewer linkages.[19] A further, critical, literature has questioned not only the effectiveness of AfT, but also the intent.[20] This work suggests that, rather than facilitate access to the gains of globalization, AfT works to create or embed neo-colonial relationships wherein countries in the Global South become both dependent on, and exploited by, counterparts in the Global North.

[19] Cali, M. and Te Velde, D. W. (2011). Does Aid for Trade really improve trade performance? *World Development*, 39(5), 725–740; Vijil, M. and Wagner, L. (2012). Does Aid for Trade enhance export performance? Investigating the infrastructure channel. *The World Economy*, 35(7), 838–868; Brazys, S. R. (2013). Evidencing donor heterogeneity in Aid for Trade. *Review of International Political Economy*, 20(4), 947–978; Brazys, S. and Elkink, J. A. (2021). "Aid for Trade" effectiveness? Micro-level evidence from Nepal. *The European Journal of Development Research*, 33, 1493–1513; Martínez-Zarzoso, I., Nowak-Lehmann D, F., and Rehwald, K. (2017). Is Aid for Trade effective? A panel quantile regression approach. *Review of Development Economics*, 21(4), e175–e203.

[20] Holden, P. (2014). Tensions in the discourse and practice of the European Union's Aid for Trade. *Contemporary Politics*, 20(1), 90–102; Langan, M. and Scott, J. (2014). The Aid for Trade charade. *Cooperation and Conflict*, 49(2), 143–161.

Aid AND Trade—The Hand-up

While market access is important for growth in a globalized world, and aid may certainly contribute to development, neither can do the job alone. Numerous countries have received substantial amounts of aid and yet failed to develop. Likewise, several countries have very high degrees of trade openness, but firms therein have been unable to take advantage of this market access.

While working as an economic adviser to the aid-dependent Federated States of Micronesia (FSM) in 2009, I attended a workshop of political and business leaders considering the pros and cons of the FSM's potential bid to join the WTO. At that time, the FSM was one of just a handful of "outsiders" and several officials were advocating that the FSM join the organization. They believed that the direct costs of accession would be largely subsidized through development assistance. Furthermore, as the FSM had few import-competing industries, and was relatively unreliant on import duties, they argued that there was unlikely to be much pain in the way of domestic adjustment from increased market openness. However, the accession position quickly amassed a wide range of critics. One delegate arose and, to a resounding round of applause, asked the rhetorical question "If we join the WTO, what will we trade?"

The question was apt. Outside rich stocks of tuna, it was tough to identify any readily exportable goods in the country. Even with regards to tuna, the FSM monetized this resource via licensing agreements and, as such, didn't really need to secure better market access. But while the question recognized the *reality* of the FSM's pool of exportable goods, it did not do justice to the *potential.* While the FSM's remoteness and size put a natural barrier on the breadth of economic activity, it would be unfair to say that there is nothing the FSM *could* export. Indeed, some of the FSM's island neighbors had realized remarkable success in various export sectors following the end of World War II. American Samoa had built a thriving canning industry, climbing the processing chain and capturing considerably more value added from its tuna stock than the FSM. Likewise, the Commonwealth of the Northern Mariana Islands (CNMI) was able to develop a textile industry that helped propel its economy into upper-income classification.[21] Where the CNMI and American Samoan economies differed from the FSM was that, due to their differing relationships with the United States, each had highly preferential

[21] Brazys, S. R. (2014b). Paradise lost: The cost of removing tax and trade provisions from the Compact of Free Association. *Asia & the Pacific Policy Studies*, 1(1), 204–215.

market access to the US mainland under what was known as "Headnote 3a" status. This same status had been initially included for the FSM under the 1986 agreement that defined their relationship with the United States, the "Compact of Free Association," but was unilaterally removed when the agreement was ratified by the US Congress.[22]

Thus, market access and foreign assistance pose a "chicken and egg" problem. With massive amounts of aid, the FSM ostensibly had the resources necessary to put in place the *tools* for the development of export-oriented industries like tuna processing or garment manufacturing. However, these industries would have been doomed to failure in the absence of market *access*. Yet, without any readily identifiable export-oriented industry, there was little impetus for the political leadership of the FSM to seek additional market access opportunities.

In the FSM's case, both aid and the (lack of) market access were the result of the *political calculus* of its main donor benefactor, the United Sates. The "Freely Associated States" (FAS) of the FSM, RMI, and Palau all have received massive amounts of foreign assistance under their respective Compacts of Free Association. All three had previously been part of the United Nations Pacific Trust Territory administered by the United States following the end of World War II. One of the strongest predictors of foreign aid allocation is historical ties between donors and recipients, and thus it is no surprise that the FAS have received substantially more financial assistance from the United States than their island neighbors with weaker historical links to the superpower.[23]

The Compact agreements that provided this aid also included substantial defense rights for the United States, including rights of sea and airspace denial as well as rights to establish military facilities. Indeed, the United States maintains a large military presence at Kwajalein in the RMI and the FAS are a key part of the "2nd Pacific Island Chain," which stretches from Japan to Papua New Guinea. The strategic importance of the FAS to the US Pacific Strategy is substantial and certainly factors into the decision to allocate resources to these states (but not some of their Pacific neighbors).[24]

However, the decision to limit market access opportunities for the FSM (and RMI) by removing headnote 3A status was also entirely dependent on

[22] Ibid.

[23] For instance, Kiribati, also of the Micronesian island groups but not part of the US-administered UN Trust Territory, when receiving any financial support averaged less than $1 million per year, compared to roughly $100 million per year for the FSM, despite similarly sized populations (source: OECD CRS https://stats.oecd.org/Index.aspx?DataSetCode=crs1#).

[24] Scott, D. (2012). US strategy in the pacific–geopolitical positioning for the twenty-first century. *Geopolitics*, 17(3), 607–628.

US political choices. As illustrated in Congressional testimony, the provision of this market access faced significant opposition from the neighboring territories of the CNMI and American Samoa who viewed the FAS as potential competitors. In the face of this political opposition, the United States withdrew this access and, in doing so, created development winners and losers in the region. Without meaningful market access, the economies of the FSM and RMI have stagnated, and real incomes have barely risen over the past 25 years as the countries have struggled to maintain lower-middle income status, even when supported with massive aid inflows. In contrast, while starting from a roughly similar base in the 1970s, both the CNMI and American Samoa have economies that are currently in or near high-income status.

This extended vignette is intended to illustrate that aid and market access are unlikely to be effective in isolation. But at the same time, each is a political choice that largely depends on the preferences and interests of the rich donor countries who provide that aid and access. However, in many instances, donors appear to treat aid and access as substitutes rather than complements. Sometimes, as in the FSM and RMI cases, a donor may think that one or the other is sufficient, if providing aid there is no need to provide market access. Other times, aid may act as a as a "payoff" for the failure to extend (or even remove) market access. Indeed, numerous critiques of the European Union's (EU's) Economic Partnership Agreements (EPAs) with countries in the Africa, Caribbean, and Pacific (ACP) group suggest that this is precisely the exchange that occurred. Significant assistance packages accompanied the negotiations of these agreements, but many saw these as a "pay-off" for the fact that the ACP countries were not able to secure the types of market access they would have liked with the EU, particularly in the agricultural sector.[25]

But surely some countries that have received both aid and market access have also failed to develop? Sub-Saharan Africa, in particular, is replete with countries that have some of the highest aid-to-GDP ratios in the world and also have extraordinary market access via agreements like the European "Everything but Arms" (EBA) initiative, or the US Africa Growth and Opportunity Act (AGOA). These cases prompt two important observations. First, aid and access aren't everything, and they aren't always *sufficient* to spur growth and development. Geography, history, natural resource endowment, and other external factors can act as sufficient enablers or barriers to growth.

However, the second observation is that market access isn't always what it seems. While the EU's EBA provides tariff and quota-free access for all

[25] Prowse, S. (2006). "Aid for Trade": A proposal for increasing support for trade adjustment and integration. *Economic Development and Multilateral Trade Cooperation*, 41181(4), 229; Langan, M. and Scott, J. (2014).

products excepting arms and ammunition, this access may be for naught if EBA countries are unable to overcome various non-tariff barriers (NTBs), especially in sectors where those countries have a comparative advantage—namely agricultural production. Among other things, these barriers can include food safety, production, packaging, or other types of technical regulations. Thus, while some countries may have significant de jure market access opportunities under various free or preferential trade agreements, the de facto benefits could be considerably smaller.[26] Likewise, while GSP schemes can provide preferential access for developing countries, this access is both arbitrary in that it remains extended at the discretion and pleasure of the providing partner but also selective in that GSP is extended for specific products. GSP access will not necessarily include sectors wherein receiving countries have strong comparative advantage and, even if it does, the fact that it can be withdrawn can create significant uncertainty.[27] Likewise, subtle nuances in how preferential access operates, such as the type of "rules of origin" (ROO), which dictate how much of the raw material or value-added of a finished product must take place in the country, might render seemingly attractive market access offers inoperable in practice.[28] The intricacies of market access agreement do not simply happen by chance but are yet again the result of the political choices of the granting entities.

In similar ways, aid is also a mixed bag. The simple fact that a country receives a substantial amount of aid does not necessarily mean that that aid will be effective in promoting exports or growth. The effectiveness of aid depends on who it comes from, what it is used for, how it is spent, and if it is coordinated with other efforts. Yet again, the answers to these questions are more often political than technical. In combination with the varieties of access, this suggests a need to delve into the qualitative nature of both aid and access to ascertain if the two, in combination, promote growth and development. The core contention of this book is that a considerable amount of the country-level discrepancy in export-led success under globalization can be attributed to those countries who have received effective aid combined with meaningful market access, and those who have not. That difference is not necessarily one of random chance, but instead is often the result of purposive political action. While the right mix of aid and market access can

[26] Boys, J. and Andreoni, A. (2023). Does regionalism increase industrial policy space? An analytical framework applied to the East African textiles and apparel sector. *Third World Quarterly*, 44(8), 1680–1698.

[27] Karsenty, G. and Laird, S. (1987). The GSP, policy options and the new round. *Weltwirtschaftliches Archiv*, 123, 262–296.

[28] Ju, J. and Krishna, K. (2005). Firm behaviour and market access in a free trade area with rules of origin. *Canadian Journal of Economics/Revue canadienne d'économique*, 38(1), 290–308.

come together, it does not do so automatically and is usually the result of contextually specific circumstances.

An important corollary is that market access doesn't provide opportunity for countries, it provides opportunity for firms. Likewise, the human and physical capital built by aid benefits individuals and companies. Ultimately it is firms, made up of individuals, that must decide what and how to produce and for what market. While countries can pursue policies and trade agreements, and provide infrastructure and incentives, the final decision to export rests with firms. While at times the actions of these firms are closely coordinated with and by the state, in many instances firms are also truly private market actors. However, in either case, the capacity and institutional quality of the state will play an important mediating role. If a developing country's government is ineffective in collecting, advocating, or implementing its firms' interests—with respect to either the tools needed via aid, or the market access and regulatory environment needed for trade—then export-led growth is unlikely to occur. Accordingly, this book maintains an equal focus between states and firms as economic growth and development rest in the hands of both.

Data

To build its arguments, the book utilizes several existing and novel data sources. While the book considers growth since World War II, the primary temporal focus is on the post-Cold War period of unipolar globalization. The arguments are meant to be global, and the book focuses on a handful of key cases from South(-East) Asia, Sub-Saharan Africa, the Equatorial Pacific, and South America. Quantitatively, the book draws on a wide range of descriptive data from the World Bank, United Nations, and Organisation for Economic Co-operation and Development including the World Bank's World Development Indicators the various resources of UN Data, and the OECD's Creditor Reporting System. To evaluate Aid for Trade, the book relies heavily on information on aid flows from AidData. This organization, founded in 2009, has assembled a variety of data on different aid projects across the globe. The data is highly detailed, at the project level. Most notably, many of the AidData datasets have assigned spatial coordinates to aid projects at the project location level. This innovation allows for the deployment of spatial identification strategies, where the *location* of aid projects can be matched to other, similarly geo-referenced data. The book takes advantage of several of these existing datasets including, for example, high-frequency, firm-level survey data on Colombian exporters, geo-referenced household surveys from Afrobarometer, and geo-referenced data on infrastructure like well-placement in Bangladesh.

In addition to utilizing these existing datasets, the book also utilizes several novel datasets generated over the past 10 years. These include geo-referenced directories of exporting firms in Bangladesh, Nepal, and Colombia, geo-referencing of the Bangladesh Household Income and Expenditure Survey, and direct, geo-referenced, surveys of exporting firms including 765 in Bangladesh and 131 in Nepal. From a qualitative perspective, the book draws on 92 in-depth field interviews from Bangladesh, Colombia, Indonesia, Nepal, Nigeria, the Philippines, Timor-Leste, and Vietnam. These interviews were conducted with officials from aid agencies and partner governments, but also with exporting firms and non-governmental organizations, and give rich qualitative context to many of the empirical claims made in the book. Finally, parts of the book rely extensively on my own direct observation in participatory research based on several years consulting for the government of the Federated States of Micronesia, 18 months of which while living in the country.

Plan of Book

The book explores its core claim both from a stepped-back, global perspective, and via more in-depth case studies. Chapter 2 builds a detailed theoretical argument to suggest why trade-effective aid and meaningful access are not simply randomly distributed but instead are deeply rooted in the structure and agency of international and domestic politics. The argument examines how states' positioning in the international system, combined with the quality of their own domestic institutions, enables or inhibits engagement with the providers of aid and market access to secure and develop those goods in effective and meaningful ways.

Chapter 3 then presents a global view of the "best" and the "rest" in terms of developing countries to illustrate the divergent growth performance of those countries that have received both aid and access and those that have not. Drawing on secondary literature and global datasets, the chapter develops a quadrant-based typology based on effective aid and meaningful market access and examines descriptive analyses and cross-country correlations as a classification exercise to determine if there is a prima facie case for the importance of combined aid and access. As the book focuses on market access and export-led growth, the chapter introduces the notion of "Trade-Effective Aid" (TEA) as a subset of broader foreign aid.

This chapter provides the observational base from which the rest of the book is built.

Departing from this broad view, Chapter 4 zooms into the politics of market access. The chapter begins by describing those countries that have received market access, and those who have not, both through multilateral initiatives such as the General Agreement on Tariffs and Trade (GATT) and its successor body, the World Trade Organization (WTO), the Generalized System of Preferences (GSP), and through bilateral and regional or preferential trade agreements (PTAs). The chapter then turns to the politics behind this market access, drawing on the theoretical insights from Chapter 2. Why have some countries received broader and deeper market access than others? Why have some countries received more meaningful preferential concessions? The analysis in this chapter goes beyond simple market access structures like tariffs and quotas and explores how non-tariff barriers (NTBs) like product standards or labeling requirements can effectively block exports from developing countries even when they appear to have access "on paper."

The subsequent chapter, Chapter 5, provides a more detailed overview of the tools developing countries have received to help facilitate their development. In particular, the chapter focuses on what makes aid effective in helping countries realize the opportunities of a globalized market. Thinking about the different ends to which aid is employed, the chapter's primary focus is on AfT and the extent to which aid classified in this manner has been "trade-effective." The chapter will show how the effectiveness of AfT is deeply heterogeneous, drawing on "mezzo" level quantitative and qualitative data from Nepal, Bangladesh, and Colombia. In many instances the countries which host AfT projects, or even firms that are proximate to those projects, appear to see little benefit from the interventions. AfT, like aid more broadly, can, but will not always, be effective.

The book then turns to a series of both "on" and "off" the line case studies which illustrate, either via presence or omission, the importance and nuance of both trade-effective aid and meaningful market access for achieving development aims. While the cases are selected based on cross-case variation in economic growth and the presence or absence of trade-effective aid and meaningful market access, each of the cases is also dynamic which enables within-case analysis of critical junctures where political changes in either domestic or international politics led to changes in the key explanatory variables.[29]

[29] Collier, D. and Munck, G. L. (2017). Building blocks and methodological challenges: A framework for studying critical junctures. *Qualitative and Multi-Method Research*, 15, 2–9.

The first of these chapters, Chapter 6, considers several "on-the-line" success stories to show how the combination of aid and access can lead to sustained growth and development. Focusing on two cases in the South-East Asian region, the chapter explores how Vietnam and Indonesia were each able to take advantage of market access opportunities while receiving meaningful amounts of effective foreign assistance, while showing how and why these countries received that aid and access. These cases are selected, in part, to also illustrate how domestic governance serves to mediate meaningful market access but especially trade-effective aid. While Indonesia has transitioned to a quasi-functional democracy, Vietnam was and remains a hardline autocracy, suggesting that the form (if not quality) of domestic governance takes a back seat to other types of governance effectiveness that can facilitate the right mix of aid and access.

Chapter 7 more closely interrogates two "on-the-line" cases that have failed to achieve sustained economic growth. The chapter shows how aid alone, or the combination of *ineffective* aid and *inconsequential* market access, is not sufficient for sustained development. The chapter highlights how both small (FSM) and large (Madagascar) countries that have received vast amounts of financial assistance have been unable to translate this into export-led growth even in the face of significant de jure market access. These countries illustrate, in particular, how good governance is not sufficient to achieve trade-effective aid or meaningful market access. States' positions in the international system will influence the potency of their agency in securing these goods.

The penultimate chapter illustrates how the political choices by rich countries can empower some developing countries with aid and access can create unintended consequences for their neighbors and competitors. This chapter shows how aid and changing market conditions for India and Bangladesh led to a "beggar thy neighbor" situation with Nepal. Through distortions caused by the Multi-Fiber Agreement (MFA), and via "better" aid, Bangladesh and India have been better positioned to take advantage of the past 20 years of globalization. While Nepal's recent development story has been one of moderate success, political choices largely beyond its influence have set it on a different, and poorer, growth path than it would have faced in the absence of that interference.

The book concludes with thoughts about how its lessons, drawn on a history of the last 35 years of increased globalization, might be applied in the coming decades where the breakdown of the unipolar order and the global climate emergency specter loom over all development efforts. The conclusion argues how the changing geo-physical and political global environments will open new windows of opportunity and critical junctures that may open or shut prospects for trade-effective aid and meaningful market access for particular countries. The book concludes with thoughts on how, in many instances, the prospects for export-led growth depend on trade-effective intentionality in aid and a willingness to acknowledge and confront the costs and benefits of providing meaningful market access.

This book stitches together two related but distinct strands of existing inquiry, which, when combined with original research, tell a story of how external countries are as responsible for unequal growth in the developing world as the developing countries themselves. Rich and powerful countries' distortion of both markets and aid helps lead to a world of winners and losers in the race for economic growth. In the absence of meaningful and sustained market access, countries cannot thrive in a globalized economy regardless of the amount of assistance they receive. Yet, the burden of growth in the developing world does not fall on the shoulders of the rich and powerful alone. Quality governance is needed by developing countries to fully exploit the potential of their agency in shaping these political outcomes. Ultimately, the ability to pursue export-led growth in a globalized world is not an elusive or unattainable technical goal; it is a political choice by actors in both the developed and developing worlds.

2
The Global Political Economy of Aid and Market Access

Bretton Woods and a New World Order

When 44 nations of the allied powers met in 1944 at the tiny hamlet of Bretton Woods nestled in New Hampshire's White Mountains to lay the institutional framework for the post-war world, aid and trade were key components of the new global order. The gathered powers decided that the post-war governance edifice would rest on four pillars: international security, macroeconomic management, trade, and development assistance, all under the auspices of the United Nations. However, almost immediately, each of the pillars was undermined. The primary mechanism for international security and high politics, the United Nations Security Council (UNSC), ground to a halt as the Iron Curtain fell between the Union of Soviet Socialist Republics (USSR) and the other permanent, veto-wielding, members of the body. Likewise, the macroeconomic pillar based on pegged exchange rates, overseen by a newly established International Monetary Fund (IMF), was insufficiently capitalized. Consequently, Bretton Woods architects established a gold-exchange system wherein currencies were pegged to the US dollar, which itself was backed by gold.[1]

The development and trade pillars also deviated from their original design. Trade and development were meant to be explicitly linked in the establishment of an "International Trade Organization" (ITO). The concept of "economic development" featured prominently in the institutional foundation for this organization as laid out in the Havana Charter. Among other features, the charter included numerous departures from principles of liberalized trade—most notably through its allowance for developing countries to use import quotas ("quantitative restrictions") to protect their domestic industries and through mechanisms for the stabilization of commodity

[1] Iwami, T. and Iwami, T. (1995). *The Bretton Woods System as a Gold Exchange Standard* (pp. 1–35). Palgrave Macmillan UK.

The Invisible Hand(out). Samuel Brazys, Oxford University Press. © Samuel Brazys (2025).
DOI: 10.1093/9780198970422.003.0002

prices.[2] Thus, while designed as a "development-friendly" institution, the ITO never came into being as the Truman administration did not pursue ratification both due to domestic opposition (including from within his own Democratic party) but also as trade issues were supplanted by the security concerns of the blossoming Cold War, made manifest on the Korean peninsula. Thus, the Bretton Woods trade pillar, a pillar which would have been very deferential to the trade concerns of the developing world, was ultimately stillborn.[3]

The development pillar was equally malformed. With the loss of the ITO, this pillar was carried primarily on the shoulders of the International Bank for Reconstruction and Development (IBRD), the first institution of the World Bank Group (WB). However, this institution was established primarily with the goal of financing the reconstruction of post-war Europe. It was only when the United States' bilateral Marshall Fund supplanted this financing that the WB turned its attention to the broader developing world. While proposals for setting up a special financing mechanism for developing countries circulated during the early 1950s, most notably via the unfortunately acronymed "Special" United Nations Fund for Economic Development ("S"UNFED), it took until 1960 to establish the International Development Association (IDA). The IDA's explicit mandate is to focus on providing low or interest-free loans and grants to the developing world.[4]

The fate of trade and development in the early days of the Bretton Woods system are indicative of the political economy of these issues. While the topics received considerable attention, they became secondary to the pressing security paradigm of the Cold War. Indeed, Cold War dynamics dominate explanations of the politics of trade and aid during this period.[5] The substitute for the ITO was the General Agreement on Tariffs and Trade (GATT). Launched in 1947, the GATT was a low-frills trade institution only meant to kick-start the liberalization process and to be supplanted by the ITO. However, when the ITO failed to materialize, the GATT formed the basis of the global trade regime for the next 40 years. The GATT's mandate was considerably more limited than what had been proposed for the ITO. In its initial years, it focused primarily on cutting tariff rates on manufactured goods

[2] Toye, J. (2012). The world improvement plans of Fritz Schumacher. *Cambridge Journal of Economics*, *36*(2), 387–403.

[3] Toye, R. (2003). Developing multilateralism: The Havana charter and the fight for the International Trade Organization, 1947–1948. *The International History Review*, *25*(2), 282–305.

[4] Shaw, D. J. (2005). Turning point in the evolution of soft financing: The United Nations and the World Bank. *Canadian Journal of Development Studies/Revue canadienne d'études du développement*, *26*(1), 43–61.

[5] Dunning, T. (2004). Conditioning the effects of aid: Cold War politics, donor credibility, and democracy in Africa. *International Organization*, *58*(2), 409–423.

between industrialized countries. Not only did the GATT exclude the Warsaw Pact countries, but it also omitted the most populous nation on Earth, the People's Republic of China.

Thus, instead of a globalized trade and development order, what existed was an architecture to support the Western allies in their struggle with the Soviet menace. The key development-friendly trade policy during this era, the Generalized System of Preferences (GSP), was established in 1971 following negotiations via the United Nations Conference on Trade and Development (UNCTAD) and the GATT.[6] However, GSP began and remained as somewhat of a gift horse. While, in theory, GSP could be used to give unlimited preferential access to any developing country, in practice, GSP preferences are only extended on a relatively limited basis and to limited success.[7] During the Cold War, the important recipients of GSP included stalwart Western allies like South Korea and geographic lynchpins like Egypt or Singapore.[8]

The Neoliberal Moment

The launch of the Uruguay round of GATT talks in 1986 coincided with the first cracks in the Berlin Wall. By the time the round was completed in 1994, the last vestiges of the Cold War had been swept away and the United States stood presiding over the international economic system as the world's lone superpower. The "neoliberal moment" ushered in a heady optimism that centuries of global warfare and economic turmoil would be replaced by a liberal, rules-based, global economic and security apparatus that would spread the benefits of markets to all corners of the globe.[9] This "capitalism unleashed" promised to generate widespread stability and prosperity.[10] The key institution for structuring this new global economic order was the World Trade Organization (WTO), established at the conclusion of the Uruguay Round of talks in 1995. While this organization did not necessarily correct all the "birth defects" of the GATT regime, it did usher in a new rules-based organization where developing countries in particular would ostensibly be on a

[6] Dos Santos, N. B. and Cunha, R. (2005). Generalized system of preferences in general agreement on tariffs and trade/World Trade Organization: History and current issues. *Journal of World Trade*, *39*(4).

[7] Herz, B. and Wagner, M. (2011). The dark side of the generalized system of preferences. *Review of International Economics*, *19*(4), 763–775.

[8] Özden, Ç. and Reinhardt, E. (2005). The perversity of preferences: GSP and developing country trade policies, 1976–2000. *Journal of Development Economics*, *78*(1), 1–21.

[9] Ampuja, M. (2012). Conclusion: Globalization theory and the neoliberal moment. In *Theorizing Globalization* (pp. 339–378). Brill.

[10] Glyn, A. (2007). *Capitalism Unleashed: Finance, Globalization, and Welfare*. Oxford University Press.

level playing field with their developed country peers both in terms of formal decision making and rule enforcement.[11]

This neo-liberal moment also saw a significant reduction in foreign aid levels, thus supporting the contention that this Cold War era aid was driven more by strategic rather than developmental objectives. Or, perhaps, it was driven by an ideological belief that with the advent of truly global markets, developing countries would find financing through commercial channels and thrive in a world of increased market access and competition. To this end, the early 1990s saw the first explicit melding of aid and trade. By the 1996 WTO Singapore Ministerial conference, multilateral donors were directed to "assist (Least Developed Countries) LDCs to enhance their trading opportunities."[12] By the turn of the century, individual countries were beginning to adopt "Trade Capacity Building Assistance" or "Aid for Trade" strategies, following the adaptation of the "Integrated Framework for Technical-Related Trade Assistance" in 1997. Finally, the WTO officially endorsed its "Aid for Trade" initiative at the Hong Kong Ministerial in 2005 and began publishing biannual global reviews in 2007.

Whereas the GATT had been dominated by Cold War politics, the WTO was a nearly universal institution. At its establishment in 1995, the WTO was comprised of 123 members. With the accession of the People's Republic of China (PRC) in 2001, and Russia in 2012, the WTO's membership included 93% of the world's population and over 98% of global trade. AfT was ostensibly intended to help knit these members together into an integrated and open global market wherein principles of comparative advantage and factor endowment could reign supreme. Ricardian gains from trade would accrue to all and underdevelopment would become a thing of the past.

At least rhetorically, the AfT idea was a paradigm-shifting approach to foreign assistance, by explicitly linking aid to increased export-led growth it invoked the notion of "helping you help yourself." Global markets were ultimately seen as the mechanism by which countries could develop and converge. Aid (for trade) would be used only insomuch as it facilitated accessing these markets. In the abstract this was an attractive and plausible aim. The theoretical bases for gains from trade are canonical. And, despite critiques that it was misleading to characterize success stories such as the East

[11] Jackson, J. H. (2007). *The Jurisprudence of GATT and the WTO: Insights on Treaty Law and Economic Relations*. Cambridge University Press.

[12] Prowse, S. (2002). The role of international and national agencies in trade-related capacity building. *World Economy*, *25*(9), 1235–1261, p. 1241.

Asian Tigers as exemplars of "export-led" growth, the narrative retained a prominence of place in popular and policy discussions.[13]

The pitfall of this approach, however, is that the clear waters of the economics of liberalized markets and gains from specialization are always and everywhere muddied by the realities of domestic and international politics. The nuances of export markets are so fine that even minor distortions in the allocation of aid or the granting of market access can undermine the entire enterprise. The remainder of this chapter first explores the political economies of market access and foreign aid before advancing an argument that obtaining the happy combination of *trade-effective aid* and *meaningful market access* depends on whether the structuring of the international system permits well-governed developing states to successfully exercise agency in influencing the domestic political considerations of the developed states that provide aid and market access. As will be elaborated below, the myriad veto points in this sequence, some of which are outside the control of developing countries, means that the realization of trade-effective aid and meaningful market access is a sufficiently rare occurrence.

The Political Economy of Access

There is perhaps no more frustrating puzzle in the social sciences than the political economy of trade and market access. The theory and empirics behind free trade are unequivocal: liberalized trade leads to more overall wealth. Obstacles to trade lead to higher prices and less consumer choice. Yet, despite these benefits, significant barriers remain to the free flow of goods and services across borders. Why do we, collectively, choose costlier goods with less choice? Because, while liberalized trade may increase the overall size of the pie, it does not deal with how the pie is distributed. Liberalizing trade creates winners and losers, both within and across countries. If the mechanisms by which the winners could compensate the losers are absent or insufficient, the losers will resist liberalization. Compensation and redistribution mechanisms are ultimately the purview of *politics* where power and influence can elevate the interests of the few over that of the many.

[13] Amsden, A. H. (1994). Why isn't the whole world experimenting with the East Asian model to develop?: Review of the East Asian miracle. *World Development*, *22*(4), 627–633; Rodrik, D. (1997). Trade strategy, investment and exports: Another look at East Asia. *Pacific Economic Review*, *2*(1), 1–24; Palley, T. I. (2012). The rise and fall of export-led growth. *Investigación económica*, *71*(280), 141–161; Yang, J. (2008). An analysis of so-called export-led growth. *IMF Working Papers*, *2008*(220); Bonaglia, F. and Fukasaku, K. (2003). Export diversification in low-income countries: An international challenge after Doha. Working Paper No. 209. OECD Development Centre.

The Economics of Trade

The field of political economy largely arose from the reflections on the gains of trade in the writings of Adam Smith, David Ricardo, and other leading intellectuals of the 18th and 19th centuries.[14] What these thinkers made unequivocally clear was the potential for overall welfare gains from trade. While later thinkers like Wolfgang Stolper, Paul Samuelson, Eli Heckscher, and Bertil Ohlin tweaked and refined these early conceptualizations, the core logic that trans-national exchange based on specialized production due to comparative advantage, either from technology or relative factor endowments, would lead to overall gains in production which could increase global consumption.[15] However, these proponents of liberalization also met theoretical challengers like Alexander Gerschenkron or Fernando Henrique Cardoso and Enzo Faletto, who espoused ideas that extractive international trade patterns based on historical relationships between colonizers and the colonized could lock the latter into ever-declining terms of trade which would forestall meaningful economic growth.[16] While certain countries since World War II have certainly appeared to have faced these dynamics, they serve primarily as examples of countries who did not receive *meaningful* market access, or trade-effective aid to utilize that access.[17]

Whereas classical trade theory focused on the comparative advantage and specialization of countries, in the 1970s trade theory progressed to focus on the role of firms. Ultimately, it is firms that produce and decide whether or not to export, sometimes with, and sometimes without, state support. Likewise, these firms may be domestically owned or may have foreign ownership as trans or multi-national corporations (TNC or MNC). Theorists including Elhanan Helpman, Paul Krugman, Avinash Dixit, and Joseph Stigliz who noted the importance of market size in what is commonly coined as the *New* Trade Theory (NTT).[18] Understanding that many industries faced increasing

[14] Ricardo, D. (1821). *On the Principles of Political Economy*. London: J. Murray; Smith, A. (2010). *The Wealth of Nations: An Inquiry into the Nature and Causes of the Wealth of Nations*. Harriman House Limited.

[15] Heckscher, G., Heckscher, E. F., and Ohlin, B. (1991). *Heckscher-Ohlin Trade Theory*. Mit Press; Stolper, W. F. and Samuelson, P. A. (1941). Protection and real wages. *The Review of Economic Studies*, 9(1), 58–73.

[16] Gerschenkron, A. (1962). Economic backwardness in historical perspective. *Cambridge MA*; Cardoso, F. H. and Faletto, E. (1979). *Dependency and Development in Latin America*. University of California Press.

[17] Ortiz, J. (2012). Déjà vu: Latin America and its new trade dependency … this time with China. *Latin American Research Review*, *47*(3), 175–190.

[18] Dixit, A. K. and Stiglitz, J. E. (1977). Monopolistic competition and optimum product diversity. *The American Economic Review*, *67*(3), 297–308; Dixit, A. and Norman, V. (1980). *Theory of International Trade: A Dual, General Equilibrium Approach*. Cambridge University Press; Helpman, E. (1984). A simple theory of international trade with multinational corporations. *Journal of Political Economy*,

returns to scale and that, accordingly, firms who were able to capture these lower unit costs, due to sufficiently large markets, would become globally competitive and dominate international exchange. Firms thus appropriately scaled would engage in monopolistic competition, where product differentiation based on non-price factors like branding or quality could lead to situations wherein countries may become both importers and exporters of the same product.

The foray into firms with the NTT spawned further theorizing and distinction throughout the 1980s and 1990s. In an increasingly globalized world characterized, or perhaps spawned, by large MNCs, trans-national production and supply chains gained an increasing share of cross-border exchange. *International* trade in many instances soon became *intrafirm* trade, with vertically integrated firms locating different parts of their production processes in different countries to minimize costs. While these cost savings in some instances accrue from taking advantage of classic trade determinants like relative factor abundance in labor or capital, intra-firm trade is also prompted by institutional features such as transfer pricing or tariff jumping which enables firms to optimize tax, profit, and revenue strategies.[19] This line argument was further developed by Robert Feenstra and others to consider outsourcing via "vertical specialization" in the context of Global Value Chains (GVCs).[20] The focus on trade in intermediate goods is central to the "New New Trade Theory" (NNTT) developed by scholars like Marc Meltiz or Pol Antras which began to take more seriously the *political* economy determinants of trade.[21] This scholarship focuses increasingly on the micro-level determinants of trade. In particular, this inquiry shifted to exploring why some firms export and others don't, even when they are in the same country and industry. This literature ultimately concludes that some firms are more productive than others, which enables the former to enter into more competitive export markets. This focus on firm cost structure echoes the

92(3), 451–471; Helpman, E. and Krugman, P. R. (1985). *Market Structure and Foreign Trade: Increasing Returns, Imperfect Competition, and the International Economy*. MIT Press; Krugman, P. R. (1979). Increasing returns, monopolistic competition, and international trade. *Journal of International Economics*, *9*(4), 469–479.

[19] Lanz, R. and Miroudot, S. (2011). Intra-firm trade. OECD Trade Policy Working Papers, 114.

[20] Antràs, P. (2020). Conceptual aspects of global value chains. *The World Bank Economic Review*, *34*(3), 551–574; Feenstra, R. C. (1998). Integration of trade and disintegration of production in the global economy. *Journal of Economic Perspectives*, *12*(4), 31–50; Johnson, R. C. and Noguera, G. (2012). Accounting for intermediates: Production sharing and trade in value added. *Journal of International Economics*, *86*(2), 224–236.

[21] Antràs, P. (2003). Firms, contracts, and trade structure. *The Quarterly Journal of Economics*, *118*(4), 1375–1418; Bernard, A. B., Jensen, J. B., Redding, S. J., and Schott, P. K. (2007). Firms in international trade. *Journal of Economic Perspectives*, *21*(3), 105–130; Melitz, M. J. (2003). The impact of trade on intra-industry reallocations and aggregate industry productivity. *Econometrica*, *71*(6), 1695–1725.

insights from the NTT but also opens the door for further understanding firm-specific comparative advantage. In addition to export competitiveness stemming from firm market share or global market structure, the focus also allows for firm productivity to be based on *intra*-country differences in local productive infrastructure, quality of human capital, or regional institutional environment. Moreover, it is the consideration of firm cost structure as the driver for exports that ultimately creates a conducive environment for AfT. At the same time, other work revisited the (new) economic geography of trade, noting how physical distance, political boundaries, and concentration and agglomeration of firms can drive observed trade flows and explain regional inequalities.[22] Most recently, the mainstream economics of trade literature has been coming increasingly to grips with the political economy of trade policy, noting how a changing geopolitical environment impacts firm decision making and trade flows.[23]

Effective Market Access

However, while the economics of free trade is clear, the political economy of trade is much cloudier. Even the original thinkers realized that people employed in the comparatively disadvantaged sectors (sometimes called "import-competing" sectors) would lose out once trade was liberalized. While in the Hecksher–Ohlin–Samuelson classic model of free trade this is solved via an assumption of "perfect factor mobility"—that is, an auto-line assembly worker could seamlessly transition to making microchips—the untenability of this position was readily evident.[24] The "trade adjustment" problem is at the core of the political economy of trade.[25] This problem is driven by the logic of collective action. While the gains from trade mostly accrue to consumers in the form of reduced costs and increased choice, these

[22] Anderson, J. E. and Van Wincoop, E. (2003). Gravity with gravitas: A solution to the border puzzle. *American Economic Review*, *93*(1), 170–192; Eaton, J. and Kortum, S. (2002). Technology, geography, and trade. *Econometrica*, *70*(5), 1741–1779; Krugman, P. (1991). Increasing returns and economic geography. *Journal of Political Economy*, *99*(3), 483–499; Krugman, P. and Venables, A. J. (1995). Globalization and the inequality of nations. *The Quarterly Journal of Economics*, *110*(4), 857–880; Redding, S. and Venables, A. J. (2004). Economic geography and international inequality. *Journal of International Economics*, *62*(1), 53–82.

[23] Caldara, D. and Iacoviello, M. (2022). Measuring geopolitical risk. *American Economic Review*, *112*(4), 1194–1225; Handley, K. and Limão, N. (2017). Policy uncertainty, trade, and welfare: Theory and evidence for China and the United States. *American Economic Review*, *107*(9), 2731–2783; Rodrik, D. (2018). Populism and the economics of globalization. *Journal of International Business Policy*, *1*(1), 12–33.

[24] Mundell, R. A. (1957). International trade and factor mobility. *The American Economic Review*, 321–335.

[25] Kim, S. E. and Pelc, K. (2021). How responsive is trade adjustment assistance? *Political Science Research and Methods*, *9*(4), 889–898.

gains are small and diffuse. Few people recognize a small decrease in the price of their T-shirt or an extra variety of grapes on their supermarket shelf. Fewer are prompted to political action by such prospects. In contrast, the losses from liberalized trade—the closing of a textile mill or the seizure of the family farm—are both specific and life-altering. It is much easier to solve the collective action problem of political organization when mobilization depends on coordinating a comparatively small number of people, whose livelihoods are at stake, and who may already be otherwise affiliated via labor or trade organizations. In contrast, consumers, the main beneficiaries of free trade, are much less likely to organize to secure or maintain their small and diffuse gains from trade. Export-oriented interests, those in the comparatively advantaged sector, may be able to similarly overcome the collective action problem as they have the potential for a specific and large gain.[26] These groups can offer some counterweight to import-competing sectors, but as their interests are usually confined to their own sector, they are likely to only be concerned with gaining market access for their wares. If that can be accomplished without granting market access in the import-competing areas, they have no particular reason to advocate for broader liberalization.

As such, and despite the theoretical economic benefits of liberalized trade, market access has always been a completely negotiated and curated domain. The presence of market barriers has given rise to the analyses of "second best" trade rules. One of the most important concepts of the "second best" is that of trade diversion. First discussed by Jacob Viner, trade diversion occurs as a result or regional, or "preferential," trade liberalization. Under these types of agreements, trade is only liberalized between a subset of states. This second-best liberalization can generate both "trade creation" and "trade diversion" effects.[27] Trade diversion occurs when one state substitutes imports from a third-party state with imports from the counterparty with whom the state is engaging in preferential liberalization, which have become competitive vis-à-vis the third-party state solely because of the preferential liberalization. In this instance, imports are shifted away from the most efficient producer. Under these circumstances, the comparative nature of tariff and other trade barriers become the determinants of trade, rather than firm efficiency. The use of selective and incomplete liberalization opens the door for *country-level* winners and losers in trade. Trade diversion implies the possibility of a beggar-thy-neighbor gain—my gain in market access comes at the expense

[26] Dür, A. (2010). *Protection for Exporters: Power and Discrimination in Transatlantic Trade Relations, 1930–2010*. Cornell University Press.

[27] Viner, J. (2014). *The Customs Union Issue*. Oxford University Press.

of your loss.[28] Under trade-diversionary circumstances, market access may no longer increase overall welfare but instead be wielded as a goody which can be bestowed based on political rationale.

The economics of trade is further complicated by the sheer complexity and vastness of human productive endeavors. The Harmonized Tariff Schedule (HTS), an internationally standardized categorization of tradable products maintained by the World Customs Organization (WCO), classifies over 10,000 distinct products at the "eight-digit" tariff code level. Even at the "six-digit" level of product subheadings, there are over 5,000 products.[29] The vastness makes it easy to present a façade of tariff liberalization. Stating that over 99% of tariff lines are duty-free means that 100 products are still subject to tax. Likewise, claiming that an agreement sets a very low *average* tariff level can easily obscure tariff *peaks* on a handful of products.[30] Thus, in practice, market access is rarely complete, and even broad-reaching liberalization agreements can leave out key areas.

Beyond tariffs, other policies can act as significant barriers to trade, effectively hampering exports even when border taxes are low or absent. These so-called "non-tariff barriers" (NTBs) include explicit trade related measures, most notably import quotas or "quantitative restrictions," but can also include less obvious regulatory measures like production subsidies, labeling requirements, product safety standards ("sanitary and phytosanitary measures," SPS), or even policies like environmental or labor regulations. These "behind the border" barriers can effectively block imports, even when no explicit trade barriers are in place.[31] As the GATT/WTO trade regime progressively lowered tariff rates, these NTBs became the more prevalent and practical impediments to trade in sensitive areas excluded from an otherwise liberalizing regime.[32]

These dynamics were distinctly evident in the evolution of the multilateral trade regime. Whilst successive rounds of the GATT rapidly reduced tariffs on a great number of products, certain products and sectors were conspicuously omitted, either via direct or indirect trade barriers. The two most

[28] Nel, P. and Taylor, I. (2013). Bugger thy neighbour? IBSA and South–South solidarity. *Third World Quarterly*, *34*(6), 1091–1110.

[29] HS Nomenclature 2022 edition. Available at https://www.wcoomd.org/en/topics/nomenclature/instrument-and-tools/hs-nomenclature-2022-edition/hs-nomenclature-2022-edition.aspx. Accessed 08-11-2023.

[30] Hoekman, B. M., Ng, F., and Olarreaga, M. (2001). *Tariff Peaks in the Quad and Least Developed Country Exports* (Vol. 2747). Londres: Centre for Economic Policy Research.

[31] Francois, J. and Hoekman, B. (Eds.). (2019). *Behind-the-Border Policies: Assessing and Addressing Non-tariff Measures*. Cambridge University Press.

[32] Orefice, G. (2017). Non-tariff measures, specific trade concerns and tariff reduction. *The World Economy*, *40*(9), 1807–1835.

notable areas are textile and agricultural products. Liberalization in textiles was forestalled by the Multi-Fiber Agreement (MFA), implemented in 1974, which permitted developed countries to impose quantitative restrictions to protect their domestic industries from textile imports from the developing world. While the MFA's successor, the Agreement on Textiles and Clothing (ATC) ended in 2005, the agreements significantly distorted global dynamics in the sector with reverberations still felt today.[33] Likewise, global trade in agricultural products has long been warped by the existence of significant subsidies, or "production supports," in the developed world, most notably in the Europe and the United States.[34] Efforts to liberalize the sector have faced considerable headwinds and, to this day, remain subject to a complex set of rules under the WTO's Agreement on Agriculture. While the distortions in these sectors have had profound detrimental impacts on developing countries, they have also opened opportunities for preferential and potentially trade-diverting access which enables some countries to benefit at the expense of their peers.

These discussions lead to a crucial point of this book, that when discussing market access what is important for export-led growth is meaningful market access. By this I mean market access that (firms in) developing countries can take advantage of. If countries receive market access in the vast majority of areas but fail to secure access in the sector or industry wherein their comparative advantage lies, the broad liberalization will be of little use. Moreover, the existence of more and less obvious NTBs can generate situations wherein countries may have de jure market access in a sector of importance, but still face de facto trade barriers as the countries, or firms therein, lack the capacity to meet regulatory or other barriers. This de jure access may only become operationalizable if and when those barriers can be overcome.[35]

What (or Who?) Determines Access?

As suggested by the discussion above, despite a broadly liberal global trade regime, significant opportunities exist for differential market access based on preferential terms. This trade-diversionary potential creates a situation

[33] Hudson, D., Ethridge, D. E., and Mutuc, M. E. M. (2011). Lessons learned from the phase-out of the MFA: Moving from managed distortion to managed distortion. *Estey Journal of International Law and Trade Policy*, *12*(1), 29–43.

[34] Athukorala, P. C. (2004). Agricultural trade reforms in the Doha round: A developing country perspective. *Journal of World Trade*, *38*, 877.

[35] Pauwelyn, J. (2005). Rien ne va plus? Distinguishing domestic regulation from market access in GATT and GATS. *World Trade Review*, *4*(2), 131–170.

wherein market access can be doled out as a reward or inducement for aims that go beyond simple economic welfare maximization. This inherent politicization of trade makes the economic "first best" of fully liberalized global markets subservient both to the demands of realpolitik but also to the influence of domestic import-competing interests.

International politics models based on rational-actor assumptions suggest that nation-states in an anarchical international system are motivated by material gains. For some, namely proponents of (neo)realism, the binding constraints of anarchy drive states to be primarily concerned with gains vis-à-vis their adversaries in the international system, or "relative gains."[36] For others, namely (neo-liberal) institutionalists, the strictures of anarchy are less pressing and institutionally coordinated cooperation can lead to the pursuit of "win–win" situations, or "absolute gains."[37] In terms of trade policies, these paradigms lead to different implications. Under a neo-realist framework, states will be hesitant to liberalize with any counterparty that might be an adversary but conversely may seek to liberalize with any states with whom they are aligned in order to strengthen their relative position against a common adversary. Using an institutionalist approach, one may expect states to be less concerned about liberalizing with potential adversaries if they themselves can also benefit, but only if and when they believe that international institutions can do an effective job of promoting transparency and rule-adherence.

In practice, at the country level, access to markets has largely followed the tenants of neo-realist thinking. As discussed above, the GATT operated largely as a club open to those members countering, or at least not aligned with, the Soviet Union and communist China.[38] However, with the fall of the Berlin Wall and the accession of the PRC, and then Russia, to the WTO, geo-strategic market access began to be focused more on the proliferating regional (RTAs) and preferential trade agreements (PTAs). Whereas RTAs must be both reciprocal and non-discriminatory, PTAs can give preferential market access terms to developing countries. The most notable PTAs fall under the GATT's Generalized System of Preferences program. Beyond geographic proximity, it has been demonstrated that co-membership in these agreements is more strongly correlated with things like security alliances,

[36] Snidal, D. (1991). Relative gains and the pattern of international cooperation. *American Political Science Review*, *85*(3), 701–726.

[37] Powell, R. (1991). Absolute and relative gains in international relations theory. *American Political Science Review*, *85*(4), 1303–1320.

[38] McKenzie, F. (2008). GATT and the Cold War: Accession debates, institutional development, and the Western Alliance, 1947–1959. *Journal of Cold War Studies*, *10*(3), 78–109; Davis, C. L. and Wilf, M. (2017). Joining the club: Accession to the GATT/WTO. *The Journal of Politics*, *79*(3), 964–978.

historical (including former colonial) ties, shared language or religion, or key natural resources in the developing country.[39]

From the standpoint of domestic politics, market access agreements tend to be offered to countries that offer less risk of import-competition or economic offshoring. Indeed, a broad body of literature has shown that it is difficult to garner domestic support for trade agreements with countries that have strong import-competing sectors or that are potentially home for offshoring.[40] While the latter concept gained a measure of notoriety, if not ridicule, when US presidential candidate Ross Perot described the "giant sucking sound" of the North American Free Trade Agreement (NAFTA) moving jobs from the United States to Mexico, the logic he invoked has resonated with domestic constituencies fearful of losing their livelihoods due to liberalized markets. As such, trade access agreements with countries whose comparative advantage might impinge upon a domestic import-competing sector are less likely to come about than with those countries whose industries could compete with domestic producers.

Yet even within these preferential and regional agreements, there are numerous carveouts. While GATT and WTO rules have mandated that these types of agreements do not undermine multilateral trade principles and preferences, the agreements still rarely liberalize all trade. As many countries trade in only a handful of products, these agreements may mean little to the developing countries if they do not liberalize in the right sectors. Negotiations on key sectors will depend on the extent to which domestic interests in the Northern state will oppose liberalization.

The Political Economy of Aid

The political economy of aid is both more contentious and more uncertain than that of trade. Whereas the political economy of trade centers around understanding why the world ends up in a place of second-best economic outcomes, there is no consensus on if or how foreign aid is effective. As such, and unlike trade, it remains an open question whether foreign aid is desirable, even from a bare economic standpoint. Without this strong theoretical and empirical economic foundation, the political economy of aid becomes even more the purview of politics than trade.

[39] Baccini, L. and Dür, A. (2012). The new regionalism and policy interdependence. *British Journal of Political Science*, *42*(1), 57–79.

[40] Owen, E. (2017). Exposure to offshoring and the politics of trade liberalization: Debate and votes on free trade agreements in the US House of Representatives, 2001–2006. *International Studies Quarterly*, *61*(2), 297–311.

Aid Efficacy

Foreign aid is largely an artifact of the post-WWII era. As discussed earlier, "development" was meant to feature as a key pillar in the Bretton Woods post-war order. However, contemporary foreign aid only began to take the form we currently recognize with the advent of the Organization for Economic Co-operation and Development's (OECD's) Development Assistance Committee in 1960 and the emergence over the following years of bilateral foreign aid programs that complemented development efforts through the World Bank and International Monetary Fund.

The early economics of aid was centered on the basic accounting identity of national income, $Y = C + I + G + (X–M)$, where national income (Y) is comprised of consumption (C), investment (I), government spending (G), and net exports (exports–imports, X–M). The fundamental diagnosis was that the developing countries had suffered from chronic underinvestment, due to factors including distance and unfamiliarity which raised risk and made it difficult for these countries to raise capital on international markets. The obvious solution was to use foreign assistance to fill this investment gap, primarily via investment in large public works projects including transportation and energy. The hope was that this investment would put in place the necessary infrastructure to prompt both foreign and domestic private investment which would lead to increased trade, tax revenues, and private consumption.[41] In essence, it was hoped that these early foreign aid programs would mirror the success of post-war Europe, wherein massive amounts of foreign assistance, primarily through the US-funded Marshall Plan, led to a dramatic recovery of the economies that had been devastated by the war.[42]

However, by the late 1970s it was clear that foreign aid efforts were not bringing widespread prosperity in other parts of the world.[43] Many countries had combined foreign assistance with disastrous import-substitution industrialization (ISI) policies often financed, directly or indirectly, by recycled petrodollars.[44] When US interest rates rose in the 1980s, leading to a rapidly appreciating dollar, numerous developing countries found themselves unable to service these loans, resulting in widespread default and the

[41] Rosenstein-Rodan, P. N. (1961). International aid for underdeveloped countries. *The Review of Economics and Statistics*, 107–138.

[42] Wood, R. E. (1986). *From Marshall Plan to Debt Crisis: Foreign Aid and Development Choices in the World Economy* (Vol. 355). University of California Press.

[43] Heller, P. S. (1975). A model of public fiscal behavior in developing countries: Aid, investment, and taxation. *The American Economic Review*, *65*(3), 429–445.

[44] Yaghmaian, B. (1989). Economic development and the determinants of third world debt. *Review of Radical Political Economics*, *21*(3), 99–104.

resulting "lost decade" of growth for much of the developing world in the 1980s.[45] Many of these countries were bailed out by the World Bank and IMF, but these bailouts often came with the strict conditionality of "structural adjustment programs" (SAPs). The programs imposed the "Washington Consensus" of neoliberal policy practices which largely followed the mantra of "stabilize, privatize and liberalize," resulting in significant cuts in public spending, the sale of state assets, and opening of domestic markets to external goods and investments. These SAPs have been widely perceived as failures.[46] By the mid-1990s many aid-recipient countries were little better off than they had been in the 1960s.[47]

These results prompted a fundamental rethink in the approach to aid. Programs in the 1970s had started to see the importance of building human, in additional to physical, capital, and began to markedly expand assistance programs into "social" sectors like health and education. However, a seminal paper by Craig Burnside and David Dollar argued that aid investment would only be effective in combination with high-quality institutions.[48] As such, aid efforts from the late 1990s onward began to pay markedly more attention to institution building, in areas like judicial independence, control of corruption, press freedom and accountability, the business regulatory environment, and (democratic) governance. Thus, whereas early investigations into aid efficacy had tended to look for broad relationships between aid and growth, more recent investigations consider the impact of aid on growth conditional on other scope conditions.

In this same vein, more recent aid scholarship has come to recognize that not all aid is created equal. An early 2000s reckoning of cross-country studies ultimately concluded that little could be conclusively said with regards to the macro effect of aid on growth.[49] As a result, and with the realization that the causal linkage from aid input to GDP output consists of many steps, most

[45] Singer, H. W. (1989). The 1980s: a lost decade—development in reverse? In *Growth and External Debt Management* (pp. 46–56). Palgrave Macmillan UK.

[46] Easterly, W. (2003a). IMF and World Bank structural adjustment programs and poverty. In *Managing Currency Crises in Emerging Markets* (pp. 361–392). University of Chicago Press.

[47] Rodrik, D. (2006). Goodbye Washington consensus, hello Washington confusion? A review of the World Bank's economic growth in the 1990s: Learning from a decade of reform. *Journal of Economic Literature, 44*(4), 973–987.

[48] Burnside, C. and Dollar, D. (2000). Aid, policies, and growth. *American Economic Review, 90*(4), 847–868.

[49] Doucouliagos, H. and Paldam, M. (2009). The aid effectiveness literature: The sad results of 40 years of research. *Journal of Economic Surveys*, 23(3), 433–461; Easterly, W. (2003b). Can foreign aid buy growth? *Journal of Economic Perspectives, 17*(3), 23–48; Hansen, H. and Tarp, F. (2001); Rajan, R. G. and Subramanian, A. (2008). Aid and growth: What does the cross-country evidence really show? *The Review of Economics and Statistics, 90*(4), 643–665; Roodman, D. (2007). The anarchy of numbers: Aid, development, and cross-country empirics. *World Bank Economic Review*, 21(2), 255–277; Tarp, F. (2006). Aid and development. *Swedish Economic Policy Review, 13*, 9–61.

studies now examine the impact of foreign aid on intermediate outcomes, often at the project level and using randomized control trial (RCT) techniques.[50] While this wave of study has strengthened the internal validity of aid-outcome studies, it has come, to some extent, at the expense of broad external validity. While these studies may solidly establish the efficacy of a particular aid program on a specific outcome, it is not always clear how well the results will travel to other contexts or if the intermediate outcome will ultimately translate into improved performance in aggregate indicators like GDP growth.[51]

Heterogeneity in aid effectiveness may result from a number of aid features. Source and delivery mechanism may well influence the efficacy of aid. Aid from multilateral donors may differ in efficacy from that of bilateral donors, while aid from different bilateral donors might also have differential effects.[52] This bilateral donor heterogeneity has been heightened in recent years by the increasing importance of new or "non-traditional" donor partners such as the PRC.[53] Likewise, aid that is funneled via non-governmental organizations (NGOs), or is directly implemented by donor partners, may have different effects compared to aid which is directed via host country governments.[54] Finally, the modality of aid can also influence effectiveness. Aid that comes in the form of cash grants, "budget assistance" is observed to impact countries differently than that which comes in the form of projects, although the modes or channels of assistance may themselves be conditional on features of the recipient governments and/or the relationship of the recipients with the donor partner.[55] In other words, much of the heterogeneity among donors is directly linked to the different political economy dynamics of aid allocation, as elaborated below.

Some strands of the aid efficacy literature even go so far as to suggest that aid can be *detrimental* to development objectives. Three broad arguments exist that support this overall conclusion. First, a literature on the "aid curse" explores how "unearned" foreign income can prop up ineffective regimes

[50] de Souza Leão, L. and Eyal, G. (2019). The rise of randomized controlled trials (RCTs) in international development in historical perspective. *Theory and Society*, *48*, 383–418.

[51] Peters, J., Langbein, J., and Roberts, G. (2018). Generalization in the tropics–development policy, randomized controlled trials, and external validity. *The World Bank Research Observer*, *33*(1), 34–64.

[52] Brazys, S. R. (2013). Evidencing donor heterogeneity in Aid for Trade. *Review of International Political Economy*, *20*(4), 947–978.

[53] Dreher, A. and Fuchs, A. (2015). Rogue aid? An empirical analysis of China's aid allocation. *Canadian Journal of Economics/Revue canadienne d'économique*, *48*(3), 988–1023.

[54] Dietrich, S. (2013). Bypass or engage? Explaining donor delivery tactics in foreign aid allocation. *International Studies Quarterly*, *57*(4), 698–712.

[55] Koeberle, S., Stavreski, Z., and Walliser, J. (Eds.). (2006). *Budget Support as More Effective Aid?: Recent Experiences and Emerging Lessons*. World Bank Publications.

and undermine effective economic governance.[56] Second, both theoretical and empirical studies on an aid-induced "Dutch Disease" claim that foreign aid can undermine domestic tradable production, hampering export-led growth and worsening balance of payments problems.[57] Finally, a substantial literature examines if large or persistent amounts of foreign aid can lead to instances of "aid dependence," wherein countries become economically dependent on foreign aid inflows, forestalling or obviating the need for economic reforms.[58]

In sum, the myriad (of often overlapping or conflicting) scope conditions likely explain the mixed results on the efficacy of aid. It is very likely that some aid is effective some of the time in some contexts. However, it is also clear that aid does not always and everywhere lead to improvements in intermediate outcomes, much less aggregate development aims like economic growth. This lack of theoretical and empirical consensus on the efficacy of aid only serves to heighten the importance of the political economy of aid, in particular, the political economy and where, how, and why aid is allocated.

Who Gets (Effective) Aid?

While the efficacy of aid remains an open question, scholars are far more settled on questions of who gets aid and why. Like considerations of market access, the allocation of foreign aid is very much a result of political intrigue rather than a question of pure market forces. While observations that foreign aid could be used as a strategic foreign policy tool date nearly to its inception in 1960s,[59] studies in the 1970s began to establish more detailed theoretical and empirical linkages between foreign aid and broader foreign

[56] Djankov, S., Montalvo, J. G., and Reynal-Querol, M. (2008); Ahmed, F. Z. (2012). The perils of unearned foreign income: Aid, remittances, and government survival. *American Political Science Review*, *106*(1), 146–165; Brazys, S. and Vadlamannati, K. C. (2021). Aid curse with Chinese characteristics? Chinese development flows and economic reforms. *Public Choice*, *188*(3), 407–430.

[57] Younger, S. D. (1992). Aid and the Dutch disease: macroeconomic management when everybody loves you. *World Development*, *20*(11), 1587–1597; Arellano, C., Bulíř, A., Lane, T., and Lipschitz, L. (2009). The dynamic implications of foreign aid and its variability. *Journal of Development Economics*, *88*(1), 87–102; Brazys, S (2010). Dutch disease in the western Pacific: An overview of the FSM economy under the Amended Compact of Free Association. *Pacific Economic Bulletin*, *25*(3), 24–39; Rajan, R. G. and Subramanian, A. (2011). Aid, Dutch disease, and manufacturing growth. *Journal of Development Economics*, *94*(1), 106–118.

[58] Bräutigam, D. (2000). *Aid Dependence and Governance* (Vol. 1). Stockholm: Almqvist & Wiksell International; Knack, S. (2001). Aid dependence and the quality of governance: Cross-country empirical tests. *Southern Economic Journal*, *68*(2), 310–329; Brazys, S. (2018). Aid dependence as aid persistence? Non-declining aid and growth. *Journal of International Relations and Development*, *21*, 717–738.

[59] Keohane, R. O. (1965). Political influence in the General Assembly. *Int'l Conciliation*, *36*, 1.

policy objectives.[60] The heart of this debate boiled down to a discussion regarding whether foreign aid was provided to meet "recipient needs" or if, instead, it is used to serve "donor interests." While the former invokes a logic of aid allocation based on economic or social need, the latter is predicated on the idea that aid is given to advance the economic, security, or political aims of the donor. If aid is allocated based on donor interests, the result is that states that lack geo-strategic importance, sizeable domestic markets, or valuable natural resources are unlikely to receive substantial assistance, regardless of any economic or social need. While more recent debates have unpacked more nuanced concepts, such as if aid is "targeted" by donor countries to forestall spillovers from developing countries which might impact the donors, the underlying message is that politics inundates foreign aid allocation decisions.[61]

The implications of the aid allocation debate for aid efficacy are substantial. If aid is not allocated based on development potential, then it is less likely to be effective in promoting economic growth or human development for two reasons. First and foremost are issues of accountability. Donors will be less concerned with how aid is spent when that aid is a quid pro quo for some non-development aim. If the recipient country fulfills the donor's objective, be it through security or political alignment or access to markets or resources, the donor will be less concerned whether the aid is being put to "good" development use. As a result, aid can be used to support and entrench kleptocratic regimes which are more concerned with personal enrichment than with broad-based development.[62]

Forty years of empirical inquiry have found substantial evidence that donors' interests predominate in the allocation of foreign aid. That said, there are some caveats. First, not all donors are created equally.[63] While the vast majority of studies have focused on the behavior of the United States and, more recently, the PRC, a handful of studies examine and find significant heterogeneity among donor motivations in aid allocation. For those countries with colonial pasts, most notably France and the United

[60] Wittkopf, E. R. (1973). Foreign aid and United Nations votes: A comparative study. *American Political Science Review*, *67*(3), 868–888; Richardson, N. R. (1976). Political compliance and US trade dominance. *American Political Science Review*, *70*(4), 1098–1109; McKinlay, R. D. and Little, R. (1977). A foreign policy model of US bilateral aid allocation. *World Politics*, *30*(1), 58–86; McKinlay, R. D. and Little, R. (1979). The US aid relationship: A test of the recipient need and the donor interest models. *Political Studies*, *27*(2), 236–250.

[61] Bermeo, S. (2018). *Targeted Development: Industrialized Country Strategy in a Globalizing World*. Oxford University Press.

[62] Acemoglu, D., Verdier, T., and Robinson, J. A. (2004). Kleptocracy and divide-and-rule: A model of personal rule. *Journal of the European Economic Association*, *2*(2–3), 162–192.

[63] Brech, V. and Potrafke, N. (2014). Donor ideology and types of foreign aid. *Journal of Comparative Economics*, *42*(1), 61–75.

Kingdom, aid allocation is largely driven by these historical ties.[64] Other countries, like Japan and South Korea, are unabashed in their assertion that their foreign aid serves their own economic interests (in addition to ostensibly aiding the recipient country).[65] Still others' allocations, particularly those from Scandinavian donor countries, consistently rank well on the determinants of "need": income levels or other measures of human development.[66]

This heterogeneity in aid allocation motives stems from differences in the domestic political considerations of the donors.[67] In a world of limited resources and unlimited resource demands, governments are held to account for the money they spend. While the stringency of public fiscal accountability will vary with regime type, all governments are keen to display a return on taxpayer funds. Thus, foreign aid donors must ultimately be able to provide a domestic political justification for what, in effect, amounts to a resource transfer to non-citizens in other parts of the globe. Thus, the tack which governments take will depend on what arguments resonate most strongly with their pillars of domestic support.[68] When those pillars are based on popular, elected, support governments will frame allocation in the terms that are most salient to their median voters. The inference is that democratic donors' allocation behavior should mirror that of their median voter on the altruism/self-interest scale. However, while cross-country data on values and preferences is limited, it does not appear that this is always the case. The reason for this is that scholars have evidenced that foreign aid is a very low *salience* issue.[69] Thus, while a democratic electorate may have a preference on how or to whom foreign aid is allocated, this preference is usually not very strong. As such, and like trade preferences, aid allocation may ultimately become captured by, or subservient to, other interests.[70] Like market access, foreign aid can then become the handmaiden to security concerns or

[64] Berthélemy, J. (2006a). Aid allocation: Comparing donor's behaviours. *Swedish Economic Policy Review*, *13*(2), 75.

[65] Hoeffler, A. and Outram, V. (2011). Need, merit, or self-interest—what determines the allocation of aid? *Review of Development Economics*, *15*(2), 237–250.

[66] Alesina, A. and Dollar, D. (2000). Who gives foreign aid to whom and why? *Journal of Economic Growth*, *5*, 33–63.

[67] Tingley, D. (2010). Donors and domestic politics: Political influences on foreign aid effort. *The Quarterly Review of Economics and Finance*, *50*(1), 40–49.

[68] Mosley, P. (1985). The political economy of foreign aid: A model of the market for a public good. *Economic Development and Cultural Change*, *33*(2), 373–393.

[69] Hurst, R., Tidwell, T. and Hawkins, D. (2017). Down the rathole? Public support for US foreign aid. *International Studies Quarterly*, *61*(2), 442–454.

[70] Kegley Jr, C. W. and Hook, S. W. (1991). US foreign aid and UN voting: Did Reagan's linkage strategy buy deference or defiance? *International Studies Quarterly*, *35*(3), 295–312.

commercial interests, and aid allocation decisions will have few electoral consequences for the donor government. Thus, observed altruism in foreign aid allocation from democratic donors is likely to only result when there is both a median voter preference for altruism, but also the absence of any strong countervailing interests.

The constraints are perhaps even less binding in non-democratic donor countries. While foreign aid donors have traditionally been democracies,[71] recent years have seen the rise of important anocratic and autocratic foreign aid suppliers. The most notable of these is the PRC which, by the 2010s, rivalled the other major bilateral donors in both size and scope of their development program.[72] As non-democratic leaders only need satisfy the demands of a "selectorate," foreign aid programs are almost certain to fall into alignment with the broader foreign security and commercial goals that the regime pursues to maintain power.[73] Indeed, as the lines blur between the state and the private sector in these countries, so to do the lines between development assistance and other commercial flows.

More sinisterly, both autocratic and democratic donors might have incentives to tie truly strategic states to themselves financially. Even concessional loans might have hidden strings or be "debt traps" and/or create an aid-dependency wherein the recipient government's economic growth is stymied by an overreliance on foreign funds.[74] These aid-dependent relationships may allow donors to present an outward picture of largesse while achieving strategic aims. Like other strategic motivations discussed above, aid-dependence has an analogue with "trade-dependence" wherein countries become disproportionately reliant on a single export market which allows that state to not only dictate terms of trade but also push for other strategic or economic objectives.[75]

Finally, unlike bilateral donors, the major multilateral development institutions, the IMF, World Bank, and associated regional development banks, have no domestic constituencies but instead are beholden to their member-state principals. While a vast literature shows that powerful principals, the United States in particular, are indeed able to influence the allocation practices of these institutions, the "multiple principals" problem also allows some

[71] With the exception of the Gulf State donors.

[72] Weaver, C. (2015). The rise of China: Continuity or change in the global governance of development? *Ethics & International Affairs*, *29*(4), 419–431.

[73] Licht, A. A. (2010). Coming into money: The impact of foreign aid on leader survival. *Journal of Conflict Resolution*, *54*(1), 58–87.

[74] Brazys, S. (2018). Aid dependence as aid persistence? Non-declining aid and growth. *Journal of International Relations and Development*, *21*, 717–738.

[75] Armstrong, A. (1981). The political consequences of economic dependence. *Journal of Conflict Resolution*, *25*(3), 401–428.

"agent slack" which enables these organizations to pursue aid allocation objectives that are more in line with the preferences of the institution (and individuals therein).[76] This theory has borne out in the real world as a raft of empirical studies suggest that these institutions do allocate aid more "altruistically" with respect to poverty or other social indicators.[77]

In the end, aid allocation, like market access, depends on a complex set of domestic and international political economy considerations that ultimately result in a "second-best" allocation of aid, if we understand the normative function of aid to be to provide assistance to the least developed. Yet, also like market access, the drivers of aid allocation are varied and depend on who is giving the aid.[78] As such, it may well be that some foreign aid truly is given to those most in need, although most aid appears to be driven by at least some level of strategic consideration or foreign policy aim. Of course, it may well happen that recipient need and strategic or economic importance may overlap in happy coincidence. But as suggested by the politics of market access, this already hints that "winners" and "losers" in aid will very much be driven by political choices.

However, even if aid is allocated efficiently in a "first best" manner, unlike trade there is no clear consensus that this will necessarily lead to pareto optimal, or even pareto improving, outcomes. Aid receipt is no guarantee of economic or social development. This ambiguity over aid efficacy not only suggests that aid is no panacea on its own, but that even if coupled with market access it may still not be sufficient in promoting export-led growth. Thus, like the need for *meaningful* market access, countries need to get the *right kind* of aid, to build the right *tools* for growth, if not through the "correct" modalities and in the "right" amounts.

When the Twain Shall Meet: Structure and Agency

The premise of this book is that neither aid nor market access alone is sufficient to lift countries out of poverty and promote sustained and meaningful export-led economic growth in a globalized world. Without aid to

[76] Hawkins, D. G., Lake, D. A., Nielson, D. L., & Tierney, M. J. (2006). Delegation under anarchy: States, international organizations, and principal–agent theory. In *Delegation and Agency in International Organizations*, 3, 21. Cambridge University Press.

[77] Nunnenkamp, P., Öhler, H., and Sosa Andrés, M. (2017). Need, merit and politics in multilateral aid allocation: A district-level analysis of World Bank projects in India. *Review of Development Economics*, *21*(1), 126–156.

[78] Berthélemy, J. C. (2006b). Bilateral donors' interest vs. recipients' development motives in aid allocation: Do all donors behave the same? *Review of Development Economics*, *10*(2), 179–194.

help provide the public goods tools which support productive enterprise—infrastructure, healthy and educated workforce, robust institutions—all the market access in the world will not induce private sector forces to set up shop. Likewise, the absence of a market will negate all the advantages of a supportive environment built with aid. Accordingly, it is the combination of trade-effective aid and meaningful market that is key to development success in a globalized world.

The core problem for developing countries in securing trade-effective aid and meaningful market access is overcoming the domestic politics of the donor countries who provide these goods. As the discussion above highlights, relying on the altruism of donors alone is unlikely to secure either. The domestic politics of aid and access stems from the fact that each imposes different costs and benefits on different constituencies in donor, especially in electoral democracies. If aid is given in pursuit of foreign strategic or economic interests both the costs and benefits are diffuse for the donor population. The largest single donor country, the United States, provides roughly $35 billion per year in ODA. This is less than 1/20th the size of the United States' annual defense budget. While the economic, strategic or "goodwill" benefits of the ODA are hard to quantify, they will frequently take on the same public goods nature as those provided by national defense.[79] These diffuse costs and benefits mean that most constituencies will be largely indifferent, between granting foreign aid to any particular country. When specific interests do arise, such as commercial interests that are looking to secure access to a natural resource, these constituencies will secure these private benefits on the back of the public purse. While private rents may accrue to a select few, there are unlikely to be many interests that pay a direct cost—there is no aid analogue to "import-competing" producers. Usually, these commercial interests arise abroad because the resource in question cannot be secured at home, and thus there are no competing domestic interests.[80] Aid can be transactional in securing this commercial advantage.[81] In other words, giving aid, if anything, will only provide specific benefits but not generate a constituency that will bear concentrated costs.

In contrast, giving market access will almost always impose a concentrated cost on a specific import-competing interest in the domestic constituency.[82] Domestic market access is almost always and everywhere granted as the

[79] Mosley, P. (1985). The political economy of foreign aid: A model of the market for a public good. *Economic Development and Cultural Change*, *33*(2), 373–393.

[80] Reilly, J. (2013). China and Japan in Myanmar: Aid, natural resources and influence. *Asian Studies Review*, *37*(2), 141–157.

[81] Sogge, D. (2002). *Give and Take: What's the Matter with Foreign Aid.* Zed Books.

[82] Schattschneider, E. E. (1935). *Politics, Pressures, and the Tariff.* New York: Prentice Hall.

concession for reciprocal market access abroad. Thus, unlike the granting of aid which accrues no specific cost to a domestic constituency, granting market access will. As discussed above, import-competing interests are strong, especially in electoral democracies. A small, but concentrated, import competing interest may well be able to block market access concessions.[83] These forces will be unopposed by any countervailing domestic interest when broad reciprocal market access has little value to the vast bulk of export-oriented forces.[84] This is often the case in North–South trade negotiations, where the value of gaining (complete) market access to the Southern states' markets is minimal for the majority of export-oriented interests.[85] "Unfair" trade deals, such as preferential trade agreements are, unsurprisingly, viewed negatively by domestic publics in advanced markets.[86]

When and how can developing countries overcome these domestic political dynamics? The answer rests on identifying the conditions when developing countries have sufficient political leverage despite the power asymmetry that frequently exists between them and the donors.[87] The variation in this political leverage depends on when developing countries have the ability to compel, or more likely bargain with, donor partners for the provision of aid and/or access on terms that would make them effective and meaningful. These conditions depend on two features—the structure of the international system (and the developing country's positioning therein) and the agency from the developing country itself.

Discussions of structure and agency are at the core of international relations theory.[88] At one extreme lie entirely structurally determined theories. Most prevalent among these are theories based in structural neo-realism which posit that the nature of international anarchy will compel states to engage in particular foreign policy behaviors or face annihilation.[89] Conversely, other broad approaches, like neo-liberal institutionalism and

[83] De Bièvre, D. and Dür, A. (2005). Constituency interests and delegation in European and American trade policy. *Comparative Political Studies*, *38*(10), 1271–1296.

[84] Kucik, J. (2012). The domestic politics of institutional design: Producer preferences over trade agreement rules. *Economics & Politics*, *24*(2), 95–118.

[85] Manger, M. S. (2009). *Investing in Protection: The Politics of Preferential Trade Agreements between North and South*. Cambridge University Press.

[86] Brutger, R. and Rathbun, B. (2021). Fair share? Equality and equity in American attitudes toward trade. *International Organization*, 75(3), 880–900.

[87] Swedlund, H. J. (2022). Narratives and negotiations in foreign aid: How post-genocide Rwanda uses narratives to influence perceptions of power. In *International Negotiation and Political Narratives* (pp. 178–193). Routledge.

[88] Hollis, M. and Smith, S. (1994). Two stories about structure and agency. *Review of International Studies*, 20(3), 241–251.

[89] Waltz, K. N. (2010). *Theory of International Politics*. Waveland Press.

constructivism, suggest either that anarchy either has sufficient slack or indeed is "what states make of it," such that all countries are able to exercise considerable agency in international affairs.[90] In these latter approaches, the structure of the international system imparts states with "identities" which shape their interactions with other agents in the system.[91] Indeed, this book has already relied heavily on the "identities" of "donor" or "developed" and "developing" states or entities. Yet, as already mentioned, not all donors are the same nor are all developing countries. These identities may be further modified. For donors, the book has already delineated between "democratic" and "autocratic" donors, pointing to evidence that the two types may have different aid and access policies. Likewise, identities of developing countries may be modified based on their "strategic importance" or "economic potential."[92] Alternatively, developing countries may have "spillover" potential (for particular donors).[93] Based on their geographic positioning, natural resource endowment, market or migration potential, some developing countries may be "of interest" to a given donor at a given time. This "of interest" identity is crucial in that it gives a developing country leverage in seeking trade-effective aid and meaningful market access from a given donor.

However, two important caveats apply. First, a developing country's "of interest" identity may shift over time.[94] Its geopolitical position may be strategically salient in one permutation of the international system, but not in another. The "second island chain" in the Pacific was crucially important in World War II but then largely neglected in the following decades. However, with the rise of the PRC as a strategic competitor in the late 2010s, the countries in this chain have regained strategic significance.[95] These dynamics can lead to critical junctures or "windows of opportunity" wherein the (perceived) changing structure of the international system has the potential to

[90] Wendt, A. E. (1987). The agent–structure problem in international relations theory. *International Organization*, *41*(3), 335–370; Carlsnaes, W. (1992). The agency–structure problem in foreign policy analysis. *International Studies Quarterly*, *36*(3), 245–270; Wendt, A. (1992). Anarchy is what states make of it: The social construction of power politics. *International Organization*, *46*(2), 391–425.

[91] Wendt, A. (1994). Collective identity formation and the international state. *American Political Science Review*, *88*(2), 384–396; Bucher, B. and Jasper, U. (2017). Revisiting "identity" in International Relations: From identity as substance to identifications in action. *European Journal of International Relations*, *23*(2), 391–415.

[92] Schraeder, P. J., Hook, S. W., and Taylor, B. (1998). Clarifying the foreign aid puzzle: A comparison of American, Japanese, French, and Swedish aid flows. *World Politics*, *50*(2), 294–323; Bermeo, S. B. (2016). Aid is not oil: Donor utility, heterogeneous aid, and the aid-democratization relationship. *International Organization*, *70*(1), 1–32.

[93] Bermeo, S. B. (2017). Aid allocation and targeted development in an increasingly connected world. *International Organization*, *71*(4), 735–766.

[94] Ibid.

[95] Erickson, A. S. and Wuthnow, J. (2016). Barriers, springboards and benchmarks: China conceptualizes the Pacific "Island Chains". *The China Quarterly*, 225, 1–22.

change a state's identity to or from "of interest" for a particular donor.[96] These dynamics can lead to important within-case variation wherein developing countries who may not have been able to secure effective aid and meaningful market access in one time period may be able to do so in another.

Second, an "of interest" identity alone is not sufficient to secure trade-effective aid and meaningful market access. If the donor's aim is simply to secure security or political alignment, or access to a market or resource, then the donor may care little if the aid or access offered results in economic development. Even when a recipient state's importance stems from donor concern regarding underdevelopment spillovers, targeted donor development efforts may only address that narrow spillover (say stemming outmigration) without contributing to broader economic development. This is the first place where developing country institutional quality enters the equation.

In considering the importance of institutions in the domestic political economy of growth, Douglass North, John Wallis, and Barry Weingast distinguish between "limited" and "open" access orders. The former is predicated on elite management of violence in order to use the state to capture rents and ensure stability while the latter provides broad and inclusive economic and political opportunities via the rule of law and market competition.[97] The conceptualization of limited and open access orders is similar to that of extractive and inclusive institutions, developed by Daron Acemoglu and James Robinson, albeit with the latter having somewhat less of an emphasis on the constraining of political violence.[98] A related line of inquiry focuses on the concept of "political settlement," wherein even limited access orders might achieve growth-compatible institutions if the distribution of elite power is such that the promotion of the institutions is in the interests of those elites.[99] In the world of political settlements, growth-effective aid and development strategies are those that align with the institutions formed by these elite power distributions.[100] Thus, developing countries need to have sufficient institutional capacity to exercise their agency to exploit their structural importance

[96] Doeser, F. and Eidenfalk, J. (2013). The importance of windows of opportunity for foreign policy change. *International Area Studies Review*, *16*(4), 390–406; Capoccia, G. (2016). Critical junctures. *The Oxford Handbook of Historical Institutionalism*, 89–106.

[97] North, D. C., Wallis, J. J., and Weingast, B. R. (2009). *Violence and Social Orders: A Conceptual Framework for Interpreting Recorded Human History*. Cambridge University Press.

[98] Acemoglu, D., and Robinson, J. A. (2013). *Why Nations Fail: The Origins of Power, Prosperity, and Poverty*. Currency.

[99] Khan, M. (2010). Political settlements and the governance of growth-enhancing institutions; Whitfield, L. and Buur, L. (2014). The politics of industrial policy: Ruling elites and their alliances. *Third World Quarterly*, 35(1), 126–144.

[100] Fritz, V. and Menocal, A. R. (2007). Developmental states in the new millennium: Concepts and challenges for a new aid agenda. *Development Policy Review*, 25(5), 531–552; Levy, B. (2014). *Working with the Grain: Integrating Governance and Growth in Development Strategies*. Oxford University Press.

vis-à-vis a donor in a way that is compatible with export-led growth. If a developing country's elites are only interested in securing rents that are incompatible with export-led growth, then they may squander the opportunity to press for trade-effective aid or meaningful market access. However, the transition from limited to open access orders can be difficult and may depend on structural breaks, or critical junctures, to materialize. Likewise, political settlement can be fragile and contingent and can break down due to internal or external factors. Thus, like an international identity, growth-compatible domestic institutional capacity is not static, but can emerge or disappear over time.

In sum, when developing countries have sufficient leverage due to their "of interest" identity vis-à-vis a given donor, and sufficient domestic capacity generated by growth-enhancing institutions, they may be able to successfully overcome domestic political opposition in a donor country to the provision of trade-effective aid or meaningful market access. That said, the size of the win-set for this success ultimately rests on the donor's political calculation of whether the payoff from securing the foreign policy aim outweighs the domestic political cost. However, both the costs and benefits in this equation will vary for any given donor-developing country pair. For some pairs, the domestic political costs of providing aid, or more likely market access, will be much higher than others. In these instances, the developing country will need an identity which imparts more leverage in terms of foreign policy significance to overcome these obstacles. In rare cases, it may be that the donor's interests, and or its targeted development objectives, may provide the combination of trade-effective aid and meaningful market access even in the absence of well-exercised capacity from the developing country partner. However, these cases are likely to be the exception rather than the rule, and most developing countries will have to exercise the agency to exploit the leverage their structural identity gives them. The use of this agency rests in the control of the developing country, but its identity in the international system does not.

However, as previously alluded to, it is firms, not states, that ultimately decide to produce and export. These firms are best positioned to understand both the public goods and market access constraints that hinder that activity. For developing countries to advocate their interests with foreign donors and markets, they need to know what those interests are. Thus, government institutional capacity becomes important in a second part of the logic, this time meditating the extent to which governments can successfully collect information on public goods and market access needs from their firms. In limited access orders or contexts where political settlements may favor a balance of power of elites without export-related interests, government agency may be utilized to promote rent seeking by politically connected, rather than efficient, firms and thus not used to secure aid or access that ultimately promotes growth.

To summarize, the theoretical logic runs thusly. To achieve export-led growth, the ultimate outcome, developing countries need to have firms that are successfully able to export. That export success, an intermediate outcome, is predicated on firms having *meaningful* market access to developed entity markets and an appropriate supporting public goods environment. Market access always depends on developed countries, and public goods may depend on foreign aid from developed entity donors when public investment is otherwise lacking, as is most often the case in the developing world. To secure market access and the aid to build these public goods, developing country governments first need to effectively absorb information on these needs from the domestic firms—a process which is conditional on the institutional quality of those governments. Once governments are equipped with this information, they then need to bargain with developed entities to secure that aid and market access. Developing country governments' success in that endeavor will depend on the relative positioning of the country with any of its given developed entity partners, based on the structure of the international system and the relational identities between the developed country and the respective partner. This relationship will determine if a developing country has sufficient importance to a given developed entity to successfully overcome any domestic political opposition in the developed country to the granting of trade-effective aid or the provision of meaningful market access. The successful exercise of this agency in negotiation will once again depend on the institutional quality of the developing country's government.

Thus, as the book will further argue and demonstrate, developing countries need to secure both aid and access to best pursue export-led growth in a globalized world. As such, developing countries must be wary of instances when donors will provide aid as a substitute for granting access to their markets, usually when attempting to secure market access abroad. When Northern states are unwilling to grant market access due to the politics of import-competing domestic interests, they may instead offer aid, or Aid for Trade, as part of the negotiating package since, as discussed above, aid is relatively "costless" from a domestic political standpoint. This can create situations wherein developing country partners may get aid in lieu of, rather than in conjunction with, meaningful market access. Likewise, and perversely, when developing county partners do have market access that their Northern partners desire, then the negotiations may well be reciprocal, but may obviate the need for compensating aid as the Northern market access becomes the "payment" for whatever access that country is seeking in the developing country.

The following chapters will provide empirical substantiation for this theoretical story. Chapter 3 descriptively explores the relationship between aid, access, and growth to establish the empirical puzzle and provide a classification exercise of different growth experiences. Chapters 4 and 5 then further develop the concepts of *trade-effective aid* and *meaningful* market access, before Chapters 6 through 8 explore "on" and "offline" cases to illustrate how and why a selection of countries did or did not receive trade-effective aid and meaningful market access and how the (non)-receipt of these goods impacted the countries' export-led growth in the globalized world of the late 20th and early 21st century.

3
The Best and the Rest

Diverging Roads

The 75 years since the end of World War II have witnessed one of the largest expansions of income in history. World Bank data suggests that global per capita income increased over 200% in constant terms in the 60 years between 1960 and 2020. In terms of purchasing power parity (PPP), which accounts for difference in prices across countries, the growth has been even more rapid, with the globe seeing over a 200% gain in this measure during the last 30 years alone. These triumphs of global growth have lifted countless millions of individuals out of abject poverty and led to markedly improved living standards for many.[1] Globally, the post-war period of economic growth has been a resounding success story.

Yet, as any casual observer will note, this growth has been uneven, both across and within countries. While some countries, like China, have seen spectacular growth, others, like Madagascar, have seen real income levels drop over the past decades. Figure 3.1 plots the constant per capita Gross Domestic Product (GDP) for all countries whose initial data value put them into the low or middle-income categories. From the figure one can make a few observations. First, there is an overall growth trend—both for the majority of countries but also globally as shown by the thick, black, line. Second, several countries, including South Korea, Singapore, and Guyana were able to vault from low or lower-middle income status all the way to high-income status. Others achieved similarly impressive feats, expanding their economies many times over. For example, India and Indonesia saw over 500% real growth in 60 years, while Vietnam secured the same percent growth in 40 years. While some of these accomplishments are due to the base effects of very poor initial conditions, countries like Thailand achieved over 900% growth despite a starting income that was not amongst the lowest of the low. However, the absolute standout is the People's Republic of China, whose real per capita income increased from the abject-poverty level of $238 in 1960

[1] Radelet, S. (2015). *The Great Surge: The Ascent of the Developing World.* Simon & Schuster.

The Invisible Hand(out). Samuel Brazys, Oxford University Press. © Samuel Brazys (2025).
DOI: 10.1093/9780198970422.003.0003

to over $11,560 in 2022, an increase of more than 4700%. This is especially impressive given the country's massive population. However, the story of the Chinese growth miracle is one that has been told many times and largely falls outside the purview of this book.[2] That said, China was the single largest recipient of aid and, as shown in Figure 3.1, its growth accelerates substantially following its accession to the WTO in 2001. However, despite these success stories, Figure 3.1 also has a bundle of lines which trudge along in the lower income ranges. Some of these, like Madagascar, the Central African Republic, Kiribati, and the Solomon Islands have actually seen decreasing per person incomes, while others, like Guinea-Bissau, Chad, and the Federated States of Micronesia are essentially flat. Still others, like Colombia or the Philippines, show incremental, if uneven, growth.

What explains these divergent growth paths? Severe disruptions, like inter and intra-state war, or major natural disasters, are obvious culprits for underperformance.[3] Indeed, some of the poorest performers in Figure 3.1, like

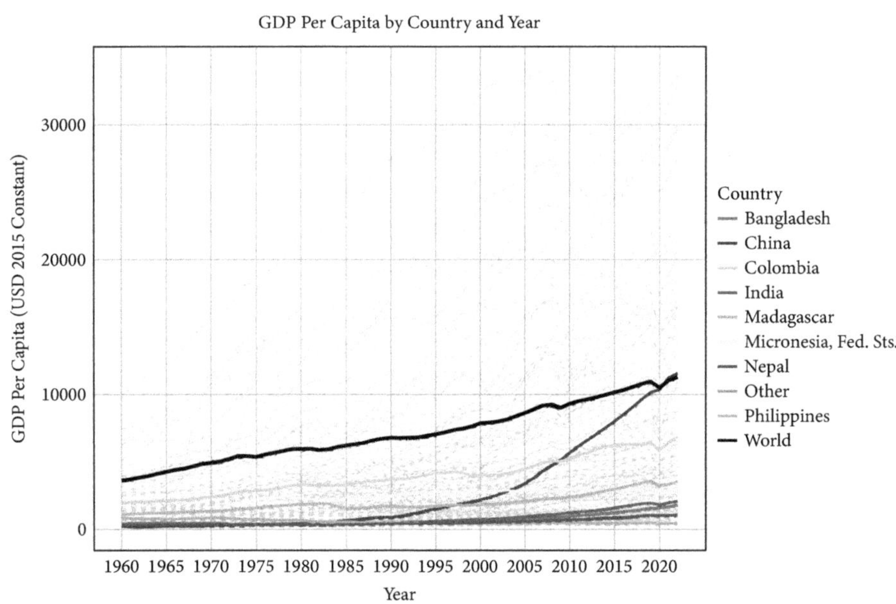

Figure 3.1 GDP per capita for initial low and middle-income countries
Source: World Bank.

[2] Lin, J. Y., Cai, F., and Li, Z. (2004). *The China Miracle: Development Strategy and Economic Reform* (Revised Edition). The Chinese University of Hong Kong Press; Naughton, B. J. (2018). *The Chinese Economy: Adaptation and Growth.* MIT Press.

[3] Koubi, V. (2005). War and economic performance. *Journal of Peace Research*, 42(1), 67–82; Imai, K. and Weinstein, J. M. (2000). Measuring the economic impact of civil war. CID Working Paper Series;

South Sudan, the Democratic Republic of the Congo, Yemen have been plagued by conflict or, like Haiti, a long history of natural disasters.[4] More recently, Russia's invasion of Ukraine set the country's income back 20 years, even after accounting for the economic collapse in the country following the end of the Cold War. However, while many of the growth laggards have similarly afflicted histories, not all can be explained with such prima facie rationales. For instance, while Madagascar has faced several political crises, and periodically endures severe storms, the country has not been overly beset by mass conflict or devastating disasters.[5] Yet, the country's per capita income has fallen by over 45% from its zenith in the early 1970s to its nadir some 50 years later. Likewise, the drop in income in the Pacific-island microstate, Kiribati, has been even more dramatic, plunging nearly 60% from a peak of over $3400 per capita to a pre-pandemic value of just over $1400 in 2019.

In contrast, some of the best performers have been blessed with natural resources or favorable geographic positioning. Botswana's diamonds or Equatorial Guinea's oil are unequivocal drivers of the more than 10-fold increases in each country's income levels.[6] Alternatively, Singapore's positioning at a crucial maritime crossroads is largely cited as a key factor in its astounding economic success, while Panama's control of the eponymous canal has helped it achieve steady growth.[7] Yet, resources alone do not seem to be a sufficient impetus for growth, as many resource-rich states suffer from a natural resource "curse" and do not reap the rewards of their bounties.[8] Likewise, favorable geography is not always a path to success, as Ukraine on the Euro-Asian frontier illustrates.[9]

Moreover, as Jared Diamond argues in his (in)famous book, geography may also be attributable for the "initial conditions" in which states

Fomby, T., Ikeda, Y., and Loayza, N. V. (2013). The growth aftermath of natural disasters. *Journal of Applied Econometrics*, 28(3), 412–434.

[4] Kim, C. K. (2010). The Effects of Natural Disasters on Long-run Economic Growth (Doctoral dissertation).

[5] Hinthorne, L. L. (2011). Democratic crisis or crisis of confidence? What local perceptual lenses tell us about Madagascar's 2009 political crisis. *Democratization*, 18(2), 535–561; Francken, N., Minten, B., and Swinnen, J. F. (2012). The political economy of relief aid allocation: Evidence from Madagascar. *World Development*, 40(3), 486–500.

[6] Hillbom, E. (2008). Diamonds or development? A structural assessment of Botswana's forty years of success. *The Journal of Modern African Studies*, 46(2), 191–214; Frynas, J. G. (2004). The oil boom in Equatorial Guinea. *African Affairs*, 103(413), 527–546.

[7] Huff, W. G. (1997). *The Economic Growth of Singapore: Trade and Development in the Twentieth Century*. Cambridge University Press; Cordoba, G. F. (2022). The impact of the Panama Canal transfer on the Panamanian economy. *Economics Letters*, 211, 110208.

[8] Atkinson, G. and Hamilton, K. (2003). Savings, growth and the resource curse hypothesis. *World Development*, 31(11), 1793–1807.

[9] Mykhnenko, V. (2020). Causes and consequences of the war in Eastern Ukraine: An economic geography perspective. *Europe-Asia Studies*, 72(3), 528–560.

found themselves.[10] Indeed, latitude appears to go a long way in explaining divergent income levels, with countries at tropical latitudes having notably lower income levels, on average, compared to their more temperate counterparts.[11] However, yet again, there are many exceptions to this (deterministic) rule. The aforementioned growth miracles Singapore, Botswana, Equatorial Guinea (not to mention Taiwan) all lie between 30 degrees North and South. Likewise, solid, if not spectacular, performers like Indonesia or Vietnam also rest in these latitudes.

To reconcile these discrepancies, many scholars have introduced the idea that divergent growth is based on differing institutional quality, as discussed at length in the previous chapter. Most notable among these voices are those of Daron Acemoglu, Simon Johnson, and James Robinson. In a series of works, culminating in Acemoglu and Robinson's popular book *Why Nations Fail*, the authors argue that countries with institutions that encourage property rights and constrain (the rents of) the holders or political power, see higher growth rates.[12] These compelling arguments, evidenced through "natural experiments" like the political division of Korea, have been largely adopted as conventional wisdom by the policy and scholarly communities. However, yet again, there are exceptions to the "good governance" rule. Several countries which score highly in governance metrics, indicating open access orders or potentially growth-enhancing political settlement, also sit near the bottom of growth measures. Small-island states like Kiribati, Micronesia, or Vanuatu, or larger states like Namibia, all score comparatively well on governance measures yet have minimal long-term average growth rates. Likewise, some of the highest growth performers, like Equatorial Guinea or Vietnam rank near the bottom in conventional measures of governance.

The debates over the causes of persistent (or divergent) underdevelopment thus suggest nuance. As William Easterly demonstrates emphatically in his book-length critique, *The Elusive Quest for Growth*, there are no "catch-all" rules that explain why some countries have been able to prosper while others have lagged behind.[13] However, even the combination of the prevalent

[10] Diamond, J. (1997). *Guns, Germs, and Steel: The Fates of Human Societies*. Norton & Company.

[11] Sachs, J. D. (2001). Tropical underdevelopment. NBER Working Paper, (w8119); Sachs, J. D. (2003). Institutions don't rule: Direct effects of geography on per capita income, National Bureau of Economic Research Working Paper No. 9490.

[12] Acemoglu, D., Johnson, S., and Robinson, J. A. (2001). The colonial origins of comparative development: An empirical investigation. *American Economic Review*, 91(5), 1369–1401; Acemoglu, D., Johnson, S., and Robinson, J. A. (2005). Institutions as a fundamental cause of long-run growth. *Handbook of Economic Growth*, 1, 385–472; Acemoglu, D. and Robinson, J. A. (2013).

[13] Easterly, W. R. (2002). *The Elusive Quest for Growth: Economists' Adventures and Misadventures in the Tropics*. MIT Press.

existing explanations still appears unable to account for the wide range of variation that is observed in developmental outcomes. To complement these existing rationales, this book advances the argument that states which have received the combination of trade-effective aid and meaningful market access will have outperformed those who haven't in an era of economic globalization. While the subsequent chapters flesh out these arguments through more in-depth investigations into what constitutes trade-effective aid and meaningful market access, illustrated with a series of case studies, this chapter uses cross-country data to set the puzzle through descriptive and inferential statistics. This "nested-analysis" seeks to first identify a range of potentially interesting cases to further investigate in a model-building, small-N, approach in the subsequent chapters.[14] Importantly, this chapter does not purport to establish causal linkages between aid and market access and growth, but, instead, seeks to identify which countries have grown, which have not, and what types and/or amounts of aid and access they have received. The chapter conducts this analysis with references to dominant explanations of geography and institutions and reflects on how these prevailing explanations of divergent growth fit into the theoretical argument of Chapter 2.

The Conventional Wisdom

The two dominant explanations for divergent growth paths, geography and governance, do a reasonable job of explaining much of the variation in economic performance. However, each has limitations. While geographic explanations largely take into account the "space and place" of history, including the role of slavery and imperialism, as well as differing climatic factors including the prevalence of disease or the difficulty of navigation, they are also deterministic and reductionist and obviate the role of international politics, human agency, or entrepreneurial *nous*.[15] Natural and spatial geography no doubt carries explanatory power. The basis of much work on contemporary trade flows is the "gravity model," which counts physical distance as the primary determinant of bilateral trade flows in goods.[16] Likewise, strategic or political geography can be a key determinant of whether or not a state has an

[14] Lieberman, E. S. (2005). Nested analysis as a mixed-method strategy for comparative research. *American Political Science Review*, 99(3), 435–452.

[15] Stock, R. (1986). "Disease and development" or "the underdevelopment of health": A critical review of geographical perspectives on African health problems. *Social Science & Medicine*, 23(7), 689–700; Forbes, D. (2010). *The Geography of Underdevelopment: A Critical Survey* (Vol. 68). Routledge.

[16] Anderson, J. E. (2011). The gravity model. *Annual Review of Economics.*, 3(1), 133–160; Ashworth, L. M. (2013). Mapping a new world: Geography and the interwar study of international relations. *International Studies Quarterly*, 57(1), 138–149.

"of interest" identity.[17] Yet, as an overarching heuristic explaining divergent economic growth, the approach falls woefully short and has been forcefully critiqued by geographers who note how it overlooks key socio-spatial or (geographic) political economy rationales for development.[18]

On the flip side, governance-based explanations tend to shift the bulk of the underperformance onto the underdeveloped societies. While Acemoglu and Robinson explicitly dismiss *cultural* explanations of underdevelopment, and thus claim their explanation is anti-racist, this logic is predicated on the tenuous claim that institutions are divorced from culture and that country institutions were often (entirely) imposed on developing countries by their colonizers.[19] These arguments largely place the onus of "acquiring" good institutions on the developing countries.[20] A critique of these arguments is that they represent a thinly veiled implication that persistent institutional failings result from societies (and individuals therein) that are too impotent/stupid/corrupt to rein in rent-seeking elites who have captured state institutions in a limited access order.[21] While Acemoglu and Robinson and others lay down anti-racist foundations for why many countries have poor institutions in the first place, colonialism, and slavery, they still neglect to explain why many well-governed countries struggle to attain persistent economic development. As theorized in Chapter 2, this book in no way discounts that domestic institutions are certainly an important part of the export-led growth story but argues that they serve primarily as a catalyzing feature that enables states to take advantage of the opportunities presented by their positioning in the international system.

While these explanations appear to soak up a fair amount of the cross-country and over-time variation in growth rates, a closer look suggests that they might not be wholly satisfactory. While geographic explanations carry a heavy determinism which overlooks the agency of both donor and developing countries polities, institutional explanations may overlook the external realities which inhibit the opportunities for developing countries to fully exercise their agency even in the presence of strong domestic institutions. As later chapters will show in more detail, aid and access are very

[17] Cohen, S. B. (2014). *Geopolitics: The Geography of International Relations*. Rowman & Littlefield.

[18] Sheppard, E. (2011). Geography, nature, and the question of development. *Dialogues in Human Geography*, 1(1), 46–75.

[19] Dzionek-Kozlowska, J. and Matera, R. (2021). Institutions without culture: On Daron Acemoglu and James Robinson's Theory of Economic Development. *Journal of Economic Issues*, 55(3), 656–676.

[20] Rodrik, D. (2000). Institutions for high-quality growth: What they are and how to acquire them. *Studies in Comparative International Development*, 35, 3–31.

[21] Qureshi, M. G., Qayyum, U., and Ghani, E. (2021). Acemoglu, Johnson and Robinson's notion of exogenous imposition of colonial institutions onto colonies—a critique in the light of historical evidence. *Pakistan Development Review*, 60(2), 133–152.

often the consequence of political choices by external international actors. Unlike geography, which cannot be altered, political choices can be changed and thus, if they are indeed explanatory, can provide an alternate path for addressing concerns of underdevelopment.

The View from 30,000 Feet—the Aid and Access Quadrants

This section turns to some descriptive evaluation using "off the shelf" data to evaluate the puzzle of divergent growth. While further chapters flush out additional nuance in terms of meaningful access and trade-effective aid, the evidence presented in this section is aggregate and of a general and imperfect level of operationalization. The first instance considers purely raw measures of aid, trade, and growth. Unless otherwise stated, growth is considered as the percent change in GDP per capita. For aid, raw metrics are problematic as both aid and aid per capita are strongly correlated with country size. Empirically, the largest total amounts of aid go to the largest countries, but the largest amounts of aid per capita go to the smallest countries. A metric which reconciles some of this discrepancy is to consider the ratio of aid to GDP. This measure is plotted in Figure 3.2 for all aid receiving country-years since 1960 for which there is data. The figure shows that there is no clear-cut, simple, relationship between aid amounts and growth, consistent with decades of research on the topic. At nearly all levels of aid there are country-year observations which show both growth and contraction and, while not statistically significant, overall there is a slight downward trend between aid levels and growth.

Looking at raw data for market access is more complicated since, although dozens of measures have been established over the years to evaluate trade openness, few of these reflect the market access opportunities that face a country.[22] Most studies consider a given country's own trade openness, ex post, by looking at an outcome-based measure of trade (exports, imports, or total trade) as a share of income.[23] However, these measures overlook non-tariff barriers (NTBs) and may not reflect that average tariffs can obscure meaningful market access for key, specific, products. Other measures look at tariff costs faced by exporting countries and/or considers distance and

[22] Rose, A. K. (2004). Do WTO members have more liberal trade policy? *Journal of International Economics*, 63(2), 209–235.

[23] Squalli, J. and Wilson, K. (2011). A new measure of trade openness. *The World Economy*, 34(10), 1745–1770.

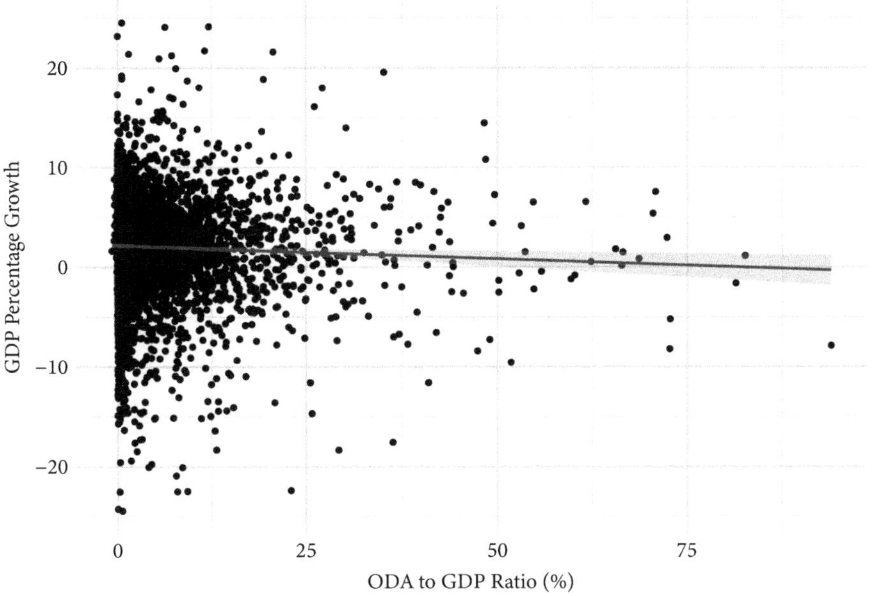

Figure 3.2 ODA/GDP and GDP per capita growth
Source: World Bank.

residual "border" costs as part of standard gravity model of trade.[24] In a 2012 paper, José de Sousa and co-authors estimated border effects for countries based on the ratio of internal to external trade, along with other gravity determinants like (internal and external) distance.[25] This approach allowed for border effect coefficient estimates by country and time-period. The authors were further able to disaggregate this to consider a coefficient for developing country access to Northern markets—in effect a measure of market access to these markets. However, due to data limitations, the authors were only able to generate estimates for 69 countries in three periods: 1980–1988, 1989–1997, and 1998 to 2006. This sample is likely biased, as poorer countries are less likely to have complete data, and this is correlated with a growth measure. That said, to take a look at the raw data, Figure 3.3 plots these market access scores against the average per capita growth rates for each country during the given period.

The market access indicator is constructed in such a way that higher scores indicate more severe border effect. Figure 3.3 shows a slight downward trend

[24] Larch, M., Tan, S. W., and Yotov, Y. V. (2023). A simple method to ex-ante quantify the unobservable effects of trade liberalization and trade protection. *Journal of Comparative Economics*, 51(4), 1200-1213.
[25] De Sousa, J., Mayer, T., and Zignago, S. (2012). Market access in global and regional trade. *Regional Science and Urban Economics*, 42(6), 1037–1052.

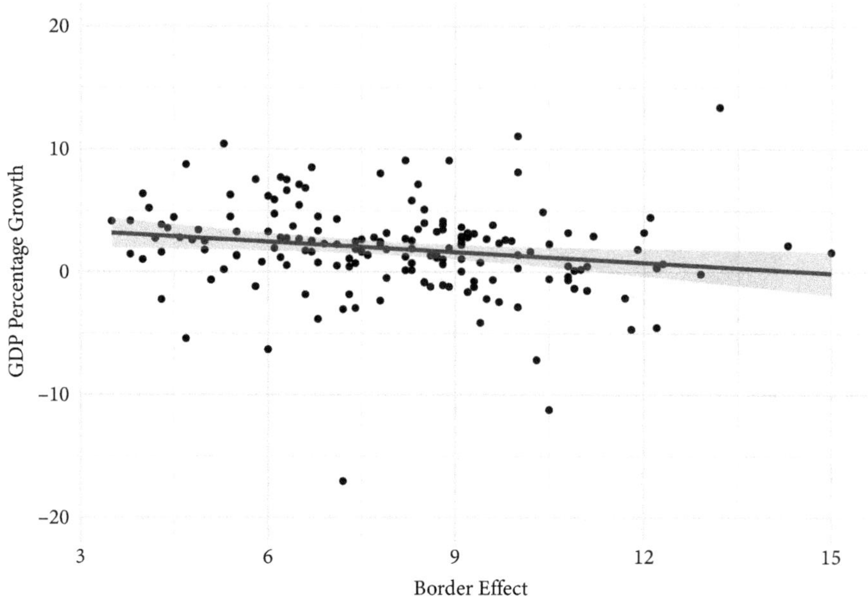

Figure 3.3 Market access and GDP per capita growth
Source: Adapted from data presented in De Sousa et al. (2012).

between increasing border effects (i.e., less market access) and growth. As this is an ex-post measure—it is based on actual internal and external trade flows—it might be considered as ex-post evidence of realized meaningful market access. On average, those developing countries who had more market access had higher growth rates than those that did not. Yet, there remains a substantial amount of variation—many country-periods with lower border effects had growth rates lower than country-periods who faced more restrictive border effects. These raw data are not intended to test the theoretical claims of the importance of effective aid and meaningful market access, but instead to primarily highlight the volatility between these measures and measures of growth.

Conceptually, the factors of trade-effective aid and meaningful market access suggest that countries can fall into one of four quadrants in any given time period—those with aid and access, those with one or the other, respectively, or those with neither. Classifying country (periods) into these quadrants provides a basis for the case selection and framing device for the remainder of the book. In the first instance, Figure 3.4 provides a static, descriptive, view of the growth of the 142 countries who started the post-war period as low or middle-income economies. Each country is ranked against its peers with percentile measures along the aid and access dimensions. To

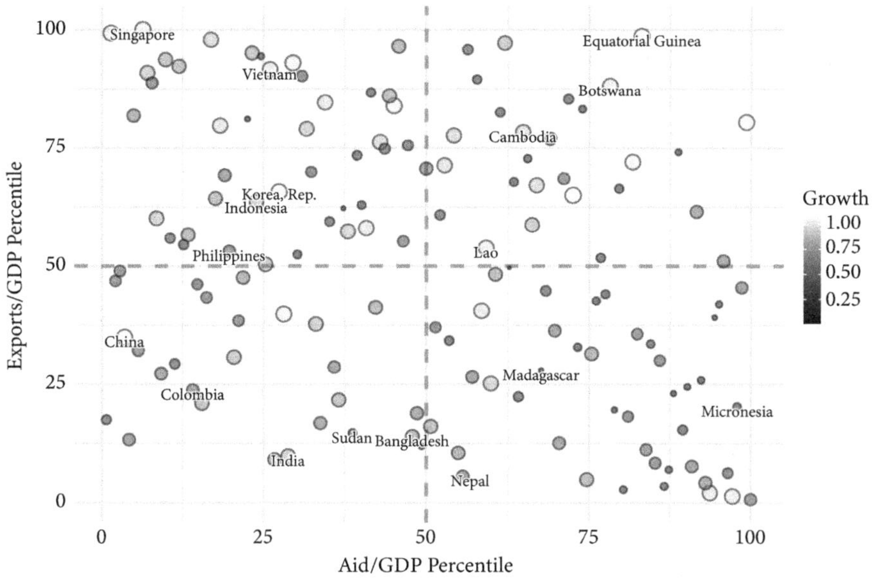

Figure 3.4 Aid and export ratios quadrants

Sources: World Bank, author's calculations.

expand the data coverage for the access measure, Figure 3.4 uses the simpler ex-post measure of trade share—in this case the average ratio of a country's level of exports to total economic output. Admittedly, this is an imperfect measure—exports may dominate the economies of some countries—especially resource-rich ones—even in the absence of broad market access in those product areas. Likewise, larger countries are more likely to have larger domestic markets and thus have a smaller export share. Finally, export statistics can be distorted via creative firm-level accounting in areas like the presence of intangible assets.[26] However, those caveats aside, as a quick look at this measure is still likely to be highly correlated with the underlying concept and gives a reasonable approximation of countries whose firms were able to find export markets for their products.

Figure 3.4 provides a first cut at categorizing countries into the four conceptual quadrants. The size and shading of each country's indicator circle captures their percentile in long-term growth rates—larger and brighter circles had higher growth rates. The patterns reflect those from the bivariate relationships in Figures 3.2 and 3.3. Countries with higher export shares (in the upper half) have better average growth performance than those that

[26] Polyak, P. (2023). Jobs and fiction: identifying the effect of corporate tax avoidance inflating export measures in Ireland. *Journal of European Public Policy*, 1–22.

do not. As mentioned above, while export share may be an ex-post reflection of meaningful market access, nothing in this revelation explains how or why some countries received and were able to take advantage of that access. Moreover, countries that had both comparatively lower export shares and higher aid shares (in the SE quadrant) perform worst of all. Likewise, many of the strongest growth "success" stories—Singapore, South Korea, Vietnam—inhabit the NW, or "low aid, high export share" quadrant. This visualization again suggests that measures of aid *amounts* simply are not meaningful proxies for *effective* aid. Even as a ratio (to GDP), the aid measure struggles to escape its relationship to population with most of world's most populous developing countries (including China and India) inhabiting the left-hand (west) side of the space. Indeed, population also impacts the export share, as larger countries are likely to have larger internal markets and, thus, smaller ratios of exports to GDP.

To tweak the aid measure to be a better proxy of ex-post evidence of effective aid, Figure 3.5 uses an indicator that captures the rate of change in the aid ratio—the median annual percent change in the amount of per capita ODA received by the country. The conceptual logic, used in previous studies of aid dependence, is that, over the long run, effective aid should be self-defeating.[27] In other words, if aid enables a country to grow, that country should need less, and eventually no, aid. In many countries which have developed, aid stopped flowing, either due to formal ineligibility or a reduction in perceived need by donors.

Some countries, like Botswana, did have high levels of aid, but these fell precipitously as the country developed. Indeed, in many instances, former net recipients of aid become net donors. Thus, one way to capture effective aid would be to look for aid that decreases over time. Again, this is not a perfect metric as one can think of numerous other reasons why aid might be reduced, withdrawn, or suspended short of its "success."[28] That said, in a world of imperfect proxies it is useful for a "30,000" foot view.

[27] Riddell, R. (1996). Aid dependency, in Gus Edgren, Roger Riddell and Rehman Sobhan, eds, Aid Dependency: Causes, Symptoms and Remedies, Project, 2015, 23–110, Swedish International Development Cooperation Agency; Brazys, S. (2018). Aid dependence as aid persistence? Non-declining aid and growth. *Journal of International Relations and Development*, *21*, 717–738.

[28] Asongu, S. A. and Nwachukwu, J. C. (2017). Is the threat of foreign aid withdrawal an effective deterrent to political oppression? Evidence from 53 African countries. *Journal of Economic Issues*, 51(1), 201–221; O'Brien-Udry, C. (2022). Aid withdrawal: theory and evidence from international climate politics Portela, C., and Mora-Sanguinetti, J. S. (2023). Sanctions effectiveness, development and regime type. Are aid suspensions and economic sanctions alike? *World Development*, 172, 106370.

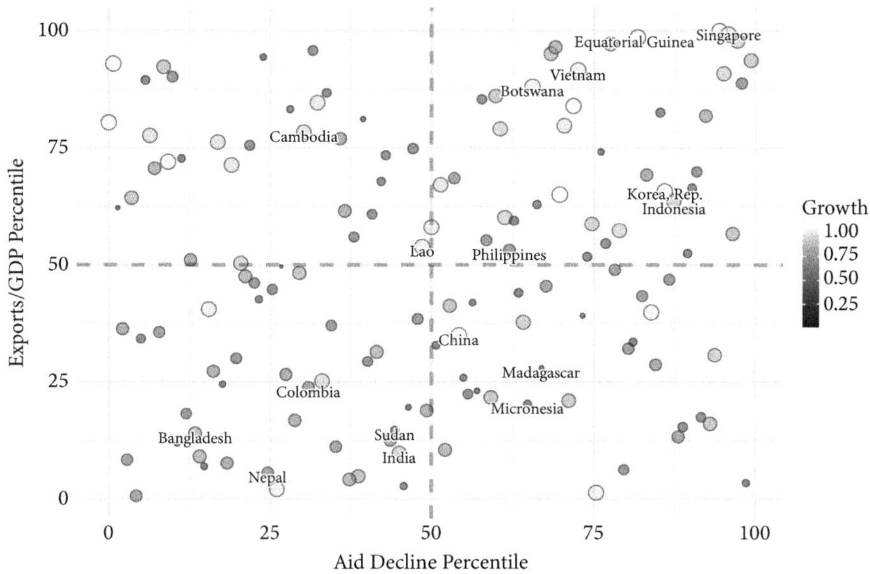

Figure 3.5 Aid rate of change and export ratio quadrants

Sources: World Bank, OECD, author's calculations.

Box 3.1 Zimbabwe: Unlimited Limited Access

Since the end of its civil war in 1980, few countries better fit the conceptualization of a "limited access order" with "extractive institutions" than the well-documented case of Robert Mugabe's Zimbabwe. Following his election in 1980, Mugabe ruled the country, in and out of political settlement with other elites, until his forcible ousting at the hands of the army in 2017, which served to perpetuate the interests of the elites. In the intervening years, the country experienced out-and-out expropriation of resources and elite capture of the country's vast mineral and other rents, all while the bulk of country's population experienced degrowth and hardship. Mugabe's Zimbabwe remains a prime example of a country where the political settlement of elites resulted in institutions that inhibited, rather than promoted, export-led growth. Thus, while the country appears to score well on metrics of aid and access, the lack of strong domestic institutions likely inhibited them from facilitating trade-effective aid or meaningful market access that went beyond the rent-seeking of elites.

Figure 3.5 points to a few interesting observations. The top half is almost a mirror image of Figure 3.4. Countries with a high ratio of exports, but with low ratios of aid that are also declining are now in the NE quadrant—including success stories Singapore, South Korea, Hong Kong, Botswana, Thailand, Indonesia, Vietnam, Chile, Costa Rica, and Malaysia to name a few.

Notably, among the high performers in this quadrant, institutional quality is varied, with pure dictatorships like Equatorial Guinea, autocracies like Vietnam, anocracies like Sri Lanka or Thailand, fragile and emerging democracies like Mongolia, or established democracies like Chile or Singapore all populating the space. Likewise, many of these higher performing economies lie squarely within the tropics. However, equally interesting are those countries "off the line" in this quadrant—that is, those with aid and access but who underperformed on growth. While some, such as Libya, are easily explainable via a combination of aid withdrawal and natural resource export dominance, others, like (periodically) democratic Philippines, are less easily explainable. Some of these "off-the line" cases are suggestive of the importance of institutional or geographic explanations, and that effective aid and market access are not sufficient for growth. One example is Zimbabwe, a country classified in the 62nd percentile of exports to GDP and the 66th percentile of declining aid while only 16th percentile of growth, whose experience is provided in more detail in Box 3.1.[29] In contrast, there is less movement on the bottom half of the graph. Both Micronesia and Madagascar remain in the SE quadrant—suggesting that both, in addition to having high ratios of aid, also had higher comparative rates of decline. That said, both have some of the worst growth performance of any of the countries in the sample. These are "on-the-line" cases in that they do not appear to have the necessary combination of effective aid and meaningful market access. More curiously, Bangladesh and Colombia remain the SW quadrant (a low ratio of exports and a lower relative rate of aid decline), and Nepal drifts into that category as well. While none of these countries are stellar performers, both Nepal and Colombia had growth performance near the median of the sample. Bangladesh's performance is even better, in the 64th percentile, despite scoring in only the 13th

[29] Acemoglu, D. and Robinson, J. A. (2019). Rents and economic development: The perspective of why nations fail. *Public Choice*, 181, 13–28; Bracking, S. (2018). Corruption and state capture: What can citizens do? *Daedalus*, 147(3), 169–183; Dendere, C. and Taodzera, S. (2023). Zimbabwean civil society survival in the post-coup environment: A political settlements analysis. *Interest Groups & Advocacy*, 12(2), 132–152; Kamete, A. Y. (2016). "Programmed to serve": Urban planning and elite interests in Zimbabwe. *Governing Urban Africa*, 151–169; Matamanda, A. R., Chirisa, I., and Rammile, S. (2021). Elitist domination and its import: Survey of four decades of perpetuation of inequities in Zimbabwe. *Politikon*, 48(3), 450–467; Simpson, M., Hawkins, T., Simpson, M., and Hawkins, T. (2018). Regime survival: Poverty creation, mass migration and elite enrichment. In M. Simpson and T. Hawkins (Eds.), *The Primacy of Regime Survival: State Fragility and Economic Destruction in Zimbabwe* (pp. 139–163). Taylor & Francis.

percentile in both the aid and access measures. Bangladesh then is an interesting "off-the-line" case, one that appears to have had at least some modicum of development success despite the lack of prima facie evidence of effective aid and meaningful market access. The rate of change aid measure mitigates some population problem when constructing an aid metric, as China is now (just) in the SE quadrant.

Box 3.2 The "Growth" Quadrant

Did developing countries which had declining aid *and* a ratio of exports to GDP grow more than those that did not? Simple regressions suggest so.

Box Table 1 Correlates of long-term growth performance

	(1)	(2)	(3)
NE Quadrant	1.126***	1.036***	0.411**
	(0.332)	(0.367)	(0.172)
Population		0.003*	
		(0.002)	
Governance		0.024***	
		(0.006)	
Conflict		0.005	
		(0.010)	
Initial GDP pc		–0.000***	
		(0.000)	
Latitude		1.254**	
		(0.541)	
Observations	142	142	6,438
Country FE	No	No	Yes
Year FE	No	No	Yes
Adjusted R^2	0.08	0.30	0.17
Prob > F	0.00	0.00	0.02

Robust standard errors in parentheses
**p < 0.01, *p < 0.05, † p < 0.1.

Both bivariate regression and a multi-variate regressions including controls for governance, latitude, population, and conflict indicate that countries in the NE quadrant had average per capita growth rates 1.0–1.1 percentage points higher than countries in other quadrants over a cross-section of developing countries. A panel model, with year and country fixed effects suggests that, on average, countries had 0.40 percentage point higher growth rates in years they were in the NE quadrant.

Again, these ex-post measures in no way explain how or why aid was effective or market access was meaningful to these countries (or not). Instead, this exercise is simply meant to categorize the countries into those that did or did not have the combination of these prima facie indicators of aid and access. These raw data suggest it is reasonable to claim that the countries with this mix did indeed experience better overall growth. Box 3.2 displays the results of the simple cross-country growth regressions in Models 1 and 2.[30] As shown there, countries in the NE quadrant are associated with higher growth levels over the entire post-war period. That said, due to the non-random assignment of aid and market access, these relationships cannot shed light on any causal relationship. The relationships could be spurious, suffer from reverse causality (where countries with better growth prospects receive more effective aid and meaningful market access), or be further confounded by other unobserved variables. Moreover, the number of outliers—both those in the NE quadrant who did not experience growth and those in the other quadrants who did—suggests that aid and access may be neither sufficient nor necessary for growth and/or that these ex-post measures do not fully capture the concepts of growth-effective aid and meaningful market access.

Who Gets the Golden Goose?

While the ex-post measures above provide some idea of what countries have or have not grown, and what the aid and export profiles of these states look like, they provide little insight into how or why some countries get market access and effective aid and others do not. In the previous chapter I argued that it is domestic and international politics that determines which countries receive trade-effective aid and meaningful market access. As argued there, these dynamics are driven by both the structure and agency of international politics. When developing countries are sufficiently important, they may be able to exercise agency to overcome domestic politics to secure trade-effective aid and meaningful market access. Also, in some rare instances, it may be that a lack of donor domestic political opposition (or donor domestic interests which align with meaningful access and trade-effective aid) allows for either "targeted development" or simply a "happy accident" that results in a developing country receiving both useful aid and access. A quick perusal of

[30] To proxy institutional quality, a metric of the average governance score from the World Bank's World Governance Indicators is used. To capture spatial geography, the absolute value of the latitude of each country's capital serves as a proxy for that country's geographical positioning. The confounders included in the model 2 include a measure of each country's average population, and their initial GDP per capita level to capture base effects.

the NE quadrant countries suggests that it is populated with both types of states.

From a strategic perspective, US allies South Korea and the Philippines have both received aid and access and are classified in the NE quadrant. While South Korea and the United States signed a FTA in 2007, both countries have historically had preferential access for key goods with the United States, with South Korea commanding a sufficient quota share under the Multifiber Agreement (MFA) in the 1960s and 1970s and the Philippines being an early beneficiary of US GSP.[31] Likewise, high-performing NE quadrant dwellers Singapore, Vietnam, and Indonesia, the latter two who are both explored at greater depth in Chapter 7, are key actors in a strategic corner of the globe. Both the European Union and United States have invested considerable aid, as well as helped facilitate market access, in order to strengthen ties with these states.[32] That said, other countries in the NE quadrant have little prima facie strategic importance. Mauritius, Guyana, or even Botswana, all countries in the NE quadrant who have experienced impressive long-term growth, are not generally considered to be key pieces on the global geostrategic chessboard. Thus, rather than the exercise of domestic agency by states of key "importance," each of these countries may have received their effective aid and meaningful market access more as a happy coincidence that the access agreements that they belonged to provided access in areas that were important to their economies. For example, Botswana's ubiquitous endowment of diamonds (HS 7102) enter markets duty-free under MFN tariffs. The lack of import-competing diamond mining interests in the developed world (because there are no major diamond mines) no doubt facilitates this duty-free access. In contrast, very few of the states in the other three quadrants would be considered vitally strategic states for major Western countries, at either the regional or global level. The obvious exceptions would be either large states like Brazil, India, Mexico, or Turkey (or China), whose large domestic markets mean they have lower export ratios, or states like Ukraine, Iraq, or Afghanistan which, while strategic, have also been directly impacted by major conflict.

In sum, the view from 30,000 feet suggests that the underlying premise of the book is worthy of further exploration. The analysis above serves primarily as a classification exercise, rather than a causal analysis, recognizing

[31] Smith, D. A. (1996). Going south: Global restructuring and garment production in three East Asian cases. *Asian Perspective*, 211–241; Paderon, M. M. A. (2022). Philippine-United States trade relations: Looking back and a way forward. East-West Center. Number 588, June 13, 2022.

[32] Forster, A. (1999). The European Union in South-East Asia: Continuity and change in turbulent times. *International Affairs*, 75(4), 743–758; Goh, E. (2007). Great powers and hierarchical order in Southeast Asia: Analyzing regional security strategies. *International Security*, 32(3), 113–157.

that countries that have performed well also appear to have had effective aid and meaningful market access. Without discounting the importance of existing explanations, particularly the importance of good governance for long-term growth and development, the strong relationship between effective aid *and* meaningful market access and long-term development performance is readily apparent. Given that there are plenty of cases which do not fit existing explanations—that is, countries which are well-governed but nonetheless struggle to thrive from a development standpoint—it is worth exploring what purchase alternative explanations can give. However, the measures used in this overview, despite being "off the shelf," are ex-post and not ideal operationalizations for the concepts under investigation. Beyond that, the preceding analysis is static and, as such, does not account for important temporal dimensions and critical junctures which may have substantially altered countries' growth paths. As such, the next section adds more conceptual nuance to these operationalizations by constructing temporally varying "meaningful market access" and "effective-aid" indicators and then by evaluating the relationship between *those* measures on growth.

Nuancing the Understandings of Aid and Access

Finding appropriate empirical indicators for nuanced concepts is one of the greatest challenges in the social sciences. Adding modifiers like "effective" or "meaningful" to terms like "aid" and "market access" implies a qualitative dimension to what might otherwise be objective empirical data. While official and readily available (if imperfect) statistics may exist for the base data, adding a modifier requires careful thinking about how those data may be modified or enhanced to capture a more complex conceptual understanding. In these instances, it is useful to again turn to the literature for guidance on what factors may make aid "effective" or market access "meaningful" in order to reflect on how underlying measures might be adjusted.

With respect to aid, the previous chapter highlighted how there is still a lack of academic consensus about what constitutes growth-effective aid. However, 50 years of scholarship suggests that differences in effectiveness may derive from heterogeneity in aid source, delivery mechanism, modality, and/or sector. This book does not proport to definitively settle the question of what makes aid effective but instead notes several features around which the literature converges upon regarding effective aid features. First, going beyond the approach above that considers declining aid, there is considerable evidence that stable aid is likely to be more effective than aid flows which are volatile.[33] A series of studies has established that aid volatility introduces uncertainty and can undermine performance, unless this volatility stems from efforts which counter other macroeconomic shocks. Common approaches to measuring aid volatility detrend the series and then compare the ratio of the mean and standard deviation, either in isolation or as a comparison with a similar ratio of government revenue.[34]

Second, recent years have seen scholars focus on how aid in different sectors contributes to different developmental outcomes, in both the short and long run. While there is evidence of different types of aid contributing to positive sectoral outcomes,[35] which then may ultimately support long-term economic performance, perhaps the best established and most immediate direct route is via the infrastructure sector. Infrastructure projects tend to both provide an immediate fiscal boost but also tends to be more effective in promoting subsequent private sector investment.[36] Studies of "Aid for Trade" (AfT), described at much further length in Chapter 5, also tend to find that infrastructure AfT is more effective at boosting exports than other types of AfT.[37]

Third, while not as strong as the consensuses above, and often indirect, several studies have found that aid from different donors appears to be more or less effective. These differences may stem from different donors structuring the aid delivery in different ways, emphasizing different aid sectors, or supporting better projects. Specifically, some work has found evidence than Nordic, or perhaps simply Scandinavian, aid may be more effective at promoting growth compared to other OECD Development Assistance

[33] Kodama, M. (2012). Aid unpredictability and economic growth. *World Development*, 40(2), 266–272.

[34] Lensink, R. and Morrissey, O. (2000). Aid instability as a measure of uncertainty and the positive impact of aid on growth. *The Journal of Development Studies*, 36(3), 31–49; Hudson, J. and Mosley, P. (2008). Aid volatility, policy and development. *World Development*, 36(10), 2082–2102; Kharas, H. (2008). Measuring the cost of aid volatility. Wolfensohn Center for Development Working Paper, (3); Chauvet, L. and Guillaumont, P. (2009). Aid, volatility, and growth again: When aid volatility matters and when it does not. *Review of Development Economics*, 13(3), 452–463; Hudson, J. (2015). Consequences of aid volatility for macroeconomic management and aid effectiveness. *World Development*, 69, 62–74.

[35] Riddell, A. and Niño-Zarazúa, M. (2016). The effectiveness of foreign aid to education: What can be learned? *International Journal of Educational Development*, 48, 23–36; Marty, R., Dolan, C. B., Leu, M., and Runfola, D. (2017). Taking the health aid debate to the subnational level: The impact and allocation of foreign health aid in Malawi. *BMJ Global Health*, 2(1), e000129.

[36] Donaubauer, J., Meyer, B., and Nunnenkamp, P. (2016). Aid, infrastructure, and FDI: Assessing the transmission channel with a new index of infrastructure. *World Development*, 78, 230–245; Chauvet, L. and Ehrhart, H. (2018). Aid and growth: Evidence from firm-level data. *Journal of Development Economics*, 135, 461–477.

[37] Cali, M. and Te Velde, D. W. (2011). Does aid for trade really improve trade performance? *World Development, 39*(5), 725–740; Vijil, M. and Wagner, L. (2012). Does aid for trade enhance export performance? Investigating the infrastructure channel. *The World Economy, 35*(7), 838–868.

Committee (DAC) donors.[38] Other studies have suggested that aid from multilateral donors is more effective than that of bilateral donors, although this finding is based more on the perceived higher quality of "selectivity" of multilateral aid rather than on any observed impact on growth.[39] Still further studies into donor heterogeneity have found that while aid from the People's Republic of China (PRC) tends to be (comparatively) more effective at promoting economic growth, it is also likely plagued with selection effects both within and across countries and may have adverse institutional consequences.[40]

While debates continue over how other features of assistance impact aid effectiveness—such as the impact of project aid (where aid is used to finance specific projects, usually under control of the donor) compared to budget support (funding, which can be earmarked or not, that goes directly to a recipient government) or channeling aid through multilateral organizations or non-governmental organizations (sometimes referred to as bypass), there is less consensus on how these differences might ultimately affect aid effectiveness.[41] As such, in thinking about an "aid effectiveness" indicator, the chapter focuses on the three dimensions above—aid volatility, infrastructure aid share, and "effective" donor share.

Constructing such an indicator is a difficult task that relies on what are effectively subjective judgments about operationalization and the relative importance of different features. Moreover, combining data from multiple sources can lead to different types of measurement error and incomplete geographic or temporal coverage. However, recognizing these limitations, the hope is that the indicator may provide a measure that may more closely capture the concept of growth, if not trade, effective aid. The approach taken here is to use a combined and scaled metric of volatility, infrastructure, and "effective" donor share where each indicator is scaled to a mean value of "1."

[38] Brazys, S. R. (2013). Evidencing donor heterogeneity in Aid for Trade. *Review of International Political Economy, 20*(4), 947–978; Dietrich, S. (2016). Donor political economies and the pursuit of aid effectiveness. *International Organization*, 70(1), 65–102; Elgström, O. and Delputte, S. (2017). An end to Nordic exceptionalism? Europeanisation and Nordic development policies. In M. Carbone and J. Orbie (Eds.), *The Europeanisation of Development Policy* (pp. 28–41). Routledge.

[39] Dollar, D. and Levin, V. (2006). The increasing selectivity of foreign aid, 1984–2003. *World Development*, 34(12), 2034–2046; Biscaye, P. E., Reynolds, T. W., and Anderson, C. L. (2017). Relative effectiveness of bilateral and multilateral aid on development outcomes. *Review of Development Economics*, 21(4), 1425–1447.

[40] Wako, H. A. (2018). Aid, institutions and economic growth in sub-Saharan Africa: Heterogeneous donors and heterogeneous responses. *Review of Development Economics*, 22(1), 23–44; Dreher, A., Fuchs, A., Parks, B., Strange, A., and Tierney, M. J. (2021). Aid, China, and growth: Evidence from a new global development finance dataset. *American Economic Journal: Economic Policy*, 13(2), 135–174.

[41] Cordella, T. and Dell'Ariccia, G. (2007). Budget support versus project aid: A theoretical appraisal. *The Economic Journal*, 117(523), 1260–1279; Dietrich, S. (2013). Bypass or engage? Explaining donor delivery tactics in foreign aid allocation. *International Studies Quarterly*, *57*(4), 698–712.

These measures are then additively combined with equal weighting. The aid volatility measure takes the simple ratio of the coefficient of variation for aid. The infrastructure measure is simply the ratio of infrastructure aid to total aid in a given year for a country. Finally, the "effective donor" measure is a simple ratio of the proportion of Nordic and World Bank aid to total aid in a given year. This combined measure is then used as a proxy for the "effectiveness" of aid received by the country. This measure implicitly assumes that the effectiveness of aid matters more than the quantity of aid. Larger amounts of aid may be more likely to induce aid dependence and thus dampen growth. As such, the focus of this measure is on the presumed effectiveness of aid, irrespective of the amount received.[42]

Turning to meaningful market access, operationalization is more straightforward, although again there are several ways to approach the task. Like a base measure of aid amounts (or duration, or number of donors), baseline market access is available via readily accessible metrics such as total effective tariff level, total number of tariff lines that are duty free, total amount of quantitative restrictions, etc. However, as adding the modifier effective complicates the operationalization of an aid metric, adding meaningful to market access invites a subjective assessment of if some types of access are "better" than others. Meaningful market access is also a tricky concept in that the counterfactual of the potential outcome—exports under different market access rules—is not known. Thus, relying on ex-post measures like the export ratio used above can be misleading. We might observe that, for instance, Malaysia exported at a high level compared to GDP, but perhaps it could have exported even more (or in more growth-conducive products) if it had had different market access rules.

The most basic building block of market access is what tariff schedules a given country's exporters face—what I will call their de jure market access. As was discussed briefly in the proceeding chapter and will be discussed in greater detail in the next chapter, global goods trade is classified by a harmonized system that identifies over 10,000 potentially distinct products, and a country's exporters may face a whole host of different access regimes. But, rarely, if ever, do countries receive market access for all products. Moreover, the export potential for different products will vary substantially by country, as different countries have different comparative advantages. Thus, even though the Philippines and Mongolia might both receive duty-free access to the European market for fresh or chilled mackerel fish (HS 0302.44.00) under

[42] Azam, J. P., Devarajan, S., and O'Connell, S. A. (1999). *Aid Dependence Reconsidered* (Vol. 2144). World Bank Publications; Brazys, S. (2018). Aid dependence as aid persistence? Non-declining aid and growth. *Journal of International Relations and Development*, *21*, 717–738.

the EU's "GSP+" scheme, that particular market access benefit for an oceanic product is likely to be of greater use for the country with 22,000 miles of coastlines than the one who is 400 miles from the nearest ocean. Likewise, other dimensions of depth or potentiality shade other market access agreements, where depth has been conceptualized both by the range of issues a market access agreement includes but also the extent to which these issues are a departure from what practice is/would be in the absence of the agreement.[43] Finally, while many countries in the Global South have free trade agreements with their peers, these agreements often do little in terms of reducing tariff lines and, even when they do, only open comparatively small export markets. In contrast, a single market access agreement could give a country broad access to a market like the United States, EU, or China. Which trade agreements one belongs to, who they are with, and what they cover, is likely to matter decisively.

To incorporate that level of nuance into an aggregate indicator would involve assessing the comparative advantage (i.e., export potential) for each developing country on over 10,000 products and then matching that to the market access in up to 200 countries—a task of roughly 280 million permutations. Thus, once again, a cruder proxy is used. Data on which regional and preferential trade agreements each developing country belongs to is used to assess how much market access, as a share of global GDP, each country received by joining the RTA/PTA in a given year. While this measure doesn't fully capture the depth of these agreements, it may be plausible given that all RTA/PTAs are relatively comparable in terms of the breadth and depth of market access they grant—especially those North–South agreements between developing countries and the large markets in G7 countries—as many of these agreements follow somewhat established templates.[44] This weighted measure of RTA/PTA market access, scaled to a mean value of "1," is combined with an annual indicator that equals "1" if the country was in the GATT/WTO and "0" otherwise, to capture if the country had broad "most favored nation" market access under the global trade regime. Finally, to try and capture the impact of non-tariff barriers and, in particular, the impact of Sanitary and Phytosanitary Measures (SPS) on market access, a third indicator is constructed based on the proportion of agricultural land available in each country, again scaled to a mean of 1. The logic

[43] Pelc, K. J. (2011). Why do some countries get better WTO accession terms than others? *International Organization*, 65(4), 639–672; Baccini, L., Dür, A., and Elsig, M. (2015). The politics of trade agreement design: Revisiting the depth–flexibility nexus. *International Studies Quarterly*, 59(4), 765–775.

[44] Chauffour, J. P. and Maur, J. C. (Eds.). (2011). *Preferential Trade Agreement Policies for Development: A Handbook*. World Bank Publications.

here is that this measure proxies for the export potential of agriculture of a country, the sector which is vitally important for many developing countries and is significantly impacted by SPS measures as discussed elsewhere in the book.[45]

The averages of these measures are combined into an aggregate measure that is subsequently rescaled between 0 and 1 like the effective aid measure for ease of interpretation. These measures are then used to classify an annual indicator variable for the NE quadrant and this regressed against per capita growth rates, along with country and year fixed effects. Model 3 in Box 3.2 displays the results of this panel regression. As with the static, cross-country regressions, countries in the NE quadrant in a given year are associated with higher growth rates in that year, of roughly 0.4 percentage points. However, even with the dynamic element, these relationships still cannot be interpreted as causal as again they could be spurious or suffer from reverse causality or unobserved confounding.

As with the static analysis above in Figure 3.5, these metrics are primarily employed for classification, rather than explanatory purposes. However, the dynamic nature of these measures means that Figure 3.6 gives a sense of how classifications can change over time, using decade-level metrics of aid and access, where the classification in a given decade is based on the lag of the effective aid measure (i.e., the measure from the previous decade) to account for the fact that aid projects take time to be implemented, whereas market access should impact growth in a more or less contemporaneous manner. These dynamics allow for identifying critical junctures wherein states went to/from having the combination of aid and access that suggests a possibility of within-case comparison.

First, unlike the static analysis, some of the highest performers, like Singapore and Korea drop out of the analysis in later decades as they become net aid donors. Second, the figure captures both continuity and change. Indonesia shifts from the SE (1980s and 1990s) and SW (2000s) quadrant to the NE quadrant in the 2010s when it averaged 4.24% real per capita GDP growth based on a market access in the 53rd percentile in that decade and effective aid in the 90th percentile from the decade previous. This suggests that Indonesia experienced a critical juncture in aid and market access from the 1990s to 2010s that coincided with a significant uptick in growth. In terms of continuity, while Vietnam was in the NE quadrant from the 1980s, it soars to the 99th percentile in effective aid and the 96th percentile in meaningful

[45] Disdier, A. C., Fontagné, L., and Mimouni, M. (2008). The impact of regulations on agricultural trade: Evidence from the SPS and TBT agreements. *American Journal of Agricultural Economics*, 90(2), 336–350.

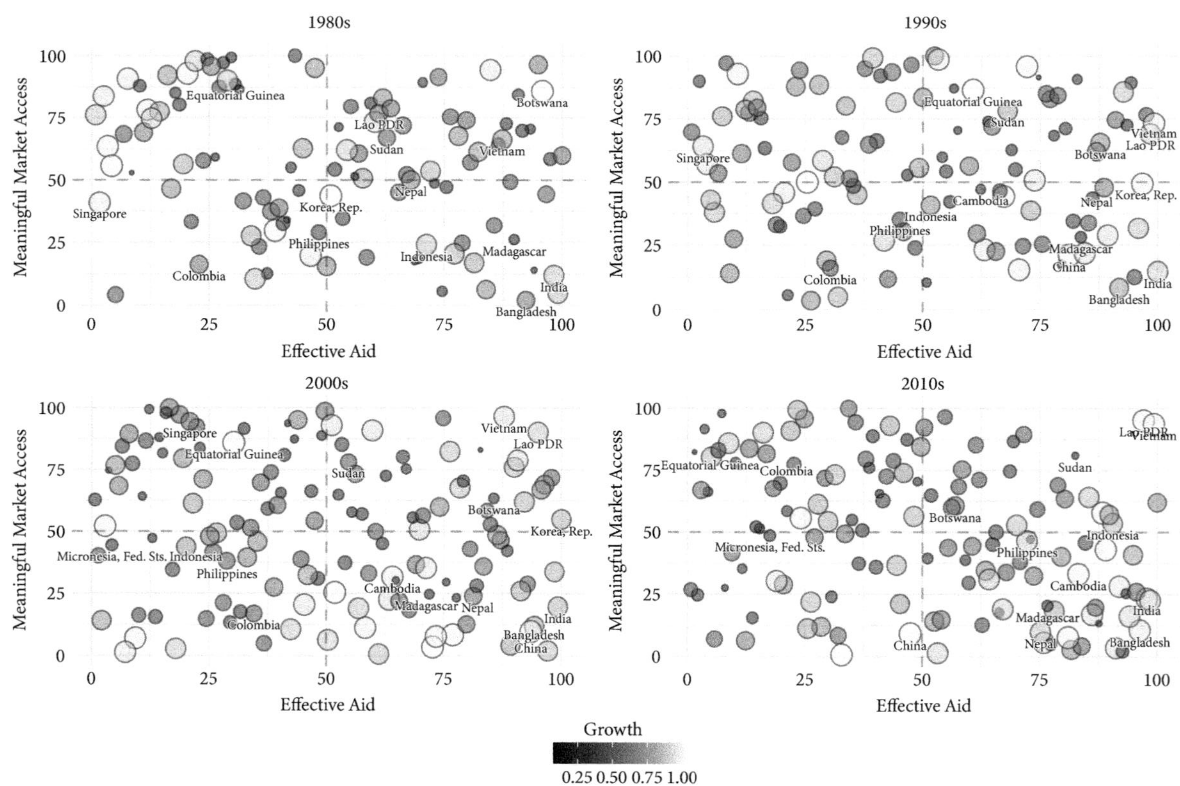

Figure 3.6 Dynamic aid, access, and growth

Sources: World Bank, OECD, DETSA, author's calculations.

market access from the 1990s to 2000s, the latter decade during which the country experienced real growth of 5.6% per year.

Countries in other quadrants are equally illuminating. Bangladesh, who was categorized as a "SW" quadrant country in the static analysis, is consistently in the "SE" quadrant with the more nuanced measures, as it is consistently ranked in the 90th percentile for effective aid. But, like the static analysis, its meaningful market access ranking remains abysmal, peaking in the 12th percentile in the 2000s. However, its growth performance over the four decades is steady if not remarkable, growing from the 58th percentile (1.01%) in the 1980s to the 72nd (2.75%), 75th (4.02%), and 93rd (5.44%) percentiles, respectively, in the following three decades. Bangladesh thus provides an interesting off-the-line, "deviant," case wherein it achieved reasonable growth success despite apparently not having overly meaningful market access.[46]

Bangladesh's regional neighbor, Nepal, also displays interesting dynamics in Figure 3.6, hovering on the border between the NE and SE quadrants in the 1980s–1990s, before falling firmly into the SE quadrant in the subsequent two decades. Most notably, the figure illustrates a drop in meaningful market access from the 50th percentile in the 1980s to less than the 10th percentile in the 2010s. While Nepal continued to grow at a reasonable (relative) clip during the 40 years depicted in the figure, from a better comparative performance in the 1980s it dropped off from its larger neighbor Bangladesh's pace, from the 1990s through the 2010s.

The dynamic analysis also captures two of the poorer overall performing countries, the Federated States of Micronesia and Madagascar, both of whose growth never breaches the relative performance mark of the 50th percentile and instead remains near or below the 20th percentile in most decades. While both countries were in the SE quadrant in the static classification, the FSM is categorized in the SW quadrant in both periods (2000s and 2010s) for which there is data using the nuanced dynamic measures. Though it receives one of the largest amounts of aid per capita in the world, the more nuanced effective aid measure places it no higher than the 25th percentile in that category, while its meaningful market access is in the bottom 50th percentile. Madagascar remains in the SE quadrant with effective aid ranging in the 70th to 80th percentile, but with meaningful market access hovering in the 20th percentile. Both of these are "on-the-line" cases which are suggestive that only having one, or neither, of aid and access is associated with lower comparative growth rates.

[46] Seawright, J. (2016). The case for selecting cases that are deviant or extreme on the independent variable. *Sociological Methods & Research*, 45(3), 493–525.

Finally, the analysis tells us that, like accounts for divergent growth based on institutions and geography, an explanation based on aid and access is neither necessary nor sufficient for growth. Countries like Angola, Cameroon, Mali, Sierra Leone, Sudan, or Zambia, while consistently scoring in the NE quadrant based on the dynamic measures, have struggled to maintain long-term growth. While this again may be due to the fact that the measures still aren't sufficiently nuanced, it is also equally plausible that alternative factors can stymie the sufficiency of aid and access. Likewise, countries like Equatorial Guinea and Thailand, respectively, have thrived without having sustained periods of effective aid or meaningful market access, undermining the necessity of having both. Aid and access can be a pathway to export-led growth but will not automatically be so.

From 30,000 Feet to 30 Inches—a Model Building Analysis

Caveats and outliers aside, the combination of meaningful market access and effective aid appears to be broadly correlated with long-term development success, both in static and dynamic terms. However, this analysis from 30,000 feet still has several limitations. From a market access perspective, there is only so far that the indicators can go in analyzing access at the sector or product level—especially when access at these levels is constrained not by tariffs, but instead by non-tariff barriers, and, in particular, regulatory barriers like sanitary and phytosanitary standards. Likewise, trying to come up with a universal proxy for "trade-effective aid" is perhaps a fool's errand since, if the aid-effectiveness literature tells us anything, it is that effectiveness is very much intervention and context specific. Thus, while this eagle-eye analysis might be able to give the rough contours of the aid and access arguments, a closer look is needed to truly understand if and how these factors can come together, or not, to promote or stymie growth and development.

Second, and perhaps more importantly, even if the classifications above are reasonable in terms of identifying effective aid and meaningful market access, they do nothing to tell us how or why some countries received this combination while others did not. While the dynamic analysis suggests that some countries shifted in their positioning on these indicators over time, the metrics cannot explain those shifts. Thus, a different approach is needed to evaluate the plausibility of the argument that states which successfully achieved meaningful market access and trade-effective aid did so by effectively exercising the agency afforded them by a favorable structural positioning in the international system to effectively represent firms' goods and access needs.

As such, after more thoroughly unpacking the concepts of "trade-effective aid" and "meaningful market access" in Chapters 4 and 5, the remainder of the book digs deeper into some of the countries that populate the different quadrants of the aid-access space. Given that the large-N analysis above (LNA) is not causal, nor even strongly inferential, the book follows a "Model-building Small-N Analysis (SNA)" approach in its selection and investigation of the cases using the classifications above as a starting point.[47] By delving into the specifics of both "on" and "off-the-line" cases, the book hopes to illustrate how (the lack of) aid and access were instrumental to the country's long-term growth performance. The case selection is driven, to some extent, by the fact that, in addition variation in the outcome variable (long-term growth performance), the lack of clear and objective metrics for the explanatory (state relative importance and capacity) and mediating variables (meaningful market access and effective aid) means that "on-the-line" investigation is useful to unpack these explanatory dynamics and measures. The dynamic investigation above also is suggestive that within-case observations may also provide useful insights.[48] Time may see shifts in either/both the structural environment in which countries operate or the capacity of these countries to exercise their agency in securing meaningful market access and effective aid. This model-building approach differs from a model-testing approach in that the LNA in this chapter is not sufficiently well-identified to evaluate causal relationships which might then be further tested through a model-testing SNA. Instead, the book's approach is to provide sufficient empirical support for the theoretical mechanisms outlined in Chapter 2 to prompt further and more considered model-testing LNAs and SNAs.

The cases in the following chapters will therefore be a diverse-case approach mix of on- and off-the-line cases, reflecting cases that may be classified as typical, extreme, deviant, and influential.[49] Table 3.1 displays the seven cases which will be explored in some depth in the rest of the book. Four of these cases appear to be clearly "on-the-line"—two which achieved high growth rates and had effective aid and meaningful market access (Vietnam

[47] Lieberman, E. S. (2005). Nested analysis as a mixed-method strategy for comparative research. *American Political Science Review*, *99*(3), 435–452.

[48] Gerring, J. and Cojocaru, L. (2016). Selecting cases for intensive analysis: A diversity of goals and methods. *Sociological Methods & Research*, 45(3), 392–423.

[49] Seawright, J. and Gerring, J. (2008). Case selection techniques in case study research: A menu of qualitative and quantitative options. *Political Research Quarterly*, 61(2), 294–308; Seawright, J. (2016). The case for selecting cases that are deviant or extreme on the independent variable. *Sociological Methods & Research*, *45*(3), 493–525.

Table 3.1 Model building case selection

Country	Growth	Static Quad-rant	Dynamic Quad-rant(s)	Case Type	Within-case?
Bangladesh	2.53%	SW	SE	Deviant (OFF)	Yes
Colombia	2.01%	SW	SW/NW	??	No
Indonesia	3.18%	NE	SE/SW/NE	Typical (ON)	Yes
Madagascar	−0.90%	SE	SE	Extreme (ON)	No
Micronesia	0.45	SE	SW	Typical (ON)	No
Nepal	1.97%	SW	SE/NE	Typical (ON)?	Yes
Vietnam	4.88%	NE	NE	Extreme /Influential (ON)	Yes

and Indonesia) and two which displayed poor performance and did not have both (or either) meaningful market access and effective aid (Micronesia and Madagascar). The two "success" stories are considered in Chapter 6, while the two underperforming countries are examined in Chapter 7. Bangladesh and Nepal are considered together in Chapter 8. While Bangladesh is the book's best example of a deviant (off-the-line) case, in that it grew reasonably well without apparent meaningful market access, Nepal is a more difficult case to classify. The country's growth places it roughly in the middle of the pack and its aid/access also tends toward the middle of the classifications. But as Chapter 8 will illustrate, both of these cases are heavily influenced by their relationship vis-à-vis one another and the dynamics of one particular industry—textiles. Finally, like Nepal, Colombia is also a difficult country to classify, with middling growth and no clear quadrant positioning. While Colombia's overall case isn't explored as explicitly as others, Chapter 5 draws on the case extensively in order to flesh out the concept of trade-effective aid.

The case-study chapters use both quantitative and qualitative micro-level evidence, often gathered from 30 inches in the form of face-to-face interviews. In addition to the in-person interviews, the chapters also draw on novel survey data as well as unique, usually geo-referenced, quantitative data that is used to illustrate sub-questions such as when aid might be trade effective in given settings. Collectively, this detailed micro-evidence is used in a model-building fashion to provide support (or not) for the theoretical framework developed in Chapter 2.

4

Market Access

Who Gets It and Why?

The Road to Riches

Long-distance economic exchange has been a feature of society since the earliest annals of human civilization. Evidence of trade can be found in the archeological record dating to 100,000 years ago in different parts of the globe.[1] Apparently there is a primordial urge to acquire new and exotic wares—and to make a tidy profit in doing do. While market access in the age of the caveman was surely a function of the physical limitations of safely transporting goods across wild and lawless distances, most recent market access lives within an exceedingly complex ecosystem of laws, rules, and norms. This web of human-made barriers ultimately determines which individuals and organizations can access markets outside their own, and on what terms. Ultimately, granting access to these markets is a political decision; a decision with massive welfare and distributional consequences for both traders and consumers.[2]

As described in Chapter 2, the contemporary global trading order is one that largely rests on the global institutional foundations of the World Trade Organization (WTO). This international institution lays down a base level of commitments and standards that its 164 members and 25 observers, most of whom are in the process of acceding to the group, follow when engaging in cross-border exchange. This group of countries consists of over 99% of both global population and global trade, with the handful of "outsider" states consisting mainly of small-island or microstates like the Federated States of Micronesia or international pariahs like North Korea.[3]

[1] Smith, M. L. (2016). The substance and symbolism of long-distance exchange: textiles as desired trade goods in the Bronze Age Middle Asian interaction sphere. In *Connections and Complexity* (pp. 143–160). Routledge.

[2] Betz, T. (2017). Trading interests: Domestic institutions, international negotiations, and the politics of trade. *The Journal of Politics*, *79*(4), 1237–1252.

[3] Brazys, S. (2014a). Outside looking in: non-accession to the WTO. *Cambridge Review of International Affairs*, *27*(4), 644–665.

The Invisible Hand(out). Samuel Brazys, Oxford University Press. © Samuel Brazys (2025).
DOI: 10.1093/9780198970422.003.0004

Yet, despite the impressive breadth of the WTO, there is still considerably variation in market access among and between members and non-members alike. In order to satisfy an incredibly diverse membership and a unanimity principle, agreements on markets access and other trade-related matters in the WTO must appeal to the lowest-common denominator.[4] As a result, alongside this global regime rests a "spaghetti bowl" of entangling regional and preferential trade agreements (RTAs/PTAs).[5] In addition to simple border taxes (tariffs) this institutional mesh also includes a multitude of non-tariff barriers (NTBs) including quotas, subsidies, and regulatory requirements, including what are known as "sanitary and phyto-sanitary" (SPS) requirements covering health and safety concerns in the animal and plant trades. These NTBs, and regulatory requirements in particular, can act as de facto barriers to trade even in the face of de jure market access.[6] Firms attempting to navigate the regulatory seas of international commerce can quickly flounder and, as a result, many may choose not to export despite the potential of foreign market access.

Who Has Received Access?

The turn of the 20th century saw a massively interconnected global economy. While much of this commerce flowed along lines of colonial or imperial preference, the overall share of trade to the economy was similar to levels that would not be seen again until the latter stages of the 21st century.[7] However, World War I, and the subsequent economic depression, saw a stark reversal of the situation. In particular, following the collapse of the gold standard as a medium of financial exchange in the late 1920s and early 1930s, many countries imposed strong trade barriers.[8] These policies worsened the crisis, and many credit the ensuing economic devastation as giving rise to the forces that would propel the world into global conflict for a second time.[9] Armed with

[4] Murphy-Gregory, H., Kellow, A., Hofmeister, W., and Melissen, J. (2016). Forum shopping and global governance. *Rethinking International Institutions: Diplomacy and Impact on Emerging World Order*, 39–50.

[5] Bhagwati, J. N. (1995). US trade policy: The infatuation with FTAs. Discussion Paper Series No. 726. Columbia University, Department of Economics.

[6] Heckelei, T. and Swinnen, J. (2012). Introduction to the Special Issue of the World Trade Review on "standards and non-tariff barriers in trade". *World Trade Review*, *11*(3), 353–355.

[7] Bordo, M. D., Eichengreen, B., and Irwin, D. A. (1999). *Is Globalization Today Really Different than Globalization a Hunderd Years Ago?* (No. 7195). National Bureau of Economic Research; Went, R. (2002). Globalization in the perspective of imperialism. *Science & Society*, *66*(4), 473–497.

[8] Madsen, J. B. (2001). Trade barriers and the collapse of world trade during the Great Depression. *Southern Economic Journal*, *67*(4), 848–868.

[9] Eichengreen, B. J. (1996). *Golden Fetters: The Gold Standard and the Great Depression, 1919–1939*. NBER Series on Long-term Factors in Economic Development.

the recognition that the economic collapse of the 1930s helped precipitate the war, designing a robust international economic order was a key aspiration of the 1944 conference of allied powers at Bretton Woods.

The GATT—Trade among Friends

As described in Chapter 2, the Bretton Woods conference failed to give birth to a comprehension global trade institution. In its stead, the Global Agreement on Tariffs and Trade (GATT) laid the institutional foundation for the global trading order. However, at its inception, that GATT was by no means universal in its membership. The GATT began its life on January 1, 1948, as a collection of the eight major industrialized, western, victors of World War II and the Republic of Cuba. By the end of 1951 they were joined by an additional two dozen odd members, including much of the remainder of Western Europe and some key recently independent colonies including India, Pakistan, South Africa, and Sri Lanka (Ceylon). While membership gradually expanded during the 1950s, the institution's membership swelled to roughly 75 members during the second wave of decolonization which overlapped with the Kennedy Round of GATT negotiations from 1963 to 1967. From November 1960 to October 1967, an additional 37 members joined the GATT, mostly from the Global South. A final major expansion occurred from 1986 to 1994 during the Uruguay Round of talks which ultimately gave birth to the WTO. By the time the WTO replaced the GATT on January 1, 1995, 128 countries were party to the agreement.[10]

The politics surrounding GATT membership were heavily colored by the dynamics of the Cold War. The initial membership and subsequent 1960s expansion were largely comprised of countries in the Global West or those in the newly decolonized world who were aligned with these countries and/or were key states in Cold War "battles" for global influence, like Egypt or Indonesia. The Uruguay Round expansion, particularly following the fall of the Berlin Wall in 1989, a major change in the structure of the international system, included a number of states who had been in the Soviet sphere of influence. These Cold War dynamics meant that meaningful market access during the GATT was often subservient to the symbolism of alignment.[11] Early GATT market access negotiations focused primarily on reducing tariffs

[10] Geraets, D. (2018). The General Agreement on Tariffs and Trade 1947 (GATT 1947) and the World Trade Organization (WTO)—why join the club?: A Legal Analysis. In *Accession to the World Trade Organization* (pp. 11–35). Edward Elgar Publishing.

[11] McKenzie, F. (2008). GATT and the Cold War: Accession debates, institutional development, and the Western Alliance, 1947–1959. *Journal of Cold War Studies*, *10*(3), 78–109.

on manufactured goods. These efforts primarily benefitted the producers of those goods—namely the industrialized western countries.[12] Key sectors for the developing countries, including agriculture and textiles, were largely excluded from negotiations and/or found themselves governed by extraordinary agreements. Textiles, in particular, were carved out for special treatment first via the Short and Long-Term Cotton Agreements and ultimately via the Multi-Fiber Agreement (MFA) which came into force in 1974.[13] While the MFA was finally phased out in 2005 following the launch of the WTO in 1995 under its successor "Agreement on Textiles and Clothing," these agreements, which provided quantitative protection for the textile industry in developed countries, particularly the United States, grossly distorted the global textiles market by creating the possibility for preferential market access.[14]

Textiles, as a low-technology, labor-intensive, manufacturing industry, are often seen as the "first rung" of the industrialization ladder.[15] Unskilled labor abundance is the primary source of comparative advantage in the sector and thus the industry is a natural starting point for poor countries with comparatively large populations. In an undistorted global market, one would expect textile production to gravitate toward countries with large and cheap labor forces.[16] However, the MFA and its predecessor and successor agreements significantly perverted these market mechanisms. The quotas assigned under the MFA via a series of bilateral agreements, usually three to five years in length, determined how much textile and clothing developing countries could export to the developed country market.[17] For some country producers, these quotas were "binding" in that the "fill rate," that is, how much of the quota was used, approached 100%, suggesting that firms in the country would have exported more but for the quota.[18] Other countries, either without bilaterally agreed quotas, or with excess quotas, could take advantage of the constraints on the competitor firms in "bound" countries to increase production and capture market share. The system operated in such a way that

[12] Gowa, J. and Kim, S. Y. (2005). An exclusive country club: The effects of the GATT on trade, 1950–94. *World Politics, 57*(4), 453–478.

[13] Lopez-Acevedo, G. and Robertson, R. (Eds.). (2012). *Sewing Success?: Employment, Wages, and Poverty Following the End of the Multi-fibre Arrangement.* World Bank Publications.

[14] Trela, I. and Whalley, J. (1988). Do Developing Countries Lose from the MFA? *NBER Working Paper* (w2618).

[15] Kabeer, N. and Mahmud, S. (2004). Rags, riches and women workers: Export-oriented garment manufacturing in Bangladesh. In M. Carr (Ed.), *Chains of Fortune: Linking Women Producers and Workers with Global Markets* (pp. 133–164). Commonwealth Secretariat.

[16] Park, Y. I. and Anderson, K. (1991). The rise and demise of textiles and clothing in economic development: the case of Japan. *Economic Development and Cultural Change, 39*(3), 531–548.

[17] https://www.usitc.gov/publications/332/pub1131.pdf (accessed 05-09-2023).

[18] Faini, R., De Melo, J., and Takacs, W. (1995). A Primer on the MFA Maze. *World Economy, 18*(1), 113–135.

bilateral agreements to restrict exports, via binding quotas, were initially put on major exporters. This enabled other countries to capture those countries' market share. Early limitations on Japan (1957), Hong Kong (1962), Taiwan (1962), and South Korea (1963) eventually gave rise to the textile industries in other countries like Thailand or Indonesia until they subsequently came under the auspices of the MFA in 1972 and 1974, respectively.[19] Thus, early beneficiaries of the MFA where those states with non-binding quotas, or those outside of the system who otherwise traded under MFN or other rules. However, over time, more and more states came under the MFA, such that by the adoption of the ATC in 1995, the agreement covered several dozen countries. By this time, it was the countries *outside* the agreement, or those without binding quotas, that effectively benefitted from preferential access.

The domestic politics of the MFA was very much driven by import-competing interests. For example, Margaret Heckler, a Republican US Congresswoman from the 10th Massachusetts district, during the 95th Congress in 1977 when making an argument to:

> direct the negotiators who are now, not only negotiating a worldwide multifiber agreement, but are individually negotiating with 11 countries, to fulfill the commitment made by the President to create jobs. We must not allow textile and apparel imports to grow at a rate greater than that of the domestic market.

explicitly appealed to the specific, importing-competing, job losses her constituents would face:

> In my district thousands are employed in the textile industry. In the Fall River area, 14,000 people are employed in the textile industry. Of those, 1,000 are provided by knitting companies. Some 300 knitwear companies have gone out of business across the country in the past few years, due to the importation of large amounts of knitwear products.[20]

The MFA will be revisited in Chapter 8, by considering how the ending of the agreement meant that one country, Nepal, lost out on significant meaningful market access at the expense of its neighbors, Bangladesh and, to a lesser extent, India.

[19] https://www.ers.usda.gov/amber-waves/2006/february/the-world-bids-farewell-to-the-multifiber-arrangement/ (accessed 05-09-2023); https://www.usitc.gov/publications/332/pub1131.pdf (accessed 05-09-2023).

[20] United States Congress. September 13, 1977, Vol. 123, Part 23. p. 29017—Bound Edition. 95th Congress—1st Session.

Beyond textiles, agriculture was the other key sector the remained largely outside the purview of GATT-based market liberalization.[21] Whereas textiles are the first rung on the industrialization ladder, agriculture is a sector that relies on factor endowments in land and climatic conditions. While capital and technology are important inputs in the production of some types of agricultural production, especially industrial-scale grain production and animal husbandry, many agricultural products remain highly labor-intensive and require little capital. As such, many developing countries, with varying climatic conditions, have distinct advantages in one or more agricultural products.[22] Yet, during the GATT period, liberalization in agriculture was almost nil. Whereas the politics of textiles protection and access was driven by a specialized sector in a handful of developed countries, agricultural production occurs in almost every country. Food security concerns have long kept agriculture a step apart. While shortages of consumer goods or industrial inputs may disrupt economies, food scarcity leads to the collapse of governments and societies—you can't eat a smartphone.[23] As such, many countries seek both to actively promote agricultural production and to protect the sector from foreign competition.[24] Thus, despite being a key potential trade sector for much of the developing world, agriculture remained largely off the agenda during early GATT negotiation rounds.

However, agricultural began to get more serious attention during the Tokyo round of talks.[25] Key among the discussions, pushed by a United States which was interested at this point in liberalizing the sector, was how to address agricultural supports—subsidies—in the developed world, particularly the common agricultural policy (CAP) in the European Community.[26] While little was accomplished in this round, shots had been fired across the bow and a significant step forward would occur during the Uruguay Round which established the WTO and produced the Agreement on Agriculture (AoA).[27] This agreement introduced a colorful system of "boxes" into which different domestic supports could be placed, ostensibly distinguishing (and

[21] Josling, T., Tangermann, S., and Warley, K. (1996). *Agriculture in the GATT*. Springer.

[22] Goldin, I. (1990). *Comparative Advantage: Theory and Application to Developing Country Agriculture* (No. 16). OECD Publishing.

[23] Ashok, G. (2000). Globalization, WTO and food security: emerging issues and options. *Quarterly Journal of International Agriculture*, *39*(4), 343–357.

[24] Anderson, K., Rausser, G., and Swinnen, J. (2013). Political economy of public policies: Insights from distortions to agricultural and food markets. *Journal of Economic Literature*, *51*(2), 423–477.

[25] Josling, T., Tangermann, S., and Warley, K. (1996). *Agriculture in the GATT*. Springer.

[26] Houck, J. P. (1979). Agricultural trade: Protectionism, policy, and the Tokyo/Geneva negotiating round. *American Journal of Agricultural Economics*, *61*(5), 860–873.

[27] Coppolaro, L. (2018). In the shadow of globalization: The European Community and the United States in the GATT negotiations of the Tokyo round (1973–1979). *The International History Review*, *40*(4), 752–773.

reducing/eliminating) trade-distorting domestic supports in the "amber box"—namely export subsidies, while permitting "non-distorting" domestic support measures in the "green box" and separating production-linked payments into a "blue box."[28] Export subsidies effectively reduce global market prices, and are a direct production support for the producers which receive them. Controversially, the agreement allowed for "decoupled" (i.e., direct, non-production linked) payments. Many have argued that these payments can still be trade-distorting, as they in effect still subsidize (excess) agricultural production which depresses global market prices in a manner similar to export subsidies.[29] The agreement also prohibited the use of other non-tariff border measures, including quotas or discriminatory licensing procedures.

The domestic, developed, country politics of agriculture is even more visible than that of textiles.[30] While the total number of individuals employed in the agricultural sector in the developed world is small, these individuals often hold outsized influence due to their visibility and the structure of urban and rural constituencies in Western democracies. This power can stem from electoral geography, high levels of organization based on shared ties of identity, and historical ties with important political parties.[31] In few places is this more evident than the United States, where rules of representation in that country's upper chamber, the Senate, are such that rural constituencies are given vastly outsized voices.[32] In Europe, and particularly in France, a panache for direct action—such as, parking tractors on the Champs Elysees—has given farmers outside influence over European agricultural policies and, in particular, the CAP.[33]

More generally, the GATT regime contained a substantial number of carveouts which limited the efficacy of its liberalization efforts. As such, the GATT era saw very little in the way of broad-based, effective, market access. Instead, a handful of countries who were well positioned by virtue

[28] Zahrnt, V. (2009). For a new classification system of domestic support in the WTO agreement on agriculture. *Journal of World Trade, 43*(6).

[29] Rude, J. (2001). Under the green box—The WTO and farm subsidies. *Journal of World Trade, 35*(5); Galperín, C. and Miguez, I. D. (2009). Green box subsidies and trade-distorting support: Is there a cumulative impact? In *Agricultural Subsidies in the WTO Green Box: Ensuring Coherence with Sustainable Development Goals*, 239–257. Cambridge University Press.

[30] Thies, C. G. and Porche, S. (2007). The political economy of agricultural protection. *The Journal of Politics, 69*(1), 116–127.

[31] Klandermans, B., Sabucedo, J. M., Rodriguez, M., and De Weerd, M. (2002). Identity processes in collective action participation: Farmers' identity and farmers' protest in the Netherlands and Spain. *Political Psychology, 23*(2), 235–251; Mulgan, A. G. (2013). *The Politics of Agriculture in Japan*. Routledge.

[32] Thies, M. F. (1998). When will pork leave the farm? Institutional bias in Japan and the United States. *Legislative Studies Quarterly*, 467–492.

[33] Bush, E. and Simi, P. (2001). European farmers and their protests. In *Contentious Europeans. Protest and Politics in an Emerging Polity*, 97–121. Rowman and Littlefield Publishers, Inc.; Strijker, D. and Terluin, I. J. (2015). Rural protest groups in the Netherlands. In *Rural protest groups and populist political parties* (pp. 300–325). Wageningen Academic Publishers.

of strategic significance were able to take advantage of preferential market access to develop key industries. While this book is primarily concerned with understanding divergent economic performance since the end of the Cold War, the GATT years illustrate that the politics of market access are deeply rooted in structural considerations of the international system and the domestic politics of developed markets.

The WTO—Universalism at Last?

For many, the collapse of the Soviet Union seemed to once and for all repudiate the potential of state-directed socialist and communist economies and, instead, herald the triumphalism of the market.[34] While the GATT Uruguay round was launched in the throes of the Cold War, by the time it concluded the world was entirely transformed. The Soviet Union was dissolved, and the other great communist power, the People's Republic of China (PRC), was well underway with its "Reform and Opening" up which saw it transformed from an agrarian backwater to the world's market-oriented factory in the span of a few short decades.[35] With the launch of the WTO in 1995, the liberal vision of truly global markets appeared to be within reach.[36] The coming years saw further former communist-bloc states join the organization and with the accession of the PRC in 2001 and Russia itself in 2012, the project of universal membership was nearly complete. While (the speed of) GATT and WTO accessions was correlated with commitments to democracy or rule of law,[37] by 2016 nearly every country in the world either belonged to, or was an observer of, the organization. The handful of remaining "outsiders" were comprised of a few low-capacity, small-island developing states, micro-states Monaco, San Marino, Eritrea, and North Korea.[38]

However, despite this nearly universal membership, and the core principles of "Most Favored Nation" (MFN) and "National Treatment" (NT), not all WTO members are equal. While MFN is intended to give all other members "any advantage, favor, privilege, or immunity" granted to any member, and

[34] Macey, J. R. and Miller, G. P. (1992). The End of History and the New World Order: The triumph of Capitalism and the competition between Liberalism and Democracy. *Cornell Int'l LJ*, *25*, 277.

[35] Ploberger, C. (2016). China's reform and opening process: A new model of political economy?. *Journal of Chinese Economic and Business Studies*, *14*(1), 69–87.

[36] Ikenberry, G. J. (2009). Liberal internationalism 3.0: America and the dilemmas of liberal world order. *Perspectives on Politics*, *7*(1), 71–87.

[37] Davis, C. L. and Wilf, M. (2017). Joining the Club: Accession to the GATT/WTO. *The Journal of Politics*, *79*(3), 964–978.

[38] Brazys, S. (2014a). Outside looking in: non-accession to the WTO. Cambridge Review of International Affairs, 27(4), 644–665

NT ensures that locally produced and foreign produced goods are treated equally once they are "behind the border," in practice some members face radically different rules than others when accessing a third-party market.[39] While much of this inequality can be explained by PTA/RTAs, as discussed further below, technical regulatory rules in the WTO can act as de facto barriers to some parties but not others.

Despite the institutional parity of "one party one vote" and a consensus driven decision-making process which effectively gives every state a veto, some states are considerably more important in driving the WTO's processes and outcomes. The WTO "Green Room," with select admittance suggestively based on size or importance, is (in)famous for being the "room where it happens," where bargains are struck and decisions are made.[40] Not only do some countries lack representation in this select group, but some, due to size or capacity constraints, are unable to effectively represent themselves in official WTO settings.[41] While the United States and European Union both have fully staffed permanent missions to the WTO, small-island states like Vanuatu or Samoa only participate via a European-based embassy or via collective representation through a body like the Pacific Islands Forum.[42] States are left out of these decision-making fora will be unable to advance the market access interests of their firms.

The Spaghetti Thickens—Regional Trade Agreements

The GATT offered a wide range of carveouts for its membership. However, perhaps the most impactful of these was Article XXIV which enabled countries to form regional trade agreements (RTAs) that allowed contracting parties to lower trade barriers between themselves while maintaining separate external tariffs (Free Trade Areas (FTAs)) or adopting a common external tariff (Customs Union). Roughly half of all global merchandise trade occurs within these arrangements.[43] While the GATT witnessed a wave of "Old Regionalism" during the 1960s and 1970s which largely focused on protecting internal markets, the "New Regionalism" which began in the late

[39] General Agreement on Tariffs and Trade (GATT). (1947). Article I—General Most-Favoured-Nation, https://www.wto.org/english/res_e/booksp_e/gatt_ai_e/art1_e.pdf (accessed 21-11-2023).

[40] Jones, K. (2009). Green room politics and the WTO's crisis of representation. *Progress in Development Studies*, *9*(4), 349–357.

[41] Ismail, F. and Vickers, B. (2011). Towards fair and inclusive decision-making in WTO negotiations. In *Making Global Trade Governance Work for Development*, 461–485. Cambridge University Press.

[42] Hassall, G. (2023). Membership and participation in the major organs. In *The United Nations and the Pacific Islands* (pp. 167–203). Springer International Publishing.

[43] https://www.wto.org/english/news_e/spno_e/spno10_e.htm (accessed 22-08-2023).

1980s largely focused on creating liberalizing RTAs which went deeper than the WTO in terms of access and trade-related issue areas like environmental or labor standards.[44]

However, unlike the (near) universality of the WTO, RTAs are by their nature, exclusionary and selective in their membership. Many of the "New Regionalism" RTAs exist between only a handful of entities and are frequently "North–South" agreements wherein some (one) participant(s) in the agreement is an advanced, high-income, economy while the remaining (other) participant(s) are emerging or developing economies. While such arrangements may follow the trade logics of comparative advantage via specialization, they often times lead to politically imbalanced agreements wherein the advanced economies hold considerably more negotiating power vis-à-vis their developing country counterparts.[45] As a result, the advanced economies may be able to dictate key terms of these agreements and include or exclude access to vital or politically sensitive sectors.

The heaviest utilizer of these agreements is an entity that, itself, is an RTA. The European Union, via its predecessor entity the European Community, was established under GATT Article XXIV by the Treaty of Rome on January 1, 1958. Together with the European Free Trade Association (EFTA), a former institutional rival which now mainly serves to expand the European Market to select states not in the EU (currently Iceland, Liechtenstein, Norway, and Switzerland), EU and EFTA account for the counter-party in roughly 20% of all RTAs.[46] While many of these agreements are with neighboring European states like Albania, Georgia, or Ukraine, the EU and EFTA have agreements that span all regions of the globe, including several "interregional" agreements wherein the EU or EFTA RTA has an agreement with another RTA, like the Gulf Cooperation Council (GCC), or the Caribbean Forum (CARIFORUM).

However, other states also feature centrally in the "spaghetti bowl" of RTAs. Conceptualizing the spaghetti bowl as a network, where states (or entities like the EU) are the nodes and agreements are the edges, it is possible to ascertain various measures of network centrality, i.e. descriptive statistics which indicate how "important" different actors are within the network.[47] The two more basic measures network prominence are "degree" and "closeness" centrality.

[44] Söderbaum, F. (2016). Old, new, and comparative regionalism. *The Oxford Handbook of Comparative Regionalism* (pp. 16–41). Oxford University Press.

[45] Mittelman, J. H. (2011). Rethinking "the new regionalism" in the context of globalization. In *Contesting Global Order* (pp. 97–115). Routledge.

[46] WTO RTA Database. https://www.wto.org/english/tratop_e/region_e/region_e.htm

[47] Manger, M. S., Pickup, M. A., and Snijders, T. A. (2012). A hierarchy of preferences: A longitudinal network analysis approach to PTA formation. *Journal of Conflict Resolution*, *56*(5), 853–878.

Whereas degree centrality is simply a count of the number of other nodes a given node is connected to, closeness is a measure that captures the "distance" between one entity and other nodes in the network. Nodes that have high scores of closeness centrality are "in the middle" in that they need a comparatively low number of connections to reach all other entities in the network. These two measures are often related to each other in a direct, linear, way and indeed in the PTA network this is largely the case, as shown in Figure 4.1, which plots the two dimensions against each other in the year 2016.

Of the nation-states in the network, entities like Chile, Colombia, Egypt, and Sudan all score highly on both measures of centrality, while states like Micronesia and Nepal score poorly. More sophisticated measures of centrality show a similar pattern. Eigenvector prominence is a measure based on the prominence of the other nodes to which an entity is tied. Rather than a measure of simple connections, eigenvector prominence indicates not only that a given entity is well connected, but also that its connections are also highly connected. Likewise, a more informative measure of closeness is what is known as "betweenness" centrality. Like closeness, it is a measure of pathways, but in this instance, it measures the extent to which a given node connects two otherwise unconnected nodes. Nodes with high betweenness

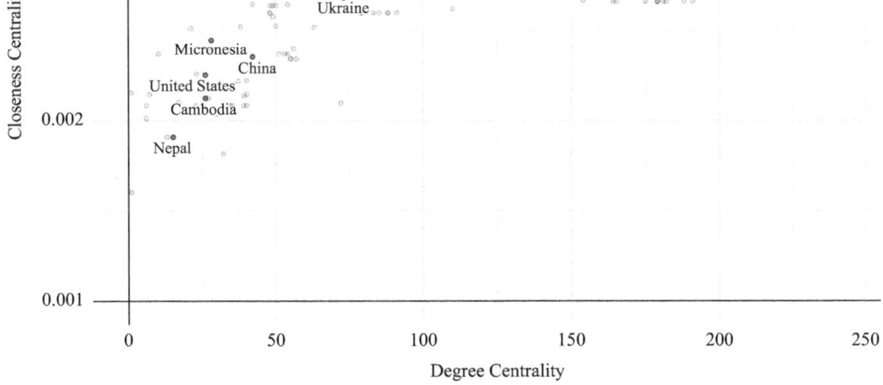

Figure 4.1 RTA degree x closeness centrality in 2016

Source: Author's adaptation from Brazys and Winecoff (2016)

centrality can act as "bridges" or "gatekeepers" in a network. Plotting the level of betweenness centrality against a rank-ordering of eigenvector centrality in Figure 4.2 we again see Chile, Colombia, Egypt, and Sudan all scoring highly in both eigenvector and betweenness centrality, along with other countries not labeled like Turkey, Tunisia, and Switzerland. In contrast, Nepal scores near the bottom in both and Micronesia also scores very low in betweenness centrality.

Notably, many of the states that are important in the network are middle-sized, emerging market economies. Interestingly, some of these states are at "cross-roads," both geographically, but also politically, at the boundaries between regions or continents like Egypt or Turkey. While higher RTA network centrality doesn't guarantee increased meaningful market access, it certainly implies greater institutional opportunity via de jure trade agreements. Indeed, there is a high amount of overlap between countries which score highly on these measures of network centrality and those that scored highly for "meaningful market access" in Chapter 3. To the extent that these measures of centrality correlate with meaningful market access, attaining network centrality is once again arguably an outcome of structure and agency. As discussed above, developing states that engage in North–South RTAs are

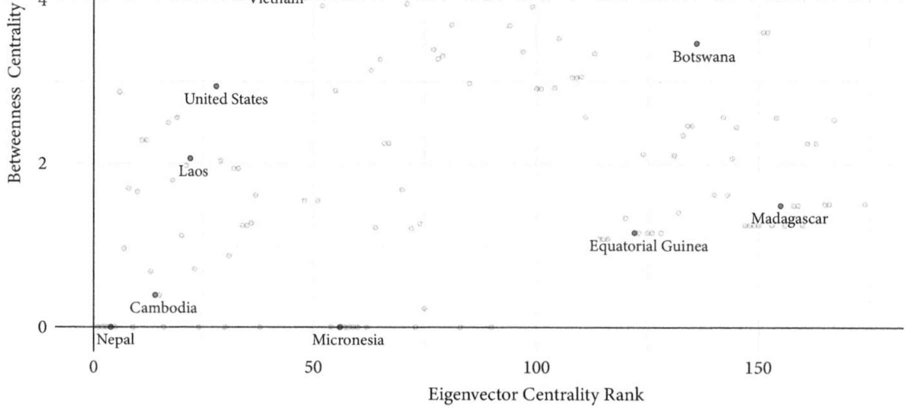

Figure 4.2 RTA betweenness x eigenvector centrality for 2016
Source: Author's adaptation from Brazys and Winecoff (2016).

both strategically important, but also are likely to have sufficient state capacity and institutional quality to exercise their agency in the negotiations.[48]

PTA/GSP

Beyond GATT Article XXIV RTAs, further trade rules allow for discriminatory trade practices via "preferential trade agreements" (PTAs). Unlike RTAs, which require reciprocity between the partners, PTAs allow for unilateral preferences to be given to developing countries under the "enabling clause" enacted in 1979 under the GATT which made a 1971 waiver to the principle of MFN in this regard permanent.[49] This departure from non-discrimination recognized that unilateral trade preferences could be used to foster growth and development in low-income countries. The most prominent of class of trade preference under the enabling clause is the "Generalized System of Preferences" (GSP). This scheme provides alternate (preferential) tariff rates for the countries which are included. GSP-like carveouts were discussed as early as 1947 in the negotiations for the Havana Charter as a concept known as "reversed preferences" and the concept was refined via the United Nations Conference on Trade and Development (UNCTAD) in the 1960s.[50]

Like other tariff schedules, GSP schemes are determined and enacted by different entities that grant these trade preferences. Thus, there is no universal "GSP-scheme," but instead a patchwork of GSP schemes. As of 2023, 15 entities (including the European Union) operated GSP schemes. A further 10 schemes exist exclusively for countries which meet the World Bank's definition of a "least developed country." Beyond these, there are eight further specific inter-entity PTAs.[51] However, while GSP schemes are non-reciprocal (i.e., the advanced economy grants trade concessions without receiving any in return), this largesse means that GSP schemes are much more imposed (or "extended") than they are negotiated.[52] Moreover, while GSP schemes

[48] Palit, A. (2017). Mega-regional trade agreements and non-participating developing countries: Differential impacts, challenges and policy options. *Competition & Change*, *21*(5), 417–434; Adriaensen, J. and Postnikov, E. (2022). Geo-economic motives and the negotiation of free trade agreements: Introduction. In *A Geo-Economic Turn in Trade Policy? EU Trade Agreements in the Asia-Pacific* (pp. 3–26). Springer International Publishing.

[49] Islam, M. R. and Alam, S. (2009). Preferential trade agreements and the scope of GATT article XXIV, GATS article V and the enabling clause: An appraisal of GATT/WTO jurisprudence. *Netherlands International Law Review*, *56*(1), 1–34.

[50] Dos Santos, N. B. and Cunha, R. (2005). Generalized system of preferences in general agreement on tariffs and trade/World Trade Organization: History and current issues. *Journal of World Trade*, *39*(4), 637 – 670.

[51] WTO PTA Database. http://ptadb.wto.org/ (accessed 22-11-2023).

[52] Grossman, G. M. and Sykes, A. O. (2005). A preference for development: the law and economics of GSP. *World Trade Review*, *4*(1), 41–67.

are usually generally authorized (i.e., an entity has a GSP scheme in force or it doesn't), GSP concessions can operate at the country-product-year level, meaning that for a given HS product code, only some GSP-eligible countries may receive the GSP rate (and perhaps only in some years). As such, while countries may lobby for GSP inclusion, they are unlikely to hold any leverage in negotiating GSP access as the schemes are non-concessional. Moreover, the longevity of GSP schemes is not guaranteed as most are term-limited. While, in practice, mostly this is not a problem, in a few instances, there has been a GSP lapse before the scheme has been renewed, particularly in the United States. Since 1993, the US GSP has lapsed on at least eight occasions.[53] The current scheme again lapsed at the end of 2020 and, as of writing, has not yet been renewed. While GSP-eligible exporters have traditionally been refunded their duties paid during the lapse periods, these lapses, again largely based on domestic politics, add uncertainty for firms who base their investment and market decisions on the provision of this access.[54] Inclusion in GSP, at both the country and product level, is inherently political. For example, the US scheme initially excluded communist countries, OPEC members, and any country which expropriated US property.[55] Both the EU and US schemes include other types of conditionality including labor rights, intellectual property protection, or environmental standards.[56] These levers of conditionality can be used to punish or reward GSP-eligible states for reasons that go far beyond their need for economic development.

Beyond the politics of GSP access, there is also the politics surrounding which product lines are eligible for GSP treatment and at what level. No entity's GSP program provides duty-free access across all, much less a super-majority, of products. Accordingly, while GSP access may grant preferences that are improved compared to MFN status, they still may not grant effective access for products that are meaningful for firms in a given country. These product-level eligibilities are determined at the outset of the scheme. After the initial adoption, at the product level, countries (or third-party entities) can lodge petitions to have product lines added or removed for either all

[53] https://ustr.gov/about-us/policy-offices/press-office/fact-sheets/2010/december/gsp-expiration-frequently-asked-questions.

[54] Hakobyan, S. (2020). GSP expiration and declining exports from developing countries. *Canadian Journal of Economics/Revue canadienne d'économique*, *53*(3), 1132–1161; https://www.cbp.gov/trade/priority-issues/trade-agreements/special-trade-legislation/generalized-system-preferences/faq-gsp-reauthorization (accessed 07-09-2023).

[55] Ibid.

[56] Compa, L. and Vogt, J. S. (2000). Labor rights in the generalized system of preferences: A 20-year review. *Comp. Lab. L. & Pol'y J.*, *22*, 199; Bartels, L. (2003). The WTO enabling clause and positive conditionality in the European Community's GSP program. *Journal of International Economic Law*, *6*(2), 507–532.

countries or particular countries in a given year. In the United States, these are called GSP annual reviews. Each year, the US Trade Representative (USTR) publishes a notice in the Federal Register which invites:

> submission of petitions to modify the GSP status of GSP BDCs because of country practices; add products to GSP eligibility; remove products from GSP eligibility for one or more countries; waive CNLs; deny de minimis waivers for eligible products; or redesignate currently excluded products.

These petitions can be submitted by individuals, corporations, trade groups, and/or foreign governments—the last of whom can petition both for their own inclusion in GSP but also petition to have other countries' GSP access removed. The USTR then decides which petitions to accept and may ask the United State International Trade Commission (USITC) to investigate the petition prior to making its decision.

The uncertainty, and political maneuvering, surrounding GSP eligibility at both the country and product levels is cited as a reason for explaining why the scheme is underutilized—that is, why products that could enter under GSP preferences do not.[57] Market access that is unilaterally and arbitrarily granted by one country is less likely to be meaningful. As the decision to export to a given market is costly, and may take considerable investment in both time and capital, firms will be hesitant to make exporting decision on the basis of access which is on shaky foundations and could be withdrawn with little or no notice (or, granted to a competitor, with similarly little notice), especially when the firm may not have any direct control over the lever of conditionality that might be pulled (i.e., firms are not responsible for setting a country's environmental standards). Thus, firms tend to prefer market access under more secure agreements like the GATT/WTO, or even reciprocal trade agreements, as their terms are less likely to be arbitrarily altered.[58]

To illustrate these dynamics, I examine a specific case of US GSP preferences at the 10-digit HS product level. In 2018, the USTR decided to remove Turkey's GSP access for cherry juice, both the tart and sweetened varieties (HS 2009.89.6011 and HS 2009.89.6019, respectively).[59] This action was the

[57] Tobin, J. L. and Busch, M. L. (2019). The disadvantage of membership: How joining the GATT/WTO undermines GSP. *World Trade Review*, *18*(1), 133–160.

[58] Ibid; Postigo, A. (2022). Utilization of GSP schemes as a political and economic determinant of the utilization of North–South FTAs. *Review of International Political Economy*, *29*(5), 1420–1447.

[59] https://ustr.gov/sites/default/files/IssueAreas/gsp/Results%20of%20the%20Review%20Lists%20 2017_2018.pdf (accessed 22-08-23).

result of a petition from the "Cherry Marketing Institute" (CMI), a Michigan-based trade association representing the state's cherry juice industry, whose mission is to:

> increase the sales and use of cherries by expanding the market domestically and Globally. To do this we need an effective staff of people dedicated to its grower membership, working in union with all other industry segments to market cherries effectively.[60]

who sought to restrict Turkey's cherry exports to protect their own domestic producers. In their submission to the USITC, the CMI noted how:

> Tart cherry juice from Turkey is also sold at very low prices that steeply undercut domestic prices. The domestic industry has been harmed by the Turkish imports that have come to dominate the market and enter at prices that are significantly below domestic producers' own costs of production.

and that

> Removal of GSP benefits from Turkey would ... benefit the domestic industry by giving some modicum of relief to the growers, handlers, and concentrators that have struggled to compete with rising volumes of low-priced tart cherry juice from Turkey.[61]

This petition was set against opposition from the Turkish Fruit Juice Association who, among other arguments, invoked a letter of support from a US cherry-juice producer who imported Turkish cherries. This California based producer, Stieb Company, wrote that:

> I have been involved in the fruit juice industry for more than 20 years and believe things such as market cycles due to weather, crop demands due to consumer taste have more impact, along with organized program set asides, than does any impact of imported fruit juice. The facts are that the U.S. tart cherry juice industry does not have the capacity to serve the demand in the U.S. market.[62]

This cherry-picked vignette illustrates three key points about market access. First, meaningful market access for developing countries can rest on very

[60] https://www.usacherries.com/about-us (accessed 22-08-2023).
[61] https://www.usitc.gov/publications/332/pub4827.pdf (accessed 05-09-2023).
[62] Ibid.

micro-level domestic political considerations in the developed world. While the CMI is unlikely to be a prime Beltway shaker, on balance, Michigan was a vitally important "swing state" in recent US presidential elections, one of the "blue wall" states which Donald Trump won in 2016 to defeat Hillary Clinton and Kamala Harris in 2024.[63] To the extent the USTR, an executive agency headed by a Trump appointee, made a political calculus in this case, it no doubt would have looked more favorably upon a petition from this key battleground, in the face of opposition only from a Turkish trade group and an importer from Democrat-stronghold California.[64] That Turkey is both a country that is strategically important to the United States, and one with a decently high level of government capacity and institutional quality, only further highlights the height of the hurdle of domestic politics in the importing developed country. Of course, it must be noted that the lack of an effective Turkish response might also have been the result of the Turkish private interest (the Turkish Fruit Juice Association) being unable to effectively enlist the Turkish government to support their opposition, highlighting the important distinction between exporting states and exporting firms.

Second, perhaps unexpectedly for the Cherry Marketing Institute, and as a testament to Stieb Company's prescience, while imports of cherry juice from Turkey did drop from $15.9 million in 2016 and $12.1 million in 2017 to $7.9 million in 2018 and $6.7 million in 2019, imports of cherry juice from alternatively GSP-eligible Brazil skyrocketed from $1.5 million in 2016 and $2.7 million in 2017 to $10.5 million in 2018 and $11.6 million in 2019. This (presumably) unintended trade-diversion was sufficiently large such that total cherry-juice imports increased in 2018 and 2019 compared to the previous two years. The data would seemingly suggest that Brazilian cherry-juice growers, freed from Turkish competition, took advantage of their newfound comparative advantage to vastly expand production. Market access decisions made as a result of a developed county's domestic politics can have unintended and diversionary effects on third-party developing countries.

Finally, the vignette demonstrates how developed country domestic politics can help explain the capriciousness of GSP access—what has been called "political trade dependence."[65] While Turkish producers would lose overall GSP eligibility in May of 2019, the fact that a relatively small US interest group was able to successfully petition to remove preferential market access

[63] Dulio, D. A. and Klemanski, J. S. (2018). Hiding behind a thin blue wall. In *Presidential Swing States*, 247–272. Lexington Books.

[64] (Although winning over the cherry producers clearly wasn't enough as Trump would lose the state to Joe Biden in 2020.)

[65] Manger, M. S. and Shadlen, K. C. (2014). Political trade dependence and North–South trade agreements. *International Studies Quarterly*, *58*(1), 79–91.

displays the type of uncertainty that gives GSP-reliant firms pause. Decisions on whether to ramp up cherry production (like many types of production) must often be made years in advance and can require substantial up-front investment. If these decisions are based on the presumption of market access, then the frailty of the access might chill the initial investment decision. As such, even though Turkish cherry farmers may have seen significant de jure US market access for their wares in 2016 under the GSP, savvy ones might have forestalled making an investment decision understanding how fickle that access might be, effectively rendering the access a *non*-meaningful opportunity.

Meaningful Market Access

The different types of trade rules discussed above, be they multilateral (WTO), RTA, or PTA, all lay out the formal institutional structure of international trade and market access. The degree to which a state is entrenched in these institutional structures may provide a rough guide to its potential, de jure, market access. However, a key claim of this book is that just because a state may appear to have a good deal of market access on paper, this does not necessarily translate into meaningful market access for its firms. This is because de jure market access can be undermined by at least two types of trade frictions that lead to de facto market access that is significantly more curtailed.

The first trade friction that can render apparent market access toothless is the presence of different types of regulatory barriers.[66] Market access under the contemporary WTO regime is largely one based on complex technical considerations like Sanitary and Phytosanitary (SPS) standards, Rules of Origin (ROO) (which determine what threshold of a product's content or value added needs to be from an exporting state), or other Technical Barriers to Trade (TBT).[67] Regulatory barriers can be as simple as what information is contained on a label and how it is displayed, to more complicated measures that specify particular production practices, chemical makeups, or ROO. States (and firms therein) that have legal access to a foreign market at a favorable (or at least non-discriminatory) tariff rate can find these regulatory barriers a formidable hurdle to actual export access due to a number

[66] Hoekman, B. and Nicita, A. (2011). Trade policy, trade costs, and developing country trade. *World Development*, *39*(12), 2069–2079; McDonald, J. (2005). Domestic regulation, international standards, and technical barriers to trade. *World Trade Review*, *4*(2), 249–274.

[67] Santeramo, F. G. and Lamonaca, E. (2022). Standards and regulatory cooperation in regional trade agreements: What the effects on trade? *Applied Economic Perspectives and Policy*, *44*(4), 1682–1701.

of direct and indirect costs.[68] The first cost is simply the issue of search costs to overcome imperfect information.[69] The WTO gives broad leeway to states in imposing regulatory restrictions as long as the principles of non-discrimination and national treatment are upheld. As such, firms need to stay abreast of the regulatory environment of over 160 countries in order to sell their wares globally. The search and information costs can be substantial. One Nepalese exporting house described how a client wanted to export coffee to Japan, and they needed an SPS certification. The exporter went first to the Ministry of Food and Agriculture but received no assistance. After fruitlessly searching the internet, the Kathmandu-based exporter then flew to the coffee growing region in western Nepal and there got the name of a government official back in Kathmandu. After taking half a day to find his small office in the back corner of a building he was told he needed to bring in a sample of the coffee. After doing so, the official directed the clerk to type up a SPS certificate, after first asking the clerk if he thinks it is "ok" to certify the coffee.[70] However, these informational and transaction costs will often pale in comparison to the compliance costs. Depending on the type or regulation, these costs can include ordering laboratory tests, obtaining specialized production equipment, or installing environmental mitigation measures.[71]

These regulatory barriers to trade are often instrumental in obstructing market access and can therefore substantially limit de facto market access even when a country may face few de jure barriers to trade. The WTO keeps track of these barriers via a notification system wherein countries self-report their regulatory barriers on the basis that these barriers are not in line with international standards and do have a significant effect on trade.[72] WTO rules stipulate that SPS barriers are only permissible when there is sufficient scientific "risk assessment" of a threat to health or safety, or, when scientific evidence is "insufficient" for such a justification, the ability to provisionally adopt SPS barriers on the basis of obtaining future scientific evidence.[73] This latter clause was championed by the European Union, in particular, as evidence of the "precautionary principle" which

[68] Beghin, J. C. and Bureau 1, J. C. (2001). Quantitative policy analysis of sanitary, phytosanitary and technical barriers to trade. *Économie internationale*, (3), 107–130.

[69] Sturm, D. and Ulph, A. (2002). Environment and trade: the implications of imperfect information and political economy. *World Trade Review*, *1*(3), 235–256.

[70] Interview N-1584. 09-05-2016. Kathmandu, Nepal.

[71] Kheir-El-Din, H. (2000). Enforcement of product standards as barriers to trade: the case of Egypt. In *Egyptian Exports and Challenges of the 21st Century. Cairo: Center for Economic and Financial Research and Studies* (pp. 213–228). Center for Economic & Financial Research & Studies.

[72] https://notifications.wto.org/en/notification-requirements/sanitary-and-phytosanitary-measures#SPSPART2 (accessed 23-08-2023).

[73] World Trade Organization. (1995). Sanitary and Phytosanitary Measures Agreement.

guides EU regulatory practice and was enshrined in the 1992 Rio Declaration on Environment and Development. While the SPS provision was ostensibly intended to only allow for restrictions of limited and short-term use, the EU has argued that it provides broad support for restrictions based on the "precautionary principle." Although WTO panels have consistently found against a broad invocation of the principle, most famously in the *EC-Hormones* and *EC-GMO* cases wherein the WTO ruled against EU SPS restrictions on hormone-fed beef and the use of genetically modified organisms (GMOs), respectively,[74] entities continue to use the SPS agreement and the precautionary principle as justifications for controversial trade restrictions. Additionally, the TBT agreement allows for regulatory barriers which protect "essential security interests." This concept is also left sufficiently vague in the agreement, which permits members to not disclose information in their TBT notifications "which they consider contrary to their essential security interests."[75] Together, the SPS and TBT agreements give states considerable room to impose regulatory restrictions that keep with the letter of WTO law.

In all, the WTO SPS and TBT platform records nearly 85,000 notifications of regulatory barriers.[76] Unsurprisingly, developed countries top the list, with the G7 countries plus the EU—whose notifications cover all European countries—accounting for nearly a quarter of all notifications, with the United States as the largest of these with over 10,000 notifications. Other major notifiers include major agricultural producing countries like Brazil (6,250+) and large middle-income countries like China (3,400+) or Mexico (2,000+). The vast bulk of the notifications are made in the areas of agriculture or foodstuffs. Most of these are justified via protection on the basis or health or safety. Of the 61,000 plus notifications whose objective was recorded, over 72% were justified on these grounds, compared to around 13% on the grounds of environmental protection, 12% on labeling grounds, and just 0.5% on national security grounds.

While these barriers are meant to follow the WTO principles of non-discrimination and national treatment, they often, in practice, end up targeting very specific goods from very particular countries. For example, in Chapter 5, the book will consider the cacao trade from Colombia. Among

[74] Cheyne, I. (2006). The precautionary principle in EC and WTO Law: Searching for a common understanding. *Environmental Law Review*, *8*(4), 257–277; Bergkamp, L. and Kogan, L. (2013). Trade, the precautionary principle, and post-modern regulatory process: regulatory convergence in the transatlantic trade and investment partnership. *European Journal of Risk Regulation*, *4*(4), 493–507.

[75] World Trade Organization. (1995). Technical Barriers to Trade Agreement.

[76] https://eping.wto.org/ (accessed 05-09-2023).

the notifications from the European Union are a handful which relate to "Commission Regulation (EU) amending Regulation (EC) No 1881/2006 as regards maximum levels of cadmium in certain foods (Text with EEA Relevance)." These regulations enable the EU to ban imports of cacao with elevated levels of cadmium. While the presence of heavy metals in food is certainly a legitimate public health concern, and these regulations apply to the import of cacao from anywhere in the world, in practice they end up targeting the few countries, mostly in South America, with elevated levels of naturally occurring ground-source cadmium.[77] The difficulty with these types of regulatory standards is that, despite a scientific "risk assessment," there may be a lack of scientific consensus on how much of a particular harm is too much. If the EU is overly zealous in setting the levels of acceptable cadmium, then the regulations may serve more as a discriminatory trade barrier (favoring, in this instance, West African cacao producers) than as a legitimate protection of human health. The SPS agreement can embolden the EU to chance legally erring on the side of caution with the result effect being a meaningful restriction on the cacao trade. Thus, even though Colombia, along with all countries (*erga omens*) can export cacao beans to the EU with a 0% tariff, this de jure market access is not meaningful for the country given the EU's SPS restrictions on cadmium.

The politics of what types of regulatory justifications are permissible is instrumental in shaping how these rules are developed and applied. Those that have a say in how these technical aspects of trade policy are made will certainly be able to better avail themselves of the market access (or protection) that these rules offer. Thus, it is no surprise that several of the "winners" identified in Chapter 3 have taken an active role in WTO technical negotiations. While the SPS and TBT committees are open to all members, the chairperson position rotates on an annual basis. While often chaired by an individual from an OECD country, since 1995 the SPS and TBT committees have also been chaired by a representative from the Philippines (x3), Indonesia (x1), and Chile (x4), all countries that that were in the NE quadrant in Chapter 3 and that export meaningful amounts of agricultural products. These countries were prima facie structurally important enough to chair the committee, but then also would have had sufficient government capacity to likely shape the committee's outcomes in ways that would be beneficial to their domestic producers.

[77] Rofner, N. F. (2021). Cadmium in soil and cacao beans of Peruvian and South American origin. *Revista Facultad Nacional de Agronomia Medellin*, *74*(2), 9499–9515.

Box 4.1 The Sweetest HTS Example

To illustrate the complexity of the HTS system, consider a simple chocolate bar in the United States' HTS. Starting with "Section IV: *Prepared Foodstuffs; Beverages, Spirits, and Vinegar; Tobacco and Manufactured Tobacco Substitutes*," chocolate bars can then be found in Chapter 18 "*Cocoa and cocoa preparations*" under the four-digit heading 1806 "*Chocolate and other food preparations containing cocoa.*" At the six-digit level, the most specific universal tariff level, chocolate bars are then found under heading 1806.31 "Other, in blocks, slabs or bars: Filled" and 1806.32 "Other, in blocks, slabs or bars: Not filled." However, the "Not filled" category is then expanded to no less than 12 product types at the eight-digit level (1806.32.(04, 06, 08, 14, 16, 18, 30, 55, 60, 70, 80, 90)) with tariffs ranging from a simple ad valorum rate of 5% to tariffs that combine quantity and ad valorum taxes ranging from $0.372 per kilogram plus 4.3% ad valorum for 1806.32.06, bars "Containing less than 21% by weight of milk solids" to $0.528 per kilogram plus 6% for 1806.32.80 for bars that are "Other" with a footnote reference to "See 9904.04.50-9904.05.01." Such is the complexity for classifying a chocolate bar in the *United States* market, but, since product descriptions (and rates) can vary by country at the eight-digit level, there could well different detailed classifications of chocolate bars in every other country. Enough to give a tooth ache.

The second major, and related, trade friction that can obscure meaningful market access stems from the complexity of products in the global trade system.[78] Products in the global trade system are classified according to a schedule known as the "Harmonized (Tariff) Schedule" (HTS or HS). This schedule builds incrementally, via expanding digits, from more general to more specific. Comprised of 22 sections, the HTS has 99 chapters, from "01" to "99" which comprise the "two-digit" product code. These digits then expand to eight and, at times, ten total digits that further classify the products. While the first six digits are universal, the eight- and 10-digit codes can vary by country. Most countries set tariff rates for most products at the six-digit level, although some entities, such as the United States and EU, use the "eight-digit" level for product tariff rates. The "10-digit" level does exist in some entities but is primarily used for statistical reporting purposes.

[78] Yu, D. (2008). The Harmonized System-Amendments and Their Impact on WTO Members' Schedules. *WTO Staff Working Paper No. ERSD-2008-02.*

As a preliminary friction, these discrepancies at the eight-digit level can add considerable complexity for firms looking to export their wares, as they can often have difficulty classifying their goods appropriately, as illustrated in Box 4.1. One Nepalese exporter described how he tried to figure out if his product was one that was GSP-eligible by using Google and a battered, decade-old, handbook on his office shelf, as he received little help from his government's export promotion center.[79] While again highlighting the distinction between state and firm, this example shows how developing country institutional capacity can also impact the ways in which the state is able to help its firms (or not) take advantage of de jure market access.

Beyond the regulatory complexity of the classifications, the larger trade friction can stem from the fact that the multitude of product line classifications can obscure tariff peaks within low average tariffs and/or can disguise tariff lines intended to target a particular country (or even firm).[80] Trade liberalization is often discussed in terms of average tariff rate or in terms of scope.[81] The former situation might describe a trade agreement as resulting in a 1% average tariff rate (perhaps on the entire HTS, or in a particular section). However, such a statement could obscure very high tariff rates on a single or even handful of products. While the GATT/WTO and most RTAs set both "bound" and "maximum" tariff rates, they still can lead to wide variability in market access on a particular product.[82] Other "scope-based" soundbites might trumpet agreements with "zero-tariff" trade on 90% or even 99% of trade products.[83] However, if these agreements are based on the thousands of products at the HTS8 or even HTS6 digit level, then such a scope claim may mean that an agreement excludes dozens, if not hundreds, of product lines.

Take, for example, duty free market access for Least Developed Countries (LDCs) to the United States under the US GSP scheme. As of 2021, there were the 10,905 HTS8 tariff product lines in the US HTS. Under the WTO, the US tariff schedule allows duty free entry for 4,191 of these products for MFN partners, that is, members in the WTO. A further 3,426 lines are duty-free

[79] Interview N-1595.

[80] Hoekman, B. M., Ng, F., and Olarreaga, M. (2001). *Tariff Peaks in the Quad and Least Developed Country Exports* (Vol. 2747). Centre for Economic Policy Research.

[81] Santos-Paulino, A. U. (2002). The effects of trade liberalization on imports in selected developing countries. *World Development*, *30*(6), 959–974.

[82] Francois, J. and Martin, W. (2003). Formula approaches for market access negotiations. *World Economy*, *26*(1), 1–28.

[83] For example, an explainer by the Irish Government on the EU-Canada Comprehensive Economic Trade Agreement (CETA) trumpeted that the agreement "removes over 98% of tariffs". https://enterprise.gov.ie/en/what-we-do/trade-investment/free-trade-agreements/ceta.html (accessed 22-11-2023).

for members of the US GSP scheme, and an additional 1,350 are duty-free for Least Developed Countries (LDCs) for a total of 8,967 lines for this latter category of country. Thus, even under the most favorable preferential rules, over 1,900, or almost 20% of, lines are still subject to tariff barriers for the poorest countries.[84] Moreover, for any country-dyad pair, the value of trade on the vast majority of products lines is very small, or, more likely, zero, as very few countries produce, much less export, the full range of HTS products. Accordingly, the overlap between products a country does trade (or might like to trade), and the areas in which there is de jure market access, may be considerably smaller than the overall market access picture. If a LDC's comparative advantage products (or even sectors) fall inside the 20% of tariff lines above, broad-based access to the US market for the other 80% of tariff lines will mean little and while a country could thus have considerable de jure market access, their meaningful market access will be limited. This distinction is also hinted by the low GSP "utilization rate" discussed above.

The Politics of Market Access

To export effectively, states must secure both de jure and de facto market access for their firms. For both, politics permeates. As a developing country, securing an RTA or GSP with an important developed country market is driven as much by the political considerations of international high politics as the economics of free exchange. The vast bulk of the United States' North–South RTAs are with developing countries in the Western Hemisphere. While the gravity logic of trade dictates that more proximate states will trade more, distance is an insufficient explainer of these agreements.[85] Indeed, the distance between the Pacific ports of Long Beach and Lima in RTA partner Peru is greater (~6,700 km) than that between the Atlantic ports of Miami and Dakar, Senegal (~6,500 km). Instead of taking advantage of geographic economic dynamism, the United States' American RTAs are as likely to be a further instantiation of the 200-year-old Monroe Doctrine's policy of hemispheric domination.[86] Outside the Occidental sphere, most of the United States' RTAs with developing or middle-income states have dubious economic bases but instead are in key geo-political locales

[84] http://ptadb.wto.org/ptaTradeInfo.aspx (accessed 30-03-2022).

[85] Tinbergen J. (1962). *Shaping the World Economy*. The Twentieth Century Fund, New York.

[86] Bulmer-Thomas, V. and Dunkerley, J. (Eds.). (1999). *The United States and Latin America: The New Agenda*. Harvard University Press.

(Jordan, Oman, Morocco). Notably absent from the United States' RTA web are trade agreements with South and East Asian states. Outside a Bilateral Trade Agreement and, later, Trade and Investment Framework Agreement concluded with Vietnam in 2007 and explained at greater depth in Chapter 6, the only other agreements in the region are with advanced economies Singapore and South Korea, also both clearly security-related.[87] The United States' major regional RTA initiative, the then-called "Trans-Pacific Partnership" (TPP) whose negotiations launched in 2008 would have seen the United States at the center of a deal with advanced and emerging Asian-Pacific economies, was clearly ensconced within the Obama administration's "Asian Pivot" in 2012 which laid out a broader economic and security vision for the region.[88] While the United States signed the agreement in 2016, this signature was withdrawn by the Trump administration early in 2017 and the agreement has proceeded without US involvement.

US GSP access is similarly spotty. While as of 2020, 119 countries were eligible for the US's GSP scheme, access at the HTS product level is by country. In the US Harmonized Tariff Schedule (HTSUS) GSP products lines are designated as "A" (available to all GSP eligible states), "A+" (available to LDC states) and "A*" (some GSP states are not eligible). The A* countries are primarily middle-income countries that are GSP-excluded for certain product lines, generally resulting from the GSP annual review petition process. In 2022, countries with A* product-line exclusions included Argentina, Belize, Bosnia, Brazil, Ecuador, Egypt Guyana, Indonesia, Jamaica, North Macedonia, Kazakhstan, Suriname, Pakistan, the Philippines, Thailand, and Ukraine. While Thailand, and to a lesser extent Argentina, Brazil, and Ecuador are listed as "A*" for a variety of product lines, other countries are only designated "A*" on one, or a handful, or product lines. For example, North Macedonia, retains GSP for most HTS product lines, but is excluded from one, 8702.10.31 "Motor vehicles for the transport of ten or more persons, including the driver: Designed for the transport of 16 or more persons, including the driver," that is, passenger buses. Looking at US import data, at total imports of $150 million, this product was a major import from North Macedonia in 2017, accounting for roughly 60% of the value of US imports from the country in that year. While the preference lost was relatively minor—GSP countries face no duty on the product while the general rate is 2%—for a highly

[87] Pang, E. S. (2007). Embedding security into free trade: The case of the United States—Singapore Free Trade Agreement. *Contemporary Southeast Asia*, 1–32.

[88] Löfflmann, G. (2016). The pivot between containment, engagement, and restraint: President Obama's conflicted grand strategy in Asia. *Asian Security*, 12(2), 92–110.

commoditized product like passenger buses, this difference may be sufficient to substitute suppliers. Indeed, from the 2017 zenith, Macedonian exports of the product fell to just $25 million in post-pandemic year 2021 and recovered only to $60 million in 2022, a 60% decrease from the 2017 value. The politics of this exclusion appears to be based on the fact that the country exceeded the Competitive Needs Limitation for the product in the 2019 GSP annual review and, as a result, was reverted to the normal trade relations (NTR) rate.[89] In this instance, the exclusion does not seem to be driven by US domestic politics, but the case illustrates how meaningful market access can depend on a single product line. In North Macedonia's case, its exclusion from just one of the 5,000 HTS8 product lines for which GSP countries are eligible meant that 60% of its exports to the US market now faced an increased entry barrier. Thus, even though the country retained 99.9% of its de jure GSP tariff line access, losing preference on its single most important product largely rendered that access moot.

The largest RTA partner, the EU/EFTA, has similar heterogeneity in its trade agreements. In addition to its nearly four dozen RTAs, the EU's GSP+ scheme, briefly mentioned above, grants additional preferential market access based on countries who meet criteria for sustainable development and good governance, while the Union's "Everything But Arms" initiative, described at greater length in Chapter 7, grants duty free access on for nearly all products to least developed countries (LDCs). In order to qualify for/maintain access to the GSP+ scheme, countries must submit to intrusive monitoring missions that assess the extent to which the country is implementing 27 different international conventions that cover issues like human and labor rights, environmental protection, and good governance practice.[90] The intrusion on sovereignty aside, the access under this scheme is fundamentally dependent on the policies of the government in power. While this is true for any access conditionality, firms may have limited control over whether or not their governments can/will continue to adhere to the 27 conventions, something largely determined by those governments' institutional capacity and quality. This introduces uncertainty over this market access and thus can detract from the meaningfulness of the de jure access.

Moreover, the application of this conditionality is often subject to domestic political considerations. As an example, Bangladesh, sought to join the

[89] https://www.govinfo.gov/content/pkg/FR-2019-11-20/pdf/2019-25134.pdf (accessed 05-09-2023).
[90] https://gsphub.eu/about-gsp/gsp-plus (accessed 05-09-2023).

GSP+ scheme following its graduation from LDC status and thus losing its eligibility for the EBA initiative. However, as of 2019, the process was in jeopardy due to EU's scrutiny that the country was not sufficiently addressing the "serious shortcomings" in human and labor rights. In response, the EU "engagement" was to press the country to focus on ensuring domestic law complied with International Labor Organization (ILO) conventions. Whether or not Bangladesh's labor practices are markedly worse than many other developing countries, including GSP+ beneficiaries like Kyrgyzstan or the Philippines, is debatable, but, unlike those countries Bangladesh suffered a major and visible international disaster in the Rana Plaza collapse in 2013 which killed over 1,000 textile workers.[91] In response to this high-profile calamity, there was massive outcry among European publics that pressed politicians to action.[92] In addition to legislative initiatives in the EU, it should not be surprising that, in the face of these domestic political demands, the Commission also increased its scrutiny of Bangladesh's GSP+ application status.

However, for Bangladeshi firms, the outcome of the GSP+ process is something that is largely out of their control. While one Khulna-based, jute-exporting, firm interviewed in 2019 noted how they had received additional training on labor rights via the labor department in conjunction with international aid programs, their main concerns were with the supply of their input materials and international prices. This firm did, however, export entirely to the Chinese market and noted how it had a challenge finding new markets, but the interviewee did not connect the dots between labor rights and access to Western, and in particular European, markets.[93] A Dhaka-based RMG (ready-made garment) exporter declared that the EBA and GSP+ didn't make much difference as their competitors also had that access, but another said that Pakistan's attainment of GSP+ in 2014 had led to a significant competition from firms in that country and a loss of market share, again highlighting the third-party implications of granting/removing market access.[94]

Finally, while the European EBA and GSP+ grant duty free access for all products covered by their respective schemes, the standard GSP scheme, which applies to any middle-income country not covered by GSP+, only

[91] Kenner, J. and Peake, K. (2017). The Bangladesh Sustainability Compact: An effective exercise of global experimentalist EU governance? *Cambridge Yearbook of European Legal Studies*, *19*, 86–115.

[92] Evans, A. (2020). Overcoming the global despondency trap: Strengthening corporate accountability in supply chains. *Review of International Political Economy*, *27*(3), 658–685.

[93] Interview. KH-1001.

[94] Interview D-1002; Interview D-1001.

received duty-free entry on "non-sensitive" products. For "sensitive" products, the countries receive a reduction from the MFN rate. The "sensitivity" of most of these products is not that they are key, high-technology infant industries, or sectors that are vitally important to regional security, but instead are politically sensitive. As of January 1, 2023, the "Sensitive products" designation applied to no less than 350 HS product lines, some at the four-digit level, meaning that a number of additional six- and eight-digit products may be covered, over a vast range of agricultural products including "beef and other meat; dairy products; fruit and vegetables; processed fruit and vegetables; maize and other cereals; starch; oils; processed sugar products; cocoa products; pasta; and alcoholic beverages"[95] as well as textiles, some metals, and various other miscellaneous items.[96] Thus, while the EU GSP grants some preference in these areas, it may not be a sufficient preference to make the market access useful.

In sum, meaningful market access for a developing country rests on three pillars. The first is the de jure market access it receives via its membership in the WTO, RTAs, or PTAs like the GSP and related schemes. The second pillar is the degree to which this market access is conditioned by any quantitative restrictions. The third pillar is the extent regulatory or origin restrictions further act as barriers to any of this access. But, in all instances, these pillars of access interact with the potentially exportable products for firms in a given country. Market access is only meaningful if the key product lines have all three pillars—that is, they have low de jure tariffs, do not face any quantitative restrictions, and are not meaningfully restricted by regulatory or origin barriers. The politics of access can intervene at any of these steps. Depending on their international structural positioning and ability to effectively exercise their agency, developing countries may not be able to successfully negotiate de jure tariff-rate or quantitative market access for the products that interest their firms—particularly in agricultural products or textiles—because of domestic political pressures from developed country markets aligned against them. Likewise, developing countries have little power to forestall the domestic regulatory requirements in developed economies which can ultimately act as trade barriers. While there may only be a handful of constituencies that are actively trying to deny meaningful market to (most) developing countries,

[95] https://unctad.org/system/files/official-document/itcdtsbmisc25rev5_en.pdf (accessed 05-09-2023).

[96] European Union. (2023) Regulation (EU) No 978/2012 of the European Parliament and of the Council of 25 October 2012 applying a scheme of generalised tariff preferences and repealing Council Regulation (EC) No 732/2008. Current Consolidated version: 01/01/2023.

certainly there are a number of domestic political actors who effectively hinder meaningful market access for developing country firms as an unintended consequence of placating domestic concerns. Countries that find themselves with the fortuitous trifecta of access for product lines in which their firms have legitimate export potential end up in that place either because they were sufficiently empowered to successfully overcome developed country domestic interests, or because there were no domestic actors in the export market that were interested to cut one of the pillars out. From developing countries' perspective, securing meaningful market access is no easy task.

5

What Makes (Trade) Effective Aid?

Aid for Trade—a New Approach or Old Wine in New Bottles?

As outlined in Chapter 2, modern foreign aid initiatives have weathered highs and lows since the end of World War II. However, the turn of the millennium offered the possibility of an exciting inflection point. Spurred by the "triumph" of global capitalism in the 1990s and the unipolar, liberal, global order, it appeared that the elusive goal of universally inclusive development was at last within reach.[1] Swept up in this heady optimism was the junction of foreign aid and international trade. While subject to an intense debate, globalization proponents argued that underdevelopment and inequality were just one more problem that could be solved by applying the panoptic prescription of neo-liberal market rationality. To these advocates, underdevelopment was a problem of states not taking significant advantage of the welfare gains afforded by the new, globalized, trading order.[2] Surely, if developing states could only find their comparatively advantaged place within global supply chains, they could attract foreign investment, realize economic growth and lift their populations out of poverty.[3]

To exploit these opportunities, a number of development actors began to talk more explicitly about using foreign aid as a "big push" to help countries make the final leap to economic prosperity.[4] Part of this initiative focused exclusively on aid that could help countries take advantage of global markets. While proponents of trade-related aid recognized the ongoing theoretical and empirical debates, their implicit assumption is that export-led growth (ELG) is a vital pathway for economic development for (particularly small)

[1] Ikenberry, G. J. (2004). Liberalism and empire: Logics of order in the American unipolar age. *Review of International Studies*, *30*(4), 609–630; Sachs, J. D. (2006). *The End of Poverty: Economic Possibilities for Our Time*. Penguin.

[2] Fischer, S. (2003). Globalization and its challenges. *American Economic Review*, *93*(2), 1–30.

[3] Narula, R. and Dunning, J. H. (2000). Industrial development, globalization and multinational enterprises: new realities for developing countries. *Oxford Development Studies*, *28*(2), 141–167.

[4] Easterly, W. (2006). The big push déjà vu: A review of Jeffrey Sachs's the end of poverty: economic possibilities for our time. *Journal of Economic Literature*, *44*(1), 96–105.

The Invisible Hand(out). Samuel Brazys, Oxford University Press. © Samuel Brazys (2025).
DOI: 10.1093/9780198970422.003.0005

developing countries in a globalized world.[5] When discussing aid effectiveness in this context, the outcome of interest is trade and, more specifically, exports. Aid which boosts exports (and, according to proponents of the ELG hypothesis, growth) is what this book calls trade-effective aid (TEA).

While aid pursuing this end was initially referred to as "trade-related assistance" or "trade capacity building assistance" the concept would ultimately be enshrined with the catchier moniker of "Aid for Trade" (AfT or A4T) at the 2005 Hong Kong WTO ministerial.[6] As laid out in that ministerial declaration, AfT was intended "to help developing countries, particularly LDCs, to build the supply-side capacity and trade-related infrastructure that they need to assist them to implement and benefit from WTO Agreements and more broadly to expand their trade."[7] This effort invoked the logic of helping developing countries to help themselves, by enabling them to seek growth by building export-oriented sectors which could then be used to fuel the social needs of the country.

The AfT initiative soon attracted a broad range of supporters and donor countries began to denote significant portions of their ODA as AfT. By the early 2010s, AfT commitments accounted for roughly one-third of all foreign aid. Under the broader umbrella, AfT was soon classified into three main categories: trade-related infrastructure (TRI), trade development (TD) (or trade productive capacity) and trade policy and regulation (TPR). In terms of total funding, the former categories dominated, accounting for nearly 98% of all AfT as of 2021.[8] TRI would encompass not only the infrastructure most obviously connected to trade—air and seaports or infrastructure for Export Processing Zones (EPZs)—but also a broader range of "productive infrastructure" including utilities and internal transportation (roads or rail).[9] The logic of this classification is that these types of infrastructure would reduce unit production costs for firms, enabling them to gain in productivity and efficiency and thus achieve international cost-competitiveness that would facilitate exports.[10] Likewise, the "trade development" label would

[5] Sannassee, R. V., Seetanah, B., and Jugessur, J. (2014). Export-led growth hypothesis: A meta-analysis. *The Journal of Developing Areas*, 361–385.

[6] Brazys, S. R. (2013). Evidencing donor heterogeneity in Aid for Trade. *Review of International Political Economy*, *20*(4), 947–978.

[7] World Trade Organization. (2005) Hong Kong Ministerial Declaration. WT/MIN(05)/DEC22. Available at: https://www.wto.org/english/thewto_e/minist_e/min05_e/final_text_e.htm (accessed 20-02-2023).

[8] OECD/WTO (2022), Aid for Trade immediately 2022: Empowering Connected, Sustainable Trade, OECD Publishing, Paris, https://doi.org/10.1787/9ce2b7ba-en.

[9] Gnangnon, S. K. (2018). Aid for trade and trade policy in recipient countries. *The International Trade Journal*, *32*(5), 439–464.

[10] Lorz, O. (2020). Investment in trade facilitating infrastructure: A political-economy analysis. *European Journal of Political Economy*, *65*, 101928.

come to be liberally applied to any project that aimed to increase production of goods or services, regardless of whether or not these products were ultimately exported. The argument for this classification being that these products had the potential for export, that is, they are in the tradable sector, and thus the projects could be said to be facilitating trade.[11] AfT projects that fit into the TPR category were ostensibly the most directly trade-related.[12] These types of projects would include efforts to update customs systems, assist exporters in meeting labeling or certification requirements or assist governments in implementing free trade agreements. However, the total funding of these efforts in the overall pot of AfT finance remains minimal.

This huge influx of funding naturally attracted the attention of practitioners, policymakers, and academics, eager to see if the combination would bear fruit—in other words, was this aid trade effective? Although relentlessly championed by the WTO and OECD, early analyses of the impact of AfT on exports were mixed. While numerous papers identified some positive export effects, these were often conditional on the type or source of AfT.[13] The inconclusive results in the literature are driven no doubt in part by the difficulty in choosing an appropriate methodological approach for identifying AfT effects. At least initially, studies on AfT effectiveness tended to focus on macro indicators of both AfT and exports. Cross-country studies that considered the impact of aggregate amounts of AfT on aggregate exports levels were likely to be confounded by unobserved and unobservable location-time specific factors. Likewise, as a (large) component of overall aid, aggregate amounts of AfT are definitionally correlated with aggregate amount of ODA, while (the growth in) aggregate exports are also correlated with overall economic health—"growth led exports."[14] Moreover, it is firms, not countries, that ultimately export. As such, focusing on the country-level unit of analysis invites a problem of ecological inference. For AfT to be increasing exports, it should be the firms "treated" by the aid that are driving aggregate export increases. However, it is fallacious to infer average firm-level behavior based

[11] Gnangnon, S. K. (2018). Aid for trade and trade policy in recipient countries. *The International Trade Journal*, *32*(5), 439–464.

[12] Helble, M., Mann, C. L., and Wilson, J. S. (2012). Aid-for-trade facilitation. *Review of World Economics*, *148*, 357–376.

[13] Cali, M. and Te Velde, D. W. (2011). Does aid for trade really improve trade performance?. *World Development*, *39*(5), 725–740; Vijil, M. and Wagner, L. (2012). Does aid for trade enhance export performance? Investigating the infrastructure channel. *The World Economy*, *35*(7), 838–868; Brazys, S. R. (2013). Evidencing donor heterogeneity in Aid for Trade. *Review of International Political Economy*, *20*(4), 947–978.

[14] Bahmani-Oskooee, M. and Economidou, C. (2009). Export led growth vs. growth led exports: LDCs experience. *The Journal of Developing Areas*, *42*(2), 179–209.

on aggregate export measures. As such, these studies, while utilizing the best available data and methods of the time, were likely to be plagued by inferential problems which have long dogged aid and growth studies and could lead to biased or spurious results.

The broad classifications of AfT do no favors to those attempting to identify export effects. A substantial portion of AfT projects have no discernable export-oriented objective.[15] Aid projects that focused on increasing smallholder farmer production, or water, sanitation, and hygiene (WASH) projects for remote villages will have only the most indirect impact on recipient exports, like the one described in Box 5.1.[16] Including projects with such dubious connections to export-oriented activity strains the credulity of the causal linkage between AfT and exports. Classifying these types of projects as AfT is thus likely to add measurement bias to the indicator, further undermining attempts to discern an AfT export effect.

Box 5.1 Whose Trade Is Being Aided?

In 2019, Elisa Savelli, Klaas Schwartz, and Rhodante Ahlers investigated the Netherlands' aid into the WASH sector in Kenya. The Dutch justified these interventions as AfT on the basis that they promoted *Dutch* companies abroad, building a Dutch "water brand" in the WASH sector. The main private sector beneficiary is a Dutch holding company, Water Forever International, whose main product is a prepaid water meter. How these projects were intended to boost Kenyan exports is unclear.

However, beyond issues with classification, measurement, and identification, there is a raft of voices that is more directly critical of the AfT project.[17] In this reading, rather than being simply ineffective, AfT is a neo-colonial project that uses the aid to further exploitative exports of primary resources and/or as a sweetener in trade negotiations which lock developing counties into unfair trade deals. The critics note how promises of AfT are rarely "new" money but instead are (an extension of) existing aid efforts which have

[15] Brazys, S. R. (2013). Evidencing donor heterogeneity in Aid for Trade. *Review of International Political Economy*, *20*(4), 947–978.

[16] Savelli, E., Schwartz, K., and Ahlers, R. (2019). The Dutch aid and trade policy: Policy discourses versus development practices in the Kenyan water and sanitation sector. *Environment and Planning C: Politics and Space*, *37*(6), 1126–1147.

[17] Langan, M. and Scott, J. (2014). The aid for trade charade. *Cooperation and Conflict*, *49*(2), 143–161; Langan, M. and Price, S. (2020). The EU's development policy: Forging relations of dependence? In *The Routledge Handbook of Critical European Studies* (pp. 499–510). Routledge.

simply received the AfT moniker.[18] AfT is thus not an exciting new initiative which promises to help developing countries fully realize the opportunities of a global market but instead is simply a continuation of existing aid practice—old wine in a new bottle.

To make sense of what can make aid trade effective, this chapter thus builds on a growing cohort of micro and mezzo level studies to consider AfT allocation and impact from the project and firm levels. The chapter first considers the allocation side of AfT. Using rich data on the locations of AfT project sites, the chapter explores if AfT follows the usual patterns of politically biased allocation or if, instead, the projects are located near to exporting firms. The latter would suggest a functional allocation logic that, for many types of AfT projects, would seem to be a precursor for AfT effectiveness. The chapter then turns to questions of AfT impact by considering if firms near the AfT projects experienced increases in their exports. The findings, and arguments, are nuanced. The evidence suggests that some types of AfT, from some donors, can lead to some increase in exports. However, this impact is very much project-dependent. AfT can be effective, but it is not always so—either because AfT projects were never really intended to be export-oriented or because the project design or implementation simply failed to achieve an export impact. After presenting overall pictures of allocation and effectiveness across three countries—Nepal, Bangladesh, and Colombia—the chapter dives into a country-industry-project case in the cacao and chocolate production and trade development projects in Colombia.

Allocating AfT—Subnational Functionality

As discussed in Chapter 2, debates over aid allocation at the country level have often boiled down to questions of if aid is allocated based on "recipient needs" or "donor interests." Within this debate the focus remains on the political economy of donor countries. These countries allocate either to places where aid is most needed, as measured by indicators of poverty or inequality, or use aid to serve some other strategic donor purpose. The implication of these debates is that aid will be more effective when it is directed to higher-needs countries if for no other reason than the development will start from a lower baseline. However, the vast bulk of aid projects are not implemented at

[18] Stiglitz, J. E. and Charlton, A. H. G. (2013). *The right to trade: rethinking the aid for trade agenda.* Commonwealth Secretariat.

the country level but instead are implemented locally. As such, intra-country allocation may matter as much for effectiveness as inter-country allocation.

The political economy of intra-country allocation is not one that simply reflects donor preferences but, instead, is the interplay of both donor and recipient actors.[19] At this subnational level, discussions of where aid goes have tended to focus on the dichotomy of "donor control" versus "(recipient) elite capture," with the implicit assumption that donors and recipient elites may have differing objectives as to where aid resources are allocated.[20] The "needs-interests" tension can thus also play out within countries, but for both the donor and recipient actors. Donors may want aid projects to go to the areas where they are most needed—schools to areas where children can't read, hospitals to areas with high infant mortality—and/or they may want projects to locate to areas that promote a donor's strategic interest—roads to a mine owned by a firm from the donor's country, alternate employment projects to a region that produces illegal drugs. Recipient elites likewise will have an interest in directing resources. Again, while these could be altruistic and reflect localized needs, they may also be prebendalist or self-serving.[21] Politicians may try to direct projects to areas to attract or reward supporters or to line their own pockets.[22] Commercial elites may try to influence allocation to support their businesses.

However, beyond the need/interest dichotomy, there is also the potential for a functional logic for aid siting. While functionality may overlap with need when considering social ODA in the health, education, or humanitarian sectors, when considering AfT, functionality may not necessarily be aligned with broader social need. AfT functionality is determined by its ability to help firms increase their exports. As such, to the extent that a given AfT project has a spatial impact, this functionality will be determined by the proximity of the AfT project to exporting firms. While the functional proximity argument is clearest for trade-related infrastructure—firms must be sufficiently near new utilities or transport infrastructure to take advantage of the cost-savings that infrastructure provides—it is also germane to many

[19] Swedlund, H. J. (2017). *The Development Dance: How Donors and Recipients Negotiate the Delivery of Foreign Aid*. Cornell University Press; Song, T., Brazys, S., and Vadlamannati, K. C. (2021). Which wheel gets the grease? Constituent agency and sub-national world bank aid allocation. *The Journal of Development Studies*, *57*(3), 519–533.

[20] Findley, M. G., Harris, A. S., Milner, H. V., and Nielson, D. L. (2017). Who controls foreign aid? Elite versus public perceptions of donor influence in aid-dependent Uganda. *International Organization*, *71*(4), 633–663.

[21] Schou, A. (2007). Demand-driven poverty programmes and elite capture in Malawi: Between prebendalism and benevolence. *The European Journal of Development Research*, *19*, 594–613.

[22] Jablonski, R. S. (2014). How aid targets votes: the impact of electoral incentives on foreign aid distribution. *World Politics*, *66*(2), 293–330.

trade-development projects. For instance, if firms are supplied locally with a key production input, AfT projects that look to boost that input are likely to only benefit those proximate firms. Projects that seek to upskill a labor pool with vocational education will again likely only benefit firms that are drawing on that (local) labor pool.

The politics of trade-effective aid allocation therefore very much flows from the theoretical discussion in Chapter 2. Developing country governments must have sufficient capacity and quality to effectively gather information on firm export needs—be they physical infrastructure or an appropriate regulatory and institutional environment. Firms, of course, can be their own advocates in this regard, but their success may well depend on their political positioning vis-à-vis the government. If and when government can successfully ascertain these needs, they then need to be able to successfully communicate them to donors. Then, these developing states need to be structurally positioned vis-à-vis the donor such that their interests can overcome any countervailing donor interests driven by the donor's own domestic political considerations.

To explore this functional allocation logic, I expand my work with Minhaj Mahmud and Arya Pillai to consider aid allocation in three developing countries: Bangladesh, Colombia, and Nepal.[23] These countries represent various stages of development with Nepal languishing as a Least Developed Country (LDC), Bangladesh recently securing graduation to lower-middle income status (LMIC), and Colombia firmly entrenched as an upper-middle income country (UMIC). Likewise, the countries are dispersed on levels of democracy with Colombia and Nepal scoring in the upper 40% of democracies while Bangladesh scores in the bottom 20% in the 2021 vDem index.[24] However, all three countries have lagged behind global averages in trade, with each falling well below the global average of 25% of exports as a percentage of GDP.

In each country, I was able to secure a directory of exporting firms from official government sources. In Colombia data for 48,009 firms came from the *Estadísticas de Exportaciones* compiled by the *Dirección de Metodología y Producción Estadística*. In Bangladesh, the data was sourced from the Export Promotion Bureau's (EPB) directory of exporting firms which contained a total of 11,124 firms. Finally, in Nepal the data comes from the Nepal's Trade and Export Promotion Centre's Export–Import Directory which contains 864 firms. These firms

[23] Brazys, S., Mahmud, M., and Pillai, A. (2023). Who gets the goodies? Overlapping interests and the geography of aid for trade allocation in Bangladesh. *The Journal of Development Studies*, *59*(2), 242–257.
[24] https://v-dem.net/.

were then matched to location data using other databases, Google's geocoding API, and/or hand-coding methods. In Colombia, coordinates were found for 20,779 of the firms, while 11,115 were identified in Bangladesh and 538 firms were identified in Nepal, for a grand total of 32,432 firms.

To consider subnational need I use the subnational "Relative Wealth Index" compiled by Facebook's parent company Meta.[25] This data is built from remotely sensed data including night-time lights, mobile phone usage, Facebook connectivity, and topography, and is checked against household survey data. Finally, I match both of these datasets to geographically referenced aid data from AidData's country-level databases based off of Aid Information Management Systems (AIMS) and from AidData's Geocoded Research Release of World Bank Data. I restrict this data to types of aid considered to be AfT and only include those project locations which are located to a high level of precision. This leaves me with 7,731 project locations from 273 distinct projects.

To examine the relationships between these data, I spatially compile them using the point information for the projects, firms, and wealth indices. These data populate a cross-sectional dataset across each of the three countries at a high degree of spatial precision by using subnational administrative divisions. In Bangladesh and Nepal, the unit of analysis is the fourth administrative level, known as the Unions in Bangladesh, of which there are roughly 4,500 while in Nepal these are known as Wada (or Wards) of which there are roughly 6,500. In Colombia, the lowest administrative divisions are the second level and are known as Municipios. There are over 1,110 of these and are for the most part of comparable size to smaller administrative units in other countries, although a few, sparsely populated Municipios, can be up to 75,000 km squared.

To join the data, I identify which administrative division each firm or AfT project is in. For the RWI, I take an average of all RWI readings which fall within an administrative unit's boundaries. Mapping this information in Figures 5.1–5.3, a few observations quickly become apparent. First, firms (shown by white circles) and AfT projects (illustrated by white x's) are highly concentrated around major metropolitan centers, which also happen to have higher degrees of relative wealth, as indicated by the lighter shading. While this is evident in all countries, it is particularly pronounced in Nepal and Bangladesh, where the vast majority of firms and projects are clustered

[25] Chi, G., Fang, H., Chatterjee, S., and Blumenstock, J. E. (2022). Microestimates of wealth for all low-and middle-income countries. *Proceedings of the National Academy of Sciences*, *119*(3), e2113658119.

Figure 5.1 Colombia firms, AfT, and relative wealth
Circles = firms, X= AfT projects, darker shading = poorer.

around Kathmandu and Dhaka, respectively. However, all three countries do display a reasonable dispersion of firms around other parts of the country.

Unfortunately, given available data, it is difficult to say much about the causal spatial relationship between firms, AfT projects, and wealth. This is mainly due to the lack of temporal information. While the AidData does contain information on the beginning and end of aid projects, unfortunately the Meta poverty data is a snapshot and the firm data has no information on when firms were established or began exporting. Thus, the relationship between AfT projects and poverty and exporting firms could run either way. AfT might have been located to places where firms were already established, or AfT might have caused exporting firms to set up shop—the "Field of Dreams" approach—"if you build it, they will come." Yet, one can argue either is evidence of functional aid allocation. AfT being put near exporting firms is very much a functional allocation. However, AfT inducing new firms to set up shop is also evidence of functionality—if not effectiveness. In the first instance, I consider the distance between AfT project locations and the most proximate exporting firm. Of the over 7,770 project locations, over half are within 25 kilometers of the nearest exporting firm and 10% are within a mile, while only 25% are more than 50 kilometers from the nearest exporting firm.

Figure 5.2 Nepal firms, AfT, and relative wealth
Circles = firms, X= AfT projects, darker shading = poorer.

On second glance, I consider several different spatial correlations in Table 5.1 below, where I account for spatial dependence between nearby administrative units and also account for country-specific differences between the three subject countries. In these, I estimate the likelihood that an administrative unit will contain AfT project(s) based on the presence of exporting firm(s) and relative wealth. As shown there, there is a consistent positive and statistically significant relationship between the presence of an exporting firm and the likelihood that an administrative unit will host an AfT project, whether or not accounting for the relative wealth of that area. Nor is the effect small. An administrative unit with an exporting firm will have an increase in probability of 14 percentage points of having an AfT project compared to an administrative unit without. Considering that the underlying probability of having an AfT project is about 34%, this represents an increase of over 40% from that mean.

The results above are certainly consistent with an explanation that firms in the three countries under study were able to convey their siting preferences to their governments who were then able to effectively convince their donor partners of the same. However, functional siting of AfT projects is a necessary, but not sufficient, condition for those projects to be trade effective. To that end, interestingly, areas with higher relative wealth are also more likely to have AfT projects. This relationship could be evidence of an

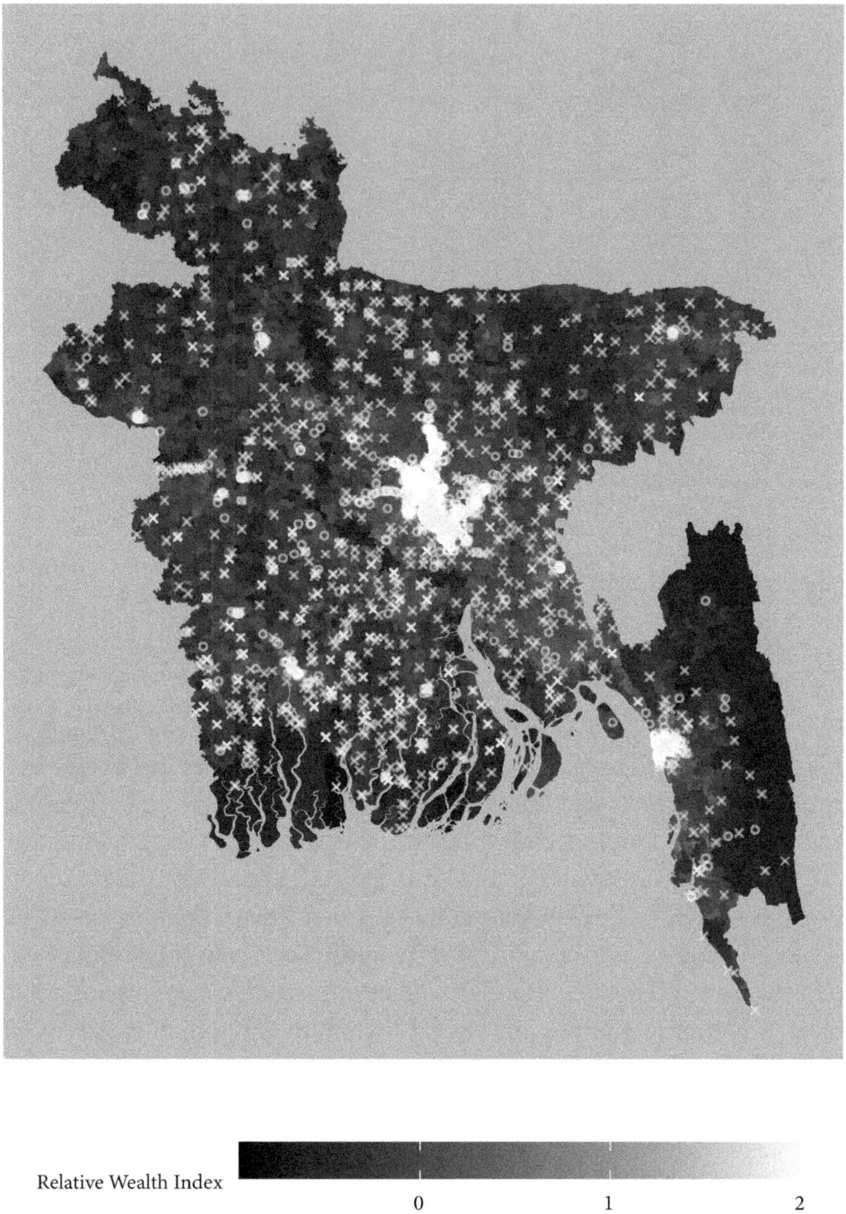

Figure 5.3 Bangladesh firms, AfT, and relative wealth

Circles = firms, X= AfT projects, darker shading = poorer.

increasingly established finding that aid projects go to wealthier areas subnationally.[26] However, given the likelihood that most of the data used for

[26] Briggs, R. C. (2017). Does foreign aid target the poorest?. *International Organization*, *71*(1), 187–206.

Table 5.1 AfT project presence—firms and wealth

VARIABLES	(1) Wealth	(2) Exporter	(3) Multivariate	(4) Logs	(5) Imputed	(6) Neg Binomial
Wealth	0.144***		0.111***		0.057*	0.471
	(0.039)		(0.036)		(0.039)	(0.387)
Exporter		0.146***	0.136***	0.109**	0.112***	0.003***
		(0.018)	(0.021)	(0.025)	(0.018)	(0.001)
Observations	9,829	10,260	9,829	10,260	10,260	9,829
Constant	YES	YES	YES	YES	YES	YES
Country FE	YES	YES	YES	YES	YES	YES
R^2	0.188	0.181	0.192	0.121	0.183	0.046

Conley standard errors in parentheses (country clustered SEs in model 6).
***p < 0.01, **p < 0.05, *p <0.1

the RWI snapshot was gathered after the AfT projects were implemented, an alternative explanation could be that AfT made these areas richer. This is what one would plausibly expect if indeed AfT were trade effective. If AfT either increased the productivity of nearby exporting firms, or induced new exporting firms to set up shop, that would ostensibly have knock-on effects on employment, wages, and poverty. Indeed, this is precisely the mechanisms that advocates of AfT would hope to see. The next section will investigate precisely that—does the presence of AfT increase firm exports?

Aid for Trade Effectiveness? The Missing Middle

Although the previous section established that exporting firms and AfT projects are often proximate to each other, this does not necessarily mean that the AfT projects are effective in improving firm export performance. To drill down into aid effectiveness, and to avoid issues of ecological inference discussed above, the chapter combines the project-level AidData with firm-level information on exports in the three countries. This level of analysis allows for an identification and separation of firms who have been (spatially) "treated" by AfT projects and those who haven't. This enables the use of more finely tuned investigative techniques to ascertain if AfT projects improve firm export performance.

In Nepal and Bangladesh this data comes from original surveys conducted by myself and my research teams. In Nepal, in February and May of 2016, all

624 exporting firms for which contact information was available were contacted. Of these, 131 agreed to take a telephone survey. To get around the fact that there was no previous baseline measure of export performance, the survey asked a retrospective performance question—had the firm's exports increased, decreased, or stayed the same over the previous five years? The survey also included several other questions including when the firm began to export and the number of employees at the firm. In Bangladesh, given the large number of exporters, a stratified sample of firms based on sector and location was identified in order to obtain a sample of 765 firms that was representative along these lines. However, of these, it turned out that only 447 were currently exporting or had ever exported. These firms were then surveyed in-person from August to November 2019 by trained enumerators who asked a wider battery of questions including retrospective questions on export performance.

In Colombia, firm-level export data comes from the same *Estadísticas de Exportaciones* used to identify firm locations above. This data includes monthly export data for all 20,779 firms and the exported product (HTS code). However, unlike the Nepal and Bangladesh data, this data does not include other firm characteristics, including size or makeup. The most straightforward approach for assessing AfT effectiveness is to analyze the data in a difference-in-difference framework wherein there is a comparison in the difference in export performance over a given period between firms that were/were not "treated" by AfT. In the main analyses, the data from all three countries are combined. To make effective comparisons between the data, the outcome indicator is a binary indicator that equals "1" if a firm's exports increased from the pre-treatment period compared to the post-treatment period and "0" otherwise. While this binary approach loses some information on magnitude of the increase, it does allow for a better qualitative comparison across small and large firms. For Nepal and Bangladesh this measure comes directly from the survey questions where AfT treatment status is assigned to "1" if the firms were proximate to an AfT project which began any time prior to the date of the surveys. For Colombia, with more frequent data on export performance, it is possible to determine the year in which a firm became "treated" based on the timing of when AfT projects began. This allows for a determination of a "before" and "after" period for each firm, where the binary export measure is determined by evaluating if the monthly average of exports in the "after" period increased vis-à-vis the average in the "before" period. For the "non-treated" firms, the before and after periods are assigned based on the final year of AfT projects in the database, 2014. While these approaches introduce some measurement error, they are necessary to make the data from the three countries reasonable comparable. With this combined data, it is then possible to estimate a classic difference-in-difference. This is done, with the results presented graphically, in Figure 5.4 below.

The results in Figure 5.4 are revealing. While there is no statistically significant overall positive export effect attributable to AfT, the results appear to vary when examining the country level. While the results for both Nepal and Bangladesh have confidence intervals which cross over the "0" threshold, the estimate for Colombian firms is positive and statistically significant. The substantive effect is modest but noticeable. The impact of being "treated" by an AfT project increases the likelihood of increased exports by three percentage points, which equates to a roughly 7% increase from the 44.6% of "non-treated" firms who reported increased exports. While none of these countries are particularly strategic lynchpins in the international system, part of Colombia's interest to donors is no doubt due to its position as a key country in the global narcotics trade. Along the lines of "targeted development" it is certainly plausible that donor interests in Colombia revolve around limiting the spillovers from this activity. As a result of this position, the Colombian government might also have increased agency when dealing with international donors and is better able to dictate the types of terms of its assistance.

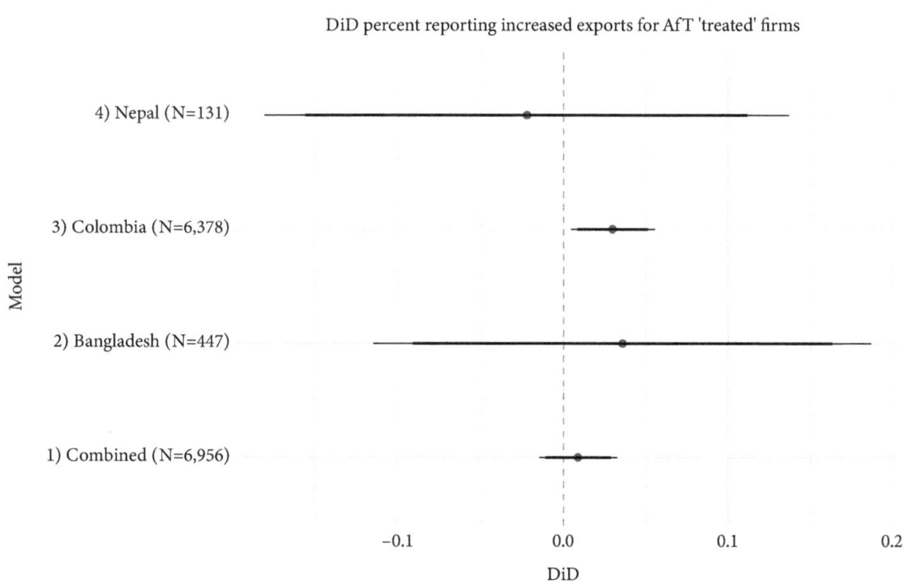

Figure 5.4 Aggregate Aid for Trade export effects

But in addition to the theory suggesting differences based on recipient-country heterogeneity based on a given country's positioning in the international system and its own domestic institutional capacity, heterogeneous outcomes might also occur within a given country due to donor heterogeneity. As any given developing country's strategic importance may differ by development partner and given that each developed country partner may have a different mix of domestic interests and politics, the donor–recipient relationship, the effectiveness of aid, may well vary based on which donor is supporting a given project. Indeed, earlier work that has found significant donor heterogeneity in AfT effectiveness.[27] A more detailed look at Nepal by Brazys and Elkink (2021) considered AfT impact at the project level, finding that proximity to different projects, from different donors, was more or less likely associated with firm export performance as shown in Figure 5.5.[28] This figure captures distance effects from a Bayesian posterior distribution, where the coefficient measures the impact of distance to a project on increased firm exports, such that negative coefficients indicate that less distance to a project is associated with improved export performance.

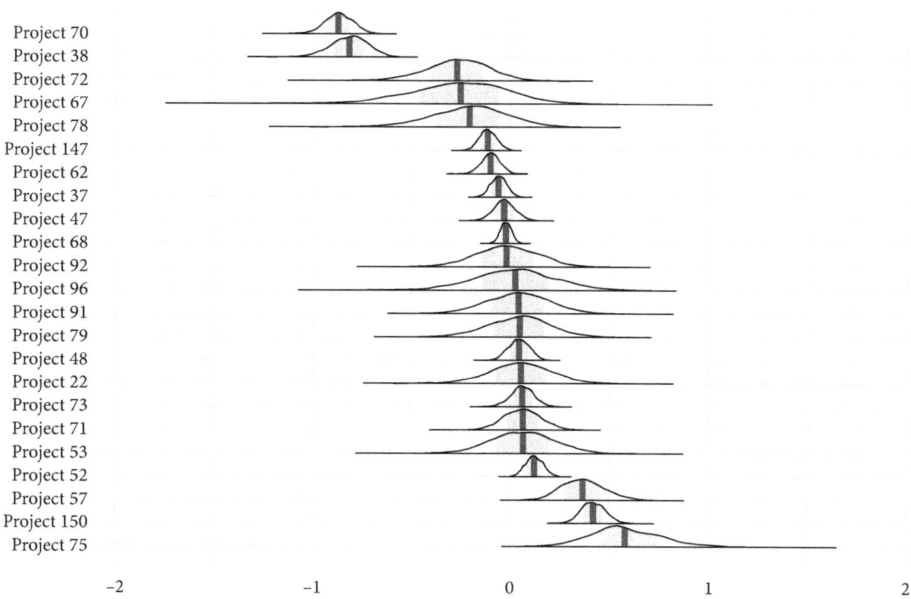

Figure 5.5 Distance effects on exports by project (Brazys and Elkink, 2021)

[27] Brazys, S. R. (2013). Evidencing donor heterogeneity in Aid for Trade. *Review of International Political Economy*, *20*(4), 947–978.

[28] Brazys, S. and Elkink, J. A. (2021). "Aid for Trade" effectiveness? Micro-level evidence from Nepal. *The European Journal of Development Research*, 33, 1493–1513.

X-axis: Posterior distribution of the impact of the distance to each project to a firm on the probability of an export increase (reproduced from Brazys and Elkink 2021).

To dig further into this efficacy heterogeneity, I look deeper into the data in Colombia. This data contains information on the sectors in which the firms export. Using data on the Harmonized Tariff Schedule (HTS) classification of each export record, it is possible to categorize the exporters into the 22 HTS sections and evaluate the AfT export effectiveness in each. While there are insufficient exporters to evaluate HTS Section III ("Animal or Vegetable Fats and Oils and Their Cleavage Products; Prepared Edible Fats; Animal or Vegetable Waxes") or HTS Section XIX ("Arms and Ammunition; Parts and Accessories Thereof") there are sufficient numbers of exporters to evaluate effects in the other sections.

As illustrated in Figure 5.6, the results again show significant heterogeneity by section. While most sections have positive coefficient estimates (16/20), these estimates are only statistically significant in three cases, that of Section X ("Pulp of Wood or of Other Fibrous Cellulosic Material; Waste and Scrap of Paper or Paperboard; Paper and Paperboard and Articles Thereof"), Section XII ("Footwear, Headgear, Umbrellas, Sun Umbrellas, Walking Sticks, Seat Sticks, Whips, Riding-Crops and Parts Thereof; Prepared Feathers and

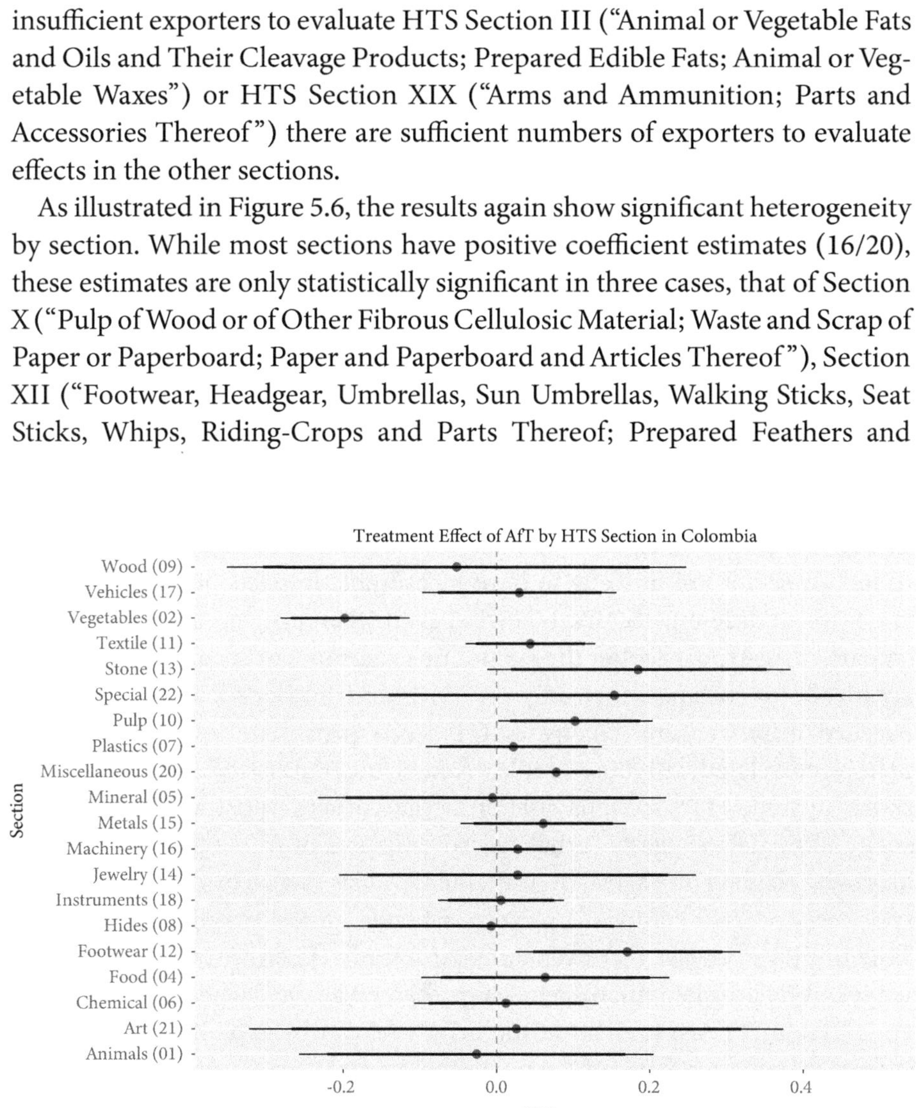

Figure 5.6 AfT effectiveness by HTS section in Colombia

Articles Made Therewith; Artificial Flowers; Articles of Human Hair") and Section XX ("Miscellaneous Manufactured Articles"). In contrast, one section, Section II ("Vegetable Products"), shows a statistically significant negative effect. This section includes Chapter 9 of the HTS which covers Colombia's most famous export, coffee.

In terms of export volume, despite the misleading title, the over $10 billion in Section XX goods ("Miscellaneous") comprises the third largest share of the roughly $200 billion in free on board (FOB) export value from 2011 to 2021, while Section X ("Pulp") and Section XII ("Footwear") total to just over $5 billion and just under $800 million, respectively. In contrast, Section II ("Vegetables") products accounted for over $7.5 billion in exports, with coffee accounting for the lion's share of this section at just under $3.3 billion. While all of these products pale in comparison to Section V ("Mineral Products") and, in particular, Chapter 27 exports ("Mineral fuels, mineral oils and products of their distillation; bituminous substances; mineral waxes") at over $100 billion, they nonetheless remain important export sectors.

While there is no immediately obvious rationale why some sections evidence positive effects while others don't, this heterogeneity demonstrates that the trade effectiveness of AfT is unlikely to be consistent across countries or even sectors within a country. As the Chapter 2 theory suggests, different types of projects in different locations from different donors will produce differential outcomes. Trade development interventions that focus on a specific product or sector are unlikely to have measurable impacts on other proximate firms in different sectors. Likewise, even when projects aren't targeted at a particular export sector, the economic geography of sectoral clustering may mean, for instance, that only certain industries benefit from (locally) upgraded infrastructure. Finally, AfT projects proximate to some sectors might be correlated with other unobserved or spurious issues, which impact exports in some HTS sections differently than others. What all this heterogeneity ultimately suggests is that macro estimates of AfT effectiveness are likely to be plagued by a substantial attenuation bias caused by considering all exporters to be "treated" by AfT projects, whereas, in reality, only a subset are. These findings suggest that evaluating AfT trade effectiveness necessitates the type of "aggregated micro" analysis presented above—wherein heterogeneous "treatment" assignment at the firm level can be exploited to recover average treatments effects (of the treated). Macro AfT studies, which do not delineate heterogenous firm treatment, overlook that firms, rather than countries, are the ultimate exporters and inferring firm level behavior from macro results is the classic ecological fallacy.

Follow the Cacao *Cadena*

To interrogate the mechanisms of trade-effective aid more closely, I next dive further into one sector within Colombia: cacao and chocolate products. Focusing on one sector in one country allows for isolation of the heterogenous impacts (if any) of different projects from different donors. Like its more famous cousin, coffee, cacao is a traditional Colombian agricultural product which takes advantage of the country's rich and diverse growing climate. While cacao cultivation can be traced back thousands of years to the Inca and other Mesoamerican native cultures, its derivative products have been a staple of the Colombian diet both as edibles but also and especially as a beverage since earlier colonial times.[29] More recently cacao has been viewed by many international development partners as an important crop in assuaging the country's long and violent history with coca production as their agricultural geographies significantly overlap. Likewise, interest in cacao as a part of sustainable agroforestry has also piqued the attention of the international development community. As such, numerous donors have invested considerable resources into improving various points of the cacao supply chain, or *cadena*.[30]

Tracing cacao from "bean to bar" requires starting with cacao farmers and tracing through various intermediaries to processors and exporters. Cacao production in Colombia tends to occur on very small holdings, averaging a few hectares and producing only several thousand kilograms. The *agricultores* who tend these plots most frequently sell their products to commercial intermediaries ("*commerciantes*"). Depending on the situation, they may sell to a local intermediary who aggregates local supply and who then sells to an additional intermediary at one of the country's cacao markets, or they may take their product directly to the cacao market and sell to an intermediary there. To achieve a better price from the *commerciantes*, in many parts of the country the *agricultores* form producers' associations to leverage collective market power. In rare instances, the *agricultores* may sell directly to chocolatiers or other producers, but this is an exception rather than a rule.

The structure of the commercial link of the *cadena* is largely dictated by a processors' duopoly between the *Sucesores de Jose Jesus Restrepo y CIA S.A. Casa Luker S.A.* ("Casa Luker") and *Compania Nacional de Chocolates S.A.S*

[29] Chaves-López, C., Serio, A., Grande-Tovar, C. D., Cuervo-Mulet, R., Delgado-Ospina, J., and Paparella, A. (2014). Traditional fermented foods and beverages from a microbiological and nutritional perspective: the Colombian heritage. *Comprehensive Reviews in Food Science and Food Safety*, *13*(5), 1031–1048.

[30] García, M., Quintero, L. F. M., and Montoya, A. (2012). Análisis comparativo de competitividad de las cadenas productivas de cacao de Colombia y Ecuador. *Revista de Ciencias Agrícolas*, *29*(1), 99–112.

("Nacional"). These behemoths collectively account for roughly 80% of the cacao market in Colombia and produce a range of cacao-based products, primarily for domestic consumption, although both also engage in exporting cacao and cacao-based products.[31] These companies do not buy directly from the *agricultores*, but instead from the *commerciantes*. While the *commerciantes* are not directly affiliated with the producers, they will frequently have established links with one of the two large buyers and will often receive up-front finance to purchase cacao from the *agricultores* which is then repaid in-kind. This distancing of *agricultor* from processor is the result not only of the fragmented cacao production, but also the country's security situation, wherein the large companies can pass risk associated with transportation and storage on to the *commerciantes* who may have better local security links. Indeed, one *commerciante* from a traditional cacao growing region spoke of how a "lost" shipment was recovered with the help of the "local community," which was a thinly veiled implication of ties with local paramilitary groups whose support this particular *commerciante* could rely on.[32]

Alongside these large producers, there exists a range of smaller cacao exporters and chocolatiers. These small and medium-size enterprises (SMEs) largely exist in a market segmented by quality. Colloquially, run of the mill cacao, or *cacao corriente*, is cacao destined for the mass market. This cacao receives a lower market price and generally has been less carefully processed before heading to market—often being insufficiently dried or fermented. In contrast, the "fine and flavor" cacao, *fino y sabor*, is of higher quality and is used in single-source or other premium products. In addition to high-quality processing, this cacao will also often be from a specialty strain, or clone, of cacao plant. Different clones have been bred to produce distinct flavors and profiles, and high-quality cacao from certain clones can achieve a significant market premium.

A final player in the Colombian cacao *cadena* is the *Federacion Nacional de Cacaoteros* ("Fedecacao"). This quasi-public entity serves both as the main trade association, conducting research on cacao-related matters and providing technical and capacity building assistance, but also serves in a commercial function, purchasing and exporting cacao. While this latter role generates some direct revenue for Fedecacao, it also is funded via a 3% tax on cacao exports. Fedecacao also operates an export price stabilization fund, wherein exporters pay in at times of elevated market prices and receive an export subsidy at times of lower international prices.

[31] Interview C-1000.
[32] Interview C-1009.

Box 5.2 Cacao for Peace or Profit?

While the narcoeconomy is a plague to the development of Colombia, cocaine is one of the largest (illicit) exports in the world. The coca trade undermines the stability and security of the Colombian state and people, it produces massive rents for those involved in the coca *cadena.* Many of the growers of coca leaf are the same *agricultores* that could otherwise produce cacao or other products. As such, a major focus of aid efforts, particularly from the United States, has been to support projects that provide alternatives to these *agricultores*, cutting the coca trade at its stem. As chronicled by Philip Abbott and co-authors, these efforts matured with the "ADAM" (2005) (*Areas de Desarrollo Alternativo Municipal)* and "MIDAS" (2006) (*Mas Inversion para el Dessarollo Alternativo Sostenible*) projects. These projects provided *agricultores* with inputs, training, and research support. While these projects did appear to increase cacao production, they also received criticism that they failed to focus sufficiently on commercialization, much less export-orientation. This perhaps stands in contrast to a raft of more recent projects by the Swiss State Secretariat for Economic Affairs (SECO) that explicitly focused on the commercialization of cacao products, especially at the higher quality end (*"fino y sabor")* as shown in the project titles in Table 5.2. In terms of impact of the US efforts, while violence has diminished, coca production is reaching all-time highs. Meanwhile, as shown below, Swiss projects may be associated with increased exports. AfT with different intent appears to lead to different ends.

Matching the cacao *cadena* with development interventions uncovers many points in which projects might conceivably have boosted exports directly or indirectly. At the level of cacao production, numerous development agencies have implemented projects to encourage better yield or initial processing. Projects from the United States, Germany, and others have introduced *agricultores* to better clones, better pest management, better techniques, or equipment for drying and fermenting that can boost yields and quality and increase eligibility for premium source labels like fair trade, organic, or sustainable. Other projects, including from the United States have helped the *agricultores* better commercialize their product by linking them directly with processors, allowing them to bypass the *commerciantes* who typically only pay *corriente* prices, regardless of product quality. At the level of processors, especially of specialty cacao-based products, capacity building interventions, including from the Swiss, Germans,

Canadians, and French can again assist with techniques, certifications, labeling, and marketing.[33] Finally, and more directly related to exports, projects from development partners including South Korea and Switzerland help link producers with international markets and buyers through trade fairs and other means or overcome other types of entry barriers to foreign markets.[34]

However, like the AfT interventions in the statistical analysis above, these interventions do not reach all enterprises at a given link in the cacao *cadena*. As shown in Figure 5.7, projects from different donors focused on different geographic intervention areas. This geographic dispersion is again driven by the types of allocation rationales discussed above. Notably, only a handful of projects were explicitly intended to boost export production. In fact, the projects from USAID, the largest development actor in the cacao sector by value, were explicitly not motivated by exports. As a senior USAID official explained, and further discussed in Box 5.2, these projects were part of a decades-long strategy to combat the coca trade, and violence that stems from it, by providing *agricultores* with an alternative crop, and former combatants with an alternative livelihood.[35] As such, the USAID project sites were located in areas that were particularly affected by the coca trade, including Antioquia, Cauca, and Nariño. Once again, this donor intent very much follows the "targeted development" donor logic—the United States suffers significantly from the Colombian narco-trade and that it is therefore no surprise that its aid projects are aimed at mitigating those impacts. In contrast, other projects, especially those from the Swiss and, to some extent the Germans, were focused on exports, but often in service of an alternative motive, and indeed several exporters credited the Swiss program for their success.[36] German efforts, particularly with the *Cacao, Bosques y Paz* project, were largely focused on cacao as part of a broader effort to promote global ecosystem agriculture and biodiversity through sustainable agroforestry. As an offshoot, the project helped *agricultores* meet certification standards for this type of production which then enabled them to market a product for export that received a higher premium due to quality and certification. However, this impact was largely a spillover from the broader aims of sustainability.[37] Once again, these aims are ostensibly driven by the domestic interests of those countries.

[33] Interview C-1018.
[34] Interview C-1024.
[35] Interview C-1020.
[36] Interview C-1014; C-1022; C-1024.
[37] Interview C-1018.

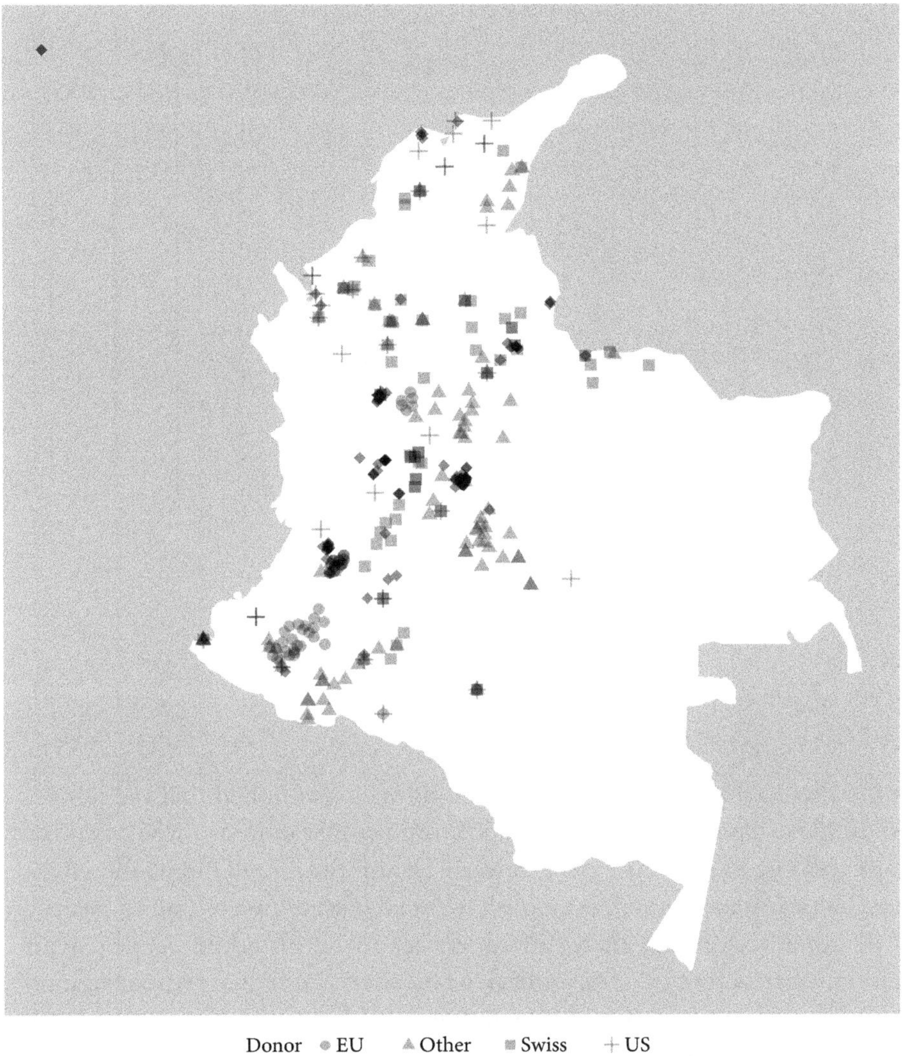

Figure 5.7 Cacao AfT projects and exporter locations in Colombia

Black diamond = Cacao Exporter; Grey circle = EU AfT project; Grey cross = US AfT project; Grey square = Swiss AfT project; Grey triangle = Other donor AfT project.

Thus, even within a sector and within a country it is evident that there is likely to be heterogeneity in "treatment" assignment, project effectiveness, and firm outcomes. In very few cases were the AfT projects working directly with exporters. Instead, the bulk of projects in the sector were implemented at the *agricultor* level. In most projects the international donors worked with the producer associations to identify *agricultores* to participate

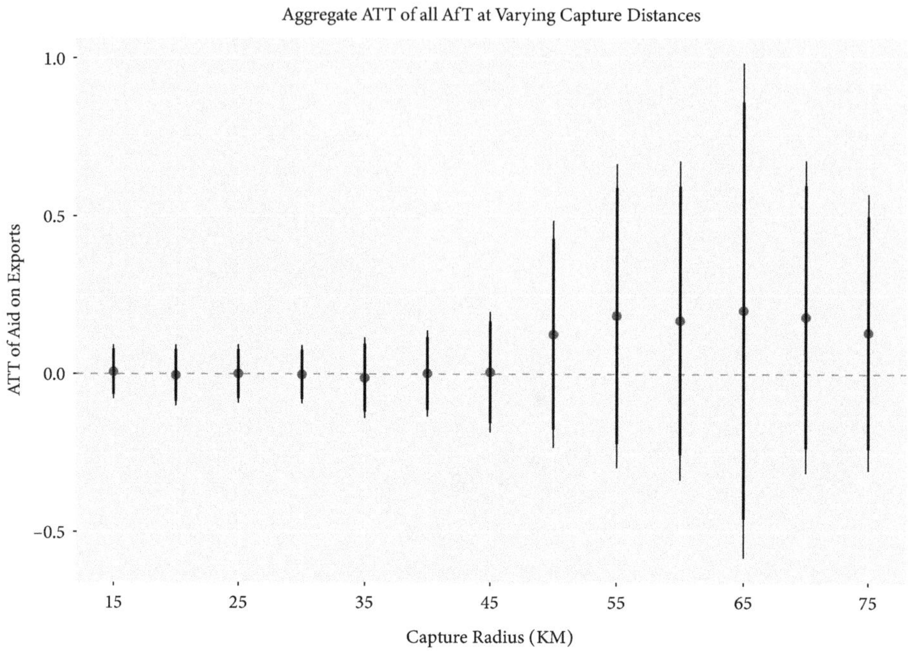

Figure 5.8 Cacao AfT effectiveness in Colombia

in the projects. Indeed, numerous interviewees mentioned that the donors' use of these associations led to association proliferation as these organizations jockeyed to receive international donor funding. Often times these were associations that had previously worked with donors on other projects or in other sectors but then shifted to cacao when funding became available for that activity.[38] One interviewee called these "paper associations" whose business is to secure international aid.[39] Indeed, one of the exporters regaled how they had set up an association precisely for this purpose as the commercial arm of their enterprise was not eligible to implement some international aid programs which could only partner with non-for profit organizations.[40]

For the AfT projects implemented at the *agricultor* level, the export effects will be indirect. If the projects improve the quantity and/or quality of cacao, then it is conceivable that this increased supply of *fino y sabor* will lead to increased exports of this type of cacao or of premium cacao-based products

[38] Interview C-1018.
[39] Interview C-1019.
[40] Interview C-1012.

like specialty chocolate. However, the export of cacao beans is still primarily of *corriente*-grade product and few projects were aimed at increasing this type of production. Moreover, while it is reasonable to assume that most smaller processors and exporters source their cacao from local or regional *agricultores*, given the poor state of transportation infrastructure and the difficult geography of the country, this is not necessarily true and indeed unlikely true for Nacional and Casa Luker who source cacao from across the country. Nonetheless, using the same strategy employed above, the analysis below looks at AfT export effects in the cacao sector. Notably, the qualitative investigation led to the acquisition of far more detailed project siting information for these AfT projects. This information is substantially more granular than that available from the OECD CRS data or AidData, again suggesting that this reporting bias may influence broader AfT studies. Via interviews with actors along the cacao *cadena*, our research team identified 49 distinct cacao-related aid projects at 235 *municipio* locations from 2006 to 2022. These are then spatially joined to the 201 cacao exporting firms from the *Estadísticas de Exportaciones*. Again, the underlying assumption is that these cacao projects will have boosted the quantity or quality of proximate *agricultores* whose products, in turn, are predominantly used to supply nearby exporters. As with the data above, to make meaningful comparisons between firms of different sizes, the analysis is a simple two-period difference-in-difference where the outcome variable is a binary indicator which indicates if a firm's average monthly exports increased after the completion of a local AfT project.

The results in Figure 5.8 show that firms with proximate cacao AfT projects showed no consistent or significant differences in cacao-related exports compared to those without a proximate AfT project. Cacao-related products fall under Chapter 18 of the HTS, in Section IV which, as shown in Figure 5.3, evidenced no significant impact when considering all AfT on section-level exports. The strategy employed in these analyses relies on an assumption that cacao AfT projects will impact the exports of proximate firms. While this assumption may be reasonable for the smaller exporters, it may be more tenuous for Casa Luker and Nacional who source their cacao supplies from across the country. However, excluding these firms from the models does not substantively alter the results in Figure 5.8.

These statistical findings are somewhat at odds with detailed qualitative evidence from interviews with *agricultores*, processors and exporters. Numerous processors or exporters discussed how aid projects had connected

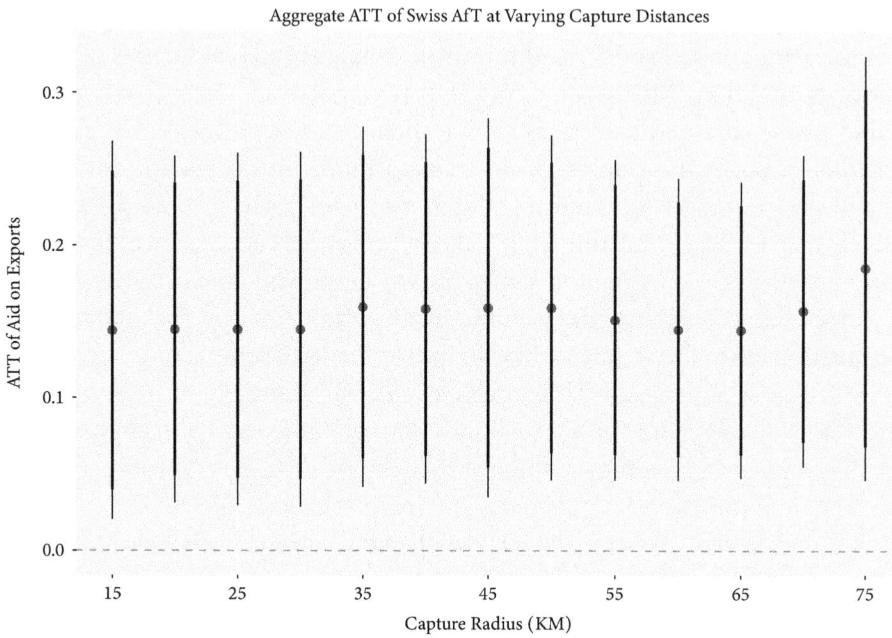

Figure 5.9 Swiss cacao AfT effectiveness in Colombia

them with *agricultores* for their cacao supply.[41] Some even explicitly credited AfT projects with helping them establish their business or exports.[42] So what explains the gap between the statistical analysis and the qualitative evidence? Theory would point to donor and/or project heterogeneity. As discussed above, some donors, like the United States, explicitly disavowed an export focus for their projects. Instead, their projects were motivated primarily, if not exclusively, by a desire to replace coca production with cacao, in regions plagued by violence and instability. In contrast, Swiss projects were much more explicitly focused on developing an exportable product and identifying export markets. Of the 235 cacao AfT project locations, 73 were Swiss project location sites. Figure 5.9 shows the analyses using only these sites. The evidence is suggestive that exporters nearer to the Swiss sites were more likely to have increased exports compared to exporters who were further away. Motivation, driven by a donor country's interest and domestic politics matters. It is perhaps no surprise that exporters nearer to US projects—in regions otherwise beset by violence and instability—might not have experienced increased exports even if the projects achieved their aims of inducing *agricultores* to

[41] Interviews C-1012; C-1014; C-1024; C-1027; C-1029; C-1030.
[42] Interview C-1012; C-1030.

swap coca for cacao. While the Colombian government may have been sufficiently effective, via its quasi-governmental entity Fedecacao—at identifying what interventions were needed along the *cadena* in order to improve export performance—the Colombian government may have had insufficient agency to dissuade the United States from pursuing cacao-projects focused on its targeted-development objective of impacting the coca trade, rather than on boosting exports.

But is Aid Enough? *El Cadmio*

Beyond parsing what makes aid trade effective, or not, this book's core contention is that effective aid must also be paired with meaningful market access. Even if AfT boosts the intensive margin of production, without market access such an impact may not be enough to increase exports and, ultimately, promote economic growth and development. While some AfT projects may also expand the extensive margin—that is, they help establish new export markets—many issues of market access will remain beyond what can be accomplished with aid, as discussed in Chapter 4. To illustrate this point, I turn back to cacao in Colombia.

As discussed above, and not with standing the quantitative evidence, the qualitative evidence certainly points to AfT projects improving both the intensive and extensive margins of Colombian cacao production and exports, at least in some cases. However, despite these successes, Colombian cacao and cacao-based products have faced difficulty in accessing certain markets due to issues that go beyond gravity factors of trade. A most notable example is EU regulation surrounding the presence of cadmium in foodstuffs. Cadmium is a heavy metal that is a known carcinogen as well as being linked to kidney problems and bone softening.[43] The EU first addressed cadmium levels in cocoa and chocolate products in Commission Regulation (EC) No. 1881/2006 which applied to a range of contaminants and foodstuffs. However, this regulation was annexed with specific regards to cadmium via Commission Regulation (EU) No. 488/2014 which set maximum cadmium levels for chocolate with varying levels of cocoa solids as well as cocoa powder. These limits came into force on January 1, 2019.

While these regulations are ostensibly aimed at preserving human health, as discussed in Chapter 4, sanitary and phytosanitary (SPS) measures are

[43] Hayat, M. T., Nauman, M., Nazir, N., Ali, S., and Bangash, N. (2019). Environmental hazards of cadmium: past, present, and future. In *Cadmium Toxicity and Tolerance in Plants* (pp. 163–183). Academic Press.

widely recognized for their potential to serve as non-tariff barriers (NTBs) to trade. While the protection of health and human safety is recognized as a legitimate government objective by the WTO, a measure of subjectivity can enter these considerations as different states may advance different views on what are safe standards. The EU has built a reputation for being particularly cautious on these types of regulatory matters, frequently adopting a *precautionary principle* stance in justifying restrictions on health grounds. This principle proports that, even in the absence of definitive evidence of harm, the state may yet regulate based on a not-yet-evidence potential for harm. To the extent these regulations target products for specific states, they can act as a discriminatory barrier to entry.[44]

South American producers, particularly Colombia, Peru, and Ecuador, are those with the highest cadmium levels in their cacao and, as such, these EU regulations effectively bar a meaningful portion of their production from market entry. Several actors in the Colombian cacao *cadena*, including donor partners, suggested that the EU regulations were indeed intended to be discriminatory,[45] with one exporter declaring "everyone knows that the cadmium thing is political, (we) have been eating it for years in Colombia and it hasn't been a problem,"[46] while another called the regulations "subjective."[47] While the EU does not produce any cacao itself, it imports the vast majority of its cacao and cacao-based products from West Africa, specifically Cote d'Ivoire, Cameroon, Ghana, and Nigeria, which do not face the same cadmium issues. The suggestion from these interviews is that the EU regulations where a form of protection offered to West African producers to insulate them from South American competition in the European Market, perhaps based on the political influence these states wielded as former colonies of key (then) EU-member states France and the United Kingdom.[48] The issue has been brought to the WTO where it is pending as of this writing.

Whether or not these cadmium regulations had a material impact on Colombian exports to the EU is difficult to say. Colombia accounts for less than 0.5% of all European cacao and cacao-product imports. Colombian exports did decline to an average share of 0.20% of EU imports in the four years after the regulations came into effect (2019–2022) compared to an average of 0.28% in the four years prior (2015–2018), a decline of nearly

[44] Priess, H. and Pitschas, C. (2000). Protection of public health and the role of the precautionary principle under WTO law: A trojan horse before Geneva's walls. *Fordham Int'l LJ*, *24*, 519.

[45] Interviews C-1012; C-1013; C-1015; C-1017; C-1018; C-1019.

[46] Interview C-1025.

[47] Interview C-1032.

[48] Interview C-1012.

30%, while shares of some West African states—Cote d'Ivoire, Cameroon—increased, shares of other West African states (Ghana and Nigeria) decreased. Overall, while the share of West African imports increased (66.17% to 66.88%) and the share of South American imports decreased (4.26% to 4.18%) these are nearly negligible amounts. However, some of the interviewees did indicate that these regulations had significantly impacted their access to European markets. One interviewee described how they lost an export shipment after it had arrived in Hamburg because they were not able to have the cadmium analysis done in advance and it took over a month to get the analysis on arrival by which point the shipment had spoiled.[49]

While EU cadmium regulations may not have been intentionally trade discriminatory, or explicitly trade diversionary, the case illustrates the complexity of the interplay between effective aid and meaningful market access. Even if aid projects are successful in boosting the intensive or extensive margin of a particular export product, these efforts may be undermined (or at least inconsistent with) aspects of trade policy which deter the same product. While several of the more recent Colombian cacao AfT projects have components to help address the cadmium barrier, it is unclear that the barrier needed to be erected in the first place. At a minimum, it appears that aid efforts in the cacao sector in Colombia or other parts of South America were considered when implementing the cadmium regulations. While only implicit—this situation again suggestively illustrates that a developing country's positioning in the international system, and its importance to a given actor, does not always sit in isolation—but may often be relative vis-à-vis third party states. Even if Colombia can exercise some degree of agency in isolation vis-à-vis the EU based on its position in the international system, it may be relatively less important to the EU compared to other developing states. When Colombia's and those states interests come into conflict with regards to an EU policy, the latter may be able to win out.

In sum, it appears reasonable to claim that AfT can build the tools that enable firms, and ultimately countries, to increase their exports and promote economic development, that is, it can be trade effective. But it does not do so automatically. Many AfT projects may not have any discernable impact on this avenue of economic growth, either because they were not intended to do so (like USAID projects) or perhaps because they were simply poorly designed. One producer told of how one cacao project had built toilets for local *agricultores* which, while useful, did nothing improve the quantity or quality of the product. This same producer also related stories of projects

[49] Interview C-1025.

which helped to build cacao fermenters, but then did not teach the *agricultores* how to properly use them.[50] Not everything is politics—sometimes explanations may go no further than incompetence. Aid projects outside of AfT that are even less directly tied to exports and economic growth are also likely to be equally, if not more, heterogeneous in their ability to promote those kinds of outcomes. Thus, trade-effective aid is not a given, and the determinants of which countries do and do not receive aid projects that are ultimately effective in building the tools of development are subject to any number of vagaries and nuances based on the donor and recipient political motivations behind allocation siting decisions, aid objectives, and aid project and program design decisions.

Summing Up: What Makes Trade-Effective aid?

Perhaps the main illustration of this chapter is just how difficult it is to ascertain the export effects of AfT projects. Coming at the question from multiple levels—all projects and all firms across multiple countries, all projects and all firms in different sectors in one country, projects and firms in just one sector in one country—leaves no clear answer on the question of what determines aid's trade effectiveness or, indeed, even how to best approach evaluating that effectiveness. Even with incredibly granular information on project location and timing, and firm exports, the conceptual steps in the causal identification chain are still tenuous. Any number of observed and unobserved factors may confound a researcher's attempt to evaluate effectiveness. Perhaps the most pervasive is attenuation bias—wherein "untreated" units (be they firms, subnational regions, etc.) are considered treated. The main consequence of attenuation bias is a tendency toward a non-finding, suggesting that studies of AfT effectiveness that treat "untreated" firms as "treated" may be underreporting export effects.

However, detailed qualitative work points to several other factors that can influence exports and may not be easily accounted for in quantitative analyses. The first are the conditions of international markets. Price and demand are key determinants of firms' decisions to export. While some firms lamented that they would lose orders because they couldn't compete on price[51] others lamented the lack of demand for their product.[52] Still others noted how the timing of their exports might be contingent on international

[50] Interview Colombia 1024.
[51] Interview N-1090; N-1610; N-9001; K-1001; D-1002; CH-1010.
[52] Interview N-1594; N-1523; N-1623; N-9001; CH-1004.

market prices.[53] Other exporters across multiple countries noted that issues with export finance impacted their ability to access markets, citing the delay between when they would produce their products and when they would ultimately get paid.[54] Other times, country-specific shocks may influence export behavior. As an example, exporters in Nepal faced a tumultuous period of civil war and ultimately the establishment of a Maoist government. Almost universally, Nepalese exporters described how this government massively hampered their industry through regulatory and other measures to the extent that many exporters simply closed shop.[55] Any positive export benefits of AfT projects in Nepal during these years would, in all likelihood, be massively offset by these domestic conditions. Incorporating sector, industry, or product-level controls for price, demand, financing conditions or other "exogenous" shocks into a quantitative analysis is difficult, if not impossible, especially if the analysis includes multiple countries and time-periods as different product markets may face differential shocks (in different time periods).

Perhaps another way to make sense of the evidence is that it shows the incredible heterogeneity in effectiveness. Indeed, this is what the theory in Chapter 2 would suggest. There are no panaceas or blanket statements when it comes to aid effectiveness—some aid works sometimes. Yet the scope conditions for that effectiveness may be very much time, place, or sector dependent and not easy to capture in quantitative (or indeed qualitative analysis). With those caveats in mind, what generalizations can be made about aid's trade effectiveness? First, many types of AfT projects need to be sufficiently proximate to the exporting firm or its suppliers. Beyond that, one needs to consider common export constraints and the extent to which AfT can overcome those. Ultimately, there are three choke points: production, logistics, and market demand. AfT projects that boost production or improve logistics can impact exports on the intensive margin, whereas market demand will affect exports on the extensive margin. Accordingly, projects that increase production capacity or smooth transportation logistics may increase the volume of exports. This will include infrastructure projects, but also sector or industry specific projects that specifically target production—like many of the cacao projects above. However, increasing the potential of the intensive margin will not translate to increased exports unless market demand for exports exists. This is where projects that explicitly focus on identifying or creating that demand influence exports by the extensive margin—they can create

[53] Interview C-1021; C-1032; CH-1006.
[54] Interview N-1523; C-1030.
[55] Interview N-1615; N-1021; N-1400; N-1339; N-9001; N-1610.

export opportunities where none existed before. The converse is that if market demand does not exist for a product, then AfT projects which operate by boosting the intensive margin will not demonstrate export effects, even if they are successful in the production aims. Thus, trade effective AfT is that which builds the tools that increase the intensive margin for products that have existing market demand or shifts the extensive margin by facilitating new export markets.

6
When It Works

A Room with a View

Sitting across from the ambassador of a OECD-DAC donor country on a muggy July afternoon in 2011, I looked out at the urban vista from the modern office building's eighth-floor windows. In my mind, I wondered how the thriving city below must have looked 40 years prior, when the country was in the midst of one of the most violent conflicts of the second half of the 20th century. The ambassador on the other side of the table was a veteran diplomat and had served in numerous developing countries across the Global South. I asked, based on her experience, what it was like for donor countries working in this country, especially given the strongly authoritarian regime that had been in power for 35 years. Somewhat sheepishly, given this particular donor's especially strong reputation for democratic values and human rights, the ambassador admitted that actually donors found that they were able to get things done in the country. I asked for more details. "Well," she explained "in other countries if the government decides it wants to build a road through a populated area it can take years between getting permits, negotiating with landowners, and conducting environmental studies. Here, if the government decides it wants to build a road, the next day bulldozers are on site pushing over houses."[1] While obviously hyperbole, the anecdote conveyed the brutal efficiency with which this country of some 90 million people had transformed itself in a generation.

Less than 40 years earlier, on July 2, 1976, a new nation was born from decades of conflict. Reunification of the southern and northern parts brought forth a country now known as the Socialist Republic of Vietnam. However, with only a year having passed since the guns of war fell silent for the first time in 35 years, the fledgling nation was one of the poorest in the world. By the time the government started releasing official economic figures almost

[1] Interview V-1003.

The Invisible Hand(out). Samuel Brazys, Oxford University Press. © Samuel Brazys (2025).
DOI: 10.1093/9780198970422.003.0006

10 years later, GDP per capita was the equivalent of just under $600 in 2015 terms, squarely putting the country in the least developed category. Yet, within 35 years, this figure would increase over 450%, and the country would find itself on the cusp of upper-middle income status by the end of the Covid-19 pandemic. While such a feat of development is not unprecedented (Vietnam's massive neighbor to the north vastly outpaced this growth over the same period), given Vietnam's recent history, which notably included being a direct military antagonist of the world's economic hegemon, being able to move tens of millions of individuals out of abject poverty in the space of a generation is remarkable.

As shown in Chapter 3, Vietnam is not the only developmental success story. Some of its SE Asian neighbors also experienced similar feats of growth. Indonesia and Thailand catapulted from least developed per capita income levels in the late 1960s to the base of upper middle-income status by the 2020s. Others, like the Philippines, or even Myanmar or Cambodia have also seen impressive growth from their baselines. What enabled these countries to achieve such marked development in such a relatively short period of time? Some of the traditional explanations do not appear to give a prima facie account. While the Philippines or Indonesia might be generously pegged as democracies, at least at a certain point in time, Myanmar, Cambodia, and Vietnam are clearly not. Moreover, all these countries inhabit a tropical geography, with latitudes shared with countries like the Central African Republic, Chad, or the DRC. Certainly, all are in proximity to economic powerhouse China, but PRC-adjacency does not ensure access to that market, nor has it been sufficient for growth for countries like North Korea or Tajikistan.

This chapter will focus on two of the "on-the-line" success stories above, Vietnam and Indonesia, to illustrate how these countries both received trade-effective aid and meaningful market access which have allowed them to secure real development gains despite (or perhaps because of) governance systems which don't score well in traditional metrics of openness or accountability. Yet, each of these countries has been able to effectively pursue export-oriented growth strategies based on effectively exercising the agency afforded them by virtue of their position in the international system. Both have had clear critical junctures in their recent political history, allowing for a consideration of within-case dynamics. The chapter proceeds with the countries sequentially, highlighting how political choices by third-country actors enabled these countries to make the most of aid and access opportunities.

Land of 17,000 Islands

The Indonesian archipelago stretches over 3,300 miles from the Northwest tip of Breuh Island off Banda Aceh, the epicenter of the 2004 tsunami, to the border on the island of Papua, shared with the nation of Papua New Guinea, a distance 500 miles greater than that from San Diego to the Maine-New Brunswick border. Across this expanse lies roughly two million square kilometers of land comprising 17,000-odd islands, some 1000 of which are permanently inhabited. Some of the islands are densely foliated with thick, tropical vegetation, and many of the major islands have mountainous and rugged interiors. Accordingly, although well-endowed with overall land-mass, Indonesia's internal physical geography is a significant constraint to the productive potential of much of the country.

Institutionally, contemporary Indonesian politics still bears the legacy of the 30 years of dictatorship under former president Suharto. Suharto's rule was both politically oppressive and massively corrupt.[2] Suharto's regime embodied the practices of Korrupsi, Kollusi, Nepotisme (KKN), or corruption, collusion, and nepotism, and he and his family were subject to personal corruption investigations by the Indonesian state after his resignation in 1998.[3] During the years of Suharto's reign, Indonesia was a clear-cut autocracy but quickly transitioned to a partial and then fully formed democracy in the following decades. Yet despite this relatively hasty transition, underlying institutional quality in the country was slow to improve. At the end of Suharto's reign, institutional quality was in the bottom 20th percentile in the World Bank's Governance Indicators, and it would stay here through 2006. While governance gradually improved from 2007 on, by 2020 the country still ranked in the bottom half of these governance measures.

Yet, despite these geographic and institutional challenges, the country's growth trajectory has been strong, both pre- and post-Suharto. Much of this growth has been export-led. While a shift from being a net exporter to importer of oil led to a noticeable drop in the country's export ratio, it has since rebounded and has averaged roughly 25% of GDP since the mid-1970s—respectable given the size of the country. Indonesia has also been a major recipient of ODA. Between 1960 and 2010, only Egypt, India, and Pakistan received more in total flows from the DAC donors. While the

[2] McLeod, R. H. (2000). Soeharto's Indonesia: a better class of corruption. *Agenda: A Journal of Policy Analysis and Reform*, 99–112.

[3] Robertson-Snape, F. (1999). Corruption, collusion and nepotism in Indonesia. *Third World Quarterly*, *20*(3), 589–602.

country's population means that the per capita aid figures are unremarkable, the sheer volume means that the country has been able to use aid to finance major projects and initiatives.

Bandung and Beyond

As the world's largest Muslim-majority country, Indonesia has long held a unique place in the global political arena.[4] As the competing superpowers vied for spheres of influence at the onset of the Cold War, Indonesia led the charge to mark out a third way for countries who hoped to escape becoming pawns of either side. In 1955, only six years after its independence from the Netherlands was recognized, the country hosted a meeting of 29 states from Africa and Asia, most of whom had also only recently emerged from the yoke of colonialism. The conference laid the foundation for the non-aligned movement (NAM), which, along with the G-77, became the loosely organizing force behind a number of initiatives during the Cold War, most notably for the purposes of this book the United Nations Conference on Trade and Development (UNCTAD) and the establishment of the Generalized System of Preferences (GSP).[5]

As one of the driving forces behind its creation, Indonesia was also an early beneficiary of GSP status, participating in the schemes of the United States, EU, Japan, UK, Australia, and New Zealand, among others.[6] Indonesia's historical utilization of its GSP preferences is also relatively high, particularly in resources where it has comparative advantage. For example, in 2005, Indonesia exported $319 million worth of Plastics & Rubbers (HS Section VII), $134 million of Base Metals & Products (HS Section XV), and $143 million of Precious Stones, etc. (HS Section XIV) under its GSP preferences to United States, utilizing 92%, 98%, and 98% of the preferences in those sectors, respectively. Across all products, Indonesia utilized US GSP preferences on $1.7 billion worth of goods, out of a total of $2.3 billion worth of eligibility, or roughly 75% utilization. In that same year, Indonesia exported $265 million worth of Plastics & Rubbers (HS Section VII), $230 million of Prepared Foodstuffs (HS Section IV), and $305 million of Miscellaneous Manufactured Products (HS Section XX) under its GSP preferences to the European Union, again with respective utilization rates of 86%, 75%, and 86%, with its

[4] Vaughn, B. (2011). Indonesia: Domestic Politics, Strategic Dynamics, and US Interests. Congressional Research Service, Library of Congress, January.

[5] Tan, S. S. and Acharya, A. (Eds.). (2008). *Bandung Revisited: The Legacy of the 1955 Asian-African Conference for International Order.* Nus Press.

[6] WTO PTA Database.

overall GSP utilization of $3.1 billion representing 62% of the $5.1 billion in total available GSP preferences.[7]

Yet in the early 2000s Indonesia's single largest export market, by far, was Japan. While total exports to the EU and US in 2005 summed to $13.4 billion and $12.9 billion, respectively, total exports to Japan in that same year totaled $20.9 billion. However, the vast bulk of this in that year was in Mineral Products (HS Section 5), ergo oil, of which Japan imported $12.4 billion worth. Indonesia's eligible Japanese GSP preferences in 2005 were $1.9 billion, less than either the United States or EU, and utilization of those preferences was also lower (albeit only slightly compared to the EU) at 61%. However, as Indonesia transitioned from a net oil exporter to importer, its trade structured altered. By 2019, Indonesia was exporting $17.9 billion worth of goods to the EU and $21.3 billion to the United States, with $7.5 billion (79%) of the $9.5 billion worth of EU GSP being utilized and $2.8 billion (67%) of the $4.2 billion of US GSP being used.

Box 6.1 "GSP Politics Carries a Lot of Baggage"

In 2015, a group of nearly two dozen entities that included major international corporations (Callaway Golf, Coach Inc., Victorinox Swiss Army Inc., Michael Kors, and others), trade associations (Council for Leather Exports, Luggage Coalition, and others) and governments (Philippines and Thailand) petitioned to have "Certain Travel and Luggage Goods Products" (HS 4202) added to US GSP eligibility for LDCs, AGOA countries, and regular GSP recipients. The arguments made to the USITC's investigation for inclusion largely centered around the politics of diversifying supply of these goods "outside China" to avoid "depending on a single source country." The USTR granted GSP access for these products, but only to the LDC and AGOA countries. Despite many of the petitioners explicitly calling for regular GSP access, including Indonesia specifically, the decision seems to have been swayed by a lone import-competing dissenter, US-based Korchmar luggage, whose products are made in the United States and the Dominican Republic. The company, with revenue of less than $5 million and less than a dozen US-based employees, argued in their submission (with original capitalization) to the USITC that granting GSP access to "the largest producing Asian countries" would "severely impact a new and re-growing US MANUFACTURING Industry that is hiring and training Americans with a trade skill." The

continued

[7] Ibid.

Box 6.1 *continued*

submission furthered its rhetoric by noting that granting the access "will NOT employ any more Americans, it will NOT reduce prices to consumers and it WILL cost the good new manufacturing jobs of American workers created in this sector over the last 7 years. Wall Street will win and U.S. manufacturing jobs and our middle class will lose." The (potential) losses that galvanized this single, small, import-competing producer appear to have been sufficient to sway the USTR to forgo granting access to Indonesia and other regular GSP members in that year. However, this success was only temporary, as the products were added for GSP eligibility in 2017.

While Indonesia's overall volume of GSP exports increased to both the United States and the EU from 2005 to 2019, the EU's utilization rate increased while the United States' fell. This may stem from the fact that, in recent years, a wide range of Indonesia's GSP preferences have come under attack. From 2015 to 2020, Indonesia was subject to no less than seven petitions to remove only its GSP access (as opposed to making a product ineligible for all GSP countries) either via removal of a competitive needs limitation (CNL) waiver or from removal from a GSP product line. At least four of these were successful while three were denied. However, the petition process works both ways, and Indonesia has also been party to petitions to include it for GSP market access on new product lines such as certain plywood products in 2019 (HS 4412), even if these efforts are not always (immediately) successful, as described in Box 6.1.[8] Yet, in all, Indonesia is excluded from over a dozen specific products lines under the US GSP as outlined in General Note 4 of the USHTS.[9]

More importantly, perhaps, the country has been subject to two US-GSP "Country Practice Reviews," one launched in 2012 that has held periodic hearings through 2020 and the other in 2018.[10] These reviews, which can be launched by any interested party on the basis of labor, intellectual property, or other rights violations, can render a country ineligible for GSP access.[11] Thus, the (increasing) uncertainty of year-on-year, product-level, GSP access

[8] https://ustr.gov/sites/default/files/Outcomes-2015-2016-GSP-Annual-Review.pdf (accessed 05-09-2023); https://www.usitc.gov/publications/332/pub4609.pdf (pp.72–80) (accessed 05-09-2023); https://www.datanyze.com/companies/korchmar/354520906 (accessed 05-09-2023); https://ustr.gov/sites/default/files/gsp/Results%20of%20the%20Review061617.pdf (accessed 05-09-2023).

[9] https://www.usitc.gov/publications/docs/tata/hts/bychapter/1400gn.pdf#page=11.

[10] Indonesia Intellectual Property Rights International Intellectual Property Alliance (IIPA) USTR-2013-0011 Ongoing https://www.regulations.gov/search?filter=USTR-2013-0011.

[11] Jones, V. C. (2017). *Generalized System of Preferences (GSP): Overview and Issues for Congress.* Congressional Research Service.

due to the whims of domestic US politics may well account for the decreased utilization of the US GSP, reducing the meaningfulness of this de jure market access for Indonesian firms.

In contrast, Indonesia's total exports to Japan in 2019 dropped to $18.1 billion, largely as a result of the decline in mineral products to $5.4 billion in that year. However, this implies that the non-mineral product exports increased over the period from $8.5 billion to $12.6 billion. Of the $4.9 billion worth of these products that were dutiable in Japan, $3.9 billion, or 80%, entered duty-free—not as a result of GSP, but instead because of other preferences with Japan, notably through the Japan–Indonesia economic partnership agreement, discussed further below.[12]

This GSP access was coupled with Indonesia's early entry into the GATT/WTO regime. Indonesia has one of the longest tenures in the GATT/WTO of any developing country, having joined in 1950. These decades of experience have undoubtedly conditioned Indonesian firms to the rules-based trading system and all its accompanying lacunae. However, outside of the multilateral regime, Indonesia is involved in relatively few regional trade agreements. The country was a founding member of the Association of Southeast Asian Nations (ASEAN) in 1967, and whose headquarters is now located in Jakarta. Despite the fact that ASEAN is considered a relatively shallow PTA[13], it ranks in the 33rd percentile for depth as measured by total features coded in the Design of Trade Agreements (DETSA) database,[14] Indonesia exports more to the combined region than it does to any other single trade partner, with $41.5 billion in exports in 2019. Via ASEAN, Indonesia also belongs to trade agreements with the Australia and New Zealand, India, Japan, South Korea, and both Hong Kong and the mainland of the People's Republic of China. Again, while these agreements are comparatively circumspect in their liberalization, these countries rank among Indonesia's largest export destinations, with the PRC taking the number one spot in 2019 at $28 billion, followed by Japan ranked third, India fifth, South Korea seventh, Hong Kong thirteenth, and Australia fifteenth.[15]

However, the country has historically pursued only limited bilateral market access agreements. While the situation has changed somewhat since 2018 with FTAs concluded with the EFTA states, Australia, and South Korea, the

[12] All GSP utilization data from UNCTAD.

[13] Sally, R. (2013). ASEAN FTAs: State of play and outlook for ASEAN's regional and global integration. *ASEAN Economic Community*, 320.

[14] Dür, A., Baccini, L., and Elsig, M. (2014). The design of international trade agreements: Introducing a new dataset. *The Review of International Organizations*, 9, 353–375.

[15] World Bank (2019). World Integrated Trade Solution (WITS). Accessed at: https://wits.worldbank.org/WITS/WITS/Restricted/Login.aspx.

only FTAs in force in earlier periods were the Japan-Indonesia Economic Partnership agreement, concluded in 2007 and entered into force in 2008, and an FTA with Pakistan concluded in 2012. Opening of the Japanese market, in particular, substantially increased the country's de jure market access, and as suggested above, may be partially accountable for the uptick in non-oil exports to Japan.[16] However, compared to its peers, its overall market access remains comparatively lower as FTAs with other major developed markets—notably the United States and EU—remain missing—although Indonesia is exploring a FTA with the latter.

In sum, Indonesia's de jure market access is certainly not deficient, but it is also not remarkably outstanding. Indeed, in the dynamic market access indicator developed in Chapter 3, Indonesia's score only crosses the 50th percentile starting in the 2010s and in the 1960s to 1980s was only roughly around the 33rd percentile. While clearly a long-standing beneficiary of both the GATT/WTO and the GSP, the lack of comparative preferences in the former, and the capriciousness of the latter, mean that the country did not have meaningfully privileged access in any key products. Moreover, as a country heavily reliant on its oil exports in earlier years, the country may have suffered from aspects of the resource curse which discourage export diversification.[17] While access to the ASEAN markets and that entity's trade agreements, the completion of the Japan EPA in 2008, and more recent agreements with other developed country markets, have certainly improved market access for the country in recent years, Indonesia's success story is not one of extraordinary market access. Instead, it is a country with market access that has been sufficiently meaningful to foster development in a scenario in which it has also had highly trade-effective aid.

A Train to Somewhere—Aid at Its Most Effective

While its market-access is somewhat middle of the road, Indonesia has been a leading recipient of foreign aid since early in its independence, averaging nearly $10 billion annually in net inflows. While receiving aid from nearly 70 multilateral and bilateral donor entities, the country has been one of the largest recipients of Japanese ODA since 1960 and Japan has been its single largest donor. Since 1996, Japan has committed over $30 billion in total

[16] Gumilang, H., Mukhopadhyay, K., and Thomassin, P. J. (2011). Economic and environmental impacts of trade liberalization: The case of Indonesia. *Economic Modelling*, *28*(3), 1030–1041.
[17] Ross, M. L. (1999). The political economy of the resource curse. *World Politics*, *51*(2), 297–322.

support, over one-third of Indonesia's total ODA take during that period and almost three times more than the next single-largest donor Germany.

Japan's position in Indonesia is not overly surprising. Since 1960, Japan has rivalled the United States, and more recently the PRC, as the largest bilateral donor of development assistance. Japan's forte has been the provision of development assistance devoted to building infrastructure and has tended to focus its efforts on countries in Asia. This focus is partly explained by the dual objective of Japanese ODA—while infrastructure is intended to boost productivity and attract investment, it is also explicitly seen by the Japanese government as a mean of supporting its own domestic industries and as a way to build state capacity.[18] In a document unabashedly titled "Enhancing Enlightened Self Interests," the Japanese Ministry of Foreign Affairs discusses how "Yen-loan" projects are to employ "cooperation with the (Japanese) private sector in order to 'facilitate participation by Japanese local companies and SMEs (Small and Medium Enterprises) in ODA projects.'"[19] Japan's focus on crafting an ODA program that meets the approval of its domestic constituencies means that it tends not to rank spectacularly in international metrics of donor quality. The Overseas Development Institute's (ODI) 2023 "principled aid index" places Japan at 17th of 29 DAC donors.[20] However, there is little to suggest that the efficacy of Japanese ODA is reduced by this self-interest, with several studies finding Japanese "Yen-loans" and other projects to be effective in spurring growth.[21] Indonesia, as one of the largest (potential) markets in the SE Asian neighborhood, is a natural location for Japan to pursue its "enlightened self-interested" strategy.

Digging into Japan's yen-loan projects in Indonesia quickly reveals why they might well be effective in spurring growth. Focusing heavily on transportation and energy, Japan has supported dozens of major power plant, road, rail and port, and communications projects around the country since the mid-1960s. The locations of a convenience sample of these projects are displayed in Figure 6.1, with the shading indicating the year of the project (lighter = later), the funding amount (larger is more), and the shape equaling the sector.

[18] Dietrich, S. (2016). Donor political economies and the pursuit of aid effectiveness. *International Organization*, *70*(1), 65–102; Nishitateno, S. (2023). Does official development assistance benefit the donor economy? New evidence from Japanese overseas infrastructure projects. *International Tax and Public Finance*, 1–29.

[19] Government of Japan, Ministry of Foreign Affairs (MOFA). (2010). *Enhancing Enlightened National Interest, ODA Review Final Report*, Tokyo: MOFA, p. 15.

[20] https://odi.org/en/topics/principled-aid-index/ (accessed 29-08-2023).

[21] Brazys, S. R. (2013). Evidencing donor heterogeneity in Aid for Trade. *Review of International Political Economy*, *20*(4), 947–978; Sahoo, P. and Bishnoi, A. (2016). Role of Japanese official development assistance in enhancing infrastructure development in India. *Contemporary South Asia*, *24*(1), 50–74.

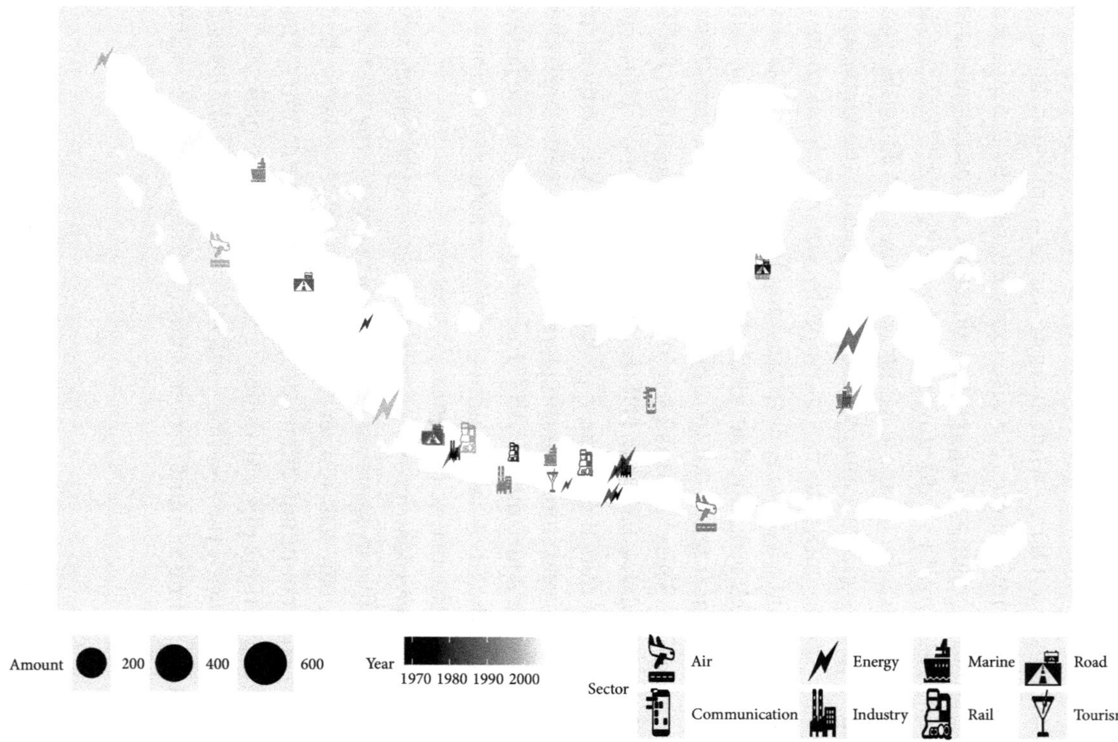

Figure 6.1 Selection of Japanese yen-loan projects 1968–2005

Source: AidData

Notably, rather than building stand-alone projects, Japan often clusters projects in a particular focus area over a sustained period of time as shown in Figure 6.1. For example, the first Japanese project in Surabaya, the capital of East Java and Indonesia's second city, began in 1971. While this was a relatively small dock project, subsequent projects focused on energy (Surabaya–New Perak Steam Power Plant Project 1972–1974), improved transportation links (Semarang–Surabaya Railway Track 1977–1985; Surabaya Airport Construction Project 1992–2002) and communications (Surabaya–Banjarmasin Optical Fiber Submarine Cable Project 1986; Regional Telecommunications Networks in Surabaya and Surrounding Areas Project 1992–1993). By the 2000s, Surabaya was one of the richest and best-performing regions of the country, with a significant manufacturing sector and a thriving port.[22]

How was Japan able to engage on such a long-term and sustained program of infrastructure construction? Much of the success is attributable to how the country operates its Yen-loan program. As described by both Japanese and Indonesian aid officials, the process essentially consists of the Indonesian government devising a "wish list" of projects, which it develops with the assistance and input of the Japanese International Cooperation Agency (JICA). This list is then submitted to the Japanese government via the Ministry of Foreign Affairs who ultimately approves a selection of projects. JICA then hires and oversees a contractor (often, though not always, a Japanese firm) who constructs the project. While the contractor bidding process is generally competitive, some projects are assigned "Special Terms for Economic Program" (STEP) which enables the project to be tied. One interviewee gave the example of how a high-tech bridge which (supposedly) only Japanese firms had the technology to construct, was assigned to the STEP which effectively restricted the contract to Japanese firms.[23] While the Yen-loan process is heavily influenced and managed by the Japanese donor, interviewees in a number of JICA-recipient countries, including the Philippines, Vietnam, and Timor-Leste, all confirm that the recipient country governments meaningfully participate in the formulation and promotion of the projects on the "wish list."[24] A sufficiently capable Indonesian government was able to effectively exercise this agency to coordinate on the types and locations of projects that would benefit their exporting firms. While the recipient countries do

[22] https://www.asiagreen.com/en/news-insights/indonesia-s-second-tier-cities-on-the-move (accessed 29-08-2023).
[23] Interview V-1001.
[24] Interview TL-1008; Interview P-1002; Interview V-1001.

not control the funds or manage the contractors—that is, the infrastructure largely comes "turnkey"—they do exercise ownership through the project selection process.

Furthermore, while Japan's primary focus in the country is on its Yen-loan projects, it also engages in other types of development cooperation. Through the JICA-supported Nikkeiren International Cooperation Center (NICC), a Japanese trade organization, technical trainings were carried out in the 1990s and 2000s. These efforts were intended to build management and human resource capacity with Indonesian firms and were organized via a major Indonesian employers' organization. As described by an official of this entity, the organization collaborated closely with the Indonesian Ministry to Trade to coordinate efforts with development partners that furthered the organization's objectives of management and vocational training, particularly for women's entrepreneurship, as well as helping its members increase productivity and find new export markets.[25]

Box 6.2 AMARTA—"Buying the Manager's Network"

The USAID-funded project "Agribusiness Market and Support Activity" (AMARTA) was a multi-product, multi-location, agricultural development project focused on "increasing production of targeted high-value commodities" including tropical fruit, coffee, cocoa, cattle, and fish in the Medan, Bali, Jakarta, Makassar, and Papua regions. Among the six target indicators was an objective of "percent change in the value of exports" which range from 10 to 100% for the various sub-activities. USAID, rather than implementing projects directly, subcontracts their efforts to implementing partners, in this case Development Associates Inc., who in turn will often subcontract various implementation activities. As noted by a USAID official, one consideration USAID would make in awarding programs to the contractors was based on the project managers. In this case, USAID made the award because the project manager had been a senior executive in a major international food company and attributed the export success of the project to "buying the manager's network."

However, despite being the largest with average annual ODA of over $1 billion, Japan has not been the only donor active in Indonesia since the 1960s. The EU and its member states, Australia, the United States, and South Korea have all been major historic donors, contributing hundreds of millions of

[25] Interview I-1001.

dollars annually in ODA. Germany, Indonesia's second largest donor with roughly $420 million in annual assistance, has focused less on economic infrastructure and more on technical assistance to develop policies that enable national and regional development. These projects were often implemented at either the sector or industry level but with no particular area focus, ranging from tourism to dairy farming to seaweed processing to the production of rattan furniture.[26] Likewise, US assistance, averaging some $250 million per year, is largely structured as it is elsewhere—providing support to a range of functions including social programs in health and education, governance efforts, and different types of private sector development.[27] These private sector projects include building productive capacity, but also involve linking producers to markets, as in the Agribusiness Market and Support Activity (AMARTA) described in Box 6.2.[28]

Other donors, like Norway, have focused on the environment, by providing incentive-based funding to address issues like forestry conservation or climate change.[29] While it may be more difficult to assess the ultimate trade effectiveness of these types of efforts, there has clearly been a fair degree of harmonization amongst these major donors in that they did not appear to be largely duplicating efforts or engaging in projects that worked at cross purposes, despite the challenges of having 70 some odd bilateral and multilateral donor entities operating within the country.[30] While this may be a happy coincidence, it is more likely suggestive of a sufficiently effective Indonesian government that was successfully able to exercise agency in managing the types and locations of aid projects from its numerous development partners. Likewise, until the early 2000s, aid to Indonesia was quite stable, consistently ranking in the 25th percentile or better in aid volatility. This changed, however, after the 2000s as another major donor entered the Indonesian landscape.

In addition to these DAC donors, Indonesia has also been a very large recipient of development assistance from the PRC since that country transitioned into a major provider of development finance. According to the AidData China dataset, between 2003 and 2017, the PRC funded over 250 projects, ranging from small grants of less than $10,000 for schools or minor

[26] Brazys, S. R. (2013). Evidencing donor heterogeneity in Aid for Trade. *Review of International Political Economy*, *20*(4), 947–978.

[27] Ibid.

[28] Box 6.1 References. I-1003. 26-05-2011. Jakarta, Indonesia; https://www.dai.com/our-work/projects/indonesia-agribusiness-market-and-support-activity-amarta (accessed 31-08-2023); https://pdf.usaid.gov/pdf_docs/PDACN125.pdf (accessed 31-08-2023).

[29] Interview I-1002.

[30] Winters, M. S. (2012). The obstacles to foreign aid harmonization: Lessons from decentralization support in Indonesia. *Studies in Comparative International Development*, *47*, 316–341.

disaster relief, to general infrastructure loans worth tens of billions of dollars.[31] Like much PRC support, the structure of this assistance isn't always clear, with a blurry line between concessional and commercial finance.[32] Nearly 60% of the projects received were classified by AidData as "OOF-like," meaning they were granted on commercial terms. Moreover, in line with the observation that China has transitioned from "benefactor" to "banker" in the developing world, of the 69 project-commitments made prior to 2008, 54 (76%) were classified as "ODA-like," meaning they were likely to meet the DAC criteria for concessionally. Since 2008, however, the proportion is nearly reversed, as only 22% of projects were classified as concessional.[33] Of the nearly $100 billion the PRC has committed to Indonesia since 2003, over half came in 2015 via two major pledges for infrastructure funding from the Industrial and Commercial Bank of China (ICBC—$20 billion) and the China Development Bank (CBD—$30 billion). These funds, loaned to the state-owned Bank Mandiri, were ostensibly part of China's global investment strategy commonly referred to as the "Belt and Road Initiative" (BRI), to which Indonesia was one of the original signatories. While the terms of PRC loans are notoriously secretive, these particular loans appear to have financed a wide range of infrastructure projects, including rail and hydroelectric facilities.[34]

Why have these donor countries invested so substantially in Indonesia and in the areas they have? Indonesia's strategic value is unquestioned. Its physical and maritime geography, controlling half of the Malacca Straight and nearly all of the maritime routes between Australia and Asia put it squarely at the crossroads of Indo-pacific security strategy.[35] Moreover, the country is home to the largest Muslim population in the world, who live, since the late 1990s, in an (at least) semi-democratic, religiously plural, state, placing it at the frontier of two distinct international value systems.[36] While the end of Suharto's reign was an important critical juncture in forging this identity (large Muslim democracy) in the international system, a second critical juncture—9/11 and the subsequent war on terror—shifted the importance

[31] Dreher, A., Fuchs, A., Parks, B., Strange, A., and Tierney, M. J. (2021). Aid, China, and growth: Evidence from a new global development finance dataset. *American Economic Journal: Economic Policy*, *13*(2), 135–174.

[32] Dreher, A., Fuchs, A., Parks, B., Strange, A. M., and Tierney, M. J. (2018). Apples and dragon fruits: The determinants of aid and other forms of state financing from China to Africa. *International Studies Quarterly*, *62*(1), 182–194.

[33] Dreher, A., Fuchs, A., Parks, B., Strange, A., and Tierney, M. J. (2022). *Banking on Beijing: The Aims and Impacts of China's Overseas Development Program*. Cambridge University Press.

[34] Gelpern, A., Horn, S., Morris, S., Parks, B., and Trebesch, C. (2022). How China lends: A rare look into 100 debt contracts with foreign governments. *Economic Policy*, eiac054; https://www.reuters.com/article/us-indonesia-china-beltandroad-idUSKCN1TY1DU (accessed 06-09-2023).

[35] Laksmana, E. A. (2011). The enduring strategic trinity: explaining Indonesia's geopolitical architecture. *Journal of the Indian Ocean Region*, *7*(1), 95–116.

[36] Assyaukanie, L. (2009). *Islam and the Secular State in Indonesia*. Institute of Southeast Asian Studies.

of this identity for a number of DAC donors. These critical junctures coincide with Indonesia's shift into the NE quadrant by the 2010s—a decade when its average per capita growth rate also increased to nearly 4.25%—putting it in the 80th percentile of the developing countries considered in Chapter 3.

Thus, to see the PRC and Western donors vying for trade and aid primacy is no surprise, as these tools can be used to secure broader foreign policy objects. Indeed, the BRI is seen by many as a vehicle through which the PRC can challenge not only the economic primacy of the West, but also its broader influence in the international system.[37] Indonesia also seems to have been able to effectively exercise this agency to make its aid trade effective. However, this does not mean that all aid will be (trade) effective. Particular projects can still reflect the more micro-level political interests of the donors. As one donor embassy official put it, sometimes projects can be "pushed for" as part of the donor government's political agenda. This interference can result in project fragmentation with many small volume projects, which the same official described as "a challenge" to implement.[38]

From Foe to Friend

One thousand miles north of Jakarta, across the Java and South China Seas, lies the Mũi Cà Mau National Park and UNESCO (United National Educational, Scientific and Cultural Organization) biosphere preserve on the Cà Mau Cape, the southernmost point of the Socialist Republic Vietnam. Established as a national park in 2013 the site allows intrepid tourists to explore the thousands of hectares of unspoilt mangrove habitat that is home to dozens of species of mammals, reptiles, amphibians, and birds and to see Vietnam's "South Pole." However, less than 45 years earlier, the spot was the scene of "Operation Solid Anchor," a successful US–South Vietnamese initiative of the Vietnam War to re-establish a naval base on the Cua Lon River that had been destroyed during the Tet-Offensive of 1968. The soldiers partaking in the operation could probably little fathom that in 50 years the area would be awash with tourists from the United States and other democratic countries, but also under the control of Communist Vietnam for decades—a Communist Vietnam which was now receiving $100 million annually in development assistance from the United States, a country to whom it would sending almost

[37] Beeson, M. (2018). Geoeconomics with Chinese characteristics: The BRI and China's evolving grand strategy. *Economic and Political Studies*, *6*(3), 240–256; Vadlamannati, K. C., Brazys, S., Dukalskis, A., and Li, Y. (2023). Building bridges or breaking bonds? The Belt and Road Initiative and foreign aid competition. *Foreign Policy Analysis*, *19*(3), orad015.

[38] Interview I-1002.

$100 billion worth of exports to in 2021, an amount $30 billion more than the exports to all its other trade partners combined.

Unified Vietnam is comprised of a thin strip of land stretching for over 3,000 kilometers along the South China Sea, covering over 300,000 square kilometers. Vietnam boasts a population of just under 100 million people, placing it well within the 20 most peopled countries in the world, roughly comparable to Egypt, the DRC or Turkey. Prior to its decades-long struggle with the United States, Vietnam had had a violet break with France, its colonial influencer of some 100 years. Politically dominated by the Vietnamese Communist Party (VCP) which emerged victorious from the war with the United States and its democratic ally South Vietnam, the country ranks poorly on many governance metrics, especially those which measure democratic norms and values.

So how is it that Vietnam, a country whose name was synonymous with communism, authoritarianism, war, and the loss of Western moral and military prestige, could transform from one of the poorest countries in the world, and bitter enemy of the United States, into one of the best performing economies of the last 30 years? Vietnam is perhaps the best "on-the-line" extreme and influential case for this book's argument, as it received plentiful and effective aid and meaningful market access to achieve growth rates surpassed only by a handful of countries, including its massive neighbor to the north. By the 2010s, the country was in the 99th and 96th percentile, respectively, of the effective aid and meaningful market access dynamic indicators developed in Chapter 3.

Making the Most of Market Access

Vietnam, like many communist and post-communist countries, only began to enter the global rules-based trading system following the end of the Cold War. Vietnam's market access history has been heavily colored by the politics of its bloody conflict with the United States. Following the end of the Vietnam War in 1975, the US Executive imposed an embargo on all Vietnamese exports under the 1917 "Trading with the Enemy Act" (TWEA) and the "Export Administration Act" of 1969.[39] US Congressional testimony from the time reveals only very limited support for avoiding/removing this embargo, including a bill introduced to that effect by Jonathan Bingham, a Democratic Congressman from the Bronx. However, this support, rather than being based on an argument in favor Vietnamese exporters, or Vietnam's

[39] Tuzin, A. H. (2009). Vietnam's eligibility to receive trade benefits under the US generalized system of preferences. *Loy. U. Chi. Int'l L. Rev.*, *7*, 193.

economic development more broadly, was largely based on the fact that a number of American firms, including Barclays, Chase Manhattan, and Bank of America Banks, IBM, Esso, Pfizer, and Merck still had investments in the former South Vietnam and the embargo would "encourage expropriation," although a rationale of easing "restrictions on humanitarian assistance" was also proffered, and indeed restrictions on these types of trade were eased.[40]

However, Mr. Bingham's efforts at lifting the embargo were unsuccessful and the policy would continue for nearly 20 years, during which time the only market access Vietnam secured was via its inclusion in some countries' GSP schemes, with exclusion from the United States scheme a notable exception. The US antagonism also inhibited any GATT/WTO ambitions which the country may have harbored, particularly following the adoption of its "Doi Moi" reforms in the mid-1980s.[41] Prior to these reforms, Vietnam exported very little, with roughly half of exports occurring via the barter system that existed amongst the members of the USSR-led Council of Mutual Economic Assistance (Comecon), and the remaining exports dominated by near Asian neighbors. During this period Japan and Singapore were the only two market economies that received any exports of note.[42]

However, a critical juncture would soon occur which would shift Vietnam's fortunes in both aid and access. In the early 1990s, the United States sought to normalize relations with the country. As part of this process, in February of 1994, in the run-up to the formal re-establishment of diplomatic ties with the United States in July of 1995, Vietnam was removed from the TWEA list by the Clinton administration. And trade relations with the United States would ultimately formally normalize in 2001 with the adoption of the US–Vietnam Bilateral Trade Agreement (BTA).

This normalization fundamentally shifted Vietnam's identity in the structure of the international system. The country went from a communist pariah to a member of the global economic community. But the US domestic politics that precipitated this change were highly idiosyncratic. These efforts were largely driven by the personal efforts US Senators John McCain and John Kerry, both of whom were decorated veterans of the Vietnam War.[43]

And they weren't primarily driven, at least initially, by either economic or security concerns. In speaking on the subject in January of 1994, Senator John

[40] United States Congress. October 1, 1975, Vol. 121, Part 24, p. 31113—Bound Edition. 94th Congress—1st Session; United States Congress. November 19, 1975, Vol. 121, Part 29, p. 37481—Bound Edition. 94th Congress—1st Session.

[41] Tuzin, A. H. (2009). Vietnam's Eligibility to Receive Trade Benefits under the US Generalized System of Preferences. *Loy. U. Chi. Int'l L. Rev.*, *7*, 193.

[42] World Bank. (1990). Vietnam: stabilization and structural reforms. Country Operations Division, Country Department II, Asia Region, Report No. 8249-VN.

[43] Castelli, B. (1994). The lifting of the trade embargo between the United States and Vietnam: The loss of a potential bargaining tool or a means of fostering cooperation. *Dick. J. Int'l L.*, *13*, 297.

Kerry elaborated, in nearly 6,000 words of floor speech, how the rational for lifting the embargo would be to provide "answers to our families and to our veterans about POW-MIA," illustrated by a graphic story of how cooperation with the Vietnamese had enabled the United States to:

> (dig) up some farmer's field with the help of the Vietnamese finding it because they told us that the three other bodies were lain out one, two, three beside each other right there in the field.

The Democrat Senator also went to great pains to emphasize that the lifting of the embargo would not be a "reward" to Vietnam.[44] These arguments were repeated in another 2000 words of floor speech by then-Senator, and future Republican US Presidential candidate, John McCain. While primarily echoing the POW-MIA rationale, Senator McCain also picked up on Senator Kerry's brief remarks about the economic rationale for lifting the embargo, but echoed that Senator's dismissive tone:

> this is not about economics, and that is why I am not dwelling on it.

with his own exclamation that:

> there are, of course, business advantages which we ought to be in a position to compete for. It won't dwell on these because American businesses interested in Vietnam are quite able to make their own case for going forward.[45]

However, this move was not without opposition. The move was castigated in May of 1994 by one-term Long Island Congressman David Levy, who noted that:

> when President Clinton lifted the Vietnam embargo several weeks ago, there was a hue and cry within my district and many other districts

and that:

> If it is the sense of Congress that lifting the Vietnam embargo is correct, then Congress is out of touch … By including embargo language in the conference report, some in Washington are attempting to give the President the political cover that he needs to cover the fact that he made the wrong decision. The conference report should not be used for that purpose."[46]

[44] United States Congress. January 26, 1994, Vol. 140, Part 1, p. 247—Bound Edition. 103rd Congress—2nd Session.

[45] Ibid, p. 251.

[46] United States Congress. April 28, 1994, Vol. 140, Part 6, p. 8818—Bound Edition. 103rd Congress—2nd Session.

in discussions within the US House of Representatives on language supporting lifting the embargo in a conference report, a document which reconciles language from bills passed in the US House and the US Senate.

The passages above illustrate that the normalization of US trade relations for Vietnam, and its subsequent shifting position in the international system, were very much driven by domestic US political considerations, but that these considerations were much more about issues regarding the legacy of the Vietnam War than anything to do with the prospects for export-led development in Vietnam. Yet, once the US embargo was lifted, the flood gates opened. Vietnam quickly began to integrate itself into the global trading system, joining ASEAN in 1995 and applying for WTO membership in that same year. However, the WTO negotiations paralleled the normalization of US trade relations, and they only concluded in 2007, the same time that the country signed an additional "Trade and Investment Facilitation Agreement" (TIFA) with the United States. Arguably, all of this occurred because two highly visible and influential US Senators carried sufficient personal political cache to overcome domestic squeamishness toward "rewarding" Vietnam with market access in order to try and track down "73 tough cases" of POW-MIA.[47] A critical juncture which set Vietnam on a 30-year growth path.

After joining the WTO, Vietnam would continue to push for substantial de jure market access, including to the EU market via the EU's "GSP+" scheme, despite its strict conditionality.[48] The country would also conclude bilateral free trade agreements with Japan (2008), Chile (2014), South Korea (2015), the EU (in 2019—replacing GSP+) and the UK (2020) in addition to joining the regional agreements the Eurasian Economic Union (EAEU) and the Comprehensive and Progressive Agreement for Trans-Pacific Partnership (CPTPP). Alongside the market access Vietnam receives via its ASEAN membership, both with members and with the countries with whom ASEAN has its own agreements, this collection gives the country a very substantial basket of export destination markets. Collectively, this market access contributed to a huge surge in exports, from $7.6 billion in 1993, the last year of the US embargo, to $321 billion in 2021, an increase of over 4000% in the space of less than 30 years.[49]

As discussed above, the United States is Vietnam's largest single export market, a mantle it has held since the early 2000s.[50] But exactly what market

[47] United States Congress. January 26, 1994, Vol. 140, Part 1, p. 250—Bound Edition. 103rd Congress—2nd Session.

[48] Access actually continued under this scheme until January 1, 2023, after the FTA access began on August 1, 2020 to "to ensure legal certainty and avoid undue administrative burden." https://eur-lex.europa.eu/legal-content/EN/TXT/?uri=CELEX%3A32021R0114 (accessed 31-08-2023).

[49] WDI.

[50] https://wits.worldbank.org/CountryProfile/en/Country/VNM/Year/2002/TradeFlow/Export.

access did Vietnam get under the US BTA and TIFA and its WTO accession agreement? As explained by a US official, the BTA was intended to jump-start Vietnamese market access to the United States by establishing "Normal Trade Relations" (NTR) prior to the conclusion of Vietnam's WTO accession and global most-favored nation status (MFN). This agreement was seeing as a "stepping stone" and, in the estimation of the official, got Vietnam about "70%" of the way to its WTO commitments.[51] But this agreement, and the subsequent TIFA, gave Vietnam no particular preferential access. What they did do, however, was bring Vietnam into line with the market access of other MFN countries, allowing the country to exploit its comparative advantage in low labor-cost manufacturing. However, unlike other similarly situated countries who utilized this labor pool to enter heavily in textiles, Vietnam instead used the access to integrate itself into other global value chains, particularly the production of electronics.[52] As noted by one donor official, the opening of the US market under the BTA brought investment from neighboring countries, including Taiwan, Hong Kong, and South Korea who were already exporting to the United States but wanted to move segments of their production to Vietnam to take advantage of lower labor costs.[53] In some product areas which would become major Vietnamese exports, like HS 8525 (transmission apparatus for radio-broadcasting or television) or HS 8542 (electronic integrated circuits; parts thereof), achieving MFN status brought duty-free treatment—compared to non-MFN rates of 45% or 35% in the US which would effectively block Vietnamese manufacturers.[54] Also, unlike agricultural or textile products, these sectors are largely, if not completely, devoid of other NTBs like SPS or quantitative restrictions. Thus, Vietnam was able to transform what was, in effective, very ordinary market access (MFN shared by 160 other countries), into meaningful market access by promoting industries in products that had absolutely zero international market distortions. And, as described above, since its WTO accession, Vietnam has pushed this access further by concluding bilateral agreements which have broadened its market access in other product areas.

An Aid STAR

While Vietnam has undoubtedly secured meaningful market access since its critical juncture in the mid-1990s, it is this book's contention that those

[51] Interview V-1005.
[52] Giroud, A. (2007). Vietnam in the regional and global transnational corporations value chain. In *Multinationals and Asia* (pp. 52–69). Routledge.
[53] Interview V-1005.
[54] https://hts.usitc.gov/.

access possibilities can only be effectively exploited if a country also has the necessary tools in place for its firms to take advantage of the opportunity. When countries start from a place of grinding poverty, like Vietnam, the resources to build those tools most often can come in the form of development assistance. Given Vietnam's success, it should therefore be no surprise that the country has also been one of the most remarkably beneficiaries of trade-effective aid.

As with Vietnam's market access, the country's aid receipt was heavily influenced by its post-war environment. Despite being one of the poorest and most populous nations in the world, the country averaged less than $500 million annually from DAC-reporting donors, in real terms, throughout the 1980s—compared to three to four times more in similarly sized (and impoverished) Philippines and less than one-tenth of what Bangladesh or Indonesia received during the same period. However, like its market access, this situation changed radically in the 1990s. In the run-up to re-establishing diplomatic ties with the United States, ODA from all donors jumped from $266 million in 1990 to $1.3 billion in 1994. Aid levels continued to grow from there, reaching a zenith of $4.25 billion in 2013.[55]

However, like Indonesia above, the largest single donor over the past 20 years has been its Asian neighbor Japan. Yet, unlike most other countries considered in this book, its next largest donors are multilateral development banks (MDBs), with the World Bank Group and the Asian Development Bank taking the second and third positions. The use of multilaterals in providing aid to Vietnam, especially in earlier years, is perhaps unsurprising when considering the domestic politics of giving. In the United States, the thought of using tax dollars to assist a country where tens of thousands of young men had died in recent memory was undoubtedly politically unpalatable to many, as suggested by the political debates over lifting the US trade embargo. By channeling support via multilateral banks wherein it had substantial influence, the United States could provide development assistance while at the same time lessening the spotlight on that support. Use of multilateral institutions to hide domestically contentious aid flows is not unique to Vietnam and has been coined the "dirty work" hypothesis.[56] Indeed, the United States would not start recording direct ODA flows to Vietnam until 1997. While it would then become a major donor, averaging around $100 million per year, it would lag behind Japan, the MDBs, Germany, France, and in later years Korea in the total volume of its flows.

[55] OECD CRS.

[56] Dreher, A., Lang, V., Rosendorff, B. P., and Vreeland, J. R. (2022). Bilateral or multilateral? International financial flows and the dirty-work hypothesis. *The Journal of Politics*, *84*(4), 1932–1946.

Like in Indonesia, Japanese ODA in Vietnam focused on Yen-loan projects that built economic infrastructure. Again, interview evidence suggests that the Vietnamese government (GoV), particularly the Ministry of Planning and Investment (MPI), was involved heavily in the development and prioritization of projects due to high levels of capacity. That said, while the interviewee noted that project requests should "theoretically" come from the GoV, the process described in practice includes a substantial amount of Japanese involvement at the planning and design stages, including final Japanese government approval following ministerial approval from the Japanese ministries of foreign affairs (MOFA), finance (MOF) and economy, trade and industry (METI) who sent (semi)-annual delegations to meet with their Vietnamese counterparts. However, the interviewee also mentioned how the project needs in Vietnam—especially in transportation and energy—were readily apparent to both sides and thus there has typically been broad consensus on the selection and timing of projects.[57]

Though not as large Japan or the MDBs, the United States also became an increasingly important bilateral donor to Vietnam during the 2000s. And, perhaps more so than any other donor, US ODA to the country was the most explicitly linked to the new market access opportunities facing the country, including its own bilateral BTA and TIFA. The major project that accompanied these talks was the "Support for Trade Acceleration" (STAR) program which ran, in two phases, from 2001 to 2013 and was explicitly intended to accompany and facilitate Vietnam's entry into the WTO via implementation of the BTA and TIFA.[58] Much of the work needed for this was ensuring that Vietnam had the appropriate domestic legal and regulatory environment to meet the demands of its WTO accession agreement.

Finally, as in Indonesia, the People's Republic of China has been a major provider of development finance to Vietnam. Despite their own brief war in the late 1970s, a series of skirmishes throughout the 1980s, and continuing tension of territorial claims in the South China Sea, the PRC has been a large, though intermittent, donor, averaging finance commitments of over $1 billion per year since 2000. The vast bulk of this is (~77%) characterized as "Other Official Finance-like," meaning it is not necessarily concessional financing that meets the definition of ODA aid, with a further ~15% characterized as "Vague."[59] Since 2013, much of this finance has come through the BRI, as Vietnam was another early adopter of the initiative. The PRC's project profile in the country is similar to that of Japan—and of the PRC's efforts elsewhere—with projects heavily focused on the energy and transportation

[57] Interview V-1001.

[58] https://www.dai.com/our-work/projects/vietnam-support-trade-acceleration-project-star-i-ii-plus accessed 01-09-2023; Interview V-1004.

[59] AidData China.

sectors. Between 2003 and 2017, the PRC financed the construction of over a dozen coal-fired power plants alongside a handful of hydroelectric facilities in addition to rail, road, and port projects. The PRC has also directly financed a number of industrial projects including fertilizer plants, copper mines, and various manufacturing facilities.

What made this aid trade effective? First, the comparatively small number of donors, particularly major donors, appears to have facilitated cooperation to a greater degree to which might exist elsewhere. Aid volatility in Vietnam has been relatively low, particularly in the 1990s and 2000s. Moreover, the three largest DAC donors—Japan, the World Bank, and the Asian Development Bank (ADB), were able to communicate and, at least in earlier stages, coordinate areas of intervention, with the World Bank focusing on the social sector while the ADB and Japan invested heavily in economic infrastructure, even coordinating on some projects with the ADB handling project design and JICA hiring the contractor.[60] Like the effective aid in Indonesia, this specialization also occurred with other, smaller donors, again suggesting either fortuitous chance or the effective exercise of agency by Vietnam's government. In response to the Government of Vietnam's request, Germany, another of Vietnam's major bilateral donors with annual flows well above $100 million, directed a substantial amount of its efforts on providing technical and vocational education and training (TVET) focused on qualifying workers for the demands of industry in the country. As described by a German aid official, they tended to target these efforts where Germany had particular labor expertise—area like electronics and metalworking. These projects responded to demand from the private sector for particular skills and supported practical, on the job, training. Some of these projects, such as the Center for Excellence in Saigon which focused on welding and metal working, were also joint-projects with other donors, like the French.[61] Likewise, other donors who were focused on trade and the WTO accession (US, UK, EU) established a trade working group which met to coordinate activity in this area.[62] This aid specialization, coordination, and responsiveness to the needs requests of the Vietnamese government likely facilitated the effectiveness of aid—with projects simultaneously working to build the physical, institutional, and human infrastructures that firms needed to take advantage of their newfound market access.

Ultimately, Vietnam was able to fully exploit its newfound MFN market access in the 2000s by utilizing the trade-effective aid above to essentially skip the lowest rung of the industrialization ladder—textiles. While not

[60] Interview V-1001.
[61] Interview V-1002.
[62] Interview V-1004.

completely neglecting this sector, the country built an export growth model based on low wages, but not completely bottom-skilled products—primarily by integrating itself into the global value chain of electronics production. When it comes to institutional quality, Vietnam is a curious case as it is a clearly an authoritarian success story. The country is one of the least free on the planet—and increasing prosperity has not brought increasing freedom. As one donor official lamented, during the WTO accession negotiations, the country "relaxed" its iron grip on the press and political opposition in order to assure a smooth completion of the process. However, following accession, the official noted how 2008 saw a significant regression of these liberties via the implementation of major new restrictions on civil and political freedoms.[63] Yet, this same official, along with those from many other donor missions, noted the high capacity and functioning of the government in implementing aid and pursuing an export-oriented growth strategy.[64] Indeed, over time, Vietnam has ranked toward the very bottom of indicators in Voice and Accountability, keeping company with the likes of Belarus or Iran while still scoring moderately well on indicators like Government Effectiveness, where it looks more like Serbia or Indonesia. Thus, Vietnam provides an interesting case of a major developmental success where the country has grown in spite of, or even because of, its limited access order. Like its neighbor to the North, Vietnam appears to be a case of "authoritarian capacity," at least when it comes to fostering economic growth.

Aid and Access—Chance or Choice?

Of the two "success stories" above, Vietnam is clearly the more brightly shining star. Indeed, its average annual real per-capita income growth since the 1980s of 4.5% is 150% of that of Indonesia's 3.0%. As demonstrated, Vietnam also had markedly better market access and aid. That said, both countries have vaulted from least developed status to the bottom end of upper-middle income status in 30 years. What enabled these two countries, neither of which has a completely realized democracy or across-the-board good governance, to succeed where so many others have failed? Why did each get sufficiently meaningful aid and access when others did not?

First, both countries, by virtue of their populations and geographic positioning on the South China Sea, have become increasingly crucial parts of the Western, and in particular US, Indo-Pacific security posture in the 2010s and

[63] Interview V-1003.
[64] Interviews V1001-1005.

beyond. Both the US Executive and US Congress have recognized the importance of these countries. In a 2021 US Senate amendment, the two countries were specifically enumerated alongside other key allies in a Sense of Congress which read:

> the United States greatly values other partnerships in the Indo-Pacific region including with India, Singapore, Indonesia, Taiwan, New Zealand, and Vietnam as well as regional architecture such as the Quad, the Association of Southeast Asian Nations (ASEAN), and the Asia-Pacific Economic Community (APEC), which are essential to further shared interests;[65]

With these strategic considerations in mind, some clarity comes to the puzzle of how authoritarian and repressive Vietnam was able to meet the conditionality for the EU's GSP+ access, while equally sized, but much less strategically important, nearby Bangladesh could not.

Second, Vietnam's history and, in particular, the resulting historical accident that two influential US Senators who were well positioned to push for its return to the global system of trade had significant personal histories with the country, was a major catalyst for all that followed. It is not out of the realm of hyperbole to suggest a direct domino link between John McCain spending five and a half years as a North Vietnamese prisoner of war (POW) and John Kerry receiving three Purple Hearts for being wounded on three separate occasions during the war, and the $100 billion dollars' worth of goods exported from Vietnam to the United States in 2021.

Equally important is that both countries received what ultimately proved to be very trade-effective foreign aid. This effectiveness largely stemmed from its predictability, specialization among donors, and focus on the right kinds of economic infrastructure—all of which indicate the governments had sufficient capacity to effectively exercise the agency afforded them via their positioning in the international system. While to some extent both were no doubt the beneficiaries of the "geographic accident" that Japan, a major infrastructure donor, also tends to play an outsized donor role in Asia, it was also the result of the fact that, despite some token coordination, each donor mostly independently provided aid portfolios either as a result of successful management by the Indonesian and Vietnamese governments and/or based on the demands of the donors' own domestic constituencies.

[65] United States Congress. May 19, 2021—Issue: Vol. 167, No. 87—Daily Edition 117th Congress (2021–2022)—1st Session.

7
When It Doesn't Work

When Good Government Isn't Good Enough

Of the 142 countries considered in Chapter 3 who were in the low or lower-middle income category following the end of World War II or their subsequent independence, only 16 were ranked in the top 10 for their average scores in two or more of the six categories of the World Bank's World Governance Indicators. Included in this group are standout development performers Botswana, Hong Kong, Singapore, and South Korea as well as other countries who have achieved upper and upper-middle income status including Chile, Cyprus, Malta, Mauritius, and Uruguay. Yet, also included in this group are a handful of states whose economic performance has been far more dismal—the Federated States of Micronesia (FSM), Samoa, and Tuvalu. While even an amateur geographer may quickly realize that all three of these countries are island states in the midst of the vast Pacific, this feature is not determinative for economic sluggishness as fellow better performing insular countries Antigua and Barbuda, and Palau (not to mention Mauritius) who are also in this group of 16 also fit the bill as small island states.

These countries, along with other comparatively well governed countries like Ghana or Namibia, stand as some of the most direct challenges to claims that the institutions and governance of open access orders are sufficient to explain divergent development. Although none of these countries are the worst of the worst in terms of economic performance, they lag significantly behind countries like Indonesia and Vietnam, despite having vastly better overall governance environments. While falling to the middle of the pack on indicators of government effectiveness or regulatory quality, the FSM and many of its fellow island states are some of the strongest democracies in the world. If the argument is that underdevelopment is caused by unaccountable elites capturing government institutions for their own enrichment, then these countries serve as stark counterpoints. Moreover, many of the small island developing states are some of the largest per-capita recipients of ODA in the world. If bulk aid alone were sufficient for growth, these should have been some of the best global development performers.

The Invisible Hand(out). Samuel Brazys, Oxford University Press. © Samuel Brazys (2025).
DOI: 10.1093/9780198970422.003.0007

This chapter explores this conundrum by putting Micronesia under the microscope to understand why aid in that country had not been trade effective and, why, despite having no tariffs on the bulk of goods to the largest market in the world, the country still does not have meaningful market access. The chapter then further explores another significant aid recipient, Madagascar. Madagascar has had one of the absolute poorest track records of economic performance despite years of overseas investment and significant, preferential, market access under GSP schemes for least developed countries. Ultimately, these cases are both "on-the-line" cases in that each lacked either (if not both) effective aid or meaningful market access and both have struggled to develop an economy that could navigate the currents of globalization to find a niche in the global economy. While Micronesia may be a typical case, Madagascar represents an extreme case in that it has had some of the absolute worst long-term growth performance in the world—ranking third from the bottom—ahead of only the Democratic Republic of the Congo and Yemen—two countries riven by conflict.

It's Too Hot Today—the Politics Ineffective Aid

Like Indonesia in Chapter 6, the Federated States of Micronesia (FSM) is also a collection of islands that stretches across thousands of miles of tropical ocean, in this instance between the Philippines and Hawaii. However, unlike Indonesia's 200 million people on two million square kilometers of land, Micronesia's 100,000 odd residents reside on a total land mass of less than 1000 square kilometers—meeting the generally accepted definition of a "microstate." Yet, since its founding as a federation in 1979 between the four states of Chuuk, Kosrae, Pohnpei, and Yap, the country has emerged as a fully sovereign entity, with membership at numerous international institutions including the Asian Development Bank, the North Pacific Fisheries Commission, the Pacific Islands Forum, and the United Nations and many of the latter's constituent bodies. Additionally, the country hosts several important diplomatic missions, including from Australia, the People's Republic of China, Japan, and the United States and has accredited over three dozen non-resident embassies.

The FSM's comparative lack of human and natural resources, combined with its remoteness, mark significant development challenges. These challenges have only been accentuated by the onset of human-driven climate change which poses an existential threat to many of the low-lying atoll islands on which thousands of its citizens live.[1] While the FSM is a fully sovereign nation, along with sister states Palau and the Republic of the Marshall Islands, it maintains a unique political and economic arrangement with the United States of America. All three countries had been part of a United Nations designated Trust Territory following the end of World War II, along the Northern Marianas. While the latter elected to remain a territory of the United States, the three countries who sought independence would ultimately agree to "Compacts of Free Association" with the United States. These treaties, while recognizing the sovereignty of the countries, delegated broad defense rights in the territories of the countries to the United States and, at the same time, obligated the United States to providing significant amounts of economic assistance. This economic assistance, which largely came in the form of budget grants, meant that these three countries have, since their independence, had some of the highest aid to GNI (Gross National Income) and aid per capita ratios in the world.[2]

Yet, despite these massive aid inflows, the FSM has struggled to develop over the past 30 years. While aid flows relative to GNI have declined somewhat from their zenith in excess of 50% in the early 2000s, at roughly 30% they still remain outlandishly high. In real terms, by 2022 the FSM economy had only grown by 14% since it signed the Compact of Free Association in 1986, an annualized real growth rate of 0.4%. This long-term performance is on par with Chad, Sudan, or the Gambia. As elaborated below, the FSM is the most illustrative case in this book for illuminating the nuance of trade-effective aid and meaningful market access.

Much of the evidence in this case is first hand. Known as "direct" or "participant observation" investigatory methods, many of the insights below were gathered over the course of 18 months as a resident economic adviser, and then several different years as an external economic consultant.[3] In these positions, I observed and participated in trade policy discussions, foreign aid diplomacy, economic planning, and aid implementation via the office of Statistics, Budget, Overseas Development and Compact Management (SBOC) from 2009 to 2011 and as an adviser to the Joint Committee on Compact Review and Planning (JCRP) from 2020 to 2024.

[1] Fletcher, C. H. and Richmond, B. M. (2010). Climate change in the Federated States of Micronesia. *Food and Water Security, Climate Risk Management, and Adaptive Strategies*. University of Hawai'i, Hawaii.

[2] Feeny, S. and McGillivray, M. (2013). Aid and growth in small island developing states. In *Understanding Small-Island Developing States* (pp. 83–103). Routledge.

[3] Delamont, S. (2004). Ethnography and participant observation. *Qualitative Research Practice*, *217*(205–217); Zieman, G. A. (2012). Participant observation. In *Action Research Methods: Plain and Simple* (pp. 49–67). Palgrave Macmillan US.

Roughly 90% of the FSM's official development assistance comes from the United States. Of this, the vast bulk comes through the Compact of Free Association as budget grants. In the initial 15-year Compact period, 1986–2003, this assistance came in the form of almost wholly unrestricted budget support—effectively cash straight into the FSM's coffers with 30% of the amount earmarked for a loosely defined "capital account."[4] While the relative merits of "budget support" versus "project support" have been hotly debated in the policy and scholarly literatures, the experience in the FSM was one that was not conducive to growth. Although there were few allegations of out and out fraud or embezzlement, the assistance was widely recognized to have financed a high degree of current expenditure on consumption goods and unnecessary capital goods. The number of small boats with new outboard motors in the country's lagoons exploded during this period. While the economy showed some marginal growth in the first decade of the Compact as the country adjusted to these inflows, the progress quickly leveled off. Recognizing these failures, the United States pushed for far more stringent terms when the Compact was renewed, or "Amended," for a further 20 years in 2004. Foremost among the changes was the creation of discrete sectors—in Education, the Environment, Health, Infrastructure, Private Sector Development and Public Sector Capacity Building—whose budgets were ultimately approved and overseen by United States grant managers working for the Office of Insular Affairs. Under a new "Fiscal Procedures Agreement," these grant managers were empowered to engage in budget consultations with counterparts from the FSM for grants which ultimately had to be approved, by majority vote, by a "Joint" Economic Management Committee (JEMCO) consisting of two FSM-appointed and three US-appointed delegates.

While this Amended Compact era brought increased oversight, it did not lead to improved economic performance. From 2004 to 2019, the last year before the Covid-19 pandemic, real FSM GDP per capita grew by less than 6% *total* or less than 0.4% per year. Remote island economies were hit particularly hard by Covid-19 lockdowns and, as such, by 2022 real per capita GDP was almost 2.5% *less* than it had been in 2004. These macro performance figures are hard to reconcile with any definition of trade or growth effective aid. Why did these massive, stable, and prolonged investments fail to spur meaningful economic growth?

While the OECD classifies the bulk of US assistance as "Sector Budget Support" (SBS), given the oversight by JEMCO, US Compact funds

[4] Brazys, S. R. (2014b). Paradise Lost: The Cost of Removing Tax and Trade Provisions from the Compact of Free Association. *Asia & the Pacific Policy Studies*, *1*(1), 204–215.

often had higher degrees of conditionality and oversight that one might normally expect from a pure definition of SBS.[5] Beyond this, the Amended Compact prioritized funding for the Health and Education sectors, and extended this prioritization to the Infrastructure sector, such that Health and Education infrastructure projects received highest priority. In practice, this meant that during the Amended Compact period the vast bulk of all non-infrastructure Compact funding went to these two sectors, as well as the lion's share of infrastructure spending being directed to health and education facilities. While the FSM undoubtedly has substantial needs in these areas, the budget support in health and education largely financed personnel spending, which ultimately fueled domestic consumption rather than investment. These resources induced a sort of aid-based "Dutch-Disease" wherein private sector investment was directed toward retail operations to provide (imported) consumption goods and the economy saw a relative increase in the price of non-tradable goods, primarily in domestic services.[6]

While the Compact was funding teachers and health-care workers, the economic infrastructure in the islands was sorely neglected. Unreliable power plagued many of the islands, with unscheduled blackouts being frequent occurrences, especially in Pohnpei and Chuuk. Principal roads on the main islands remained substandard, and one of the main infrastructure projects during this period, the Weno Road project, was only completed after extensive delay and significant cost overruns.[7] Instead, Compact infrastructure funds were used primarily to build health and educational facilities, often to a standard (and cost) far beyond what was requested or endorsed by the FSM governments and in the face demographic trends which saw increasing out-migration over the Compact period.

However, US Compact funding was not alone in its trade or growth ineffectiveness. The European Union's main financing in the country, via the European Development Fund (EDF) rounds, also was unresponsive to the FSM's growth needs. A major initiative during the period was the construction of renewable power sources on the FSM's outer islands.[8] While working at SBOC in 2010 I observed the margins of these discussions. When the EU delegation arrived to negotiate the next round of the EDF they solicited project ideas from the FSM. The FSM proposed a project

[5] Edwards, K. (2016). *Financing Pacific Governments for Pacific Development*. World Bank.

[6] Brazys, S. (2010). Dutch disease in the western Pacific: An overview of the FSM economy under the Amended Compact of Free Association, *Pacific Economic Bulletin*, 25(3), 24–39.

[7] Government of the Federated States of Micronesia. Compact Infrastructure Sector 3rd Quarter 2021 Report. Palikir, Pohnpei. https://tci.gov.fm/documents/pmu/q-reports/fy21-qreports/final-third-quarter-report-fy21.pdf (accessed 05-12-2023).

[8] https://www.eeas.europa.eu/delegations/fiji/federated-states-micronesia-sustainable-energy-project-fsmse_en?s=139 (accessed 15-08-2023).

to improve pedestrian facilities alongside the main roads on the principal islands. These routes were the primary means of intra-island transportation but often lacked basic pedestrian facilities like sidewalks or footpaths. As the islands receive substantial amounts of rain, pedestrians would often take to walking along (or even sleeping on) the main roads. As a result, vehicular traffic often became slowed or stalled. While listening politely, the EU delegation eventually informed the FSM that this round of EDF was supporting renewable energy projects in remote locations. When the FSM protested that, first, many of the outer islands were being depopulated due to the impacts of climate change and, second, that the islanders lived, by choice, very traditional lifestyles and had gone for centuries without electricity and didn't have a pressing demand for household electricity, the EU's response was effectively "well, that's what we're doing." As a result, many of the schemes struggled to adequately maintain their installed systems. As noted in a 2012 report, of the systems installed in the Pohnpei outer-island atolls of Pingelap, Mwoakilloa, and Sapwuafik, "The majority of the systems are not working properly as there is no 'operation and maintenance (O&M)' or a parts-replacement program in place."[9]

The People's Republic of China is a third major donor to the FSM. While the PRC has provided some unrestricted budget grants to the FSM, a substantial part of its assistance has been via the provision of turnkey projects, with government buildings as a modality of choice. The FSM national government's complex at Palikir (which includes the houses for the President, Speaker of Congress and Supreme Court Chief Justice), the nearby Pohnpei State administration building, as well as the recently completed Chuuk State government complex and National Convention center have all been constructed by the PRC, with PRC supplied labor and materials. In addition to concerns about the PRC potentially embedding surveillance technology in these buildings, the buildings themselves were often of poor quality. The elevator in the Pohnpei government building broke down shortly after the building opened, and the floor was soon cracked as it emerged that wall tiles had been used for the flooring. While the PRC has pivoted to providing more economic infrastructure in recent years, the track record since the late 1980s is not one that would have been conducive to growth.[10] Only Japan has been involved primarily in constructing economic infrastructure, as is

[9] https://prdrse4all.spc.int/sites/default/files/fsm_final_report_submitted_22nd_oct_2012_by_gses.pdf, p.11 (accessed 06-09-2023).

[10] https://gov.fm/index.php/component/content/article/35-pio-articles/news-and-updates/531-14-300-000-pohnpei-secondary-road-project-complete-thanks-to-generous-assistance-from-people-s-republic-of-china-please-tell-my-dear-friend-president-xi-jinping-that-micronesia-says-thank-you-president-panuelo-says-to-ambassador-huang# (accessed 15-08-2023).

its wont elsewhere, with the largest and most visible project being an extension of the runway at the Pohnpei International Airport. However, even this project has failed to realize large material gains as the country is only served by one international carrier who did not meaningfully increase flights, destinations, or aircraft size following this project.

Donor-country domestic politics drove these aid choices. In the United States, the Compact funding is peculiar via its administration by the Office of Insular Affairs which is housed in the Department of the Interior (DOI). Thus, whereas most US ODA flows via the State Department, and the United States Agency for International Development (USAID) in particular, Compact funding is overseen by mid-level bureaucrats who may lack experience or expertise in international development. While the three US members of the JEMCO body, which is ultimately responsible for granting decisions, are typically comprised of a chairperson from DOI and then two additional members who are usually from the State Department and the Department of Health and Human Services, these members largely take their direction from the DOI field office in Honolulu.

The politics behind the health and education focus stems primarily from a provision in the Compact which allows FSM citizens to migrate freely to the United States. As a result, since 1986, tens of thousands of FSM citizens have migrated to Guam, Hawaii, and the mainland.[11] While the many migrants have contributed positively to their adopted communities and economies, their presence has raised concerns about impacts on social services or crime.[12] As a result of this "Compact Impact," much of the US political debate has centered around how to mitigate these (perceived) costs for the affected regions. The issue of "Compact Impact" was raised as early as 1995 by the US Congressional delegate from Guam, Robert A. Underwood[13] and become a key discussion point in negotiating the 2003 Amended Compact. In that year, the "Compact Impact Reimbursement Act" was introduced by Guam representative Madeline Bordallo who noted how:

> these FAS (Freely Associated States) citizens have entered our classrooms, utilized our hospitals, and availed themselves of other social services, to a significant degree.

[11] Hezel, F. X. and Levin, M. J. (1996). New trends in Micronesian migration: FSM migration to Guam and the Marianas, 1990–1993. *Pacific Studies, 19*, 24–24.

[12] Yamada, S. and Pobutsky, A. (2009). Micronesian migrant health issues in Hawaii. *Californian Journal of Health Promotion, 7*(2), 16–31; Smith, S. A. and Castañeda, H. (2021). Nonimmigrant others: Belonging, precarity and imperial citizenship for Chuukese migrants in Guam. *PoLAR: Political and Legal Anthropology Review, 44*(1), 138–155.

[13] United States Congress. June 26, 1995—Issue: Vol. 141, No. 105—Daily Edition 104th Congress (1995–1996) —1st Session, p. H6311.

> The General Accounting Office has documented the impact of this migration (GAO-02-40).[14]

Likewise, then-Senator Daniel Akaka from Hawaii, in addressing the Amended Compact, noted how:

> In 2002, the State of Hawaii expended over $32 million in assistance to FAS Citizens, with the highest costs reported in education[15]

and that:

> Hawaii's medical providers have also suffered because they are owed thousands of dollars in unpaid medical bills. Some of the debt has been incurred by individuals.... Other debt, however, is a result of the medical referral program, and is to be paid by the FSM and RMI governments. The medical referral program allows FAS citizens to travel to Hawaii for medical treatment to be paid by the FSM or RMI because such treatment is not available in their country.[16]

Senator Akaka then explicitly tied these concerns to the proposed new funding by declaring that:

> This is why it is important to provide Federal support through social service programs while continuing to develop new economic opportunities for FAS citizens. Otherwise, the impact of serving FAS citizens will continue to be felt outside of the FAS.[17]

This congressional record makes clear that Compact assistance, especially during the Amended Compact, was not primarily driven by assessments of overall efficacy toward promoting exports or economic growth, but instead, was to be used to offset politically inconvenient (if not adverse) impacts from other parts of the Compact arrangement. With this sense of Congress, and in the hands of bureaucrats who were not necessarily development experts, it is no surprise that the Compact funding has failed to generate visible or meaningful economic growth.

The decision to use the Compact funding in this way was one that was made largely unilaterally by the United States. Given the FSM's status as a

[14] United States Congress. July 14, 2003—Issue: Vol. 149, No. 103—Daily Edition 108th Congress (2003–2004)—1st Session.

[15] United States Congress. August 1, 2003—Issue: Vol. 149, No. 117—Daily Edition 108th Congress (2003–2004)—1st Session, p. S10881.

[16] Ibid.

[17] Ibid.

small-island state in the out-of-the-way Pacific, the country had little agency with which to push back against the interests of its major donors. During the unipolar moments of the 1990s and 2000s, 1 million square kilometers of Pacific Ocean was of little strategic importance to the United States or other donors. As such, the terms of the Amended Compact were largely presented as a "take it or leave it" proposition. Beyond this, the education and social needs of the FSM were undeniable, and the package could still very much be sold as a win to the US domestic constituency. While that position began to shift in the 2010s and US-PRC rivalry began to eye the Pacific's "Second Island Chain"—the 20-year nature of the Compact agreements meant that the FSM was largely locked into the terms of its 2003 agreement. The contrast to this is the "Second Amended Compact," whose negotiations began in earnest at the end of the Trump administration in 2020. By this time, the issue of the PRC and security in the Pacific was both present and visible.[18] During the negotiations, the United States and its Pacific allies suffered a shock when the Solomon Islands signed a "framework agreement" with the PRC to enhance security cooperation.[19] Fearful that they were losing influence in their own Pacific "backyard" the United States stepped up the pace of negotiations with the FSM and its sister states. Micronesia's identity in the international system changed from small-island backwater to the front line of the US-PRC Pacific contestation. The resulting negotiated package included an increased amount of financial assistance, an elimination of the health and education "priority" language in the infrastructure sector, and a relaxed Fiscal Procedures Amendment that includes a JEMCO balanced with three delegates from each country (albeit with the United States' chairperson retaining the tie-breaking vote)—all key negotiating requests from the FSM delegation. While only time will tell if this Second Amended Compact is a critical juncture that leads to more trade-effective aid, the change in conditionality seems favorable to that end, for which the increased geostrategic importance of the FSM in 2023 compared to 2003 is of no small importance.

Thus, under a generous reading, US aid to the FSM has likely been ineffective because it was designed in a way to address US domestic political concerns rather than focus on trade and growth. Under a more sinister reading, longer-term influence considerations could also explain the US position toward how aid was structured. By relying heavily on US assistance for the daily operation of its government, which is also the largest

[18] https://www.uscc.gov/sites/default/files/Research/China-Pacific%20Islands%20Staff%20Report.pdf (accessed 06-09-2023).

[19] https://www.theguardian.com/world/2022/mar/31/security-agreement-with-china-initialled-by-both-countries-solomon-islands-says (accessed 06-09-2023).

economic sector in the FSM, the FSM very much remains "dependent" on US support. Critical scholars have suggested the "aid dependence" may be a strategic policy choice that enables donor countries to maintain disproportionate influence over their aid "dependents."[20] Thus, donors may have a perverse incentive for their aid not to be trade or growth effective in order to maintain control. While there is no direct evidence that the United States has deliberately sought to keep the FSM aid dependent, the FSM does indeed express its gratitude adopting positions in the United Nations General Assembly (UNGA) which are more closely in line with the United States than almost any other country, or by vocally expressing international support for US positions and priorities.[21] Remarkably, the then-FSM President David Panuelo, after earlier sending a letter in 2022 to other Pacific leaders warning against and effectively scuppering PRC efforts to sign a region-wide cooperation agreement,[22] in March of 2023 sent a 12-page letter to FSM political leadership leveling accusations of "political warfare" and bribery attempts from the PRC as well as outlining a strategy for the FSM to switch diplomatic recognition to the Republic of China (Taiwan) for $50 million dollars.[23]

Political considerations have also shaded other donors' aid to the FSM. The PRC, beyond competing with the United States for influence, has also lavished aid on the FSM due to the fact that the FSM, unlike its FAS sister states Palau and the Republic of the Marshall Islands, does not recognize Taiwan and the FSM publicly supports the one-China policy. The PRC is engaging in a global campaign of using economic support to bolster its international political legitimacy, and the FSM is no exception.[24] This campaign is also being wrought for domestic political reasons. The Chinese Communist Party (CCP) is able to sell international acceptance, adoration, and acquiescence as a validation of the PRC's superior political system which is predicated on single-party stability and control. While the PRC no doubt questioned the value of its investments given President Panuelo's

[20] Muller, E. N. (1985). Dependent economic development, aid dependence on the United States, and democratic breakdown in the Third World. *International Studies Quarterly*, *29*(4), 445–469; Dreher, A. and Sturm, J. E. (2012). Do the IMF and the World Bank influence voting in the UN General Assembly? *Public Choice*, *151*, 363–397; Brazys, S. (2018). Aid dependence as aid persistence? Non-declining aid and growth. *Journal of International Relations and Development*, *21*, 717–738.

[21] Brazys, S. and Panke, D. (2017). Why do states change positions in the United Nations General Assembly? *International Political Science Review*, *38*(1), 70–84.

[22] https://www.abc.net.au/news/2022-05-25/china-seeks-pacific-islands-policing-security-cooperation/101099978 (accessed 15-08-2023).

[23] https://thediplomat.com/2023/03/micronesias-president-writes-bombshell-letter-on-chinas-political-warfare/ (accessed 15-08-2023).

[24] Brazys, S., and Dukalskis, A. (2017). Canary in the coal mine? China, the UNGA, and the changing world order. *Review of International Studies*, *43*(4), 742–764.

letters described above, that administration aside, FSM foreign policy has generally sought to delicately navigate the balance between the competing superpowers.

Likewise, even the European Union's decision to fund not-sought-after solar power is also a reflection of its domestic political calculus. Faced with important domestic constituencies that demand action to combat climate change, funding levels for environment and climate change have increased substantially in subsequent rounds of the EDF.[25] These pressures have translated into top-down EDF projects and priorities which ensure that the projects that are financed under this facility reflect EU domestic political interest rather than the actual needs or priorities articulated by host governments. In essence, such a "take it or leave it" approach results in solar farms on depopulating outer islands as opposed to footpaths on populated centers.

Thus, despite the massive amounts of development assistance received by the FSM since its independence, there is little evidence to suggest that much, if any, of it has been effective at spurring trade or long-term growth. That lack of effectiveness is due, at least in part, on a reliance on the United States as the principal donor and to aid that was intended to address the political concerns of the donors rather than the priorities of the FSM government. While these efforts may represent "targeted development" by the United States, to mitigate Compact migration spillovers, the focus on these social sectors, at the expense of trade and growth-oriented aid, means that the latter categories were largely neglected.

What Will We Trade?

If an absence of growth belies the lack of trade-effective aid in the FSM, then its export to GDP ratio suggests that the FSM has had increasingly meaningful market access. The ratio of exports to GDP nearly doubled during the Amended Compact period, from 15% to 30%. While this is still not an overly large figure for such a small open economy, it is certainly a trend that moves in a promising direction. However, underneath that headline figure, the reality paints a more complicated story. The FSM—alongside several other SIDS, Eritrea, and North Korea—is one of less than a dozen states who are not in the World Trade Organization (WTO) nor have sought to join. Moreover, the FSM is only party to one trade agreement, the regional South Pacific Regional Trade and Economic Cooperation Agreement (SPARTECA) but did not join

[25] https://ec.europa.eu/newsroom/intpa/items/617911/en (accessed 15-08-2023).

the successor Pacific Agreement on Closer Economic Relations (PACER) or PACER Plus agreements. That said, the FSM has received GSP access from numerous key trading partners, including the EU, Japan, Australia, and New Zealand.

The FSM's most impressive de jure market access agreement, however, again stems from the Compact of Free Association. The agreement gives the FSM, along with Palau and the RMI, special status under General Note 10 of the US Harmonized Tariff Schedule. Paragraph (b) of that section states that "any article the growth, product or manufacture of a freely associated state shall enter the customs territory of the United States free of duty"[26] subject to it being directly imported from the FAS territory and that at least 35% of the value added occurred in the country. However, this note also has three very specific exceptions—the first two relating to the import of a handful of products and the third relating to value limitation—both in respect to the ratio of total imports of the product into the United States, and in respect of a "ratio to $25,000,000 as the gross national product of the United States for the preceding calendar year."

Thus, in essence, the FSM has on-paper market access to the United States, that rivals any country in the world. Of the over 10,000 product lines in the US HTS, the FSM has duty free access to nearly all of them. Yet here again meaningful market access trumps broad-based de jure access. The exceptions under Note 10 are limited, but hugely consequential. First, duty-free access of prepared Tuna and Skipjack is limited to 10% of the preceding year's imports. Second, textiles, including leather goods, footwear, and buttons are excluded. Third is an exclusion for watches, clocks, and timing apparatuses and the final exclusion are any agricultural products subject to a tariff rate quota.

While these exclusions apply to a limited number of product lines, they are hugely consequential for the export potential of the FSM. With an exclusive economic zone of more than three million square kilometers of Equatorial Pacific, the FSM controls one of the largest fisheries in the world. This fishery hosts some of the last remaining healthy stocks of skipjack, yellowfin, and big-eye tuna. While revenue from this fishery is substantial and comprises a significant chunk of the FSM government's non-ODA government revenue, the FSM captures very little value-added from this resource. Currently, nearly all the revenues from the fishery come from the sale of licensing rights to foreign fishing operations who take their catches elsewhere for processing.

[26] United States International Trade Commission. (2023) *Harmonized Tariff Schedule of the United States: Annotated for Statistical Reporting Purposes*. Revision 10.

As alluded to in the introductory chapter, the tariff access received by the FSM under the Compact was a result of US domestic political considerations. While the FSM had negotiated "Headnote 3a" status in the original Compact negotiations, the same duty-free regime with which US insular territories like Puerto Rico or Guam trade with the US states, this was challenged and ultimately modified as a result of US domestic political pressure. The charge was primarily led by the other US territories, particularly American Samoa, which saw direct competition from the Compact states if they traded under the same rules. The Congressional representative from the territory, Fofo I. F. Sunia, in arguing against extending Headnote 3a to the FSM exclaimed:

> I are talking about a cannery, and I think, well, it is such a massive thing, who is going to move that cannery around the Pacific? ... I will tell you, it isn't hard to put up a cannery. Van Camp is putting up a cannery in American Samoa now ... put up in around 3 or 4 months. That is no problem to move these canneries around, and that is why I can assure you that I are concerned; I are almost certain that there will be shifts, and they will come soon, too, because it is not hard to pack up a cannery and move it around the Pacific.[27]

Representative Sunia was supported in his opposition by representatives of the US Tuna industry and relevant government officials, who were concerned about foreign companies setting up tuna processing facilities in the FSM in order to entry the US market duty free. James P. Walsh, from the American Tunaboat Association, argued that:

> Secondly, I have concern about the duty-free treatment provisions of the Compact. Allowing new tuna plants based in the Compact islands duty free entry ... is very Threatening.[28]

These sentiments echoed by William Gordon, the Assistant Administrator for Fisheries at the National Oceanic and Atmospheric Administration who stated:

> I think it is of major concern to the tuna industry. I was in American Samoa early Last week and found U.S. canners there extremely concerned that foreign investments
> Will be used to ship tuna duty-free into the United States....[29]

[27] United States of America Congressional Testimony 99-9 Part I Hearing before the Subcommittee on Public Lands and National Parks, March 7, 1985, pp. 31–33.
[28] Ibid, pp. 20–22.
[29] Ibid, pp. 29–33.

Ultimately these arguments prevailed since there was little, if any, domestic support in favor of keeping the Headnote 3a status for the FSM outside of the US administration's negotiators who was unable to sway Congress's will. The most that James Berg, the Political and Economic Adviser for Micronesian Status Negotiations from the US Department of State could muster in response to the concerns above was:

> Finally, with respect to the tuna industry, I know that there is concern in the Industry, but there is also interest ... in investing in the area (Micronesia).[30]

Likewise, given the FSM's position in the 1980s as a recent trust territory largely reliant on the United States for international recognition and support meant that the country had little agency to exercise against these claims. The removal of Headnote 3a status had significant effects on the FSM economy, in all likelihood diverting investment in tuna processing facilities in the country. While it is difficult to prove a negative, following the removal of Headnote 3a from the Compact countries, American Samoa saw significant additional investment in its own cannery facilities, with exports more than doubling as a result.[31] Some estimates suggest that the cost to the FSM of losing this market access in Tuna was over $1.125 billion over the first 15 years of the Compact, or roughly 33% of GDP during the period.[32]

But tuna was not the only industry that potentially suffered from the removal of Headnote 3a status. The provision would also have given the FSM duty-free access in a range of textiles, a feature that was effectively removed by Note 10. As discussed in Chapters 1, 4, and 8, market access in textiles has been a hugely important catalyst for many developing countries as, in many instances, it represents the first rung on the ladder of industrialization. While the FSM would not have had an overt comparative advantage in the sector—although labor was relatively cheap the countries remoteness and lack of cheap and reliable energy would be significant hinderances—there is again evidence by comparison that the duty-free access of Headnote 3a would have been sufficient to mount these barriers, especially during the MFA era. Once again by looking at an insular sister that did have Headnote 3a, it is possible to speculate on what might have been. The Commonwealth of the Northern Mariana Islands (CNMI), a cluster of islands just north of the FSM, who might have also pursued the Compact route but instead choose to remain a US territory, developed a significant textile industry during the

[30] Ibid, pp. 29–33.

[31] Brazys, S. R. (2014b). Paradise Lost: The Cost of Removing Tax and Trade Provisions from the Compact of Free Association. Asia & the Pacific Policy Studies, 1(1), 204–215.

[32] Ibid., p. 210.

FSM's initial Compact period of 1986 to 2001, with the territory's earnings in the sector jumping from $58 million in 1987 to an annual average of $772 million from 1998 to 2001. Again, conservative assumptions estimate that with Headnote 3a status, the FSM might have developed a textile industry during the initial Compact period worth an additional $1.25 billion in aggregate GDP.

Thus, while Note 10 provided the FSM with significant de jure market access, by excluding the tuna and textile sectors, this market access omitted the key potential FSM exports. What is effectively a natural experiment with the CNMI and American Samoa is illustrative of the consequences of this omission. Both of these entities, which shared very similar initial conditions to the FSM, could have plausibly chosen the Compact route and accompanying Note 10 market access status in 1986 like the FSM, but instead remained insular territories with Headnote 3a market access. Thirty-five years later, both of these territories have been able to diversify their economies at least to some extent and have income levels in the "high income" category, while the FSM sits squarely in the lower middle-income range, despite the massive amounts of ODA received in the intervening years.

Other market access arrangements have similarly excluded the vital sectors for FSM exports. The FSM access to the developed world's other main market, the European Common Market, is via its GSP scheme. As the FSM did not become a member of the Asian, Caribbean, and Pacific Group of States (ACP) until 2000, it did not participate in any of the Lome Conventions. Although the FSM subsequently joined the ACP via the Pacific Islands Forum, signed the Cotonou agreement, and has taken part in the EU–Pacific Economic Partnership Agreement (EPA) negotiations, as of this writing it had not yet signed the interim EPA and does not appear likely to do so in the near future. As discussed in Chapter 4, the EU's standard GSP scheme is limited on a number of products. For the FSM, this includes key products like Tuna under HTS 1604.14 which face tariffs of 20.5% as well as a tariff of up to 9.6% for many articles for Textile and Textile articles under Section XI. In both instances, these barriers effectively preclude market access for the FSM in these sectors, as competitors in GSP+ and EBA countries receive access to the European market at duty-free rates. This again illustrates how the EU's GSP scheme affords the FSM little meaningful market access. The politics of the EU's GSP access discussed in Chapter 4 highlighted how this lack of meaningful market access was very much driven by EU domestic political considerations.

While the FSM could secure additional market access under the EU–Pacific interim EPA, including duty free access in both Tuna and Textiles, it has not yet done so. This is due, in part, to the general skepticism toward free-trade agreements characterized by the "what will we trade?" critique discussed in the introduction. However, the lack of sign on is also due to the fact that the FSM has very limited capacity for negotiating, much less implementing, these agreements. The FSM's National Trade Facilitation Committee (NTFC), who are responsible for all trade-related matters, has historically been staffed by a total of three members. One of these staffers relayed how, in 2010, they simply did not have enough staff coverage to conduct simultaneous regional, bilateral, and multilateral trade negotiations.[33]

While there is little "smoking gun" evidence, in both the Compact and the Cotonou regimes, there appears to be an implicit trade-off between aid and market access, as aid and access have gone hand in hand in both instances. The Title II ODA provisions of the Compact, and the European Development Fund arrangements, were explicitly tied to these (incomplete) market access agreements. The FSM is perhaps the most influential case of a country that shows why it is trade-effective aid (not just aid) and meaningful market access (not just market access) that are necessary for development. The FSM arguably lacks both of these elements and, despite its overall strong governance, remains an economic laggard. While its remoteness and small-island status are also no doubt contributors to its poor economic performance, these features alone cannot be determinative as other SIDS have thrived, including the FSM's near-neighbor Palau, and its insular territorial counterparts the CNMI and American Samoa.

Everything but Growth and Opportunity

While the FSM is a collection of hundreds of small islands and a handful of larger ones sitting thousands of miles from any continental landmass, the South-East African nation of Madagascar is comprised of one massive island and a few dozen small outlying islands, lying just 250 miles from the African mainland, and positioned near major shipping lanes which take the Cape of Good hope to transit goods from Asia to Africa, Europe, and the Americas. Madagascar is also home to nearly 30 million people and a cornucopia of endemic natural species of flora and fauna as well as a non-inconsequential amount of natural mineral wealth. However, despite these differences, Madagascar shares the FSM's decades of struggle with economic performance and remains one of the poorest countries in the world, firmly mired in low income, or "least developed" status. Also like the FSM, Madagascar is

[33] Interview FSM-1001.

a reasonably well-governed country and has, and continues to be, a major recipient of ODA, and is in the Southeast quadrant of "effective aid" primarily because its ratio of ODA to GDP has not grown much over the past 50 years. Finally, by virtue of its LDC status, Madagascar also has a significant amount of de jure export market access to key developed regions including the United States but also the European Union.

As a least-developed country in sub-Saharan Africa, Madagascar is eligible for two of the most generous preferential market access agreements in the world, the European Union's "Everything but Arms" (EBA) initiative and the United States' African Growth and Opportunity Act (AGOA). These programs, run as "GSP plus" initiatives under the enabling clause, give duty free access beyond that afforded to developing countries under "regular" GSP schemes. The EBA is widely recognized as the most preferential de jure market access agreement on the planet, granting duty and quota free access for all goods except armaments under HS Chapter 93.[34] The AGOA, while not quite as generous, includes duty-free access for a further 1,600 tariff lines beyond what is available to developing countries under the United States' GSP scheme.[35] These markets account for the majority of the value of Madagascar's exports, with the US alone serving as the destination for approximately 20% of Madagascar's recent exports.[36]

However, despite these agreements, and the share of trade they account for, the market access indices from Chapter 3 rate Madagascar's meaningful market access to be in roughly the 25th percentile of developing countries. This ranking is due, largely, to the fact that Madagascar has one of the highest agricultural production potentials in the measure, ranking in the 90th percentile of available agricultural land. Even though all, or the vast bulk, of agricultural products from Madagascar can enter the EU and United States duty free, respectively, other non-tariff barriers hinder market access in these products. Most notably, Sanitary and Phytosanitary measures can act as significant barriers to entry for these products. For instance, for one Madagascar's largest export products, "Coffee, tea, maté and spices" (HS Chapter 9), the EU has notified to the WTO nearly 100 SPS regulations since 1998. Of these, eight pertain to coffee (HS 0901). One of these, G/SPS/N/EEC/247, notified to the WTO in 2004, pertains to grape juice (HS 2205), wine (HS2204 and 2005), and coffee (HS0901). While best known for its exports of vanilla (HS 0905), almost half of all wild coffee species are endemic to the island,[37] and

[34] Faber, G. and Orbie, J. (2009). Everything but arms: Much more than appears at first sight. *JCMS: Journal of Common Market Studies*, *47*(4), 767–787.

[35] https://agoa.info/33-kb/16160-what-products-are-covered-by-agoa.html (accessed 04-09-2023).

[36] UN Comtrade.

[37] https://perfectdailygrind.com/2019/01/how-madagascan-deforestation-puts-world-coffee-at-risk/ (accessed 04-09-2023).

Madagascar has a history of commercial coffee production dating to French colonial times.[38] However, today Madagascar's coffee exports pale in comparison to other agricultural products, with total exports of less than $1 million in 2019. While this was a particularly poor year for Malagasy coffee, exports in the latter half of the 2010s averaged only a few million dollars, compared to tens of millions in the mid-1990s. These exports levels fell precipitously around the turn of the turn of the millennium. While global coffee markets are notoriously volatile,[39] this timing also coincided with the increasing use of the WTO SPS agreement.

G/SPS/N/EEC/247 imposes a requirement about the level of ochratoxin A in coffee products. Ochratoxin A can be found on a variety of food products, including pork and grain, and some have suggested that it has carcinogenic and/or neurotoxic properties.[40] However, despite a lack of clarity on the adverse health impacts of ochratoxin A, or at what levels these become problematic, G/SPS/N/EEC/247 requires that all imports meet the standards outlined in that regulation. This requires exporters to test for the toxin. Lab-based or field-testing kits can cost upward of hundreds of dollars. Other EU SPS regulations on coffee include prohibition on pests, and regulations on the levels of acrylamide, a potential carcinogen which can form during a roasting process. Meeting these requirements can be a significant burden on small exporters, like those found in Madagascar, and can effectively negate the de jure market access under the EBA.

Overall, the EU has some 800 SPS notifications on HS Section I (Live Animals; Animal Products) and Section II (Vegetable Products) agricultural products. For small-scale agricultural producers and exporters, navigating and complying with these regulations can constitute serious export barriers.[41] When trading in small-scale, agricultural commodities, these compliance costs can quickly negate any other cost advantages these producers might have.[42] As discussed in Chapter 4, these measures are often viewed with suspicion as being imposed as a form of trade barrier, rather than as a purely health or safety related measure.[43] These regulatory barriers may introduce

[38] Laney, R. and Turner, B. L. (2015). The persistence of self-provisioning among smallholder farmers in Northeast Madagascar. *Human Ecology*, *43*, 811–826.

[39] Ghoshray, A. (2010). The extent of the world coffee market. *Bulletin of Economic Research*, *62*(1), 97–107.

[40] Park, S., Lim, W., You, S., and Song, G. (2019). Ochratoxin A exerts neurotoxicity in human astrocytes through mitochondria-dependent apoptosis and intracellular calcium overload. *Toxicology Letters*, *313*, 42–49.

[41] Disdier, A. C., Fontagné, L., and Mimouni, M. (2008). The impact of regulations on agricultural trade: evidence from the SPS and TBT agreements. *American Journal of Agricultural Economics*, *90*(2), 336–350.

[42] Unnevehr, L. J. (2000). Food safety issues and fresh food product exports from LDCs. *Agricultural Economics*, *23*(3), 231–240.

[43] Athukorala, P. C. and Jayasuriya, S. (2003). Food safety issues, trade and WTO rules: A developing country perspective. *World Economy*, *26*(9), 1395–1416.

unintended consequences as a result of the domestic politics and pressures for their implementation. While very little coffee is grown in the EU, the ochratoxin A regulation discussed above also covered wine and grape juice, products for which there are politically powerful EU domestic producers.[44] Given the similar prevalence of ochratoxin A on coffee and grape vines, there would have been little scientific rationale for excluding coffee from the regulation.[45] As such, one might reasonably infer that the politics of protection for domestic wine producers in the EU spilled over into international coffee markets. Larger, richer, producers may have been able to absorb these costs, but for smaller producers, like many of those in Madagascar, these regulatory requirements might have effectively closed market access.[46]

Like the EBA, the AGOA also offers broad, duty-free, access in agricultural products. However, in many areas the United States has an even more aggressive SPS regime than their European counterparts, with no less than 1182 SPS notifications in Section I and Section II products, and over 42 notifications for coffee. While some of these are general provisions that apply to (nearly) all agricultural products, others are very much coffee specific. While the first of these, G/SPS/N/USA/81, notified in 1997, expressly prohibited the importation of unroasted coffee fruits and berries on the grounds that they could introduce the Mediterranean fruit fly, a series of subsequent notifications focused on tolerances for certain types of pesticides. Two of these, for the pesticides Ethiprole and Cyflumetofen, respectively, were notified in 2019, the same year that Malagasy coffee exports plummeted to well under $1 million. The petitions for these regulations were filed by US and Japanese multi-national pesticide producers, Bayer CropScience LP and OAT Agrio. Ltd. respectively, presumably in an effort to discourage the use of other (commercially competing) pesticides.[47] This petition could thus have had a two-fold impact on small-scale producers. First, it once again introduced a testing burden on producers to show that their products met the safety thresholds. Notably, these pesticide issues differ from the chemical issues under the EU notifications, requiring different testing. Second, to the extent that these actions effectively banned certain types of pesticide, this may

[44] Itçaina, X., Roger, A., and Smith, A. (2016). *Varietals of Capitalism: A Political Economy of the Changing Wine Industry*. Cornell University Press.

[45] Yurdakul, O., Sahındokuyucu, F., Yalcın, H., and Keyvan, E. (2019). Survey of Ochratoxin A in coffee, dried grapes and grape pekmez samples in Burdur, Turkey. *Journal of Research in Veterinary Medicine*, *38*(1), 46–51.

[46] Disdier, A. C., Fontagné, L., and Mimouni, M. (2008). The impact of regulations on agricultural trade: evidence from the SPS and TBT agreements. *American Journal of Agricultural Economics*, *90*(2), 336–350.

[47] https://www.govinfo.gov/content/pkg/FR-2019-06-28/html/2019-13546.htm; https://www.govinfo.gov/content/pkg/FR-2019-11-25/html/2019-25543.htm.

have caused the producers either to have to shift to a different, potentially more expensive pesticide, or abandon pesticide use altogether, potentially impacting yields.

Beyond SPS, the EBA and AGOA both include product-specific regulations on rules of origin (ROO), again heavily focused on the agricultural and textile sectors.[48] The EU has EBA-specific ROO for cocoa, fisheries, fruits, mean, and essential oils. While none of these ROO are overly onerous—the food-related focus primarily on ensuring the food product was grown/raised in the country and ensuring that non-origin sugar doesn't equal more than 40% of product weight—they again add an extra layer of administrative complexity for exporters. Exporters shipping more than 6000 Euro worth of goods are required to fill "Origin Form A." The form, which can only be retrieved from a "competent national authority for the issue of forms A, often customs" must also ensure it meets the following technical requirements:

> Each certificate shall measure 210 × 297 mm; a tolerance of up to minus 5 mm or plus 8 mm in the length and in the width may be allowed. The paper used shall be white writing paper, sized, not containing mechanical pulp and weighing not less than 25 g/m2. It shall have a printed green guilloche-pattern background making any falsification by mechanical or chemical means apparent to the eye.

While completing the form A is unlikely to be a determinative barrier to exports—rules of origin certificates and part and parcel for exporters—having an additional, EBA-specific ROO requirement adds additional transaction expense which, in conjunction with other barriers, may ultimately dissuade (particularly small) exporters who might otherwise have de jure market access.

The vignettes above are meant to illustrate that even in the presence of de jure market access, SPS and other TBTs can impose significant barriers. Moreover, while EBA and AGOA provide some preferential access, in many instances the tariff lines are already duty-free at the MFN level. This is the case with many of the coffee products lines (HS 0901) in the United States and Europe. Without de jure preferences vis-à-vis other exporters, regulatory requirements are likely to disproportionally impact smaller and poorer producers who lack the volume, technical capacity, or government support to meet SPS and other technical requirements. While the focus of this section is on coffee, it is widely acknowledged that SPS standards serve as a broad regulatory barrier across agricultural products, although these effects may vary

[48] Zappile, T. M. (2011). Nonreciprocal trade agreements and trade: Does the African Growth and Opportunity Act (AGOA) increase trade? *International Studies Perspectives, 12*(1), 46–67.

by product and country.[49] Given Madagascar's enormous agricultural export potential, it is thus difficult to say that the country has meaningful market access, despite the fact that its access to major export markets is as good as almost any other country on the globe.

Aid, but Is It Effective?

In addition to being a major recipient of de jure market access, Madagascar has also been the beneficiary of significant amounts of foreign aid since it became independent in 1960. However, unlike the other countries in this book, the country's largest donor has not been a country, but instead a multilateral institution, the World Bank, which has, on average, provided more annual assistance than the next two donors (France and the United States) combined. Moreover, Madagascar has been a major recipient of aid from other multilaterals, including IMF, African Development Bank, and various UN agencies. All told, the country has averaged roughly $500 million per year from multilateral institutions, roughly 40% more than the $350 million the country has received annually on average from bilateral donors.

Breaking down Madagascar's ODA by sector, the preponderance of aid since 1995 has been received in the transportation sector, at roughly $2.9 billion. However, this is less than 15% of the total aid received. A close second is budget support at $2.6 billion. As discussed in Chapter 5, the relative merits of project versus budget support have been hotly contested for decades, with the wisdom of the day see-sawing between the preferred modality. This oscillation is also visible in Madagascar's receipt of the category, with annual amounts swinging wildly, at time by hundreds of millions of dollars up or down from one year to the next. Much of the volatility in this funding stream was driven by the EU, with General Budget Support (GBS) commitments oscillating from $82 million in 2005, to $500,000 in 2006, back to $56 million in 2007 and up to $125 million in 2008 before being entirely withdrawn until 2014. The unsettledness in budget support is reflected in the country's broader aid, as its volatility has ranked in the upper half of developed countries since the 1990s. While also in receipt of substantial amounts of assistance in the health and education sectors, the country has received comparatively

[49] Disdier, A. C., Fontagné, L., and Mimouni, M. (2008). The impact of regulations on agricultural trade: evidence from the SPS and TBT agreements. *American Journal of Agricultural Economics*, *90*(2), 336–350; Santeramo, F. G. and Lamonaca, E. (2019). The effects of non-tariff measures on agri-food trade: A review and meta-analysis of empirical evidence. *Journal of Agricultural Economics*, *70*(3), 595–617.

little in non-transport economic infrastructure. ODA in energy has only amounted to $900 million, or less than 4% of total aid, and a paltry $53 million in communications. In contrast, its aid in the environmental sector has been substantial, amounting to nearly the same as the energy sector with $870 million.

Looking at the revealed priorities of different donors adds further context to the aggregate numbers. The largest bilateral donor, France, committed $725 million, or approximately 25% of its total, to the education sector, while another nearly $800 million went to debt relief. The United States committed almost 60% of its total ODA of $2.4 billion to the food, health, humanitarian, and environmental sectors. The largest of these outlays, food aid, accounted for over $500 million. Even traditional stalwarts of economic infrastructure like Japan and the World Bank, failed to devote substantial amounts of their portfolios to building these tools of development. Of the $6.3 billion the World Bank has poured into the country since 1995, only $900 million, or less than 15% went to transportation infrastructure and $500 million went to energy. Together, these sectors account for less than a quarter of the total World Bank commitments. Likewise, while Japan has devoted $500 million of its $1.35 billion in total commitments to transport infrastructure, it has committed a mere $220,000 to energy via a number of small technical assistance grants.

Economic infrastructure is not the be all and end all of trade-effective aid. White elephant projects can saddle countries with excess capacity and debt.[50] That said, like the FSM, Madagascar has massive needs in transportation, energy, and communications. In 2020, the country had just 0.11 broadband subscriptions per 100 people, one-fifth of the low-income country average and over 35 times less than the lower-middle income country average of 4.06. While the country does better on mobile connections, at roughly the low-income country average of 60 per 100 people, this is still considerably less than the nearly universal the lower-middle income average of 97 per 100 individuals. Likewise, only 35% of the country has access to electricity[51] and, despite its size, the country is served by only 30,000 kilometers of road, of which less than 10,000 km are paved and less than 1000 kilometers of rail. Most of those networks are to facilitate access to and from the capital city Antananarivo leaving much of the country, including most of the Western coast, functionally inaccessible by land.

[50] Attanayake, C. and Ren, Y. (2021). China, Sri Lanka and the BRI. *Research Handbook on the Belt and Road Initiative* (pp. 240–252). Elgar.

[51] https://www.irena.org/-/media/Files/IRENA/Agency/Statistics/Statistical_Profiles/Africa/Madagascar_Africa_RE_SP.pdf (accessed 04-09-2023).

What explains these allocation choices to a country with such pressing infrastructure needs? First, as a desperately poor country, much assistance is given to address immediate humanitarian concerns and, like the FSM, to provide basic social services. This pattern is reflective of an LDC-trap. Countries need economic infrastructure to promote private sector development, but if they are mired in poverty donors' first reaction will be to alleviate those primary needs. They end up receiving handouts rather than hand-ups.[52] Humanitarian aid is both crucial and is often effective.[53] However, it too can fall prey to politicization—being driven by the same logics as other types of development assistance.[54] Partly, this is likely to reflect that, to the extent that many donor publics think about development and development assistance, getting food into the hands of starving children is what they picture, due, no doubt, to the extensive use of these images in NGO fundraising advertisements.[55] But it is also likely to reflect the fact that such aid brings immediate, measurable, results that will garner domestic political support. Using taxpayer money to keep children from starving is an easier sell than using it is to subsidize the construction of an energy system that will power a textile plant that may threaten jobs at the mill in a donor politician's constituency. Beyond this, US food aid, of which Madagascar is a major recipient, also happens to benefit US farmers. US food aid programs, the "Food for Peace" program, run "in kind," meaning that, rather than sending a country funds with which to purchase food on an open market, instead supply the country with food directly.[56] This acts both as a price support for US farmers, but can also potentially distort the local market, by depressing local food prices, although the evidence for this latter impact is tenuous.[57]

Madagascar also receives a disproportionately large share of its aid, especially from the United States, for environmental projects due to the

[52] United Nations Conference on Trade and Development. (2019). *The Least Developed Countries Report 2019: The Present and Future of External Development Finance—Old Dependence, New Challenges.* United Nations.

[53] Miliband, D. and Gurumurthy, R. (2015). Improving humanitarian aid: How to make relief more efficient and effective. *Foreign Affairs, 94*(4), 118–129.

[54] Dany, C. (2015). Politicization of humanitarian aid in the European Union. *European Foreign Affairs Review, 20*(3).

[55] Vossen, M., van Gorp, B., and Schulpen, L. (2018). In search of the pitiful victim: A frame analysis of Dutch, Flemish and British newspapers and NGO-advertisements. *Journal of International Development, 30*(4), 643–660.

[56] Barrett, C. B. (1998). Food aid: Is it development assistance, trade promotion, both, or neither? *American Journal of Agricultural Economics, 80*(3), 566–571; Andriantseheno, B. (2011). The Environmental/Rural Development and Food Security Program in Madagascar. *Influencing Change*, 141.

[57] Abdulai, A., Barrett, C. B., and Hoddinott, J. (2005). Does food aid really have disincentive effects? New evidence from sub-Saharan Africa. *World Development, 33*(10), 1689–1704.

massive range of (endemic) biodiversity on the island. Yet, while conservation is no doubt important, who are the beneficiaries of these efforts? While keeping an environment healthy certainly benefits its residents, biodiversity efforts in Madagascar have also been directed toward finding commercially useful resources. One such effort, the International Cooperative Biodiversity Group (ICBG), was funded by the US government via the National Institute for Health and multinational pharmaceutical giant Bristol-Meyers Squibb. The project found promising new drug compounds and, at the same time, was able to conserve forests for "future generations to use and enjoy."[58] While the effort is no doubt appreciated, the current generations who subsist on less than two dollars per day might have had different ideas about how scarce development funds be put to use.

The People's Republic of China has also been present as a development partner in Madagascar, committing some $800 million in projects between 2003 and 2017. However, unlike in other countries, the bulk of these project commitments have been classified as "ODA-like," suggesting that the PRC also provides more concessional financing to poorer countries. However, like the other donors in country (and unlike the PRC's efforts elsewhere), the PRC's projects also largely focus on social infrastructure and services. The country made just one pledge for a major energy project, a $150 million commitment for a hydroelectric plant in 2016, that appeared to be underway as of 2020.[59] While this project had previously been investigated by USAID in 1986, and the World Bank in 2014, each ultimately declined to fund the project.

Like the FSM, Madagascar, while receiving roughly $1 billion per year in development assistance since the late 1990s, has failed to translate that aid into the tools needed to foster and develop an export-oriented private sector. While the per capita aid received by Madagascar pales in comparison with the FSM, in both countries aid has focused disproportionately on the social sectors and, in the case of Madagascar, humanitarian needs. While it is difficult to argue against providing funding for basic food or rudimentary health and education, the prolonged malaise of the Magalsay economy suggests an alternative is needed—perhaps by increasing other types of aid that are more effective. Without the tools to take advantage of the broad market access

[58] Cao, S. and Kingston, D. G. (2009). Biodiversity conservation and drug discovery: Can they be combined? The Suriname and Madagascar experiences. *Pharmaceutical Biology*, *47*(8), 809–823 (p. 821).
[59] https://www.facebook.com/189232005248268/posts/china-international-water-electric-corp-cwe-a-subsidiary-of-ctg-signed-an-epc-co/753129865525143/ (accessed 06-09-2023).

afforded the country under the EBA and AGOA there seems little rationale for even providing those preferences.

Also, despite being larger than Micronesia, Madagascar has perhaps an even less advantageous position in the international system. Its geographic positioning is not overly important—globally or regionally—from either a security or economic standpoint. It is not proximate to other dynamic markets. Likewise, given its remoteness from major donor countries, it does not generate the spillovers which might prompt donors to targeted development efforts aimed at boosting the country's own economy. The international positioning gives Madagascar very little agency with which to exercise in its dealings with its development partners.

What's Missing?

Vietnam and Indonesia were able to make the most of the market access they did have because their trade-effective aid provided their industries with the tools to enter a global market. In the FSM and Madagascar, however, a lack of trade-effective aid was compounded by an absence of meaningful market access in the areas where the countries had existing advantage—fisheries and agriculture, respectively. Why then did the FSM and Madagascar fail to secure this aid and access, when others like Vietnam and Indonesia have? Structurally, the latter countries are clearly of greater strategic and economic importance than the former, at least in the periods under study. The absence of that geostrategic importance meant that, even if the FSM and Malagasy governments had sufficient capacity, neither country was afforded the agency to overcome domestic political barriers in donor countries and markets to their effective aid and meaningful access. When American Samoa argued against Micronesian Tuna canning, the FSM has little choice but to accept the will of the US Congress, lest they lose out on the aid that was explicitly tied to this market access. When the EU put in place SPS regulations that impacted coffee production, perhaps to protect domestic grape producers, Madagascar could do little but watch as they had no negotiating or scientific heft to counter the EU's claims.

Likewise, whereas Indonesia and Vietnam had attracted the interest of a number of relatively equally sized donors who specialized their aid, the FSM, and to a lesser extent Madagascar, were dominated by their largest donors. Moreover, the donors which did operate in both countries often duplicated many of their efforts—reflective of a lack of both effective international agency and governance capacity in each of the countries. Again, donors made political choices to focus on these sectors, but, likely inadvertently, this led to aid ecosystems that were ineffective in providing the tools to support export-led development.

8

Begging Thy Neighbor

The Grass between Two Elephants

In the mid-1980s, a young man named Rajan Khadka[1] opened a factory on the outskirts of Kathmandu to take advantage of a growing industry fueled by access to the United States garment market as a result of preferential access through GSP during the period of the Multi-Fiber Agreement (MFA). Nearly two decades later, the now middle-aged factory owner found himself inside his locked office, sitting across from four union representatives from the Maoist Communist Party of Nepal. The factory had been losing money for years, but the recent upsurge in Maoist activity that had led to an increasing number of labor disturbances that made business untenable. Now, all the owner wanted to do was to close his factory and wind down his business, but strict severance laws meant that he would face a potentially crushing liability in order to go out of business. He knew that the Maoist union leaders held the key to the terms the remaining workers would accept. Asking their demands, the Maoists first insisted on 24 months of severance pay, despite the fact some of them had only been working at the factory for six months. Ultimately, he was able to negotiate a six-month severance package with the four leaders—on the condition that they sign an attestation that they only received two months. The owner then showed this document to the remaining factory workers and, as a result, was able to afford to wind up his business by paying everyone two months' severance.

While the Maoist insurgency forced the closure of Mister Khadka's factory, along with scores of others, it was only the final nail for a coffin that had already been sealing shut. Maoist activity had contributed to rising labor costs for years, but the bigger threat to Nepalese manufacturers was coming from development in neighboring countries: India, Bangladesh, Vietnam, Pakistan, Cambodia. High-quality Nepalese Pashmina was under pressure from previously inferior Indian competition. Consumers had lost the differentiation between Nepali hand-woven carpets and machine-produced substitutes

[1] Name has been changed to project identify of the respondent.

The Invisible Hand(out). Samuel Brazys, Oxford University Press. © Samuel Brazys (2025).
DOI: 10.1093/9780198970422.003.0008

from China or Turkey and Nepalese jewelry and lower-purity Indian silver were crafted in a similar style. Nepalese garment manufacturers were unable to compete with low-cost Bangladeshi counterparts following the expiration of quotas the MFA.

Nepal is a hard case for development. Landlocked and mountainous, it lacks natural resources beyond its spectacular Himalayan beauty and has both a landmass and population that are dwarfed by its neighbors. Entirely surrounded by the two most populous nations on Earth, a local saying is that "Nepal is the grass between two elephants." With complex historical ties to India, Nepal has found itself in an increasingly delicate position as a (partial) buffer between the two nuclear capable giants of Asia. Maintaining economic ties, while also balancing both autonomy and strategic positioning, requires a delicate balancing act. Internally, the country has been subject to decades of Maoist insurgency and unrest and was left devastated by the massive earthquake in 2015.

Nepal is also one of the poorest countries in Asia, with a per capita income that is just at the threshold of least developed country (LDC) status, leading only Afghanistan in the region and roughly on par with the Kyrgyz Republic. While this real GDP per capita has doubled from a very low base in the mid-1990s, average annual growth since 1980 has measured only 2.8%.[2] While this may be a respectable figure for a mature, high-income, economy, it is low for a low-income country. While other countries across the globe have fared worse than Nepal, its developmental success has been marginal at best. In 1972, Nepal's GDP per capita was nearly identical to its massive neighbor to the south, India, and not vastly off of its neighbor across the Siliguri Corridor, Bangladesh. Nepal managed to roughly keep pace with these two economies until the early 1990s, but soon lost ground, with a GDP per capita figure that was less than 60% of India's, and 65% of Bangladesh's, by 2019.

This divergence in income is mirrored by a divergence in the composition of these three economies. In 1980, the value added from manufacturing accounted for only 4% of Nepal's GDP, compared to 14% in Bangladesh and 17% in India. Over the coming decade, Nepal would increase its value-added share of manufacturing to 9% of GDP, whilst Bangladesh and India remained at roughly the 14 to 16% level. However, by the early 2000s, Nepal's share was again falling, reverting to 4% by 2020. These trends were also reflected in the broader industrial sector, which includes construction, where value added rose from a base of 11.2% of GDP in 1980 to a peak of 21.5% in 1996, before

[2] World Bank https://data.worldbank.org/indicator/NY.GDP.PCAP.KD?locations=NP (accessed 23-05-2022).

falling back to 11.8% in 2020. In contrast, both Bangladesh and India have had value-added shares above 20% of GDP since 1980, with peaks at or near 30% in 2010s.

The vignette and descriptive statistics above are meant to illustrate that, despite its inherent disadvantages in geography and population, Nepal was on a very similar development path to its near neighbors well into the 1990s. Yet since that time, it has fallen significantly behind. While tales of competition and creative destruction are as old as markets, this chapter will illustrate how Nepal's changing fortunes were not the result of an unfettered market but instead were very much the (unintended?) consequence of changing aid and access not only in Nepal, but also in her neighbors and peers, in addition to domestic turmoil at a critical juncture moment.

This chapter draws on data from a survey of 148, and in-depth interviews with 21, Nepalese exporters, conducted in 2016, as well as micro-level data on AfT projects from AidData. The chapter focuses on two sectors, textiles and jewelry, to show how access and aid initiatives that paved the way for development in India, Bangladesh, and elsewhere brought success to those places at the expense of existing Nepalese enterprises. The implication of this chapter is that decisions about aid and access not only have direct impacts on those who do and do not receive it, but they can also have indirect impacts by distorting markets in a second-best world. As Viner's analysis makes clear, trade diversion, or in this case trade reversion, is an engineered outcome that results from the natural progression from a series of policy choices.[3] Using aid and access to promote exports by fostering comparative advantage in one country will necessitate the loss of comparative advantage elsewhere. This can have meaningful consequences wherein pushing development success forward in one state requires holding it back in another.

Trade Reversion—Preferences Giveth and Preferences Taketh Away

At first glance, the market access arrangements for Nepal, India, and Bangladesh look similar. The Chapter 3 dynamic indicators have all three countries in the SE quadrant (low meaningful market access, high effective aid) from the 1980s on. From a market access perspective, all three countries are eligible for the GSP under the WTO's enabling clause and all belong to the South Asian Preferential Trade Agreement (SAPTA) and the South Asian

[3] Viner, J. (2014). *The Customs Union Issue.* Oxford University Press.

Free Trade Agreement (SAFTA). However, a closer look reveals some marked differences. Most notably, both India and Bangladesh have been members of the GATT/WTO since the establishment of their states in 1948 and 1972, respectively, while Nepal only joined the WTO in 2004. However, while all three countries are eligible for GSP under the enabling clause, and Nepal has had access to the sub-schemes from least developed countries from both the United States and Europe. India has completed a dozen bilateral RTAs since 2000, while Nepal only has one (with India) and Bangladesh has none.

Yet perhaps the most important piece of market access with respect to this South Asian trio is the Multi-Fiber Agreement and its successor the Agreement on Textiles and Clothing (ATC). As described in Chapter 4, the MFA was a framework which legitimated quantitative restrictions on different types of textiles that the United States and others (the EC) had had in place, in some instances, since the 1950s. Under the auspices of the MFA, countries could either bilaterally agree to quotas, or exporters could impose voluntary export restraints (VERs). Nepal was allocated quotas to major developed markets, including the United States and European Union (Community). Quotas on other producers, including India and Bangladesh, were sufficiently "binding" (i.e., the countries would have produced more in their absence) while Nepal's quotas to the United States were the largest in South Asia such that Nepal became a significant producer and exporter under the MFA.[4] The uptick in Nepalese textile production in the 1980s and into the 1990s is largely attributable to these quotas, and, in particular, textile firms from other countries where quotas were binding setting up shop in Nepal.[5] When the MFA expired, Nepal became the victim of what has been coined "trade revision"—a reversal of trade diversion based on the loss of preferential access.[6] Several (former) exporters explicitly cited the expiration of the MFA (ATC) as the reasons their export operations declined (or ceased).[7]

The phase-out of the MFA (ATC) in 2005, and the MFN rates of the Uruguay round, leveled the playing field between Nepal and its neighbors. While lacking seaport access, the country had an established industry and a large, cheap, labor force. Indeed, analyses of the times suggested that Nepal

[4] https://docs.wto.org/gattdocs/q/GG/COMTEXSB/377.PDF (accessed 08-09-2023); Shakya, M. (2018). *Death of an Industry: The Cultural Politics of Garment Manufacturing during the Maoist Revolution in Nepal.* Cambridge University Press; Yao, D. and Whalley, J. (2015). *Assessing the Effects of the MFA/ATC from US and World Trade Data after Its Removal* (No. w21299). National Bureau of Economic Research.

[5] International Monetary Fund. Vol. 1996. Issue 063. https://doi.org/10.5089/9781451829853.002.

[6] Deardorff, A. V. (2014). Trade implications of the Trans-Pacific Partnership for ASEAN and other Asian countries. *Asian Development Review, 31*(2), 1–20.

[7] Interview N-1012.

and Bangladesh would suffer equally from the phase out as production was expected to shift to India and China.[8] Yet, since 2005, while the Indian textile industry has expanded, the clear winner has been Bangladesh, who has become one of the largest exporters of ready-made garments (RMG) in the world. Conversely, Nepal has suffered immensely. Why was Bangladesh able to capitalize on the end of the MFA while Nepal's textile industries largely disappeared? Given that by 2004, their de jure market access was effectively identical, the next sections argue that Bangladesh received effective aid which allowed it to turn its de jure arrangement into meaningful market access, Nepal did not.

A secondary industry in which Nepal suffered trade-reversionary effects is in its production of carpets. By the late 1980s, carpets had become the major export industry for the country, accounting for 60% of exports by the early 1990s.[9] These exports were largely credited to the preference margin Nepal received compared to the MFN rate under its GSP access. However, the Uruguay round cut the MFN rate on most carpet products (HS 57), to 0%.[10] As in textiles, Nepal's market share of carpet exports collapsed. Nepal's ongoing access under GSP, particularly under the European Union's EBA and the United States' GSP scheme for least developed beneficiary countries provided some shelter from these market shifts in other sectors. In 2016, numerous Nepalese exporters credited the GSP schemes with providing the necessary market access for their goods.[11] However, the LDC GSP schemes were unable to save Nepal from this trade reversion in carpets. Moreover, in the United States, textiles are largely excluded from the GSP under General Note 4. Likewise, while the EU's EBA does provide duty-free access for textiles, these goods historically entered under the EU's more stringent rules of origin (ROO), although these have been relaxed recently.[12] Compliance with these rules can be complicated and some firms can find them as a significant barrier to entry.[13]

Beyond India and Bangladesh, a third competitor is Nepal's elephant to the north—the People's Republic of China (PRC). The PRC's accession to the WTO coincided with the winding down of the MFA/ATC and the preferential access Nepal enjoyed under those schemes. While Bangladesh ended

[8] Van Heerden, A., Berhouet, P., and Caspari, C. (2003). *Rags or Riches? Phasing-out the Multi-Fibre Arrangement* (No. 993587893402676). International Labour Organization.
[9] International Monetary Fund. Vol. 1996.
[10] Ibid.
[11] Interviews N-1382; N-9000; N-1523; N-9001.
[12] Dhakal, D. (2014). *Impact of Quota Phase Out in Garment Industry of Nepal* (Master's thesis).
[13] Khanal, D. R. (2011). Rules of origin in GSP schemes and their impact on Nepal's exports: a case study of tea, carpets, pashmina and handicrafts products. Asia-Pacific Research and Training Network on Trade Working Paper Series, No. 98.

up capturing the market in RMGs, newly MFN PRC put pressure on several other industries, including pashmina—a type of fine cashmere goat wool—where the PRC made a "different" (but cheaper) pashmina,[14] handicrafts,[15] and carpet.[16] While many Nepalese exporters maintained that their products were of higher quality, they noted that they could not compete with the PRC on price when the customers didn't know or didn't care about the quality difference.[17]

Nepal's one bilateral trade agreement is with its largest trading partner, India, who dominates the market for Nepalese exports.[18] First signed in 1971, the agreement has been renewed many times since, most recently in 2009. However, the benefits of this agreement are questionable.[19] It was under this agreement that India was able to facilitate access for its firms to invest in Nepal to take advantage of the latter's quotas under the MFA. At other times, the agreement has been used by India to import key inputs from Nepal. However, India's vast market share leads some to worry that Nepal faces a situation of trade domination which leaves it vulnerable to coercion from its southern Elephant.[20] Beyond this, one exporter noted how the same trade reversion that happened with the European and US textile and carpet markets, also happened with India. As India has signed regional or bilateral trade agreements with other trading partners in the Global South, such as Sri Lanka, Nepal's tariff preferences have been eroded, leading to a loss of market share in the Indian market.[21]

Collectively, these dynamics have led to a continuing worsening of Nepal's meaningful market access since the 1990s. The dynamic measure in Chapter 3 ranked Nepal in the 78th percentile of meaningful market access in the 1960s. This dropped to just under the 50th percentile by the 1990s and to less than the 10th percentile by the 2010s. The period from the 1990s to the 2010s represents a critical juncture for Nepal, both due to the Uruguay round and MFA phase out, which led to the loss of key preferential market access, but also due to the Maoist insurgency which significantly diminished the state's capacity, as discussed further below.

[14] Interview N-9001; N-1595.
[15] Interview N-1594; N-1584.
[16] Interview N-1408; N-1401.
[17] Interview N-1595.
[18] UN Comtrade.
[19] Taneja, N., Chowdhury, S., and Prakash, S. (2011). India–Nepal economic cooperation: Towards a new paradigm. *India Quarterly*, *67*(2), 129–147.
[20] Chand, D. (2018). Trade embargo as a geopolitical tool: a case of Nepal-India trade relations. *Polish Political Science Review*, *6*(1), 50–67.
[21] Interview N-1021.

Aid, but Not for Trade. It's Electric!

In addition to market access woes, two recurring internal factors arose that put a damper on export activity—labor costs and energy access. Both issues were mentioned by multiple exporters as explicit causes for scaling back or ceasing production, and/or being unable to expand production to meet demand. Increased labor costs were at times linked to the Maoist pressures,[22] but were also often linked to a labor supply shortage caused by workers heading abroad for employment, particularly to the Middle East.[23] However, an even greater number of exporters noted problems with utility supply, especially electricity. These problems resulted both from insufficient mains supply,[24] but also from shortages which led to insufficient diesel supply for backup generators.[25] Without reliable electricity supplies, some firms were unable to scale up production to meet the demand for large orders, or could only meet orders with some delay[26] as frequent blackouts meant that firms might only have supply for a few hours each day.[27] Such delays invariably led to customer frustration,[28] which, in at least one instance, led to a customer to switching to suppliers in India.[29] One firm went to the extreme measure of having employees come to work at 2am to polish jewelry, as this was the only time there was a reliable electric supply.[30] As a result of these constraints, a number of firms noted the difficulty in filling larger orders.[31]

Utility supply and, to a lesser extent, labor are issues which could be remedied by trade-effective aid. A review of AidData's Nepal research release identifies a total of 146 AfT projects from 1997 to 2013. Of these, 17 were focused on building electricity capacity. Of these projects, seven were funded by the Asian Development Bank (ADB), and one each by Japan, Germany, Korea, Norway, the EU, the World Bank (International Development Association), and the Netherlands. A further three projects were co-founded by Denmark and Norway, the Netherlands and the UK, and the ADB and Norway. As shown in Figure 8.1, together with exporting firms these electricity projects were broadly distributed across the country. However, as also shown

[22] Interview N-1400; N-1233.
[23] Interview N-9001; N-1639; Interview N-1382.
[24] Interview N-1170.
[25] Interview N-1134; N-1610.
[26] Interview N-1400; N-1090.
[27] Interview N-1610.
[28] Interview N-1170.
[29] Interview N-1615.
[30] Ibid.
[31] Interviews N-1382; N-9000; N-1400; N-1090; N-1339; N-1170; N-1610; N-1523.

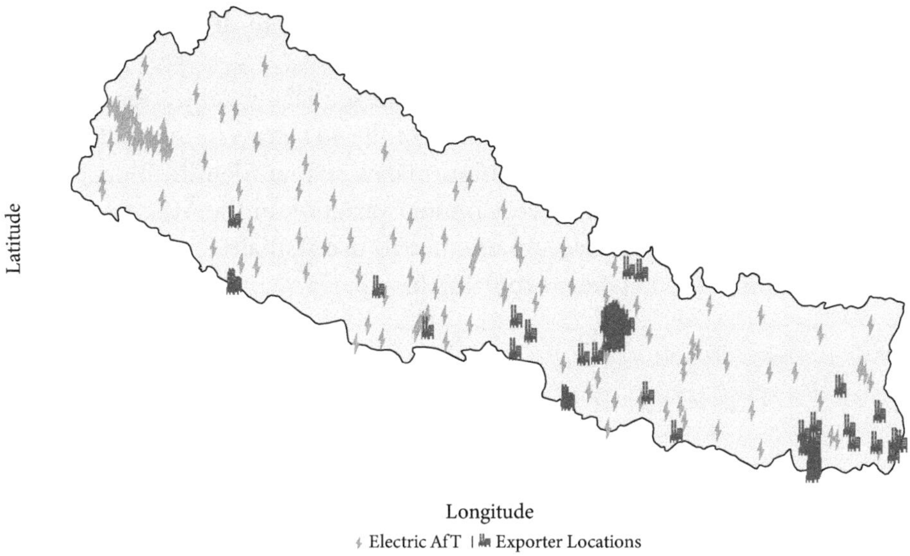

Figure 8.1 Exporters and electric AfT in Nepal

in Figure 8.1, exporting firms were far more concentrated, particularly in the Kathmandu and Biratnagar metropolitan areas.

The exporting firms in this map were identified using the exporter directory of the Nepal Trade and Export Promotion Centre. As of 2016, this directory contained 864 firms. As all firms must legally register with this body, this likely provides a good snapshot of the population of exporting firms at that time. Locations were identified for 537 of these firms and contact information for 624. All firms with contact information were contacted between February and May of 2016. A total of 148 successful contacts were made, with the remaining firms being uncontactable or having contact information that was invalid or out of date. Of the 148 firms contacted, 131 agreed to take part in a short survey. The survey asked if firms were exporting and, if so, if their exports had increased, decreased, or stayed the same over the preceding five years. Forty of the firms indicated they had either gone out of business or had stopped exporting, while a further 62 indicated they had experienced a decrease in exports, compared to 12 who reported their exports had been largely unchanged and 17 who reported increased exports. Overall, 44 of the survey respondents were carpet firms and a further 39 were in some form of textile industry (cotton or jute yarn, ready-made garments (RMG) of pashmina, silk, synthetics, or other textile materials). Jewelry or imitation jewelry exporters accounted for a further 16 firms, while the remaining firms produced and exported products ranging from beer to dry cell batteries to essential oils to copper winding wire.

The responding firms had a high degree of spatial concentration in Kathmandu, as shown in Figure 8.2, with 113 of the 131 firms in the Kathmandu metropolitan area. This concentration makes spatial identification of AfT effects difficult as there is only very limited variation in the AfT "treatment" status of firms in the sample. An attempt to use spatial techniques to analyze the relationship between exporting firm performance and AfT projects

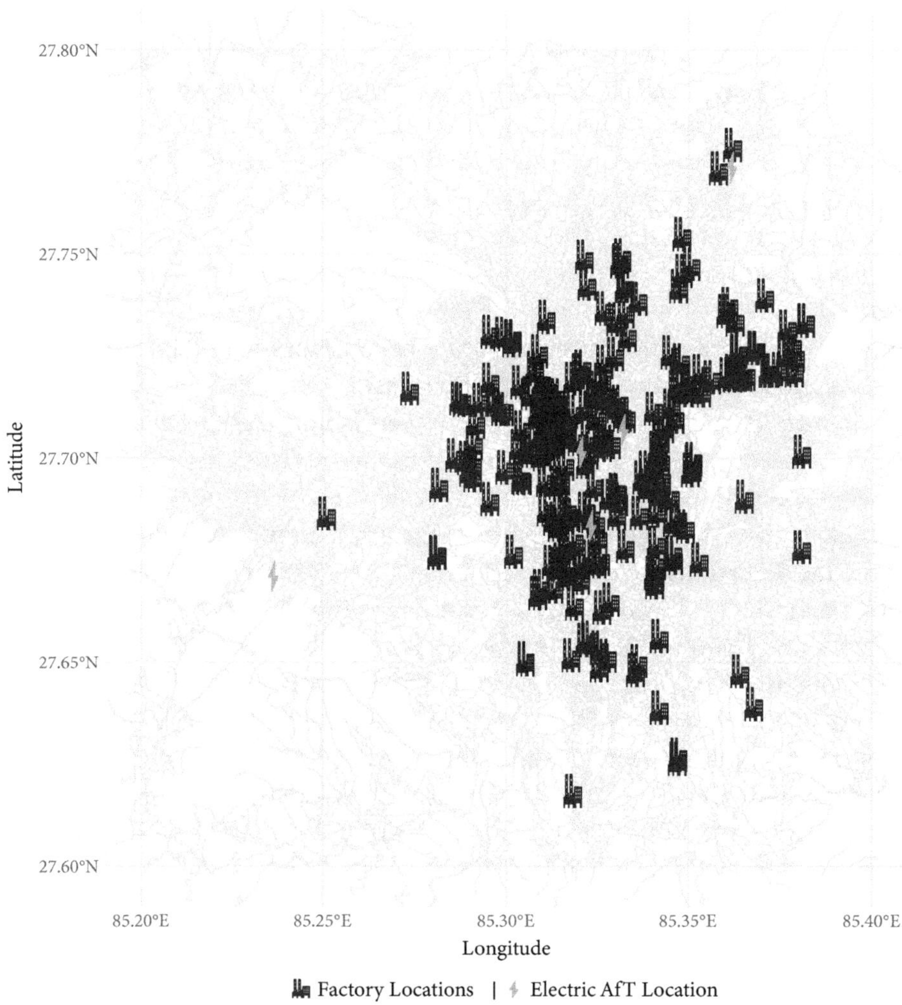

Figure 8.2 Exporters and electric AfT in the Kathmandu vicinity

conducted with Johan Elkink found only qualified support of a relationship.[32] Specifically, while finding some support for a positive impact of AfT on export performance when considering counts of AfT projects within a certain radii, and qualified evidence that some individual projects could be associated with greater export performance, the study nevertheless cautioned that these results "could still well be driven by idiosyncratic artefacts of our data."[33] As such, only descriptive observations are made here from that data.

The geographic distribution of electricity AfT projects in Figure 8.1 would suggest that exporting firms were broadly in proximity to these supply projects. Indeed, of the 537 exporting firms with location information identified from the exporter directory, the average distance to an electricity AfT project was 3.68 kilometers. For the 70 firms outside the Kathmandu area, the average distance was 13.03 kilometers, with a maximum distance of 31 kilometers. This proximity would suggest that nearly every exporting firm in Nepal would have been within a reasonable catchment to benefit from these AfT projects. Likewise, of the 131 survey respondents, the average distance to an electricity AfT project was 3.74 kilometers increasing to 14.20 kilometers for the 18 firms outside the Kathmandu area.

Yet despite this proximity, many firms still noted electricity as a production constraint. Of the 131 surveyed firms, in-depth interviews were conducted with 21 firms between May 9 and May 13, 2016. Ten of these firms explicitly mentioned electricity supply problems as a hinderance to exporting. Table 8.1 shows the distance to the nearest electricity AfT project (rounded to the nearest kilometer), the name and donor of that project, and the sector and export performance of each of these firms. The interviewed firms that mentioned electricity as an export hinderance were all reasonably close to an electricity AfT project, with proximity ranging from 1 to 7 kilometers. However, only two of the 10 firms reported increases in exports over the period from 2011 to 2016. Notably, while both of these firms were within 1 km of the nearest electricity AfT project, both also were in the textile sector but each was proximate to a different project. In contrast, all firms in both the carpet and jewelry sector saw decreased exports.

Looking more broadly at the 131 surveyed firms, in addition to the three electricity projects in Table 8.1, one additional project, the "Energy Access

[32] Brazys, S. and Elkink, J. A. (2021). "Aid for Trade" effectiveness? Micro-level evidence from Nepal. *The European Journal of Development Research*, 33, 1493–1513.
[33] Ibid, p. 1507.

Table 8.1 Firms distance to electric AfT

ID	Distance	Project Name	Donor	Sector	Exports
1170	6 km	Assistance for Feasibility Studies of Small and Medium Size Hydro Power Projects	Norway	Textiles	Decreased
1134	1 km	Introduction of Clean Energy by Solar Electricity Generation System	Japan	Textiles	Increased
1400	2 km	Introduction of Clean Energy by Solar Electricity Generation System	Japan	Carpet	Decreased
1408	7 km	Assistance for Feasibility Studies of Small and Medium Size Hydro Power Projects	Norway	Carpet	Decreased
1090	1 km	Assistance for Feasibility Studies of Small and Medium Size Hydro Power Projects	Norway	Textiles	Increased
1339	1 km	Electricity Transmission Expansion and Supply Improvement Project (ETESIP)	ADB /Norway	Carpet	Decreased
1610	2 km	Introduction of Clean Energy by Solar Electricity Generation System	Japan	Jewelry	Decreased
1623	2 km	Electricity Transmission Expansion and Supply Improvement Project (ETESIP)	ADB /Norway	Jewelry	Decreased
1523	4 km	Introduction of Clean Energy by Solar Electricity Generation System	Japan	Carpet	Decreased
1233	2 km	Electricity Transmission Expansion and Supply Improvement Project (ETESIP)	ADB /Norway	Other	Decreased

and Efficiency Improvement Project," funded by the Asian Development Bank was also the project most proximate to eight of the surveyed firms. As seen in Table 8.2 of these four projects, the "Electricity Transmission Expansion and Supply Improvement Project" (ETESIP), co-funded by Norway and the Asian Development Bank (ADB), is the clear outlier with respect to performance, with 16 of the 51 firms to which it was the closest electricity project reporting "increase" or "stay the same" with respect to exports. A mix of grants and concessional loans, this project included $19 million in grant funding from the ADB, $25 million in grant funding from Norway, a $56 million concessional loan from the ADB and a $250,000 consultancy TA from the ADB. The project focused on improving electricity transmission capacity,

Table 8.2 Electricity projects in closest proximity to surveyed firms

Project Name	Firms	Non-declining
Assistance for Feasibility Studies of Small and Medium Size Hydro Power Projects	53	15.1%
Energy Access and Efficiency Improvement Project	8	25%
Introduction of Clean Energy by Solar Electricity Generation System	19	18.8%
Electricity Transmission Expansion and Supply Improvement Project	51	31.3%

particularly along the Tamakoshi (Khimti)-Kathmandu 220/400kV transmission line, as well as some small hydro-electric powerplant rehabilitation.[34] The main transmission line runs from Tamakohsi (New Khimiti) in the east and skirting north to Kathmandu and then Ratmate. While the project was intended to enhance national connectivity and interconnection, including helping in the transmission of imported power from India, it is still reasonable that firms closest to the main project would be most likely to benefit as they would have needed less infrastructure in terms of secondary transmission lines between themselves and the main line. Of the 16 firms for which this was the most-proximate electricity project and had exports that increased or stayed the same, one was a firm that was interviewed in depth. While the representative of this firm expressed grievances about the government and reported having to pay bribes to secure VAT refunds, they reported no problems with regards to production, electricity-related or otherwise.[35] Of the 35 firms to which this was the most proximate electricity project that reported declining exports, four were in the interview population. Of these four, three reported problems with electricity supply as a hindrance to production,[36] while one explicitly noted no issues with electricity supply.[37] While this performance isn't overly inspiring for the effectiveness of the ETESIP project, closer examination shows that while the project was commenced in 2012, and expected to conclude in 2017, both grants and the loans were revised in their closing dates until 2023, 11 years after the project commitment. Thus, it is at least plausible that by the time of the surveys and interviews in the spring of 2016, the project had not yet been fully implemented and its benefits were not yet felt by the proximate firms.

[34] https://www.adb.org/projects/41155-013/main#project-pds (accessed 30-05-2022).
[35] Interview N-1584.
[36] Interview N-1233; N-1339; N-1623.
[37] Interview N-1639.

The ETESIP and other projects show that it was known and appreciated that electricity supply was a problem in Nepal and considerable resources were being dedicated to address it. Indeed, in the Chapter 3 "effective aid" measure Nepal scores quite well—ranging from the 75th to 91st percentiles from the 1980s to 2010s. However, despite the considerable resource directed to an important trade-related needs area, as of 2016 many exporting firms were still reporting issues with electricity supply, despite ostensible proximity to one or more electricity supply AfT projects. This points to several considerations. First, the scope and scale of electricity supply problems in Nepal are so large that even effective AfT efforts and projects may not be able to solve the problem for a large number of exporting firms. Despite total financial commitments for $450 million for the 17 projects identified in the data as of 2012, a recent World Bank report suggested that $1.3 to $2.1 billion in electricity investment would be required annually from 2018 to 2020.[38] The total, aggregate, committed amount from the 17 projects equals just 35% of the low end of one year's worth of investment and just 2% of investment needs over a 20-year period. The scale of electricity AfT projects in Nepal to date is simply a drop in the ocean of the total investment needed.

Second, it is possible the projects are trade effective but the temporal lag between commitment and disbursement is so long that the results have not yet been fully realized and had yet to impact firms that were surveyed and interviewed in 2016. Of the 16 projects in the data for which there is a recorded start date, 11 of these began in 2010 or later, while two others began in 2008 and 2009. If a number of these projects experienced delays like the ETESIP project, then they too would not have been fully implemented by the time of the firm survey in 2016. Indeed, of the $450 million committed to electricity projects by 2012, only $306 million had been disbursed by the same year. Even then, there is likely to be some further delay between financial disbursement and the full functioning and commissioning of the project. For the ETESIP project, only $5.2 million was recorded as disbursed by 2012.

Third, it could be that the projects simply weren't effective in getting electricity supply to exporting firms. The "last mile" problem in infrastructure, particularly for utilities, suggests that while firms or households could be in relative proximity to "heavy" infrastructure in terms of high-voltage

[38] https://kathmandupost.com/29/2019/09/18/nepal-needs-to-increase-investments-in-energy-by-fourfold-world-bank-says (accessed 30-05-2022).

transmission lines or substations, there still may be an infrastructure gap in getting a connection at a particular residence or firm.[39] While this problem is typically thought of more in the context of rural utility provision, recent work has documented that the reliability of electricity connections at the distribution-substation level in Nepal displays characteristics of a common pool resource.[40] Illegal connections can deprive local utility providers of the revenues needed to properly maintain substations and local distribution networks.[41] Such problems have also been identified as being indicative of low government capacity in a number of different settings.[42] While the Nepalese government may have had sufficient capacity to work with firms and donors to identify energy as an area for aid investment, they may have lacked the capacity to identify and implement the projects in the "last mile." In these instances, even if grid-level production and transmission capacity has been improved (via AfT or other investment), local connections, including firms, still may face reliability problems.

The reality of the problems facing firms with respect to electricity supply is likely to contain a mix of these three explanations. Yet, focusing on AfT directed to electricity one would be hard-pressed to say Nepal was neglected in this regard. Substantial attention and resources were paid to this area by international donor partners. Certainly, these efforts have increased the availability and reliability of electricity in the country. However, for many firms, these efforts still do not appear to be enough. This result again shows that aid, even aid that may be trade effective, is no panacea when considering macro-level outcomes. In the face of deteriorating market conditions vis-à-vis their competitors, even well-targeted AfT initiatives are unable to provide a sufficient boost, nationally, to offset the countervailing influences. Thus, once again aid, or at least aid alone, is insufficient to increase competitiveness and secure broad-based development.

[39] Barrie, J. and Cruickshank, H. J. (2017). Shedding light on the last mile: A study on the diffusion of Pay As You Go Solar Home Systems in Central East Africa. *Energy Policy*, *107*, 425–436.

[40] Hashemi, M. and Jenkins, G. (2022). Can privatization of distribution substations improve electricity reliability for non-residential customers? An application to Nepal. *Utilities Policy*, *74*, 101331.

[41] Burgess, R., Greenstone, M., Ryan, N., and Sudarshan, A. (2020). The consequences of treating electricity as a right. *Journal of Economic Perspectives*, *34*(1), 145–169.

[42] Makonese, T., Kimemia, D. K., and Annegarn, H. J. (2012, April). Assessment of free basic electricity and use of pre-paid meters in South Africa. In *2012 Proceedings of the 20th Domestic Use of Energy Conference* (pp. 165–172). IEEE; Bremer, J. and Bhuiyan, S. H. (2014). Community-led infrastructure development in informal areas in urban Egypt: A case study. *Habitat International*, *44*, 258–267; Salite, D., Kirshner, J., Cotton, M., Howe, L., Cuamba, B., Feijó, J., and Macome, A. Z. (2021). Electricity access in Mozambique: A critical policy analysis of investment, service reliability and social sustainability. *Energy Research & Social Science*, *78*, 102123.

Maoists in the Countryside—Domestic Capacity Matters!

In understanding Nepal's growth struggles, it is important to understand the domestic political context of Nepal. Most of the latter half of the 20th century in the country involved jockeying between monarchists and democrats. While the monarchy was reformed into a royal parliamentary system in 1990, in 1996 the Maoist Communist Party of Nepal launched a violent uprising that claimed over 10,000 lives in a decade-long civil war that ended with a political settlement which ultimately led to the declaration of a federal republic in 2008. However, another seven years would pass before a permanent constitution would be ratified in 2015.

While the Nepalese civil war was initially somewhat limited in scope, it intensified from 2001 to 2006.[43] These years coincided, crucially, with the key period of support of competing industries in India and Bangladesh and the market access disruptions due to the phasing out of the MFA. As noted in the vignette at the start of the chapter, this period of insurgency intensification often pushed already struggling firms over the brink. One factory owner noted how, during this period, factories would be captured and the owners locked up. Even firms that simply wanted to close would have to pay remuneration to do so, often via meetings with Maoists in "scary places" where they had to "exchange briefcases."[44] As a result of the insurgency, other factories closed down but didn't officially deregister, instead becoming "zombie firms" which kept permanent employees on the books but simply didn't operate. This enabled these firms to avoid paying severance, but also enabled firms to maintain company names, bank accounts, telephone numbers, etc. which made it easier to reopen upon the subsequent improvement in the political situation.[45] The Maoist insurgency was, without a doubt, disruptive to Nepalese exporters. Yet, of the 21 exporting firms interviewed, only six explicitly mentioned Maoists as a problem for their or others' businesses and only two attributed closing of their factories to the Maoists.[46] Thus, while the civil war and insurgency certainly did not help Nepalese exporters, in combination with changing market access, it certainly contributes to the critical juncture of growth divergence between Nepal and its neighbors from the 1990s to 2010s.

[43] Adhikari, P. and Samford, S. (2013). The Nepali state and the dynamics of the Maoist insurgency. *Studies in Comparative International Development*, *48*(4), 457–481.

[44] Interview N-1339.

[45] Interview N-9001.

[46] Interview N-1021; N-1610.

The more than 20 years of governmental instability, and declining capacity, dating to at least the early 1990s had consequences for exporters in numerous ways. The interviewed exporters had broadly negative opinions on the effectiveness of their government. Many cited problems with tax collection. A common refrain was that if companies were operating profitably, they received extra scrutiny. As one exporter perceived it, the government's attitude is that "if he earns money he must be doing something bad."[47] Another noted how the tax system is an "adversarial system" where the government "expects you to be lying" and, as such, "telling the truth gets you nowhere"[48] while another echoes that the tax authority thinks firms are "hiding profit."[49]

Bribery was also a recurrent theme among the exporters.[50] Although often parsed in euphemism, a surprising number of exporters openly discussed the demanding and paying of bribes. One common refrain was a variant that "rules follow the elephant"[51] or "as the elephant goes, the rules go"[52] as the 1000 Rupee note is adorned with the animal. The same exporter also mentioned the phrase "everyone wants to meet the king"[53] suggesting that that practice is not only recent, as the king featured prominently on an older version of the currency. Other euphemisms included "table money,"[54] "under the table,"[55] "pocket money,"[56] "extra money,"[57] or "giving something."[58] Bribes were mentioned in the context of using "(some) elephants" to obtain Value Added Tax (VAT) refunds,[59] to receive favorable Harmonized Tariff Schedule (HTS) classifications,[60] to expedite processes,[61] or receive product certifications.[62]

Even more widespread was the sentiment that the government was ineffective, incompetent, inattentive, inconsistent, or uncaring. A number of exporters noted a "bad government" that was unable to provide help or

[47] Interview N-9001.
[48] Interview N-1615.
[49] Interview N-1610.
[50] Brazys, S. and Elkink, J. A. (2021). "Aid for Trade" Effectiveness? Micro-level Evidence from Nepal. *The European Journal of Development Research*, 33, 1493–1513.
[51] Interview N-1615.
[52] Interview N-1584.
[53] Interview N-1615.
[54] Interview N-1523.
[55] Interview N-9001.
[56] Interview N-9002.
[57] Interview N-1610.
[58] Interview N-1339.
[59] Interview N-9000; N-1400; N-1339; N-9001.
[60] Interview N-1595.
[61] Interview N-9002.
[62] Interview N-1610.

clarity in navigating bureaucratic processes, either at home or abroad.[63] Many pointed to government inaction, politicians that "speak but don't implement,"[64] the "government was sleeping, (it is) still sleeping,"[65] the government does "nothing to help,"[66] or "the government does nothing."[67] One exporter attributed this to the ongoing political instability, noting how the "not established"[68] government was a problem, a refrain echoed in the observation that "government policies change frequently which makes difficulty."[69] As one exporter expressed esoterically on the effectiveness of the government, "If you have a tree give you sour oranges you have to cut down the tree and plant it again to get sweet oranges."[70] Or, as another put more bluntly, it is best simply to "have as little to do with the government as possible."[71]

Yet, despite the insurgency, political instability, ineffectiveness, and/or malfeasance, domestic factors simply did not appear to ultimately deter exporters. Almost without fail, if exporters received demand, they were able to fulfill their orders despite these domestic political obstacles. For instance, most exporters saw bribery as a nuisance or mild inconvenience rather than a major hindrance to producing or exporting. As one exporter put it, "bribes don't slow business if you have business."[72] Often times, the bribe amounts mentioned were nominal. For instance, when discussing a bribe needed to get a stamp on silver products, one exporter described paying bribes of 100 or 200 Rupees, about $1 or $2 US dollars. Thus, while governance has been both unstable and ineffective in Nepal, it appears to have been a contributing, rather than determinative, factor in the diminishment of the Nepalese export sector. The Maoist insurgency, government corruption, and inaction may often have been a straw on the camel's back that compounded production problems and global market structures.

Aid for Trade Reversion

As Nepal struggled through the critical juncture of diminishing market access and government instability from the 1990s to 2010s, its neighbors

[63] Interview N-1623; N-1610.
[64] Interview N-1233.
[65] Interview N-1021.
[66] Interview N-1610.
[67] Interview N-1401.
[68] Interview N-1090.
[69] Interview N-1595.
[70] Interview N-1584.
[71] Interview N-1615.
[72] Interview N-9000.

Bangladesh and India continued their steady, if not remarkable, growth progressions. During this period, both countries received a number of projects which helped them adapt their textile and carpet industries to the changing market access environment. These projects put in place the tools that enabled India, and especially Bangladesh, to effectively compete on the level playing field following the end of the MFA/ATC. While both countries have received foreign assistance from a multitude of donors, and both have been ranked in the 90th percentile in the Chapter 3 dynamic effective aid measure in all decades, both have also received some very specific supports in these key industries which enabled them to flourish.

Two important players for both countries have been the World Bank and Japan who, since 1995, have been the two largest donors for each of the countries—with the World Bank being the larger in Bangladesh and Japan being the larger in India. In Bangladesh, since 1995, the World Bank group has committed over $30 billion in assistance. Substantial amounts of this assistance has gone toward supporting the textile sector, especially as the World Bank had prognosticated that Bangladesh would suffer greatly from the phase out from the MFA.[73] The World Bank has been active in Bangladesh since before its split from Pakistan in 1971, its first project focusing on railways in 1959, before first turning its attention to textiles with a $21 million jute development project in 1978.[74] However, the Bank's efforts in the area really ramped up in 1980s and 1990s with over a dozen projects worth over $1 billion between 1980 and 1996. While some of these projects, like the "Textile Industry Rehabilitation Projects" were very much focused on industrial development, others, like a raft of "industrial sector credit projects" focused on the financing side of exports.[75] These projects drew particular ire of some Nepalese exporters who lamented the World Bank providing "soft loans" to Bangladeshi firms which provided them a competitive edge.[76] These sector-specific projects also stood along a vast array of projects building economic and public infrastructure.

Bangladesh's second largest donor, Japan, also has committed over $23 billion since 1995. While Japan has historically been a major donor, its assistance jumped markedly from 2013, increasing from an average of just under

[73] World Bank. (2005). End of MFA quotas: Key issues and strategic options for Bangladesh readymade garment industry. *Bangladesh Development Series Paper 2.*

[74] https://projects.worldbank.org/en/projects-operations/project-detail/P009334; https://projects.worldbank.org/en/projects-operations/project-detail/P009386 (accessed 08-09-2023).

[75] https://projects.worldbank.org/en/projects-operations/project-detail/P009421; https://projects.worldbank.org/en/projects-operations/project-detail/P009439; https://projects.worldbank.org/en/projects-operations/project-detail/P009457 (accessed 08-09-2023).

[76] Interviews N-1523; N-1021.

$250 million from 1995 to 2012 to an average of over $2 billion from 2013 to 2021. Like other countries, a significant component of Japan's portfolio in Bangladesh focused on the building of economic infrastructure. As a riparian nation, geographically divided by the massive river (deltas) which flow from the Himalayas to the Bay of Bengal, a major focus of these efforts has been on building bridges to stitch together the country, in addition to building other energy and transportation infrastructure.[77] Many of these large-ticket infrastructure projects have come since 2013, including the Matarbari Ultra Super Critical Coal-Fired Power Project, the Jamuna Railway Bridge Construction Project, and the Hazrat Shahjalal International Airport Expansion Project. Beyond these major infrastructure projects, and while not all in the RMG sector, several Bangladeshi firms, when interviewed, noted favorably that they had participated in smaller-valued Japanese labor training projects.[78]

In some ways, aid to the Bangladeshi industry, and particularly the textile sector, is one of the best examples of trade-effective aid in this book. The country smashed expectations of performance and, like Indonesia and Vietnam, was able to transform level-field MFN market access (in textiles) into meaningful market access via the effective tools built with aid. The combination of sector-specific, and broad-based investment in more general economic infrastructure gave these firms the tools they needed to compete globally with other textile manufacturers. This has enabled the country to become a textile-producing powerhouse and an example of export-led growth. With growth performance since the 2000s that bests Indonesia and rivals Vietnam, Bangladesh is an interesting "deviant" off-the-line case that has appeared to succeed (at least recently) without broad meaningful market access, even if it has received trade-effective aid. However, unlike Vietnam and Indonesia, Bangladesh is very much a one-trick pony. Whereas the Chapter 6 success stories each have a fair degree of sector diversification in the export portfolio, Bangladesh's exports are dominated by textiles—which, on average, account for 80–90% annually of the country's exports. Indeed, firms interviewed outside this sector in Bangladesh would often lament the lack of support their firms received with government export promotion efforts.[79] Ultimately, while Bangladesh certainly "reverted" the textile trade after the end of the MFA, this sector dependence both leaves it vulnerable to further market shifts and also, to some extent, locks it into a growth

[77] Interview B-1001.
[78] Interviews CH-1009; CH-1002; CX-1001.
[79] Interview CH-1003.

model based on the lowest value-added manufacturing sector.[80] Thus, in the coming years Bangladesh could well become a crucial test case. This book's theory would suggest that Bangladesh will be unable to continue its growth success without receiving broader meaningful market access which will allow it to expand its export sectors beyond textiles. Can Bangladesh be the next Vietnam? Only time will tell.

Bangladesh's massive neighbor to the west, India, has also seen impressive aid flows from Japan and the World Bank. Japan's largest ticket items to India are again economic infrastructure, including major investments in road and rail projects, including both passenger and freight rail. However, in India, in addition to Yen-loan projects Japan has also engaged much more directly in sector-level activities compared to other countries where it is a major donor. In particular, Japan has provided directed support for both the carpet industry[81] and again, several Nepalese exporters specifically noted this when discussing how and why they had lost market share to India.[82]

Likewise, the 933 projects the World Bank has contemplated or implemented in India since 1949 have spanned from economic infrastructure, to social programs, to governance initiatives.[83] There does not appear to have an overabundance of direct support from the World Bank to the textile or carpet industries. However, India pursued a very active export promotion position through its "foreign trade policies" after turning away from Import-Substitution Industrialization in the early 1970s. Since that time, supports have included a raft of support measures including tax breaks and export credits, and subsidies on domestic and imported inputs.[84] A number of Nepalese exporters noted these supports (and lack of corresponding support from their own government) as reasons why they had lost competitiveness.[85]

The aid received in Bangladesh and, to a lesser extent, India, was more effective in providing the firms in these countries with the tools they needed to stay competitive once MFA and other market access schemes shifted. As a result, they were positioned to capture some of the trade reversion that occurred with these access changes. Nepal, whose aid was less effective in these areas, was not.

[80] Rahman, M. S. (2022). *The Clothing Curse: Institutional Causes and Political Consequences of Clothing Export Dependence in Developing Countries* (Doctoral dissertation, University of Oregon).

[81] https://kashmirlife.net/the-silken-story-29355/ (accessed 08-09-2023).

[82] Interviews N-1523; N-1382.

[83] https://projects.worldbank.org/en/projects-operations/projects-list? os=780&countryshortname_exact=India (accessed 10-10-2023).

[84] Kumar, U. T. T. A. M. (2017). Trade policy of India since 1991: A critical evaluation and comparative study between pre and post reform periods. *Ranchi University, Ranchi Jhakhand, India.*

[85] Interviews N-1615; N-1523; N-1090; N-1401.

Why Was Nepal Left out in the Cold?

The discussions above have attempted to chart out a plausible narrative for the stagnation in Nepalese economic development since the mid-1990s, particularly in the export sector. The promotion of competing industries in Nepal's near neighbors, exacerbated by political instability and insufficient, if not ineffective, aid crippled what had been an emerging development success story in south Asia. The loss of meaningful market access, and the lack of tools to compete in a level-playing field world, meant that Nepal, who had likely been a previous beneficiary of trade diversion, now suffered on the other side of the equation.

So, where to apportion blame? A change in aid does not appear to be the culprit as overall aid flows to Nepal have largely been maintained or increased over the past two decades. Likewise, while domestic instability attracted a significant portion of exporters' ire, it is unlikely that Nepal would have thrived even in the presence of a stable and well-functioning government. Ultimately, Nepal's comparative sluggishness is a result of the invisible hand—its wares simply were (no longer) competitive vis-à-vis production from other countries as these competitors received increased aid and access supports. But was Nepal the target of this comparative shift in preferential access? That seems unlikely. The MFA was a global agreement that had been under fire for decades. As Nepal's success under the MFA was largely due to the geographic accident of proximity to India, so too its loss as the MFA expired was equally a result of this change in the structure of the global trade regime. As a country with relatively low strategic value to the main developed country markets, Nepal had little agency to exercise in attempting to steer the MFA wind-down, or structure the broader outcomes of the Uruguay round, in a manner that would have shielded its industries. Nepal's government capacity, hindered by the Maoist insurgency, compounded this agency problem and is also likely to have contributed to the aid it received being less effective than that received by its neighbors.

Instead, Nepal's fate appears largely as an unintended consequence of expanded efforts by development partners in India and Bangladesh. Donor interest in these places is no doubt driven by the vast populations and comparative strategic, if not commercial, importance of these countries. There is little evidence to suggest that donors appreciated, much less considered, the third party effects of their aid or market access concessions in these places. Indeed, there would be very little in the way of donor domestic constituencies that would demand such an analysis. Importers who relied on suppliers form Nepal likely faced few costs in shifting to lower cost production in India or Bangladesh. The Nepalese government would have little comparative influence based on strategic value vis-à-vis India or Bangladesh in major donor countries. Similarly, the access to the Nepalese domestic market pales in comparison to the potential of its larger neighbors. Simply put, it is unlikely that donors gave much thought to how their actions in India or Bangladesh would impact Nepal, and neither the Nepalese government or businesses had the clout or capacity to make their interests known and appreciated.

Disaster and a Silver Lining

In 2015 Nepal suffered a massive and devastating earthquake in which thousands were killed and hundreds of thousands were displaced. While somewhat macabre, being the victim of a major natural disaster shifted Nepal's identity in the international system. Countries that fall prey to natural disasters receive extensive media coverage and public support in donor countries for assisting such countries is high, especially when the countries share at least some political affinity.[86] Encouragingly, the humanitarian response to the disaster was substantial and broadly effective.[87] However, equally important but perhaps less visible, is that the disaster prompted a critical juncture in market access in that the United States offered new preferential access to aid in the recovery in 2016. The time-limited preference package, ending in 2025, was explicitly intended to assist the Nepalese economy in recovery from the earthquake. The earthquake changed the political economy for support. The heart-wrenching humanitarian scenes changed the political calculus and enabled supporters to overcome political opposition by framing access as a tool of disaster relief. Indeed, since 2016, Nepal's exports have recovered to over 30% of GDP, as has its income level per capita—growing from $878 in 2016 to an all-time high $1,061 in 2019—an increase of 21% in just three years.

This chapter is meant to illustrate how the political and economic choices of rich, developed, countries engaging with countries in the developing world can have unintended impacts on third-party nations. Countries whose

[86] Bechtel, Michael M. and Ziegler, Jeffrey, Foreign Policy Interests and International Disaster Assistance (September 30, 2019). Available at SSRN: https://ssrn.com/abstract=3472528; Carnegie, A. and Dolan, L. R. (2021). The effects of rejecting aid on recipients' reputations: Evidence from natural disaster responses. *The Review of International Organizations*, *16*, 495–519.

[87] Cook, A. D., Shrestha, M., and Htet, Z. B. (2018). An assessment of international emergency disaster response to the 2015 Nepal earthquakes. *International Journal of Disaster Risk Reduction*, *31*, 535–547.

industries are either dependent on comparatively preferential access, or who are only competitive in a distorted market, will feel knock-on effects from development efforts in other locations. These markets can be distorted not only by preferential market access, but also by aid. Aid, in its best form, that is, when it is trade effective, can act as a production subsidy to exporting firms—either quite directly by helping to underwrite direct export incentives—or by indirectly subsidizing private input costs in terms of utilities or labor, or via public goods investment as aid effectively subsidizes government industrial support which enables governments to focus their financing elsewhere. Aid and access can create market distortions that will benefit some at the expense of others. It sounds a cautionary note that while the combination of effective aid and meaningful market access can promote growth some countries (Bangladesh and India) this may well come at the expense of others (Nepal) who were not as fortunate in receiving or developing the aid-access combination.

9

Where Do We Go from Here?

Pursuing Prosperity in a Divided and Dangerous World

The world in 2025 is considerably less rosy than the one 30 years earlier. Rather than celebrating the end of communism while embracing the optimism of a peaceful and prosperous future, today's world often seems on the brink of calamity. From pandemic, to war, to great power competition, to spreading authoritarianism, to widespread disinformation, to climate breakdown, disaster seems to be lurking in almost every sphere of the social and natural world. As the globe becomes more perilous, the prospects for meaningful international collaboration and cooperation appear more and more remote. In the face of these challenges, and as domestic polities turn inward, it is easy to see developmental laggards being left further and further behind.

Increasing international political confrontation is creating change as the world moves to a bi-, or even multi-, polar polity.[1] As the world further divides between economic and military powers who share vastly different notions of political participation, individual liberty, and human rights, it risks sliding back into Cold War dynamics wherein geopolitics trump all other considerations. In such a world, developing countries may again be forced to choose one patron or another, or cautiously toe the line between the two or more advesaries. Such a structural shift is likely to diminish the aid and access prospects for some developing countries, while potentially opening "windows of opportunity" for others.[2] The rising animosity between the United States, the PRC, and even long-term allies has already led to an ongoing and messy trade war,[3] talk of "de-coupling" and "strategic interest" when it comes

[1] Turner, S. (2009). Russia, China and a multipolar world order: The danger in the undefined. *Asian Perspective*, *33*(1), 159–184; Maher, R. (2018). Bipolarity and the future of US–China relations. *Political Science Quarterly*, *133*(3), 497–525; Eisenman, J. and Heginbotham, E. (2019). Building a more "democratic" and "multipolar" world. *China Review*, *19*(4), 55–84.

[2] Mori, A. (2020). Latin America and the new global order: Dangers and opportunities in a multipolar world. *Latin America and the New Global Order*, 1–151. Ledizioni.

[3] Kwan, C. H. (2020). The China–US trade war: Deep-rooted causes, shifting focus and uncertain prospects. *Asian Economic Policy Review*, *15*(1), 55–72.

The Invisible Hand(out). Samuel Brazys, Oxford University Press. © Samuel Brazys (2025).
DOI: 10.1093/9780198970422.003.0009

to economic matters,[4] and of the reemergence of strategic competition in aid.[5] These tensions have resulted in a noticeable restricting of global supply chains and investment patterns and will dampen overall global growth prospects.[6] Even the more cautious European Union has adopted a strategy of "de-risking" its economic relations with the PRC after learning the price of economic, and in particular energy, reliance on an authoritarian power with Russia's invasion of Ukraine.[7]

But shifting geopolitics is not the only man-made feature that will stymie global growth efforts. Perhaps an even greater threat to global prosperity is the looming spectre of global climate change and climate breakdown. While no economy will emerge unscathed from a radically altered natural world, developing countries will bear disproportionate impacts from these changes.[8] Small island states, like Micronesia, which heretofore have faced development challenges of the tyranny of distance and the absence of resources, will now face existential threats as the very territories on which their nations reside sink under the sea.[9] Other countries will face increasing challenges of geography and local weather, as desertification and water shortages increase.[10] The significant amounts of climate finance needed to mitigate and adapt to these existential threats will compete with aid that might otherwise have focused on trade and growth. Many of those countries disproportionately affected by these impacts will be those in the tropics, perhaps unintentionally bolstering the thesis for those who argue for geographically determined courses of development.[11]

Beyond this, while there are myriad causes of anthropogenic climate change, there is no denying that the increased movement of goods and people associated with economic globalization has contributed significantly to the accumulation of gases which are heating the Earth. Likewise, although many developing countries are global leaders in terms of renewable energy

[4] Wei, L. (2019). Towards economic decoupling? Mapping Chinese discourse on the China–US trade war. *The Chinese Journal of International Politics*, *12*(4), 519–556.

[5] Blair, R. A., Marty, R., and Roessler, P. (2022). Foreign aid and soft power: Great power competition in Africa in the early twenty-first century. *British Journal of Political Science*, *52*(3), 1355–1376.

[6] Swenson, D. L. and Woo, W. T. (2019). The politics and economics of the US–China trade war. *Asian Economic Papers*, *18*(3), 1–28.

[7] Farrell, H. and Newman, A. (2023). The new economic security state: How de-risking will remake geopolitics. *Foreign Aff.*, *102*, 106.

[8] Mertz, O., Halsnæs, K., Olesen, J. E., and Rasmussen, K. (2009). Adaptation to climate change in developing countries. *Environmental Management*, *43*, 743–752.

[9] Teaiwa, K. (2019). No distant future: Climate change as an existential threat. *Australian Foreign Affairs*, (6), 51–70.

[10] Le Houérou, H. N. (1996). Climate change, drought and desertification. *Journal of Arid Environments*, *34*(2), 133–185.

[11] Ravindranath, N. H., Sathaye, J. A., Ravindranath, N. H., and Sathaye, J. A. (2002). In *Climate Change and Developing Countries* (pp. 247–265). Springer Netherlands.

generation and, indeed, may be able to largely "leapfrog" carbon-based fuels, development has enormous energy demands which can often be met most cost-effectively with generation from fossil fuels. Thus, while the negative impacts of climate change will adversely affect developing countries, parts of the efforts to combat the menace may well make parts of an export-led growth pathway more difficult. Again, these structural changes may provide windows of opportunity for certain developing countries, adapting export-led growth strategies to the changing globe will prove a significant challenge for many others.[12]

Beyond these external challenges, many developed countries are also facing increasingly divisive internal politics. Polarization in the United States, and the rise of Donald Trump and his own particular brand of nationalism, have pushed the United States into its most isolationist stance in 100 years.[13] While Donald Trump's "America First" policy wrought disastrous effects for the global trading system via his withdrawal from the Trans-Pacific Partnership, his allowing the US GSP program to lapse, his trade wars with both friends and foes, and his administration's neutering of the WTO via the blocking of judicial appointments to that organization's appellate body, none of these actions were unwound by his Democrat-party successor Joe Biden.[14] Joe Biden's signature "Build Back Better" program doubled down on global economic distortions through massive subsidies that aimed to "re-shore" manufacturing to the United States and an early evaluation of the second Trump administration indicates that the global trading order will only become increasingly fraught.[15]

The United States is not alone in this inward turn. Facing a persistent migration crisis, right-wing nationalist parties have become serious political players in several European democracies.[16] While the EU remains the standard bearer for a liberal, rules-based, global order, this position becomes more and more untenable with each boat of migrants that drown in the Mediterranean Sea.[17] This ongoing tragedy, coupled with an internal politics which has always been defective, means that the EU is unable to be a leader

[12] Brenton, P. and Chemutai, V. (2021). *The Trade and Climate Change Nexus: The Urgency and Opportunities for Developing Countries*. World Bank Publications.

[13] Kupchan, C. A. (2020). *Isolationism: A History of America's Efforts to Shield Itself from the World*. Oxford University Press, USA.

[14] Schoenbaum, T. J. (2023). The Biden administration's trade policy: Promise and reality. *German Law Journal*, *24*(1), 102–124.

[15] Gur, N. and Dilek, S. (2023). US–China economic rivalry and the reshoring of global supply chains. *The Chinese Journal of International Politics*, *16*(1), 61–83.

[16] Halikiopoulou, D. and Vlandas, T. (2019). What is new and what is nationalist about Europe's new nationalism? Explaining the rise of the far right in Europe. *Nations and Nationalism*, *25*(2), 409–434.

[17] Vollmer, B. A. (2017). The continuing shame of Europe: Discourses on migration policy in Germany and the UK. *Migration Studies*, *5*(1), 49–64.

of global free trade that is compatible with, if not based on, universal human rights and respect for labor, the environment and gender. These inward turns, on trade policy in particular, are likely to further raise the bar for developing countries seeking to secure improved de jure or de facto market access for their firms.

The PRC is happily stepping into the void in global leadership left by American disinterest and European dysfunction.[18] However, and understandably, the PRC is offering leadership on its own terms or, to borrow an overused phrase, "with Chinese characteristics."[19] While the PRC certainly has an interest in maintaining global trade—both to support its export-oriented industries but also to supply the resources demanded by its vast internal market—it is less interested in ensuring that this trade happens within a system wherein rules exist that might constrain the PRC's interests or behavior. Although the PRC launched a GSP scheme for least developed countries in 2010, in general it has not granted broad or preferential market access to developing countries. While PRC aid may often be effective in promoting economic growth,[20] it might also come with hidden obligations[21] or with costs to the quality of governance in host countries.[22] As the PRC economy has slowed, it also appears to be making its development assistance even less concessional, raising fears that its developing country partners may be falling into "debt traps."[23] Moreover, the PRC is not at all interested in supporting or expanding broader notions of political, labor or human rights. Its policies of external "non-interference" and "respect for sovereignty" are little more than rhetorical devices designed to keep critics of its own domestic politics at bay.[24] If anything, the PRC has been keen to support, if not promote, authoritarian modes of governance abroad if, for no other reason, than these types of regimes will be unlikely to challenge the Chinese Communist Party's (CCP)

[18] Sanger, D. E. and Perlez, J. (2017). Trump hands the Chinese a gift: The chance for global leadership. *The New York Times*, *1*.

[19] Kristensen, P. M. and Morgan, P. (2018). Leadership with Chinese characteristics. *Chinese Political Science Review*, *3*, 1–9.

[20] Dreher, A., Fuchs, A., Parks, B., Strange, A., and Tierney, M. J. (2021). Aid, China, and growth: Evidence from a new global development finance dataset. *American Economic Journal: Economic Policy*, *13*(2), 135–174.

[21] Gelpern, A., Horn, S., Morris, S., Parks, B., and Trebesch, C. (2023). How China lends: A rare look into 100 debt contracts with foreign governments. *Economic Policy*, 38(114), 345-416.

[22] Brazys, S., Elkink, J. A., and Kelly, G. (2017). Bad neighbors? How co-located Chinese and World Bank development projects impact local corruption in Tanzania. *The Review of International Organizations*, *12*(2), 227–253; Isaksson, A. S. and Kotsadam, A. (2018). Chinese aid and local corruption. *Journal of Public Economics*, *159*, 146–159.

[23] Dreher, A., Lang, V., Rosendorff, B. P., & Vreeland, J. R. (2022). Bilateral or multilateral? International financial flows and the dirty-work hypothesis. *The Journal of Politics*, *84*(4), 1932–1946.

[24] Brazys, S., & Dukalskis, A. (2017). Canary in the coal mine? China, the UNGA, and the changing world order. *Review of International Studies*, *43*(4), 742–764.

own domestic human rights abuses.[25] While the "Chinese alternative" may provide a path to greater economic development, it remains unclear to what extent the PRC is committed to helping countries develop beyond serving as sources for the natural resources the PRC needs—or as borrowers of the excess savings it has to offload.[26] Chinese domestic politics centers entirely around what will strengthen the CCP. The space for developing countries to exercise their agency vis-à-vis the PRC is thus very much a function of the extent to which those states might serve the CCP's aims.

Developing countries are thus left with an increasingly choppy sea to navigate on their journey to export-led development. Developed countries, which have rarely acted toward them with altruism, are likely to become even more self-interested in their trade and foreign aid policies as the world around them becomes more hostile. When faced with a choice of assuaging their own constituencies, or aiding foreign ones, politicians will pick the former every time, regardless of their political system. But, more often there is no stark choice. Instead, political choices made for domestic political reasons have unintended adverse effects. Reshoring manufacturing may harm a political adversary, but it can also impact any number of citizens in third countries when global supply chains are disrupted.[27] Initiatives to protect or promote domestic industries lead to capital not being investment elsewhere—depriving those "other" regions of growth and jobs. As the loss of a potential benefit, to "someone else," is easy to ignore, these types of protectionist policies will face very little opposition.

It Is Still a Choice

This book has argued that there is a path to export-led development via trade-effective aid and meaningful market access. While that path may be made rockier by the challenges mentioned above, fortunately forces like climate change and great power competition need not close the route for those still looking to develop. Unlike deterministic explanations based on physical or spatial geography, or institutional explanations where the onus lies solely in the hands of (elites) in developing countries, the granting of trade-effective

[25] Yakouchyk, K. (2019). Beyond autocracy promotion: A review. *Political Studies Review*, *17*(2), 147–160.

[26] Dollar, D. (2018). Is China's development finance a challenge to the international order? *Asian Economic Policy Review*, *13*(2), 283–298.

[27] Pietrobelli, C. and Seri, C. (2023). *Reshoring, Nearshoring and Developing Countries: Readiness and Implications for Latin America*. UNU-MERIT.

aid and meaningful market access for developing countries is in the control of political decision makers in both the developing and developed countries.

Facilitating market access for Micronesian tuna canners to the United States, or Malagasy coffee grower to Europe, can be undertaken with a political decision to change a tariff line or a reformulation of SPS rules. Colombian cacao exporters can regularize their market access to Europe with a scientifically based rationalization of the latter's position on cadmium. In contrast, electronic goods and components from Vietnam and prepared food stuffs from Indonesia flow freely because of access afford under most-favored nation status. These restrictions and facilitations stem from political choices—there is nothing unalterable or deterministic about these institutional structures. Donor governments can change rules to grant meaningful market access by the mere act of putting pen to paper.

While achieving trade-effective aid is not as simple as granting meaningful market access, there still is a considerable amount that lies in the realm of political choice. Ultimately, the effectiveness of aid is a complicated, if not epiphenomenal, occurrence. The conditions for trade-effective aid are highly contextual and depend considerably on the agency, capacity, and decision-making of the recipient country. That said, there still are many known or suspected "best practices," as summarized in the OECD DAC's Paris Declaration on Aid Effectiveness which donor countries can, but often do not, choose to implement because of their domestic political constraints. Emphasizing the construction of schools and dispensaries over transportation and energy infrastructure in Micronesia was a political choice of the United States government that the Micronesian government was insufficiently empowered to overcome. Choosing to focus cacao-growing efforts in Colombian regions where it would be most effective as an alternative to coca cultivation, rather than in regions where it might have had the biggest impact on production and exports, was a decision made based on US domestic drug policy considerations. While donors need not (and probably should not) hand over the reins on aid everywhere and an all instances to host governments, by and large increased deference to host country preferences—what the Paris Declaration deems "ownership"—would mostly not be remiss. Beyond this, while good health and quality education are no doubt important contributors to a country's overall development prospects, decades of evidence suggests economic infrastructure is a necessary precursor to development. This theme came up time and again when interviewing exporting firms all over the world. Without electricity, silver shops in Kathmandu have to shut down. Without transport links, Indonesian rubber stays in the jungle.

But achieving the tools and access for development does not rest solely in the donors' hands. Developing country institutions matter. Governments must be able to gather and parse information on what types of tools and access would benefit their most efficient firms, rather than those that are the most politically connected. They must then be able to effectively advance these interests when seeking developed country financial assistance or markets. Government capacity in providing institutional public goods—regulatory or licensing services, efficient customs systems, property rights, and the rule of law, etc.—may be the marginal factor in deciding whether certain firms can export. When investment is at risk of expropriation, or goods can be seized for failure to pay a bribe, growth will suffer. Likewise, local politics are important in shaping how aid is used. Bridges to nowhere and empty airports built on the wrong side of the country do not help goods get to market. Contracts that are granted on the basis of patronage, rather than efficiency, mean that aid dollars may not go as far as they otherwise might. Limited access orders, which divert resources and skim rents, are unlikely to advocate for efficient trade-effect aid or market access that benefits the most productive firms.

A Way Forward—Helping You Help You—Honestly

So what hope is there in a world besieged by everyday politics that is facing a number of both novel and recurrent challenges? There are no easy answers. As one book review of William Easterly's famous critique, *The Elusive Quest for Growth*, praised, "Wisely, Easterly avoids proposing a new panacea of his own."[28] Hopefully this book has followed the same advice and does not leave readers with the impression of a simple solution.

However, unlikely Easterly's famous skepticism, this book does not abandon hope that some strategies could be more effective, more often, than others, and will not shy away from drawing conclusions to that end. Undoubtedly, the evidence in this book suggests that the first stone for a path forward would be for developed countries to find ways to build a domestic political consensus to fully and meaningfully open their markets to all goods for all developing countries—"EBA" for all. The benefits of meaningful market access to developing countries are as blindingly obvious today as it was to Adam Smith in 1776. In many instances, providing market access to developing countries need not even be preferential, as long as it levels the playing

[28] Wacziarg, R. (2002). Review of Easterly's the elusive quest for growth. *Journal of Economic Literature*, *40*(3), p. 907.

field so as to avoid trade-diverting distortions, as shown by the success of Vietnam and Indonesia. In fact, it is better if this market access is not preferential. Showering some countries with market access preferences and aid risks distorting other economies. A path forward where some can only gain at the expense of others will only prolong unequal development.

Meaningful market access means not only removing de jure barriers to trade in all goods, but it also means removing de facto barriers. As argued at several points in the book, key among these are the regulatory barriers in the form of SPS and TBT. Trade cannot be a free for all. In many instances products standards on health and safety grounds are entirely legitimate and reasonable. However, even when sound, they can still effectively deter developing country producers and exporters. How to skirt this problem? The book does not propose to provide detailed or fully assessed solutions, but one concept might be to truly make these barriers "behind the border" costs. Fund compliance (either directly or with technical assistance) with regulatory barriers with behind the border taxes—consumption taxes like VAT. The WTO principle of non-discrimination can be extended beyond the border.

The second stone on a path forward would be for donor countries to consciously and sincerely adopt those practices which give official development assistance the best chance to be trade effective, when that is the aim. There is no panacea for trade-effective aid, and the precise structure and conditions that give aid the best chance for trade effectiveness are very much specific to countries, if not localities. That said, aid which is purposive in its design is more likely to succeed. After examining hundreds of AfT projects across dozens of countries, a feature which becomes glaringly evident is that most projects designated as AfT have little explicit trade focus and are only very rarely specifically designed with an export intent in mind. It is not so much that the concept of AfT has "failed" as it has never been given an appropriate chance. Other interests and objectives, stemming from domestic political considerations, or even bureaucratic inertia, often capture the intent of aid projects and lead them in ways that are divergent from their labels.

The economic assistance to Micronesia via the Compact of Free Association is, at a high level described in the preamble of the agreement, intended to promote "the economic advancement and self-sufficiency" of the Micronesian people. Judging against this objective, the aid has clearly failed. But, as shown in Chapter 7, due to US domestic politics, that lofty goal for the assistance was supplanted by one more along the lines of "to minimize the economic and social consequences of Micronesian migration into US states and territories." This "unwritten" objective is what ultimately guided use of the funding into building hospital and schools rather than roads and power facilities. These program choices, while perhaps increasing the efficacy of the aid in achieving the goal of mitigating "Compact Impact," were not the best policies for securing economic advancement and self-sufficiency. These secondary, hidden, or alternative objectives obscure aid efficacy when it is being measured on the basis of (export-led) economic growth and development.

It is easy to claim that developed countries should open their markets and provide effective aid, these are prescriptions that have recommended by many more esteemed authors before this book.[29] Indeed, the entire premise of "Aid for Trade" is based on exploiting the "synergy" between building tools and providing access. The failure of aid and market access to provide broad and equal growth is not because these cannot be effective strategies—they can—it is because what is often packaged as trade-effective aid or meaningful access is no such thing. If donors, and their publics, want aid and trade to work for developing countries, they need to be clear about what the aid is intended and designed to do. The prescription of this book is honesty and transparency about the intentions, costs, benefits, and trade-offs in developed countries of providing trade-effective aid and meaningful market access.

Hopefully by emphasizing the political determination of meaningful market access and effective aid, this book can prompt introspection by policymakers who claim to be undertaking policies that are billed to those ends. A major step forward would simply be if policymakers were purposive when providing aid or market access whose stated objective is to promote economic development. Building medical dispensaries, at the expense of building a reliable power network, will not bring export-led development. Providing duty free access for a product but then requiring testing which is unaffordable or unavailable to developing world producers will not bring export-led development. Revoking previously granted market access on the basis of a flimsily failed conditionality will not bring export-led development. Too often, policymakers embrace a fanciful fiction that they can have their cake and eat it too—that they can provide the *tools and access* for developing countries to succeed while at the same time assuaging all the varied demands of their domestic constituencies.

This is because, like nearly everything political, providing meaningful market access and effective aid requires trade-offs. If, as argued and illustrated throughout this book, the provision of trade-effective aid and meaningful market access is the result of a delicate balance between the agency of a developing country, determined by its place in the international system, and

[29] Birdsall, N., Rodrik, D., and Subramanian, A. (2005). How to help poor countries. *Foreign Affairs*, 136–152.

the domestic politics of the developed entity, then changing the outcome requires changing one of the variables in this equation. Directing structural change is a Herculean task; changing the capacity of developing countries to exercise their agency, or the domestic political calculus in developed markets, is less so.

There exists scope to change the domestic political calculus of granting trade-effective aid and meaningful market access by framing these as ends in-and-of themselves in the domestic self-interest. There are real and measurable gains to be had for developed countries by pursuing these objectives with all developing country partners. The largest aggregate welfare gains from liberalized trade accrue to (domestic) consumers. Lower prices and increased choice make people happier. The rub, of course, is that while the gains are broadly felt they are very small. In contrast, the concentrated, but small-in-aggregate, losses of import-competing interests have a strong incentive to organize and agitate to preserve their rents. But, as others have long explained, this fundamental political economy of trade can be overcome with welfare transfers from consumers to these producers—often referred to as trade adjustment assistance.[30] But the case for using this policy tool is rarely made with conviction or consistency and trade adjustment assistance is not used effectively.[31] It should be promoted by a broader coalition than just the political representatives of the winners from free trade.[32] The overall welfare gains in the liberalizing country are more than ample to offset these losses. This doesn't even take into account the welfare gains accruing in the countries which now have access to those domestic markets.

And why should developed country constituencies care about welfare gains in foreign markets? Why should developed country constituents care if aid is effective at providing the tools for real and meaningful development? Putting aside the fact that most people, everywhere, have a preference for their fellow human beings not to subsist in poverty, there are clear self-interested reasons for developed world constituencies to raise the boats on other tides. The logic is similar to that of mitigating "Compact Impact" but, rather than using aid to directly providing health and education services to reduce the impact of these inward flows, it is arguably far better to build the Micronesian economy so that country can fund its own health and education services to lessen the

[30] Stein, L. (1982). Trade adjustment assistance as a means of achieving improved resource allocation through freer trade: An analysis of policies for aiding the import-injured in the US, Canada and Australia. *American Journal of Economics and Sociology*, *41*(3), 243–255.

[31] Kim, S. E. and Pelc, K. (2021). How responsive is trade adjustment assistance? *Political Science Research and Methods*, *9*(4), 889–898.

[32] Rickard, S. J. (2015). Compensating the losers: An examination of congressional votes on trade adjustment assistance. *International Interactions*, *41*(1), 46–60.

burden on US states and territories. This logic has also permeated EU efforts to build the economies of countries that are the source of the migrants who are dying in the Mediterranean and elsewhere as they try to reach European shores. This type of "targeted development" aims to decrease the spillovers of underdevelopment.[33] Most economic migrants would prefer to stay in their homelands—if only those homelands held real opportunity for them and their families.[34]

But even here, care is needed to divine what type of aid truly has objectives designed to deter these spillovers. Arguably, the USAID assistance to cacao farmers in Colombia is intended to avert the negative social and economic impacts of Colombian drugs reaching US shores. This sounds exactly like "targeted development." But helping producer associations grow cacao instead of coca matters little if the former is not sustainable in the absence of market access. Colombian interviewees repeatedly bemoaned the lack of *comercialización* with the US cacao efforts.[35] The projects lacked sufficient focus on markets—either domestic or foreign—and as a result floundered. While later iterations of the project slowly began to incorporate these lessons, the initial design was flawed from a growth, or trade, perspective. But, as was made clear by the donor implementers—export and commercialization were not the objective of the project—shifting production from coca was.[36] These arguments are not to say that all aid projects, everywhere, be focused on growth and exports. But, rather, that the projects that claim these ends be carefully and honestly designed to achieve the stated objective. Global donors say they provide $50 billion per year in Aid for Trade (AfT). But that simply isn't true. While much of the infrastructure aid categorized as AfT may be more or less tangentially related to exports (ports, more so; community water systems, less so), many of the other projects have little, if any, relationship to exports. Such "mislabeling" leads to disappointment in the recipient countries, but also in the donor publics. Public perception of the inefficacy for aid reduces support and demoralizes and despairs donor publics.[37] This is an own goal when inefficacy comes from a mis-categorization of what the aid was intended to do. These efforts should thus have a sincere objective of

[33] Bermeo, S. (2018). *Targeted development: Industrialized country strategy in a globalizing world.* Oxford University Press.

[34] Long, L. D. and Oxfeld, E. (Eds.). (2004). *Coming Home?: Refugees, Migrants, and Those Who Stayed Behind.* University of Pennsylvania Press.

[35] Interview C-1027 17-01-2023. Bogota, Colombia.

[36] Interview C-1020. 24-01-2023. Bogota, Colombia; Interview C-1022 03-02-2023. Bogota Colombia (via Zoom).

[37] Riddell, R. C. (2009). Does foreign aid work. *Doing Good or Doing Better, 47,* 47–80; Milner, H. V. and Tingley, D. (2013). Public opinion and foreign aid: A review essay. *International Interactions, 39*(3), 389–401.

economic development, even if the underlying motivation is self-interested rather than altruistic. Making that case clearly and concisely to constituencies in developed markets can change the political calculus of granting market access.

Importantly, there is not a universal trade-effective aid or meaningful market access button that can be pushed. Both are deeply embedded in the socio-political-geographic environments in which they hope to engage. Granting duty-free access for tuna or oil will do little to move the needle for Nepal's development. Giving aid to build solar power to light up a *faluw* in the Yap outer islands is unlikely to transform the Micronesian economy. In part because of these rich and varied contextual factors, the book has attempted to build its main arguments not with neatly identified causal strategies—indeed the micro-level investigations in that direction perhaps only showed the futility in that approach—but instead with a more holistic approach will combines observational, descriptive, inferential, and qualitative evidence across time and countries.

Ultimately, what this book hopes to impart is that trade-effective aid and meaningful market access are nuanced concepts that capture goods that are distributed as a part of complex political process that depends on issues of structure and agency in the international system, the governance quality in developing countries, and the domestic politics of developed markets. That these goods are the result of political choices is encouraging in that it implies the unequal globalization of the past 80 years can be overcome. Some of the hurdle stems from the fact that policymakers in donor countries are not always honest with themselves, their publics, or their developing country partners about what makes trade-effective aid or meaningful market access. This lack of forthrightness is usually driven by a fear that granting aid and access that "really works" would be too politically costly. The way forward, then, is not in proposing some new miracle cure for underdevelopment but, instead, thinking about how we might more effectively confront the political economy that shapes the incentives of providing this aid and access.

The world has made remarkable progress over the past 300 years. The human condition, which had remained stagnant for most individuals for the vast bulk of the time our species has inhabited the planet, is orders of magnitude better than it was. Vast swathes of the globe can now take for granted basic subsistence and shelter needs while living in relative security and having access to greater or lesser degrees of social and human rights. But while there is much to applaud, the work is not yet done. Inequality persists, both within and across countries. Too many, and through no fault of their own, still live in societies pervaded by deprivation and insecurity. Most often, this is the result of political choices—at times by elites and political orders within those countries—but just as frequently as the (unintended) consequences of choices made by political leaders in more developed parts of the world. Providing tools and access to those countries still climbing the development ladder will not solve all the world's problems—least of all the consequences of anthropogenic climate change. But in the face of that challenge, providing aid and access is an initiative that will reap rewards for many of those still left behind in a globalized world.

ANNEX I

Data Sources

Existing Databases

AidData. 2016. BangladeshSelectDonors_GeocodedResearchRelease_Level1_v1.1.1 geocoded dataset. Williamsburg, VA and Washington, DC: AidData. Accessed on [date]. http://aiddata.org/research-datasets.

AidData. 2016. ColombiaAIMS_GeocodedResearchRelease_Level1_v1.1.1 geocoded dataset. Williamsburg, VA and Washington, DC: AidData. Accessed on [date]. http://aiddata.org/research-datasets.

AidData. 2016. NepalAIMS_GeocodedResearchRelease_Level1_v1.4.1 geocoded dataset. Williamsburg, VA and Washington, DC: AidData. Accessed on [date]. http://aiddata.org/research-datasets.

Chi, G., Fang, H., Chatterjee, S., and Blumenstock, J. E. (2022). Microestimates of wealth for all low-and middle-income countries. *Proceedings of the National Academy of Sciences*, *119*(3), e2113658119.

Croicu, Mihai and Ralph Sundberg (2017) UCDP GED Codebook version 17.1. Uppsala: Dept. of Peace and Conflict Research.

Dür, Andreas, Leonardo Baccini and Manfred Elsig. 2014. The design of international trade agreements: Introducing a new database. *The Review of International Organizations*, 9(3): 353-375.

European Union. TARIC. https://ec.europa.eu/taxation_customs/dds2/taric/taric_consultation.jsp?Lang=en.

Lindberg, S. I., Coppedge, M., Gerring, J., and Teorell, J. (2014). V-Dem: A new way to measure democracy. *Journal of Democracy*, *25*(3), 159–169.

Marshall, M. G., Gurr, T. R., and Jaggers, K. (2020). Center for Systemic Peace. *Polity V Project.*

Organization for Economic Cooperation and Development. Creditor Reporting System. https://stats.oecd.org/Index.aspx?DataSetCode=CRS1.

Overseas Development Institute. Principled Aid Index. https://odi.org/en/topics/principled-aid-index/.

Raleigh, C., Linke, A., Hegre, H., and Karlsen, J. (2010) Introducing ACLED: An armed conflict location and event dataset: Special data feature. *Journal of Peace Research* 47(5): 651-660.

Salehyan, I. and Hendrix, C. (2017) Social Conflict Analysis Database (SCAD). Denver, CO: The Sié Chéou-Kang Center for International Security and Diplomacy at the Josef Korbel School of International Studies, University of Denver.

START (2022) *Global Terrorism Database* (https://www.start.umd.edu).

United Nations. COMTRADE. https://comtradeplus.un.org/.

USHTS. https://hts.usitc.gov/.

USITC DataWeb. https://dataweb.usitc.gov/.

World Bank. (2012). *World Development Indicators 2012*. The World Bank.

World Bank Group, Kaufmann, D., Kraay, A., and Mastruzzi, M. (2010). *Worldwide Governance Indicators*. World Bank Group.

World Bank. The World Integrated Trade Solution. https://wits.worldbank.org/.

New or Expanded Databases

Government of Bangladesh. *Directory of Exporting Firms.* Export Promotion Bureau. Novel georeferencing of firms.
Government of Colombia. *Estadísticas de Exportaciones.* Dirección de Metodología y Producción Estadística. Novel georeferencing of firms.
Government of Nepal. *Export–Import Directory.* Trade and Export Promotion Centre. Novel georeferencing of firms.
Brazys et al. 2016. Nepal Exporter Survey.
Brazys et al. 2019. Bangladesh Exporter Survey.

List of Interviews

Country	Date	Interviewee	Interview Reference	Method
Indonesia	25/05/2011	Indonesian Trade Org	I-1001	Face to Face
Indonesia	25/05/2011	Norwegian Embassy	I-1002	Face to Face
Indonesia	26/06/2011	USAID	I-1003	Face to Face
Micronesia	01/08/2010	R&D	FSM-1001	Face to Face
Nepal	10/05/2016	Exporting Firm—Garments	N-1021	Face to Face
Nepal	11/05/2016	Exporting Firm—Garments	N-1090	Face to Face
Nepal	11/05/2016	Exporting Firm—Cashmere	N-1134	Face to Face
Nepal	12/05/2016	Exporting Firm—Pashmina	N-1170	Face to Face
Nepal	09/05/2016	Exporting Firm—Essential Oils	N-1233	Face to Face
Nepal	12/05/2016	Exporting Firm—Carpet	N-1339	Face to Face
Nepal	10/05/2016	Exporting Firm—Carpet	N-1382	Face to Face
Nepal	11/05/2016	Exporting Firm—Carpet	N-1400	Face to Face
Nepal	12/05/2016	Exporting Firm—Carpet	N-1401	Face to Face
Nepal	11/05/2016	Non-profit Carpet	N-1408	Face to Face
Nepal	09/05/2016	Exporting Firm—Carpet	N-1523	Face to Face
Nepal	09/05/2016	Exporting Firm	N-1584	Face to Face
Nepal	13/05/2016	Exporter	N-1594	Face to Face
Nepal	12/05/2016	Exporter	N-1595	Face to Face
Nepal	13/05/2016	Exporting Firm—Silver	N-1610	Face to Face
Nepal	09/05/2016	Exporting Firm—Jewelry	N-1615	Face to Face
Nepal	09/05/2016	Exporting Firm—textiles	N-1623	Face to Face
Nepal	13/05/2016	Exporting Firm—paper sheet	N-1639	Face to Face
Nepal	10/05/2016	Exporting Firm—Garments	N-9000	Face to Face
Nepal	12/05/2016	Exporting Firm—Pashmina	N-9001	Face to Face
Nepal	12/05/2016	Exporter	N-9002	Face to Face

Continued

Country	Date	Interviewee	Interview Reference	Method
Philippines	07/07/2011	USAID	P-1001	Face to Face
Philippines	08/07/2011	JICA	P-1002	Face to Face
Philippines	08/07/2011	GIZ	P-1003	Face to Face
Timor-Leste	31/05/2011	Gov TL—Ministry T&I	TL-1001	Face to Face
Timor-Leste	31/05/2011	USAID-DAI	TL-1002	Face to Face
Timor-Leste	31/05/2011	USAID	TL-1003	Face to Face
Timor-Leste	01/06/2011	GIZ	TL-1004	Face to Face
Timor-Leste	01/06/2011	NORAD	TL-1005	Face to Face
Timor-Leste	01/06/2011	USAID2—	TL-1006	Face to Face
Timor-Leste	02/06/2011	Gov TL—Ministry Finance	TL-1007	Face to Face
Timor-Leste	01/06/2011	JICA	TL-1008	Face to Face
Timor-Leste	03/06/2011	GOTL—Ministry Commerce	TL-1009	Face to Face
Vietnam	11/07/2011	JICA	V-1001	Face to Face
Vietnam	12/07/2011	GIZ	V-1002	Face to Face
Vietnam	12/07/2011	NORAD	V-1003	Face to Face
Vietnam	12/07/2011	USAID-1	V-1004	Face to Face
Vietnam	12/07/2011	USAID-2	V-1005	Face to Face
Bangladesh	11/03/2019	Exporting Firm—Leather	CH-1001	Face to Face
Bangladesh	10/03/2019	Exporting Firm—Plastics	CH-1002	Face to Face
Bangladesh	14/03/2019	Exporting Firm—Fish	CX-1001	Face to Face
Bangladesh	05/03/2019	Exporting Firm—RMG	D-1001	Face to Face
Bangladesh	05/03/2019	Exporting Firm—RMG	D-1002	Face to Face
Bangladesh	07/03/2019	Exporting Firm—Jute	KH-1001	Face to Face
Bangladesh	13/03/2019	Exporting Firm—RMG	CH-1010	Face to Face
Bangladesh	13/03/2019	Exporting Firm—Rope	CH-1009	Face to Face
Bangladesh	19/03/2019	JICA	B-1001	Face to Face
Bangladesh	13/03/2019	Exporting Firm—Fish	CH-1008	Face to Face
Bangladesh	13/03/2019	Exporting Firm—Software	CH-1007	Face to Face
Bangladesh	12/03/2019	Exporting Firm—Rubber	CH-1006	Face to Face
Bangladesh	12/03/2019	Exporting Firm—Marine Service	CH-1005	Face to Face
Bangladesh	12/03/2019	Exporting Firm—Newsprint	CH-1004	Face to Face
Bangladesh	12/03/2019	Exporting Firm—Packaging	CH-1003	Face to Face

Country	Date	Interviewee	Interview Reference	Method
Colombia	17/01/2023	Cacao trade federation	C-1027	Face to Face
Colombia	24/01/2023	USAID-2	C-1020	Face to Face
Colombia	03/02/2023	Chocolatier	C-1022	Face to Face
Colombia	08/01/2023	Fedecacao	C-1000	Face to Face
Colombia	09/01/2023	Cacao farmer	C-1001	Face to Face
Colombia	09/01/2023	Cacao farmer	C-1002	Face to Face
Colombia	09/01/2023	Cacao farmer	C-1003	Face to Face
Colombia	09/01/2023	Cacao farmer	C-1004	Face to Face
Colombia	10/01/2023	Chocolatier	C-1005	Face to Face
Colombia	10/01/2023	Chocolatier	C-1006	Face to Face
Colombia	10/01/2023	FONDO official	C-1007	Face to Face
Colombia	10/01/2023	Fedecacao Purchasers	C-1008	Face to Face
Colombia	10/01/2023	Commerciante	C-1009	Face to Face
Colombia	10/01/2023	Commerciante	C-1010	Face to Face
Colombia	10/01/2023	Producer	C-1011	Face to Face
Colombia	11/01/2023	Chocolatier (Exporter)	C-1012	Face to Face
Colombia	12/01/2023	Swiss SIPPO	C-1012-2	Face to Face
Colombia	13/01/2023	Cacao Exporter	C-1013	Face to Face
Colombia	13/01/2023	Cacao Exporter	C-1014	Face to Face
Colombia	16/01/2023	Swiss Embassy	C-1015	Face to Face
Colombia	17/01/2023	Fedecacao HQ	C-1017	Face to Face
Colombia	17/01/2023	GIZ	C-1018	Face to Face
Colombia	18/01/2023	USAID 1	C-1019	Face to Face
Colombia	02/02/2023	Cacao Exporter	C-1021	Video Conference
Colombia	06/02/2023	Cacao Exporter	C-1023	Video Conference
Colombia	07/02/2023	Cacao Exporter	C-1024	Video Conference
Colombia	07/02/2023	Cacao Exporter	C-1025	Video Conference
Colombia	09/02/2023	Exporter	C-1026	Video Conference

Continued

Continued

Country	Date	Interviewee	Interview Reference	Method
Colombia	15/02/2023	Cacao Association	C-1028	Video Conference
Colombia	16/02/2023	Cacao Exporter	C-1029	Video Conference
Colombia	21/02/2023	Cacao Exporter	C-1030	Video Conference
Colombia	22/02/2023	Cacao Association	C-1031	Video Conference
Colombia	22/02/2023	Cacao Exporter	C-1032	Video Conference
Colombia	02/03/2023	Cacao Association	C-1033	Video Conference
Colombia	11/05/2023	UN	C-1034	Video Conference

ANNEX II

Complete Statistical Results

Table A1 Aggregate aid for trade export effects

VARIABLES	(1) Combined	(2) Bangladesh	(3) Colombia	(4) Nepal
Treated	0.010	−0.006	0.030**	−0.021
	(0.012)	(0.065)	(0.013)	(0.081)
Observations	6,956	447	6,378	131
Prob > F	0.423	0.925	0.019	0.782
Constant	YES	YES	YES	YES
Adj. R^2	0.000	−0.002	0.001	−0.001

Table A2 AfT effectiveness by section in Colombia

Section	DiD	SE	Observations	Prob > F	Adj. R^2
01	−0.02632	0.11781	74	0.824	−0.013
02	−0.19724	0.04272	543	0.000	0.036
04	0.06349	0.08269	164	0.444	−0.003
05	−0.00556	0.11576	76	0.961	−0.014
06	0.01217	0.06124	303	0.843	−0.003
07	0.02222	0.05858	310	0.705	−0.003
08	−0.00741	0.09746	112	0.940	−0.009
09	−0.05195	0.1526	58	0.735	−0.016
10	0.10263	0.05139	372	0.047	0.008
11	0.04399	0.04306	556	0.307	0.000
12	0.17111	0.07469	176	0.023	0.024
13	0.18523	0.10082	97	0.069	0.024
14	0.02745	0.11863	78	0.818	−0.012
15	0.06089	0.05507	340	0.270	0.001

Section	DiD	SE	Observations	Prob > F	Adj. R^2
16	0.02782	0.02939	1240	0.344	−0.000
17	0.02988	0.06466	243	0.644	−0.003
18	0.0056	0.04196	581	0.894	−0.002
20	0.07827	0.03195	977	0.015	0.005
21	0.02574	0.17755	33	0.886	−0.032
22	0.15417	0.17872	31	0.395	−0.009

Table A3 Cacao AfT effectiveness in Colombia

Capture Radius (KM)	ATT	SE
15	0.0072	0.04
20	−0.0045	0.0441
25	0	0.0462
30	−0.0268	0.0467
35	−0.0364	0.0626
40	−0.0309	0.0669
45	−0.0313	0.0647
50	−0.0332	0.0803
55	0.01	0.0887
60	0.0099	0.0899
65	0.0298	0.1026
70	0.0022	0.1092
75	0.0211	0.1151
80	0.093	0.2451
85	0.0353	0.1112
90	0.0333	0.112
95	0.037	0.1163
100	0.0375	0.1347

Table A4 Swiss cacao AfT effectiveness in Colombia

Capture Radius (KM)	ATT	SE
15	0.1441	0.0561
20	0.1448	0.0562
25	0.1448	0.0532
30	0.1448	0.0556
35	0.1596	0.0644
40	0.1583	0.059
45	0.159	0.0595
50	0.159	0.0597
55	0.151	0.0526
60	0.1449	0.0486
65	0.1444	0.0489
70	0.157	0.0539
75	0.1851	0.0699
80	0.0328	0.0922
85	0.0435	0.1176
90	0.0496	0.1277
95	0.0582	0.1451
100	0.0674	0.1526

Bibliography

Abdulai, A., Barrett, C. B., and Hoddinott, J. (2005). Does food aid really have disincentive effects? New evidence from sub-Saharan Africa. *World Development, 33*(10), 1689–1704.

Acemoglu, D., Johnson, S., and Robinson, J. A. (2001). The colonial origins of comparative development: An empirical investigation. *American Economic Review, 91*(5), 1369–1401.

Acemoglu, D., Verdier, T., and Robinson, J. A. (2004). Kleptocracy and divide-and-rule: A model of personal rule. *Journal of the European Economic Association, 2*(2–3), 162–192.

Acemoglu, D., Johnson, S., and Robinson, J. A. (2005). Institutions as a fundamental cause of long-run growth. *Handbook of Economic Growth, 1*, 385–472.

Acemoglu, D. and Robinson, J. A. (2013). *Why Nations Fail: The Origins of Power, Prosperity, and Poverty*. Currency.

Acemoglu, D. and Robinson, J. A. (2019). Rents and economic development: The perspective of Why Nations Fail. *Public Choice, 181*, 13–28.

Adhikari, P. and Samford, S. (2013). The Nepali state and the dynamics of the Maoist insurgency. *Studies in Comparative International Development, 48*(4), 457–481.

Ahmed, F. Z. (2012). The perils of unearned foreign income: Aid, remittances, and government survival. *American Political Science Review, 106*(1), 146–165.

Alesina, A. and Dollar, D. (2000). Who gives foreign aid to whom and why?. *Journal of Economic Growth, 5*, 33–63.

Ampuja, M. (2012). Conclusion: Globalization theory and the neoliberal moment. *Theorizing Globalization* (pp. 339–378). Brill.

Amsden, A. H. (1994). Why isn't the whole world experimenting with the East Asian model to develop? Review of the East Asian miracle. *World Development, 22*(4), 627–633.

Anderson, J. E. and Van Wincoop, E. (2003). Gravity with gravitas: A solution to the border puzzle. *American Economic Review, 93*(1), 170–192.

Anderson, J. E. (2011). The gravity model. *Annu. Rev. Econ., 3*(1), 133–160.

Anderson, K., Martin, W., and van der Mensbrugghe, D. (2006). Incidence of trade and subsidy policies on developing country welfare, exports and debt sustainability. *Washington, DC: The World Bank, 29.*

Anderson, K. and Valenzuela, E. (2007). Do global trade distortions still harm developing country farmers? *Review of World Economics, 143*, 108–139.

Anderson, K., Rausser, G., and Swinnen, J. (2013). Political economy of public policies: Insights from distortions to agricultural and food markets. *Journal of Economic Literature, 51*(2), 423–477.

Adriaensen, J. and Postnikov, E. (2022). Geo-economic motives and the negotiation of free trade agreements: Introduction. In Adriaensen, J. and Postnikov, E. (Eds). *A Geo-Economic Turn in Trade Policy? EU Trade Agreements in the Asia-Pacific* (pp. 3–26). Springer International Publishing.

Andriantseheno, B. (2011). The Environmental/Rural Development and Food Security Program in Madagascar. In *Influencing Change* (pp. 141–150). The World Bank.

Antràs, P. (2003). Firms, contracts, and trade structure. *The Quarterly Journal of Economics, 118*(4), 1375–1418.

Antràs, P. (2020). Conceptual aspects of global value chains. *The World Bank Economic Review, 34*(3), 551–574.

Arellano, C., Bulíř, A., Lane, T., and Lipschitz, L. (2009). The dynamic implications of foreign aid and its variability. *Journal of Development Economics, 88*(1), 87–102.
Armstrong, A. (1981). The political consequences of economic dependence. *Journal of Conflict Resolution, 25*(3), 401–428.
Ashok, G. (2000). Globalization, WTO and food security: Emerging issues and options. *Quarterly Journal of International Agriculture, 39*(4), 343–357.
Ashworth, L. M. (2013). Mapping a new world: Geography and the interwar study of international relations. *International Studies Quarterly, 57*(1), 138–149.
Asongu, S. A. and Nwachukwu, J. C. (2017). Is the threat of foreign aid withdrawal an effective deterrent to political oppression? Evidence from 53 African countries. *Journal of Economic Issues, 51*(1), 201–221.
Assyaukanie, L. (2009). *Islam and the Secular State in Indonesia.* Institute of Southeast Asian Studies.
Athukorala, P. C. and Jayasuriya, S. (2003). Food safety issues, trade and WTO rules: A developing country perspective. *World Economy, 26*(9), 1395–1416.
Athukorala, P. C. (2004). Agricultural trade reforms in the Doha Round: A developing country perspective. *Journal of World Trade, 38*, 877.
Atkinson, G. and Hamilton, K. (2003). Savings, growth and the resource curse hypothesis. *World Development, 31*(11), 1793–1807.
Attanayake, C. and Ren, Y. (2021). China, Sri Lanka and the BRI. *Research Handbook on the Belt and Road Initiative* (pp. 240–252). Elgar.
Azam, J. P., Devarajan, S., and O'Connell, S. A. (1999). *Aid Dependence Reconsidered* (Vol. 2144). World Bank Publications.
Baccini, L. and Dür, A. (2012). The new regionalism and policy interdependence. *British Journal of Political Science, 42*(1), 57–79.
Baccini, L., Dür, A., and Elsig, M. (2015). The politics of trade agreement design: Revisiting the depth–flexibility nexus. *International Studies Quarterly, 59*(4), 765–775.
Bahmani-Oskooee, M. and Economidou, C. (2009). Export led growth vs. growth led exports: LDCs experience. *The Journal of Developing Areas, 42*(2), 179–209.
Banerjee, A. V. and Duflo, E. (2011). *Poor Economics: A Radical Rethinking of the Way to Fight Global Poverty.* Public Affairs.
Barrett, C. B. (1998). Food aid: Is it development assistance, trade promotion, both, or neither? *American Journal of Agricultural Economics, 80*(3), 566–571.
Barrie, J. and Cruickshank, H. J. (2017). Shedding light on the last mile: A study on the diffusion of Pay As You Go Solar Home Systems in Central East Africa. *Energy Policy, 107*, 425–436.
Bartels, L. (2003). The WTO enabling clause and positive conditionality in the European Community's GSP program. *Journal of International Economic Law, 6*(2), 507–532.
Bechtel, M. M. and Ziegler, J. (2019). Foreign Policy Interests and International Disaster Assistance (September 30, 2019). Available at SSRN: https://ssrn.com/abstract=3472528.
Beeson, M. (2018). Geoeconomics with Chinese characteristics: The BRI and China's evolving grand strategy. *Economic and Political Studies, 6*(3), 240–256.
Beghin, J. C. and Bureau 1, J. C. (2001). Quantitative policy analysis of sanitary, phytosanitary and technical barriers to trade. *Économie internationale*, (3), 107–130.
Bergkamp, L. and Kogan, L. (2013). Trade, the precautionary principle, and post-modern regulatory process: Regulatory convergence in the transatlantic trade and investment partnership. *European Journal of Risk Regulation, 4*(4), 493–507.
Bermeo, S. B. (2016). Aid is not oil: Donor utility, heterogeneous aid, and the aid-democratization relationship. *International Organization, 70*(1), 1–32.
Bermeo, S. B. (2017). Aid allocation and targeted development in an increasingly connected world. *International Organization, 71*(4), 735–766.

Bermeo, S. (2018). *Targeted Development: Industrialized Country Strategy in a Globalizing World.* Oxford University Press.

Bernard, A. B., Jensen, J. B., Redding, S. J., and Schott, P. K. (2007). Firms in international trade. *Journal of Economic Perspectives, 21*(3), 105–130.

Berthélemy, J. (2006a). Aid allocation: Comparing donor's behaviours. *Swedish Economic Policy Review, 13*(2), 75.

Berthélemy, J. C. (2006b). Bilateral donors' interest vs. recipients' development motives in aid allocation: Do all donors behave the same? *Review of Development Economics, 10*(2), 179–194.

Betz, T. (2017). Trading interests: Domestic institutions, international negotiations, and the politics of trade. *The Journal of Politics, 79*(4), 1237–1252.

Bhagwati, J. N. (1995). US trade policy: The infatuation with FTAs. Discussion Paper Series No. 726. Columbia University, Department of Economics.

Bhagwati, J. (2008). *Termites in the Trading System: How Preferential Agreements Undermine Free Trade.* Oxford University Press.

Birdsall, N. M, Campos, J., Kim, C. S, Corden, W. M., MacDonald, L., Pack, H., Page, J., Sabor, R., and Stiglitz, J. (1993). *The East Asian Miracle: Economic Growth and Public Policy. A World Bank Policy Research Report.* Oxford University Press.

Birdsall, N., Rodrik, D., and Subramanian, A. (2005). How to help poor countries. *Foreign Affairs, 84*(4), 136–152.

Biscaye, P. E., Reynolds, T. W., and Anderson, C. L. (2017). Relative effectiveness of bilateral and multilateral aid on development outcomes. *Review of Development Economics, 21*(4), 1425–1447.

Blair, R. A., Marty, R., and Roessler, P. (2022). Foreign aid and soft power: Great power competition in Africa in the early twenty-first century. *British Journal of Political Science, 52*(3), 1355–1376.

Bonaglia, F. and Fukasaku, K. (2003). Export diversification in low-income countries: An international challenge after Doha. Working Paper No. 209. OECD Development Centre.

Bordo, M. D., Eichengreen, B., and Irwin, D. A. (1999). *Is Globalization Today Really Different than Globalization a Hunderd Years Ago?* (No. 7195). National Bureau of Economic Research.

Boys, J. and Andreoni, A. (2023). Does regionalism increase industrial policy space? An analytical framework applied to the East African textiles and apparel sector. *Third World Quarterly, 44*(8), 1680–1698.

Bracking, S. (2018). Corruption and state capture: What can citizens do? *Daedalus, 147*(3), 169–183.

Bräutigam, D. (2000). *Aid Dependence and Governance* (Vol. 1). Almqvist & Wiksell International.

Brazys, S. (2010). Dutch disease in the western Pacific: An overview of the FSM economy under the Amended Compact of Free Association, *Pacific Economic Bulletin*, 25(3), 24–39.

Brazys, S. R. (2013). Evidencing donor heterogeneity in Aid for Trade. *Review of International Political Economy, 20*(4), 947–978.

Brazys, S. (2014a). Outside looking in: Non-accession to the WTO. *Cambridge Review of International Affairs, 27*(4), 644–665.

Brazys, S. R. (2014b). Paradise lost: The cost of removing tax and trade provisions from the Compact of Free Association. *Asia & the Pacific Policy Studies, 1*(1), 204–215.

Brazys, S. and Winecoff, W. (2016). The Politics of Prominence in the Globalized Network of Trade Agreements. Presented at the International Political Economy Society (IPES) annual conference, Durham, NC.

Brazys, S. and Dukalskis, A. (2017). Canary in the coal mine? China, the UNGA, and the changing world order. *Review of International Studies, 43*(4), 742–764.

Brazys, S., Elkink, J. A., and Kelly, G. (2017). Bad neighbors? How co-located Chinese and World Bank development projects impact local corruption in Tanzania. *The Review of International Organizations, 12*(2), 227–253.

Brazys, S. and Panke, D. (2017). Why do states change positions in the United Nations General Assembly?. *International Political Science Review, 38*(1), 70–84.

Brazys, S. (2018). Aid dependence as aid persistence? Non-declining aid and growth. *Journal of International Relations and Development, 21*, 717–738.

Brazys, S. and Elkink, J. A. (2021). "Aid for Trade" effectiveness? Micro-level evidence from Nepal. *The European Journal of Development Research, 33*, 1493–1513.

Brazys, S. and Vadlamannati, K. C. (2021). Aid curse with Chinese characteristics? Chinese development flows and economic reforms. *Public Choice, 188*(3), 407–430.

Brazys, S., Mahmud, M., and Pillai, A. (2023). Who gets the goodies? Overlapping interests and the geography of aid for trade allocation in Bangladesh. *The Journal of Development Studies, 59*(2), 242–257.

Brech, V. and Potrafke, N. (2014). Donor ideology and types of foreign aid. *Journal of Comparative Economics, 42*(1), 61–75.

Bremer, J. and Bhuiyan, S. H. (2014). Community-led infrastructure development in informal areas in urban Egypt: A case study. *Habitat International, 44*, 258–267.

Brenton, P. and Chemutai, V. (2021). *The Trade and Climate Change Nexus: The Urgency and Opportunities for Developing Countries.* World Bank Publications.

Briggs, R. C. (2017). Does foreign aid target the poorest? *International Organization, 71*(1), 187–206.

Brutger, R. and Rathbun, B. (2021). Fair share? Equality and equity in American attitudes toward trade. *International Organization*, 75(3), 880–900.

Bucher, B. and Jasper, U. (2017). Revisiting 'identity' in International Relations: From identity as substance to identifications in action. *European Journal of International Relations, 23*(2), 391–415.

Bulmer-Thomas, V. and J. Dunkerley (Eds.). (1999). *The United States and Latin America: The New Agenda.* Harvard University Press.

Burnside, C. and Dollar, D. (2000). Aid, policies, and growth. *American Economic Review, 90*(4), 847–868.

Burgess, R., Greenstone, M., Ryan, N., and Sudarshan, A. (2020). The consequences of treating electricity as a right. *Journal of Economic Perspectives, 34*(1), 145–169.

Bush, E. and Simi, P. (2001). European farmers and their protests. In *Contentious Europeans. Protest and Politics in an Emerging Polity* (pp. 97–121). Rowman & Littlefield.

Caldara, D. and Iacoviello, M. (2022). Measuring geopolitical risk. *American Economic Review, 112*(4), 1194–1225.

Cali, M. and Te Velde, D. W. (2011). Does aid for trade really improve trade performance? *World Development, 39*(5), 725–740.

Cao, S. and Kingston, D. G. (2009). Biodiversity conservation and drug discovery: Can they be combined? The Suriname and Madagascar experiences. *Pharmaceutical Biology, 47*(8), 809–823 (p. 821).

Capoccia, G. (2016). Critical junctures. *The Oxford Handbook of Historical Institutionalism* (pp. 89–106). Oxford University Press.

Cardoso, F. H. and Faletto, E. (1979). *Dependency and Development in Latin America.* Univ. of California Press.

Carlsnaes, W. (1992). The agency-structure problem in foreign policy analysis. *International Studies Quarterly, 36*(3), 245–270.

Carnegie, A. and Dolan, L. R. (2021). The effects of rejecting aid on recipients' reputations: Evidence from natural disaster responses. *The Review of International Organizations, 16*, 495–519.

Castelli, B. (1994). The lifting of the trade embargo between the United States and Vietnam: The loss of a potential bargaining tool or a means of fostering cooperation. *Dick. J. Int'l L.*, *13*, 297.

Chand, D. (2018). Trade embargo as a geopolitical tool: A case of Nepal–India trade relations. *Polish Political Science Review*, *6*(1), 50–67.

Chauffour, J. P. and Maur, J. C. (Eds.). (2011). *Preferential Trade Agreement Policies for Development: A Handbook*. World Bank Publications.

Chauvet, L. and Guillaumont, P. (2009). Aid, volatility, and growth again: When aid volatility matters and when it does not. *Review of Development Economics*, *13*(3), 452–463.

Chauvet, L. and Ehrhart, H. (2018). Aid and growth: Evidence from firm-level data. *Journal of Development Economics*, *135*, 461–477.

Chaves-López, C., Serio, A., Grande-Tovar, C. D., Cuervo-Mulet, R., Delgado-Ospina, J., and Paparella, A. (2014). Traditional fermented foods and beverages from a microbiological and nutritional perspective: The Colombian heritage. *Comprehensive Reviews in Food Science and Food Safety*, *13*(5), 1031–1048.

Cheyne, I. (2006). The precautionary principle in EC and WTO Law: Searching for a common understanding. *Environmental Law Review*, *8*(4), 257–277.

Chi, G., Fang, H., Chatterjee, S., and Blumenstock, J. E. (2022). Microestimates of wealth for all low-and middle-income countries. *Proceedings of the National Academy of Sciences*, *119*(3), e2113658119.

Cohen, S. B. (2014). *Geopolitics: The Geography of International Relations*. Rowman & Littlefield.

Collier, D. and Munck, G. L. (2017). Building blocks and methodological challenges: A framework for studying critical junctures. *Qualitative and Multi-Method Research*, *15*, 2–9.

Compa, L. and Vogt, J. S. (2000). Labor rights in the Generalized System of Preferences: A 20-year review. *Comp. Lab. L. & Pol'y J.*, *22*, 199.

Cook, A. D., Shrestha, M., and Htet, Z. B. (2018). An assessment of international emergency disaster response to the 2015 Nepal earthquakes. *International Journal of Disaster Risk Reduction*, *31*, 535–547.

Coppolaro, L. (2018). In the shadow of globalization: The European Community and the United States in the GATT Negotiations of the Tokyo Round (1973–1979). *The International History Review*, *40*(4), 752–773.

Cordella, T., and Dell'Ariccia, G. (2007). Budget support versus project aid: A theoretical appraisal. *The Economic Journal*, *117*(523), 1260–1279.

Cordoba, G. F. (2022). The impact of the Panama Canal transfer on the Panamanian economy. *Economics Letters*, *211*, 110208.

Cuyvers, L. and Verherstraeten, S. (2005). The EU's Generalized System of Preferences and its ASEAN beneficiaries: A success story. *CAS (Centre for ASEAN Studies)* Discussion Paper No. 47.

Dalgaard, C. J., and Hansen, H. (2001). On aid, growth and good policies. *Journal of Development Studies*, *37*(6), 17–41.

Dany, C. (2015). Politicization of humanitarian aid in the European Union. *European Foreign Affairs Review*, *20*(3), 419–437.

Davis, C. L. and Wilf, M. (2017). Joining the Club: Accession to the GATT/WTO. *The Journal of Politics*, *79*(3), 964–978.

Deardorff, A. V. (2014). Trade implications of the Trans-Pacific Partnership for ASEAN and other Asian countries. *Asian Development Review*, *31*(2), 1–20.

De Bièvre, D. and Dür, A. (2005). Constituency interests and delegation in European and American trade policy. *Comparative Political Studies*, *38*(10), 1271–1296.

Delamont, S. (2004). Ethnography and participant observation. *Qualitative Research Practice*, *217*(205–217).

Dendere, C. and Taodzera, S. (2023). Zimbabwean civil society survival in the post-coup environment: A political settlements analysis. *Interest Groups & Advocacy*, *12*(2), 132–152.

De Sousa, J., Mayer, T., and Zignago, S. (2012). Market access in global and regional trade. *Regional Science and Urban Economics*, *42*(6), 1037–1052.

de Souza Leão, L., and Eyal, G. (2019). The rise of randomized controlled trials (RCTs) in international development in historical perspective. *Theory and Society*, *48*, 383–418.

Dhakal, D. (2014). *Impact of Quota Phase out in Garment Industry of Nepal* (Master's thesis).

Diamond, J. (1997). Guns, germs, and steel: the fates of human societies. Norton & Company.

Dietrich, S. (2013). Bypass or engage? Explaining donor delivery tactics in foreign aid allocation. *International Studies Quarterly*, *57*(4), 698–712.

Dietrich, S. (2016). Donor political economies and the pursuit of aid effectiveness. *International Organization*, *70*(1), 65–102.

Disdier, A. C., Fontagné, L., and Mimouni, M. (2008). The impact of regulations on agricultural trade: Evidence from the SPS and TBT agreements. *American Journal of Agricultural Economics*, *90*(2), 336–350.

Dixit, A. K. and Stiglitz, J. E. (1977). Monopolistic competition and optimum product diversity. *The American Economic Review*, *67*(3), 297–308.

Dixit, A. and Norman, V. (1980). *Theory of International Trade: A Dual, General Equilibrium Approach*. Cambridge University Press.

Djankov, S., Montalvo, J. G., and Reynal-Querol, M. (2008). The curse of aid. *Journal of Economic Growth*, *13*, 169–194.

Doeser, F. and Eidenfalk, J. (2013). The importance of windows of opportunity for foreign policy change. *International Area Studies Review*, *16*(4), 390–406.

Dollar, D. and Levin, V. (2006). The increasing selectivity of foreign aid, 1984–2003. *World Development*, *34*(12), 2034–2046.

Dollar, D. (2018). Is China's development finance a challenge to the international order? *Asian Economic Policy Review*, *13*(2), 283–298.

Donaubauer, J., Meyer, B., and Nunnenkamp, P. (2016). Aid, infrastructure, and FDI: Assessing the transmission channel with a new index of infrastructure. *World Development*, *78*, 230–245.

Dos Santos, N. B. and Cunha, R. (2005). Generalized system of preferences in general agreement on tariffs and trade/World Trade Organization: History and current issues. *Journal of World Trade*, *39*(4), 637–670.

Doucouliagos, H. and Paldam, M. (2009). The aid effectiveness literature: The sad results of 40 years of research. *Journal of Economic Surveys*, 23(3), 433–461.

Dreher, A. and Sturm, J. E. (2012). Do the IMF and the World Bank influence voting in the UN General Assembly? *Public Choice*, *151*, 363–397.

Dreher, A. and Fuchs, A. (2015). Rogue aid? An empirical analysis of China's aid allocation. *Canadian Journal of Economics/Revue canadienne d'économique*, *48*(3), 988–1023.

Dreher, A., Fuchs, A., Parks, B., Strange, A. M., and Tierney, M. J. (2018). Apples and dragon fruits: The determinants of aid and other forms of state financing from China to Africa. *International Studies Quarterly*, *62*(1), 182–194.

Dreher, A., Fuchs, A., Parks, B., Strange, A., and Tierney, M. J. (2021). Aid, China, and growth: Evidence from a new global development finance dataset. *American Economic Journal: Economic Policy*, *13*(2), 135–174.

Dreher, A., Fuchs, A., Parks, B., Strange, A., and Tierney, M. J. (2022). *Banking on Beijing: The Aims and Impacts of China's Overseas Development Program*. Cambridge University Press.

Dreher, A., Lang, V., Rosendorff, B. P., and Vreeland, J. R. (2022). Bilateral or multilateral? International financial flows and the dirty-work hypothesis. *The Journal of Politics*, *84*(4), 1932–1946.

Dulio, D. A. and Klemanski, J. S. (2018). Hiding behind a thin blue wall. In Schultz, D.A. and Jacob, R. (Eds.), *Presidential Swing States*, 247–272. Lexington Books.

Dunning, T. (2004). Conditioning the effects of aid: Cold War politics, donor credibility, and democracy in Africa. *International Organization*, *58*(2), 409–423.

Dür, A. (2010). *Protection for Exporters: Power and Discrimination in Transatlantic Trade Relations, 1930–2010*. Cornell University Press.

Dür, A., Baccini, L., and Elsig, M. (2014). The design of international trade agreements: Introducing a new dataset. *The Review of International Organizations*, *9*, 353–375.

Dzionek-Kozlowska, J. and Matera, R. (2021). Institutions without culture: On Daron Acemoglu and James Robinson's Theory of Economic Development. *Journal of Economic Issues*, *55*(3), 656–676.

Easterly, W. R. (2002). *The Elusive Quest for Growth: Economists' Adventures and Misadventures in the Tropics*. MIT Press.

Easterly, W. (2003a). IMF and World Bank structural adjustment programs and poverty. In Dooley, M. P. and Frankel, J. A. (Eds.) *Managing Currency Crises in Emerging Markets* (pp. 361–392). University of Chicago Press.

Easterly, W. (2003b). Can foreign aid buy growth? *Journal of Economic Perspectives*, *17*(3), 23–48.

Easterly, W. (2006). The big push deja vu: A review of Jeffrey Sachs's the end of poverty: economic possibilities for our time. *Journal of Economic Literature*, *44*(1), 96–105.

Eaton, J. and Kortum, S. (2002). Technology, geography, and trade. *Econometrica*, *70*(5), 1741–1779.

Edwards, K. (2016). *Financing Pacific Governments for Pacific Development*. World Bank.

Eichengreen, B. J. (1996). *Golden Fetters: The Gold Standard and the Great Depression, 1919–1939*. NBER Series on Long-term Factors in Economic Development.

Eisenman, J. and Heginbotham, E. (2019). Building a more "democratic" and "multipolar" world. *China Review*, *19*(4), 55–84.

Elgström, O. and Delputte, S. (2017). An end to Nordic exceptionalism? Europeanisation and Nordic development policies. In Carbone, M. and Orbie, J. (Eds.) *The Europeanisation of Development Policy* (pp. 28–41). Routledge.

Erickson, A. S. and Wuthnow, J. (2016). Barriers, springboards and benchmarks: China conceptualizes the Pacific "Island Chains." *The China Quarterly*, 225, 1–22.

European Union. (2023) Regulation (EU) No 978/2012 of the European Parliament and of the Council of 25 October 2012 applying a scheme of generalised tariff preferences and repealing Council Regulation (EC) No 732/2008. Current Consolidated version: 01/01/2023.

Evans, A. (2020). Overcoming the global despondency trap: Strengthening corporate accountability in supply chains. *Review of International Political Economy*, *27*(3), 658–685.

Faber, G. and Orbie, J. (2009). Everything but arms: Much more than appears at first sight. *JCMS: Journal of Common Market Studies*, *47*(4), 767–787.

Faini, R., De Melo, J., and Takacs, W. (1995). A primer on the MFA maze. *World Economy*, *18*(1), 113–135.

Farrell, H. and Newman, A. (2023). The new economic security state: How de-risking will remake geopolitics. *Foreign Aff.*, *102*, 106.

Feenstra, R. C. (1998). Integration of trade and disintegration of production in the global economy. *Journal of Economic Perspectives*, *12*(4), 31–50.

Feeny, S. and McGillivray, M. (2013). Aid and growth in small island developing states. In Santos-Paulino, A. U., McGillivray, M. and Naudé, W. (Eds.) *Understanding Small-Island Developing States* (pp. 83–103). Routledge.

Findley, M. G., Harris, A. S., Milner, H. V., and Nielson, D. L. (2017). Who controls foreign aid? Elite versus public perceptions of donor influence in aid-dependent Uganda. *International Organization*, *71*(4), 633–663.

Fischer, S. (2003). Globalization and its challenges. *American Economic Review*, *93*(2), 1–30.

Fletcher, C. H. and Richmond, B. M. (2010). Climate change in the Federated States of Micronesia. *Food and Water Security, Climate Risk Management, and Adaptive Strategies.* University of Hawai'i, Hawaii.

Fomby, T., Ikeda, Y., and Loayza, N. V. (2013). The growth aftermath of natural disasters. *Journal of Applied Econometrics*, *28*(3), 412–434.

Forbes, D. (2010). *The Geography of Underdevelopment: A Critical Survey* (Vol. 68). Routledge.

Forster, A. (1999). The European Union in South-East Asia: continuity and change in turbulent times. *International Affairs*, *75*(4), 743–758.

Francken, N., Minten, B., and Swinnen, J. F. (2012). The political economy of relief aid allocation: Evidence from Madagascar. *World Development*, *40*(3), 486–500.

Francois, J. and Martin, W. (2003). Formula approaches for market access negotiations. *World Economy*, *26*(1), 1–28.

Francois, J. and Hoekman, B. (Eds.). (2019). *Behind-the-Border Policies: Assessing and Addressing Non-tariff Measures.* Cambridge University Press.

Frankel, J. A. and Romer, D. (1999). Does trade cause growth? *American Economic Review*, *89*(3), 379–399.

Fritz, V. and Menocal, A. R. (2007). Developmental states in the new millennium: Concepts and challenges for a new aid agenda. *Development Policy Review*, 25(5), 531–552.

Frynas, J. G. (2004). The oil boom in Equatorial Guinea. *African Affairs*, *103*(413), 527–546.

Galperín, C. and Miguez, I. D. (2009). Green box subsidies and trade-distorting support: Is there a cumulative impact? In Meléndez-Ortiz, R., Bellmann, C. and Hepburn, J. (Eds.) *Agricultural Subsidies in the WTO Green Box: Ensuring Coherence with Sustainable Development Goals* (pp.239–257). Cambridge University Press.

García, M., Quintero, L. F. M., and Montoya, A. (2012). Análisis comparativo de competitividad de las cadenas productivas de cacao de Colombia y Ecuador. *Revista de Ciencias Agrícolas*, *29*(1), 99–112.

Gelpern, A., Horn, S., Morris, S., Parks, B., and Trebesch, C. (2023). How China lends: A rare look into 100 debt contracts with foreign governments. *Economic Policy*, *38*(114), 345–416.

General Agreement on Tariffs and Trade (GATT). (1947). Article I—General Most- Favoured-Nation.

Geraets, D. (2018). The General Agreement on Tariffs and Trade 1947 (GATT 1947) and the World Trade Organization (WTO)—why join the club? A Legal Analysis. *Accession to the World Trade Organization* (pp. 11–35). Edward Elgar Publishing.

Gerring, J. and Cojocaru, L. (2016). Selecting cases for intensive analysis: A diversity of goals and methods. *Sociological Methods & Research*, *45*(3), 392–423.

Gerschenkron, A. (1952). Economic Backwardness in Historical Perspective. In Hoselitz, B. (Ed.) *The Progress of Undeveloped Countries.* Chicago University Press.

Ghoshray, A. (2010). The extent of the world coffee market. *Bulletin of Economic Research*, *62*(1), 97–107.

Giroud, A. (2007). Vietnam in the regional and global transnational corporations value chain. In Grioiud, A., Mohr, A. T., and Yang, D. (Eds.) *Multinationals and Asia* (pp. 52–69). Routledge.

Glyn, A. (2007). *Capitalism Unleashed: Finance, Globalization, and Welfare.* Oxford University Press.

Gnangnon, S. K. (2018). Aid for trade and trade policy in recipient countries. *The International Trade Journal*, *32*(5), 439–464.

Goh, E. (2007). Great powers and hierarchical order in Southeast Asia: Analyzing regional security strategies. *International Security*, *32*(3), 113–157.

Goldin, I. (1990). *Comparative Advantage: Theory and Application to Developing Country Agriculture* (No. 16). OECD Publishing.

Government of Japan, Ministry of Foreign Affairs (MOFA). (2010). *Enhancing Enlightened National Interest, ODA Review Final Report*, Tokyo: MOFA, p. 15.

Government of the Federated States of Micronesia. Compact Infrastructure Sector 3rd Quarter 2021 Report. Palikir, Pohnpei.

Gowa, J. and Kim, S. Y. (2005). An exclusive country club: the effects of the GATT on trade, 1950–94. *World Politics*, *57*(4), 453–478.

Grossman, G. M. and Sykes, A. O. (2005). A preference for development: the law and economics of GSP. *World Trade Review*, *4*(1), 41–67.

Gumilang, H., Mukhopadhyay, K., and Thomassin, P. J. (2011). Economic and environmental impacts of trade liberalization: The case of Indonesia. *Economic Modelling*, *28*(3), 1030–1041.

Gur, N., and Dilek, S. (2023). US–China economic rivalry and the reshoring of global supply chains. *The Chinese Journal of International Politics*, *16*(1), 61–83.

Hakobyan, S. (2020). GSP expiration and declining exports from developing countries. *Canadian Journal of Economics/Revue canadienne d'économique*, *53*(3), 1132–1161.

Halikiopoulou, D. and Vlandas, T. (2019). What is new and what is nationalist about Europe's new nationalism? Explaining the rise of the far right in Europe. *Nations and Nationalism*, *25*(2), 409–434.

Handley, K. and Limão, N. (2017). Policy uncertainty, trade, and welfare: Theory and evidence for China and the United States. *American Economic Review*, *107*(9), 2731–2783.

Hansen, H. and Tarp, F. (2001). Aid and growth regressions. *Journal of Development Economics*, *64*(2), 547–570.

Hashemi, M. and Jenkins, G. (2022). Can privatization of distribution substations improve electricity reliability for non-residential customers? An application to Nepal. *Utilities Policy*, *74*, 101331.

Hassall, G. (2023). Membership and participation in the major organs. *The United Nations and the Pacific Islands* (pp. 167–203). Springer International Publishing.

Hawkins, D. G., Lake, D. A., Nielson, D. L., and Tierney, M. J. (2006). Delegation under anarchy: States, international organizations, and principal–agent theory. In Hawkins, D. G., Lake, D. A., Nielson, D. L., & Tierney, M. J. (Eds.) *Delegation and Agency in International Organizations* (pp. 3–21). Cambridge University Press.

Hayat, M. T., Nauman, M., Nazir, N., Ali, S., and Bangash, N. (2019). Environmental hazards of cadmium: past, present, and future. In Hasanuzzaman, M., Fujita, M., and Prasad, M. N. V. (Eds.). *Cadmium Toxicity and Tolerance in Plants* (pp. 163–183). Academic Press.

Heckelei, T. and Swinnen, J. (2012). Introduction to the Special Issue of the World Trade Review on 'Standards and Non-tariff Barriers in Trade'. *World Trade Review*, *11*(3), 353–355.

Heckscher, G., Heckscher, E. F., and Ohlin, B. (1991). *Heckscher-Ohlin Trade Theory*. MIT Press.

Helble, M., Mann, C. L., and Wilson, J. S. (2012). Aid-for-trade facilitation. *Review of World Economics*, *148*, 357–376.

Heller, P. S. (1975). A model of public fiscal behavior in developing countries: Aid, investment, and taxation. *The American Economic Review*, *65*(3), 429–445.

Helpman, E. (1984). A simple theory of international trade with multinational corporations. *Journal of Political Economy*, *92*(3), 451–471.

Helpman, E. and Krugman, P. R. (1985). *Market Structure and Foreign Trade: Increasing Returns, Imperfect Competition, and the International Economy*. MIT Press.

Herz, B. and Wagner, M. (2011). The dark side of the Generalized System of Preferences. *Review of International Economics, 19*(4), 763–775.

Hezel, F. X. and Levin, M. J. (1996). New trends in Micronesian migration: FSM migration to Guam and the Marianas, 1990–1993. *Pacific Studies, 19*, 24–24.

Hillbom, E. (2008). Diamonds or development? A structural assessment of Botswana's forty years of success. *The Journal of Modern African Studies, 46*(2), 191–214.

Hinthorne, L. L. (2011). Democratic crisis or crisis of confidence? What local perceptual lenses tell us about Madagascar's 2009 political crisis. *Democratization, 18*(2), 535–561.

Hoeffler, A. and Outram, V. (2011). Need, merit, or self-interest—what determines the allocation of aid? *Review of Development Economics, 15*(2), 237–250.

Hoekman, B. M., Ng, F., and Olarreaga, M. (2001). *Tariff Peaks in the Quad and Least Developed Country Exports* (Vol. 2747). Centre for Economic Policy Research, London.

Hoekman, B. and Nicita, A. (2011). Trade policy, trade costs, and developing country trade. *World Development, 39*(12), 2069–2079.

Holden, P. (2014). Tensions in the discourse and practice of the European Union's Aid for Trade. *Contemporary Politics, 20*(1), 90–102.

Hollis, M. and Smith, S. (1994). Two stories about structure and agency. *Review of International Studies*, 20(3), 241–251.

Houck, J. P. (1979). Agricultural trade: Protectionism, policy, and the Tokyo/Geneva Negotiating Round. *American Journal of Agricultural Economics, 61*(5), 860–873.

Hudson, D., Ethridge, D. E., and Mutuc, M. E. M. (2011). Lessons learned from the phase-out of the MFA: Moving from managed distortion to managed distortion. *Estey Journal of International Law and Trade Policy, 12*(1), 29–43.

Hudson, J. and Mosley, P. (2008). Aid volatility, policy and development. *World Development, 36*(10), 2082–2102.

Hudson, J. (2015). Consequences of aid volatility for macroeconomic management and aid effectiveness. *World Development, 69*, 62–74.

Huff, W. G. (1997). *The Economic Growth of Singapore: Trade and Development in the Twentieth Century*. Cambridge University Press.

Hurst, R., Tidwell, T., and Hawkins, D. (2017). Down the rathole? Public support for US foreign aid. *International Studies Quarterly, 61*(2), 442–454.

Ikenberry, G. J. (2004). Liberalism and empire: Logics of order in the American unipolar age. *Review of International Studies, 30*(4), 609–630.

Ikenberry, G. J. (2009). Liberal internationalism 3.0: America and the dilemmas of liberal world order. *Perspectives on Politics, 7*(1), 71–87.

Imai, K. and Weinstein, J. M. (2000). Measuring the economic impact of civil war. *CID Working Paper Series*.

International Monetary Fund. (1996). Nepal – Selected Issues. IMF Staff Country Report No. 96/63. International Monetary Fund. Washington, DC.

Isaksson, A. S. and Kotsadam, A. (2018). Chinese aid and local corruption. *Journal of Public Economics, 159*, 146–159.

Islam, M. R. and Alam, S. (2009). Preferential trade agreements and the scope of GATT article XXIV, GATS article V and the enabling clause: An appraisal of GATT/WTO jurisprudence. *Netherlands International Law Review, 56*(1), 1–34.

Ismail, F. and Vickers, B. (2011). Towards fair and inclusive decision-making in WTO negotiations. In Birkbeck, C. D. (Ed.) *Making Global Trade Governance Work for Development*, 461–485. Cambridge University Press.

Itçaina, X., Roger, A., and Smith, A. (2016). *Varietals of Capitalism: A Political Economy of the Changing Wine Industry*. Cornell University Press.

Iwami, T. and Iwami, T. (1995). *The Bretton Woods System as a Gold Exchange Standard* (pp. 1–35). Palgrave Macmillan UK.

Jablonski, R. S. (2014). How aid targets votes: The impact of electoral incentives on foreign aid distribution. *World Politics*, *66*(2), 293–330.

Jackson, J. H. (2007). *The Jurisprudence of GATT and the WTO: Insights on Treaty Law and Economic Relations.* Cambridge University Press.

Johnson, R. C. and Noguera, G. (2012). Accounting for intermediates: Production sharing and trade in value added. *Journal of International Economics*, *86*(2), 224–236.

Jones, K. (2009). Green room politics and the WTO's crisis of representation. *Progress in Development Studies*, *9*(4), 349–357.

Jones, V. C. (2017). *Generalized System of Preferences (GSP): Overview and Issues for Congress.* Congressional Research Service.

Josling, T., Tangermann, S., and Warley, K. (1996). *Agriculture in the GATT.* Springer.

Ju, J. and Krishna, K. (2005). Firm behaviour and market access in a free trade area with rules of origin. *Canadian Journal of Economics/Revue canadienne d'économique*, *38*(1), 290–308.

Kabeer, N. and Mahmud, S. (2004). Rags, riches and women workers: Export-oriented garment manufacturing in Bangladesh. In M. Carr (Ed.), *Chains of Fortune: Linking Women Producers and Workers with Global Markets* (pp. 133–164). Commonwealth Secretariat.

Kamete, A. Y. (2016). 'Programmed to serve': urban planning and elite interests in Zimbabwe. In Silva, C. N. (Ed.) *Governing Urban Africa*, (pp. 151–169). Springer.

Khan, M. (2010). Political settlements and the governance of growth-enhancing institutions.

Kharas, H. (2008). Measuring the cost of aid volatility. *Wolfensohn Center for Development Working Paper*, (3).

Karsenty, G. and Laird, S. (1987). The GSP, policy options and the new round. *Weltwirts chaftliches Archiv*, *123*, 262–296.

Kegley Jr, C. W. and Hook, S. W. (1991). US foreign aid and UN voting: Did Reagan's linkage strategy buy deference or defiance? *International Studies Quarterly*, *35*(3), 295–312.

Kenner, J. and Peake, K. (2017). The Bangladesh Sustainability Compact: An effective exercise of global experimentalist EU governance?. *Cambridge Yearbook of European Legal Studies*, *19*, 86–115.

Keohane, R. O. (1965). Political influence in the General Assembly. *Int'l Conciliation*, *36*, 1.

Khanal, D. R. (2011). Rules of origin in GSP schemes and their impact on Nepal's exports: A case study of tea, carpets, pashmina and handicrafts products. Asia-Pacific Research and Training Network on Trade Working Paper Series, No. 98.

Kheir-El-Din, H. (2000). Enforcement of product standards as barriers to trade: The case of Egypt. In Nassar, H. and Alfonse, A. (Eds) *Egyptian Exports and Challenges of the 21st Century* (pp. 213–228). Cairo: Center for Economic and Financial Research and Studies.

Kim, C. K. (2010). *The Effects of Natural Disasters on Long-run Economic Growth* (Doctoral dissertation).

Kim, S. E. and Pelc, K. (2021). How responsive is trade adjustment assistance? *Political Science Research and Methods*, *9*(4), 889–898.

Klandermans, B., Sabucedo, J. M., Rodriguez, M., and De Weerd, M. (2002). Identity processes in collective action participation: Farmers' identity and farmers' protest in the Netherlands and Spain. *Political Psychology*, *23*(2), 235–251.

Knack, S. (2001). Aid dependence and the quality of governance: Cross-country empirical tests. *Southern Economic Journal*, *68*(2), 310–329.

Kodama, M. (2012). Aid unpredictability and economic growth. *World Development*, *40*(2), 266–272.

Koeberle, S., Stavreski, Z., and Walliser, J. (Eds.). (2006). *Budget Support as More Effective Aid?: Recent Experiences and Emerging Lessons.* World Bank Publications.

Koubi, V. (2005). War and economic performance. *Journal of Peace Research*, *42*(1), 67–82.

Kristensen, P. M., and Morgan, P. (2018). Leadership with Chinese characteristics. *Chinese Political Science Review*, *3*, 1–9.

Krueger, A. (1997). Trade policy and development: How we learn. *American Economic Review* 87(1): 1–22.

Krugman, P. R. (1979). Increasing returns, monopolistic competition, and international trade. *Journal of International Economics*, *9*(4), 469–479.

Krugman, P. (1991). Increasing returns and economic geography. *Journal of Political Economy*, *99*(3), 483–499.

Krugman, P. and Venables, A. J. (1995). Globalization and the Inequality of Nations. *The Quarterly Journal of Economics*, *110*(4), 857–880.

Kucik, J. (2012). The domestic politics of institutional design: Producer preferences over trade agreement rules. *Economics & Politics*, *24*(2), 95–118.

Kumar, U. T. T. A. M. (2017). *Trade Policy of India since 1991: A Critical Evaluation and Comparative Study between Pre and Post Reform Periods*. Ranchi University, Ranchi Jhakhand, India.

Kupchan, C. A. (2020). *Isolationism: A History of America's Efforts to Shield Itself from the World*. Oxford University Press.

Kwan, C. H. (2020). The China–US trade war: Deep-rooted causes, shifting focus and uncertain prospects. *Asian Economic Policy Review*, *15*(1), 55–72.

Laksmana, E. A. (2011). The enduring strategic trinity: Explaining Indonesia's geopolitical architecture. *Journal of the Indian Ocean Region*, *7*(1), 95–116.

Laney, R. and Turner, B. L. (2015). The persistence of self-provisioning among smallholder farmers in Northeast Madagascar. *Human Ecology*, *43*, 811–826.

Langan, M. and Scott, J. (2014). The aid for trade charade. *Cooperation and Conflict*, *49*(2), 143–161.

Langan, M. and Price, S. (2020). The EU's development policy: Forging relations of dependence? In Bigo, D., Diez, T., Fanoulis, E., Rosamond, B., and Stivachtis, Y. A. (Eds.) *The Routledge Handbook of Critical European Studies* (pp. 499–510). Routledge.

Lanz, R. and Miroudot, S. (2011). *Intra-firm trade*. OECD Trade Policy Working Papers, 114.

Larch, M., Tan, S. W., and Yotov, Y. V. (2023). A simple method to ex-ante quantify the unobservable effects of trade liberalization and trade protection. *Journal of Comparative Economics*, *51*(4), 1200–1213

Le Houérou, H. N. (1996). Climate change, drought and desertification. *Journal of Arid Environments*, *34*(2), 133–185.

Lensink, R. and Morrissey, O. (2000). Aid instability as a measure of uncertainty and the positive impact of aid on growth. *The Journal of Development Studies*, *36*(3), 31–49.

Levy, B. (2014). *Working with the Grain: Integrating Governance and Growth in Development Strategies*. Oxford University Press.

Licht, A. A. (2010). Coming into money: The impact of foreign aid on leader survival. *Journal of Conflict Resolution*, *54*(1), 58–87.

Lieberman, E. S. (2005). Nested analysis as a mixed-method strategy for comparative research. *American Political Science Review*, *99*(3), 435–452.

Lin, J. Y., Cai, F., and Li, Z. (2004). *The China Miracle: Development Strategy and Economic Reform (Revised Edition)*. The Chinese University of Hong Kong Press.

Lindberg, S. I., Coppedge, M., Gerring, J., and Teorell, J. (2014). V-Dem: A new way to measure democracy. *Journal of Democracy*, *25*(3), 159–169.

Löfflmann, G. (2016). The pivot between containment, engagement, and restraint: President Obama's conflicted grand strategy in Asia. *Asian Security*, 12(2), 92–110.

Long, L. D. and Oxfeld, E. (Eds.). (2004). *Coming Home?: Refugees, Migrants, and Those Who Stayed Behind*. University of Pennsylvania Press.

Lopez-Acevedo, G. and Robertson, R. (Eds.). (2012). *Sewing Success?: Employment, Wages, and Poverty Following the End of the Multi-fibre Arrangement*. World Bank Publications.

Lorz, O. (2020). Investment in trade facilitating infrastructure: A political-economy analysis. *European Journal of Political Economy, 65*, 101928.

Macekura, S. J. (2020). The mismeasure of progress: Economic growth and its critics. University of Chicago Press.

Macey, J. R. and Miller, G. P. (1992). The end of history and the new world order: The triumph of capitalism and the competition between liberalism and democracy. *Cornell Int'l LJ, 25*, 277.

Madsen, J. B. (2001). Trade barriers and the collapse of world trade during the Great Depression. *Southern Economic Journal, 67*(4), 848–868.

Maher, R. (2018). Bipolarity and the future of US–China relations. *Political Science Quarterly, 133*(3), 497–525.

Makonese, T., Kimemia, D. K., and Annegarn, H. J. (2012, April). Assessment of free basic electricity and use of pre-paid meters in South Africa. In *2012 Proceedings of the 20th Domestic Use of Energy Conference* (pp.165–172). IEEE.

Manger, M. S. (2009). *Investing in Protection: The Politics of Preferential Trade Agreements between North and South.* Cambridge University Press.

Manger, M. S., Pickup, M. A., and Snijders, T. A. (2012). A hierarchy of preferences: A longitudinal network analysis approach to PTA formation. *Journal of Conflict Resolution, 56*(5), 853–878.

Manger, M. S. and Shadlen, K. C. (2014). Political trade dependence and North–South trade agreements. *International Studies Quarterly, 58*(1), 79–91.

Marshall, M. G., Gurr, T. R., and Jaggers, K. (2020). Center for Systemic Peace. *Polity IV Project.*

Martínez-Zarzoso, I., Nowak-Lehmann D, F., and Rehwald, K. (2017). Is aid for trade effective? A panel quantile regression approach. *Review of Development Economics, 21*(4), e175–e203.

Marty, R., Dolan, C. B., Leu, M., and Runfola, D. (2017). Taking the health aid debate to the subnational level: the impact and allocation of foreign health aid in Malawi. *BMJ Global Health, 2*(1), e000129.

Matamanda, A. R., Chirisa, I., and Rammile, S. (2021). Elitist domination and its import: Survey of four decades of perpetuation of inequities in Zimbabwe. *Politikon, 48*(3), 450–467.

McDonald, J. (2005). Domestic regulation, international standards, and technical barriers to trade. *World Trade Review, 4*(2), 249–274.

McKenzie, F. (2008). GATT and the Cold War: Accession debates, institutional development, and the Western Alliance, 1947–1959. *Journal of Cold War Studies, 10*(3), 78–109.

McKinlay, R. D. and Little, R. (1977). A foreign policy model of US bilateral aid allocation. *World Politics, 30*(1), 58–86.

McKinlay, R. D. and Little, R. (1979). The US aid relationship: A test of the recipient need and the donor interest models. *Political Studies, 27*(2), 236–250.

McLeod, R. H. (2000). Soeharto's Indonesia: A better class of corruption. *Agenda: a journal of policy analysis and reform, 7*(2), 99–112.

Melitz, M. J. (2003). The impact of trade on intra-industry reallocations and aggregate industry productivity. *Econometrica, 71*(6), 1695–1725.

Mertz, O., Halsnæs, K., Olesen, J. E., and Rasmussen, K. (2009). Adaptation to climate change in developing countries. *Environmental Management, 43*, 743–752.

Miliband, D. and Gurumurthy, R. (2015). Improving humanitarian aid: How to make relief more efficient and effective. *Foreign Affairs, 94*(4), 118–129.

Milner, H. V. and Tingley, D. (2013). Public opinion and foreign aid: A review essay. *International Interactions, 39*(3), 389–401.

Mittelman, J. H. (2011). Rethinking "the new regionalism" in the context of globalization. In Mittelman, J. (Ed.) *Contesting Global Order* (pp. 97–115). Routledge.

Mori, A. (2020). Latin America and the new global order: dangers and opportunities in a multipolar world. *Latin America and the New Global Order*, 1–151. Ledizioni.

Mosley, P. (1985). The political economy of foreign aid: A model of the market for a public good. *Economic Development and Cultural Change, 33*(2), 373–393.

Mulgan, A. G. (2013). *The Politics of Agriculture in Japan*. Routledge.

Muller, E. N. (1985). Dependent economic development, aid dependence on the United States, and democratic breakdown in the Third World. *International Studies Quarterly, 29*(4), 445–469.

Mundell, R. A. (1957). International trade and factor mobility. *The American Economic Review, 47*(3), 321–335.

Murphy-Gregory, H., Kellow, A., Hofmeister, W., and Melissen, J. (2016). Forum shopping and global governance. In Hofmeister, W. and Melissen, J. (Eds.) *Rethinking International Institutions: Diplomacy and Impact on Emerging World Order*, (pp. 39–50). Clingendael.

Mykhnenko, V. (2020). Causes and consequences of the war in Eastern Ukraine: An economic geography perspective. *Europe-Asia Studies, 72*(3), 528–560.

Narula, R. and Dunning, J. H. (2000). Industrial development, globalization and multinational enterprises: New realities for developing countries. *Oxford Development Studies, 28*(2), 141–167.

Naughton, B. J. (2018). *The Chinese Economy: Adaptation and Growth*. MIT Press.

Nel, P., and Taylor, I. (2013). Bugger thy neighbour? IBSA and South–South solidarity. *Third World Quarterly, 34*(6), 1091–1110.

Nishitateno, S. (2024). Does official development assistance benefit the donor economy? New evidence from Japanese overseas infrastructure projects. *International Tax and Public Finance, 31*(4), 1037–1065.

North, D. C., Wallis, J. J., and Weingast, B. R. (2009). *Violence and Social Orders: A Conceptual Framework for Interpreting Recorded Human History*. Cambridge University Press.

Nunnenkamp, P., Öhler, H., and Sosa Andrés, M. (2017). Need, merit and politics in multilateral aid allocation: A district-level analysis of World Bank projects in India. *Review of Development Economics, 21*(1), 126–156.

O'Brien-Udry, C. (2022). Aid withdrawal: theory and evidence from international climate Politics.

OECD/WTO (2022). *Aid for Trade at a Glance 2022: Empowering Connected, Sustainable Trade*. OECD Publishing.

Orefice, G. (2017). Non-tariff measures, specific trade concerns and tariff reduction. *The World Economy, 40*(9), 1807–1835.

Ornelas, E. and Ritel, M. (2020). The not-so-generalised effects of the Generalized System of Preferences. *The World Economy, 43*(7), 1809–1840.

Ortiz, J. (2012). Déjà vu: Latin America and its new trade dependency ... this time with China. *Latin American Research Review, 47*(3), 175–190.

Owen, E. (2017). Exposure to offshoring and the politics of trade liberalization: debate and votes on free trade agreements in the US House of Representatives, 2001–2006. *International Studies Quarterly, 61*(2), 297–311.

Özden, Ç. and Reinhardt, E. (2005). The perversity of preferences: GSP and developing country trade policies, 1976–2000. *Journal of Development Economics, 78*(1), 1–21.

Paderon, M. M. A. (2022). Philippine-United States Trade Relations: Looking Back and a Way Forward. East-West Center. Number 588, June 13, 2022.

Palit, A. (2017). Mega-regional trade agreements and non-participating developing countries: Differential impacts, challenges and policy options. *Competition & Change, 21*(5), 417–434.

Palley, T. I. (2012). The rise and fall of export-led growth. *Investigación económica, 71*(280), 141–161.

Pang, E. S. (2007). Embedding security into free trade: The case of the United States–Singapore Free Trade Agreement. *Contemporary Southeast Asia, 29*(1), 1–32.

Park, S., Lim, W., You, S., and Song, G. (2019). Ochratoxin A exerts neurotoxicity in human astrocytes through mitochondria-dependent apoptosis and intracellular calcium overload. *Toxicology Letters, 313*, 42–49.

Park, Y. I., and Anderson, K. (1991). The rise and demise of textiles and clothing in economic development: the case of Japan. *Economic Development and Cultural Change, 39*(3), 531–548.

Pauwelyn, J. (2005). Rien ne Va Plus? Distinguishing domestic regulation from market access in GATT and GATS. *World Trade Review, 4*(2), 131–170.

Pelc, K. J. (2011). Why do some countries get better WTO accession terms than others? *International Organization, 65*(4), 639–672.

Peters, J., Langbein, J., and Roberts, G. (2018). Generalization in the tropics–development policy, randomized controlled trials, and external validity. *The World Bank Research Observer, 33*(1), 34–64.

Pietrobelli, C. and Seri, C. (2023). *Reshoring, Nearshoring and Developing Countries: Readiness and Implications for Latin America.* UNU-MERIT.

Ploberger, C. (2016). China's reform and opening process: A new model of political economy? *Journal of Chinese Economic and Business Studies, 14*(1), 69–87.

Polyak, P. (2023). Jobs and fiction: Identifying the effect of corporate tax avoidance inflating export measures in Ireland. *Journal of European Public Policy, 30*(10), 2143–2164.

Portela, C. and Mora-Sanguinetti, J. S. (2023). Sanctions effectiveness, development and regime type. Are aid suspensions and economic sanctions alike? *World Development, 172*, 106370.

Postigo, A. (2022). Utilization of GSP schemes as a political and economic determinant of the utilization of North-South FTAs. *Review of International Political Economy, 29*(5), 1420–1447.

Powell, R. (1991). Absolute and relative gains in international relations theory. *American Political Science Review, 85*(4), 1303–1320.

Priess, H. and Pitschas, C. (2000). Protection of public health and the role of the precautionary principle under WTO law: A trojan horse before Geneva's walls. *Fordham Int'l LJ, 24*, 519.

Prowse, S. (2002). The role of international and national agencies in trade–related capacity building. *World Economy, 25*(9), 1235–1261.

Prowse, S. (2006). 'Aid for Trade': A proposal for increasing support for trade adjustment and integration. *Economic Development and Multilateral Trade Cooperation, 41181*(4), 229.

Qureshi, M. G., Qayyum, U., and Ghani, E. (2021). Acemoglu, Johnson and Robinson's notion of exogenous imposition of colonial institutions onto colonies—a critique in the light of historical evidence. *Pakistan Development Review, 60*(2), 133–152.

Radelet, S. (2015). *The Great Surge: The Ascent of the Developing World.* Simon & Schuster.

Rahman, M. S. (2022). *The Clothing Curse: Institutional Causes and Political Consequences of Clothing Export Dependence in Developing Countries* (Doctoral dissertation, University of Oregon).

Rajan, R. G. and Subramanian, A. (2008). Aid and growth: What does the cross-country evidence really show? *The Review of Economics and Statistics, 90*(4), 643–665.

Rajan, R. G. and Subramanian, A. (2011). Aid, Dutch disease, and manufacturing growth. *Journal of Development Economics, 94*(1), 106–118.

Ravindranath, N. H., Sathaye, J. A., Ravindranath, N. H., and Sathaye, J. A. (2002). In *Climate Change and Developing Countries* (pp. 247–265). Springer Netherlands.

Redding, S. and Venables, A. J. (2004). Economic geography and international inequality. *Journal of International Economics, 62*(1), 53–82.

Reilly, J. (2013). China and Japan in Myanmar: Aid, natural resources and influence. *Asian Studies Review, 37*(2), 141–157.

Ricardo, D. (1821). *On the Principles of Political Economy*. London: J. Murray.

Richardson, N. R. (1976). Political compliance and US trade dominance. *American Political Science Review, 70*(4), 1098–1109.

Rickard, S. J. (2015). Compensating the losers: An examination of congressional votes on trade adjustment assistance. *International Interactions, 41*(1), 46–60.

Riddell, R. (1996). Aid dependency, in G. Edgren, R. Riddell, and R. Sobhan, eds., *Aid Dependency: Causes, Symptoms and Remedies, Project, 2015* (pp. 23–110). Swedish International Development Cooperation Agency.

Riddell, R. C. (2009). Does foreign aid work? *Doing Good or Doing Better, 47*, 47–80.

Riddell, A. and Niño-Zarazúa, M. (2016). The effectiveness of foreign aid to education: What can be learned? *International Journal of Educational Development, 48*, 23–36.

Robertson-Snape, F. (1999). Corruption, collusion and nepotism in Indonesia. *Third World Quarterly, 20*(3), 589–602.

Rodrik, D. (1997). Trade strategy, investment and exports: another look at East Asia. *Pacific Economic Review, 2*(1), 1–24.

Rodrik, D. (2000). Institutions for high-quality growth: What they are and how to acquire them. *Studies in Comparative International Development, 35*, 3–31.

Rodrik, D. (2006). Goodbye Washington consensus, hello Washington confusion? A review of the World Bank's economic growth in the 1990s: Learning from a decade of reform. *Journal of Economic Literature, 44*(4), 973–987.

Rodrik, D. (2018). Populism and the economics of globalization. *Journal of International Business Policy, 1*(1), 12–33.

Rofner, N. F. (2021). Cadmium in soil and cacao beans of Peruvian and South American origin. *Revista Facultad Nacional de Agronomia Medellin, 74*(2), 9499–9515.

Roodman, D. (2007). The anarchy of numbers: Aid, development, and cross-country empirics. *World Bank Economic Review*, 21(2), 255–277.

Rose, A. K. (2004). Do WTO members have more liberal trade policy? *Journal of International Economics, 63*(2), 209–235.

Rosenstein-Rodan, P. N. (1961). International aid for underdeveloped countries. *The Review of Economics and Statistics, 43*(2), 107–138.

Ross, M. L. (1999). The political economy of the resource curse. *World Politics, 51*(2), 297–322.

Rude, J. (2001). Under the green box—the WTO and farm subsidies. *Journal of World Trade, 35*(5), 1015–1033.

Sachs, J. D. (2001). Tropical Underdevelopment. *NBER Working Paper*, (w8119).

Sachs, J. D. (2003). Institutions Don't Rule: Direct Effects of Geography on Per Capita Income, *NBER Working Paper*, (w9490).

Sachs, J. D. (2006). *The End of Poverty: Economic Possibilities for Our Time*. Penguin.

Sahoo, P. and Bishnoi, A. (2016). Role of Japanese official development assistance in enhancing infrastructure development in India. *Contemporary South Asia, 24*(1), 50–74.

Salite, D., Kirshner, J., Cotton, M., Howe, L., Cuamba, B., Feijó, J., and Macome, A. Z. (2021). Electricity access in Mozambique: A critical policy analysis of investment, service reliability and social sustainability. *Energy Research & Social Science, 78*, 102123.

Sally, R. (2013). ASEAN FTAs: State of play and outlook for ASEAN's regional and global integration. In Das, S. B., Menon, J., Severino, R. C., and Shrestha, O. L. (Eds.) *ASEAN Economic Community*, (pp. 320–381). Degruyter.

Sanger, D. E. and Perlez, J. (2017). Trump hands the Chinese a gift: The chance for global leadership. *The New York Times*, June 1.

Sannassee, R. V., Seetanah, B., and Jugessur, J. (2014). Export-led growth hypothesis: A meta analysis. *The Journal of Developing Areas, 48*(1), 361–385.

Santeramo, F. G. and Lamonaca, E. (2019). The effects of non-tariff measures on agri-food trade: A review and meta-analysis of empirical evidence. *Journal of Agricultural Economics, 70*(3), 595–617.

Santeramo, F. G. and Lamonaca, E. (2022). Standards and regulatory cooperation in regional trade agreements: What the effects on trade? *Applied Economic Perspectives and Policy, 44*(4), 1682–1701.

Santos-Paulino, A. U. (2002). The effects of trade liberalization on imports in selected developing countries. *World Development, 30*(6), 959–974.

Savelli, E., Schwartz, K., and Ahlers, R. (2019). The Dutch aid and trade policy: Policy discourses versus development practices in the Kenyan water and sanitation sector. *Environment and Planning C: Politics and Space, 37*(6), 1126–1147.

Schattschneider, E. E. (1935). *Politics, Pressures, and the Tariff.* New York: Prentice Hall.

Schoenbaum, T. J. (2023). The Biden administration's trade policy: Promise and reality. *German Law Journal, 24*(1), 102–124.

Schou, A. (2007). Demand-driven poverty programmes and elite capture in Malawi: Between prebendalism and benevolence. *The European Journal of Development Research, 19*, 594–613.

Schraeder, P. J., Hook, S. W., and Taylor, B. (1998). Clarifying the foreign aid puzzle: A comparison of American, Japanese, French, and Swedish aid flows. *World Politics, 50*(2), 294–323.

Scott, D. (2012). US strategy in the pacific–geopolitical positioning for the twenty-first century. *Geopolitics, 17*(3), 607–628.

Seawright, J. and Gerring, J. (2008). Case selection techniques in case study research: A menu of qualitative and quantitative options. *Political Research Quarterly, 61*(2), 294–308.

Seawright, J. (2016). The case for selecting cases that are deviant or extreme on the independent variable. *Sociological Methods & Research, 45*(3), 493–525.

Shaw, D. J. (2005). Turning point in the evolution of soft financing: The United Nations and the World Bank. *Canadian Journal of Development Studies/Revue canadienne d'études du développement, 26*(1), 43–61.

Shakya, M. (2018). *Death of an Industry: The Cultural Politics of Garment Manufacturing during the Maoist Revolution in Nepal.* Cambridge University Press.

Sheppard, E. (2011). Geography, nature, and the question of development. *Dialogues in Human Geography, 1*(1), 46–75.

Simpson, M., Hawkins, T., Simpson, M., and Hawkins, T. (2018). Regime survival: Poverty creation, mass migration and elite enrichment. In M. Simpson and T. Hawkins (eds.), *The Primacy of Regime Survival: State Fragility and Economic Destruction in Zimbabwe*, 139–163. Palgrave MacMillan UK.

Singer, H. W. (1989). The 1980s: A lost decade—development in reverse? In Singer, H.W., and Sharma, S. (Eds.) *Growth and External Debt Management* (pp. 46–56). Palgrave Macmillan UK.

Smith, A. (2010). *The Wealth of Nations: An Inquiry into the Nature and Causes of the Wealth of Nations.* Harriman House Limited.

Smith, D. A. (1996). Going south: Global restructuring and garment production in three East Asian cases. *Asian Perspective, 20*(2), 211–241.

Smith, M. L. (2016). The substance and symbolism of long-distance exchange: textiles as desired trade goods in the Bronze Age Middle Asian interaction sphere. In Abraham, S. A., Gullapalli, P., Raczek, T. P., & Rizvi, U. Z (Eds.) *Connections and Complexity* (pp. 143–160). Routledge.

Smith, S. A., and Castañeda, H. (2021). Nonimmigrant others: Belonging, precarity and imperial citizenship for Chuukese migrants in Guam. *PoLAR: Political and Legal Anthropology Review, 44*(1), 138–155.

Snidal, D. (1991). Relative gains and the pattern of international cooperation. *American Political Science Review*, *85*(3), 701–726.
Söderbaum, F. (2016). Old, new, and comparative regionalism. *The Oxford Handbook of Comparative Regionalism* (pp. 16–41). Oxford University Press.
Sogge, D. (2002). *Give and Take: What's the Matter with Foreign Aid*. Zed Books.
Song, T., Brazys, S., and Vadlamannati, K. C. (2021). Which wheel gets the grease? Constituent agency and sub-national world bank aid allocation. *The Journal of Development Studies*, *57*(3), 519–533.
Squalli, J. and Wilson, K. (2011). A new measure of trade openness. *The World Economy*, *34*(10), 1745–1770.
Stein, L. (1982). Trade adjustment assistance as a means of achieving improved resource allocation through freer trade: An analysis of policies for aiding the import-injured in the US, Canada and Australia. *American Journal of Economics and Sociology*, *41*(3), 243–255.
Stiglitz, J. E. and Charlton, A. H. G. (2013). *The Right to Trade: Rethinking the Aid for Trade Agenda*. Commonwealth Secretariat.
Stock, R. (1986). 'Disease and development' or 'the underdevelopment of health': A critical review of geographical perspectives on African health problems. *Social Science & Medicine*, *23*(7), 689–700.
Stolper, W. F., and Samuelson, P. A. (1941). Protection and real wages. *The Review of Economic Studies*, *9*(1), 58–73.
Strijker, D. and Terluin, I. J. (2015). Rural protest groups in the Netherlands. In Strijker, D., Voerman, G., and Terluin, I. (Eds.) *Rural Protest Groups and Populist Political Parties* (pp. 300–325). Wageningen Academic Publishers.
Sturm, D. and Ulph, A. (2002). Environment and trade: The implications of imperfect information and political economy. *World Trade Review*, *1*(3), 235–256.
Swedlund, H. J. (2017). *The Development Dance: How Donors and Recipients Negotiate the Delivery of Foreign Aid*. Cornell University Press.
Swedlund, H. J. (2022). Narratives and negotiations in foreign aid: How post-genocide Rwanda uses narratives to influence perceptions of power. In Hampson, F. O., and Narlikar, A. (Eds.) *International Negotiation and Political Narratives* (pp. 178–193). Routledge.
Swenson, D. L. and Woo, W. T. (2019). The politics and economics of the US–China trade war. *Asian Economic Papers*, *18*(3), 1–28.
Tan, S. S. and Acharya, A. (Eds.). (2008). *Bandung Revisited: The Legacy of the 1955 Asian-African Conference for International Order*. Nus Press.
Taneja, N., Chowdhury, S., and Prakash, S. (2011). India–Nepal economic cooperation: Towards a new paradigm. *India Quarterly*, *67*(2), 129–147.
Tarp, F. (2006). Aid and development. *Swedish Economic Policy Review*, *13*, 9–61.
Teaiwa, K. (2019). No distant future: Climate change as an existential threat. *Australian Foreign Affairs*, (6), 51–70.
Thies, C. G. and Porche, S. (2007). The political economy of agricultural protection. *The Journal of Politics*, *69*(1), 116–127.
Thies, M. F. (1998). When will pork leave the farm? Institutional bias in Japan and the United States. *Legislative Studies Quarterly*, *23*(4), 467–492.
Tinbergen J. (1962). *Shaping the World Economy*. The Twentieth Century Fund, New York.
Tingley, D. (2010). Donors and domestic politics: Political influences on foreign aid effort. *The Quarterly Review of Economics and Finance*, *50*(1), 40–49.
Tobin, J. L. and Busch, M. L. (2019). The disadvantage of membership: How joining the GATT/WTO undermines GSP. *World Trade Review*, *18*(1), 133–160.
Toye, J. (2012). The world improvement plans of Fritz Schumacher. *Cambridge Journal of Economics*, *36*(2), 387–403.

Toye, R. (2003). Developing multilateralism: The Havana charter and the fight for the International Trade Organization, 1947–1948. *The International History Review, 25*(2), 282–305.

Trela, I. and Whalley, J. (1988). Do Developing Countries Lose from the Mfa? *NBER Working Paper*, (w2618).

Turner, S. (2009). Russia, China and a multipolar world order: The danger in the undefined. *Asian Perspective, 33*(1), 159–184.

Tuzin, A. H. (2009). Vietnam's eligibility to receive trade benefits under the US Generalized System of Preferences. *Loy. U. Chi. Int'l L. Rev., 7*, 193.

United Nations Conference on Trade and Development. (2019). *The Least Developed Countries Report 2019: The Present and Future of External Development Finance—Old Dependence, New Challenges*. United Nations.

United States Congress. October 1, 1975, Vol. 121, Part 24, p. 31113—Bound Edition. 94th Congress—1st Session.

United States Congress. November 19, 1975, Vol. 121, Part 29, p. 37481—Bound Edition. 94th Congress—1st Session.

United States Congress. September 13, 1977, Vol. 123, Part 23. p. 29017—Bound Edition. 95th Congress—1st Session.

United States Congress. January 26, 1994, Vol. 140, Part 1—Bound Edition. 103rd Congress—2nd Session.

United States Congress. April 28, 1994, Vol. 140, Part 6, p. 8818—Bound Edition. 103rd Congress—2nd Session.

United States Congress. June 26, 1995, Vol. 141, No. 105—Daily Edition. 104th Congress (1995–1996)—1st Session, p. H6311.

United States Congress. July 14, 2003, Vol. 149, No. 103—Daily Edition. 108th Congress (2003–2004) —1st Session.

United States Congress. August 1, 2003, Vol. 149, No. 117—Daily Edition. 108th Congress (2003–2004)—1st Session, p. S10881.

United States Congress. May 19, 2021, Vol. 167, No. 87—Daily Edition. 117th Congress (2021–2022) —1st Session.

United States International Trade Commission. (2023) *Harmonized Tariff Schedule of the United States: Annotated for Statistical Reporting Purposes*. Revision 10.

United States of America Congressional Testimony 99-9 Part I Hearing before the Subcommittee on Public Lands and National Parks, March 7, 1985, pp. 31–33.

Unnevehr, L. J. (2000). Food safety issues and fresh food product exports from LDCs. *Agricultural Economics, 23*(3), 231–240.

Vadlamannati, K. C., Brazys, S., Dukalskis, A., and Li, Y. (2023). Building bridges or breaking bonds? The Belt and Road Initiative and foreign aid competition. *Foreign Policy Analysis, 19*(3), orad015.

Van Heerden, A., Berhouet, P., and Caspari, C. (2003). *Rags or Riches? Phasing-out the Multi-Fibre Arrangement* (No. 993587893402676). International Labour Organization.

Vaughn, B. (2011). Indonesia: Domestic Politics, Strategic Dynamics, and US Interests. Congressional Research Service, Library of Congress, January.

Vijil, M., and Wagner, L. (2012). Does aid for trade enhance export performance? Investigating the infrastructure channel. *The World Economy, 35*(7), 838–868.

Viner, J. (2014). *The Customs Union Issue*. Oxford University Press.

Vollmer, B. A. (2017). The continuing shame of Europe: Discourses on migration policy in Germany and the UK. *Migration Studies, 5*(1), 49–64.

Vossen, M., van Gorp, B., and Schulpen, L. (2018). In search of the pitiful victim: A frame analysis of Dutch, Flemish and British newspapers and NGO-advertisements. *Journal of International Development, 30*(4), 643–660.

Wacziarg, R. (2002). Review of Easterly's the elusive quest for growth. *Journal of Economic Literature, 40*(3), p. 907.
Wako, H. A. (2018). Aid, institutions and economic growth in sub-Saharan Africa: Heterogeneous donors and heterogeneous responses. *Review of Development Economics, 22*(1), 23–44.
Waltz, K. N. (2010). *Theory of International Politics.* Waveland Press.
Weaver, C. (2015). The rise of China: Continuity or change in the global governance of development?. *Ethics & International Affairs, 29*(4), 419–431.
Wei, L. (2019). Towards economic decoupling? Mapping Chinese discourse on the China–US trade war. *The Chinese Journal of International Politics, 12*(4), 519–556.
Wendt, A. E. (1987). The agent-structure problem in international relations theory. *International Organization, 41*(3), 335–370.
Wendt, A. (1992). Anarchy is what states make of it: the social construction of power politics. *International Organization, 46*(2), 391–425.
Wendt, A. (1994). Collective identity formation and the international state. *American Political Science Review, 88*(2), 384–396.
Went, R. (2002). Globalization in the perspective of imperialism. *Science & Society, 66*(4), 473–497.
Whitfield, L. and Buur, L. (2014). The politics of industrial policy: Ruling elites and their alliances. *Third World Quarterly*, 35(1), 126–144.
Winters, M. S. (2012). The obstacles to foreign aid harmonization: Lessons from decentralization support in Indonesia. *Studies in Comparative International Development, 47*, 316–341.
Wittkopf, E. R. (1973). Foreign aid and United Nations votes: A comparative study. *American Political Science Review, 67*(3), 868–888.
Wood, R. E. (1986). *From Marshall Plan to Debt Crisis: Foreign Aid and Development Choices in the World Economy* (Vol. 355). University of California Press.
World Bank. (1990). Vietnam: stabilization and structural reforms. Country Operations Division, Country Department II, Asia Region, Report No. 8249-VN.
World Bank. (2005). End of MFA quotas: Key issues and strategic options for Bangladesh readymade garment industry. *Bangladesh Development Series Paper 2.*
World Bank Group, Kaufmann, D., Kraay, A., and Mastruzzi, M. (2010). *Worldwide Governance Indicators.* World Bank Group.
World Bank. (2012). *World Development Indicators 2012.* The World Bank, Washington DC.
World Bank. (2019) The World Integrated Trade Solution (WITS).
World Trade Organization. (1995). Sanitary and Phytosanitary Measures Agreement.
World Trade Organization. (1995). Technical Barriers to Trade Agreement.
World Trade Organization. (2005) Hong Kong Ministerial Declaration. WT/MIN(05) /DEC22.
Yaghmaian, B. (1989). Economic development and the determinants of third world debt. *Review of Radical Political Economics, 21*(3), 99–104.
Yakouchyk, K. (2019). Beyond autocracy promotion: A review. *Political Studies Review, 17*(2), 147–160.
Yamada, S. and Pobutsky, A. (2009). Micronesian migrant health issues in Hawaii. *Californian Journal of Health Promotion, 7*(2), 16–31.
Yang, J. (2008). An analysis of so-called export-led growth. *IMF Working Papers, 2008*(220).
Yao, D., and Whalley, J. (2015). *Assessing the Effects of the MFA/ATC from US and World Trade Data after Its Removal* (No. w21299). National Bureau of Economic Research.
Younger, S. D. (1992). Aid and the Dutch disease: macroeconomic management when everybody loves you. *World Development, 20*(11), 1587–1597.

Yu, D. (2008). The Harmonized System-Amendments and Their Impact on WTO Members' Schedules. *WTO Staff Working Paper No. ERSD-2008-02.*

Yurdakul, O., Sahındokuyucu, F., Yalcın, H., and Keyvan, E. (2019). Survey of Ochratoxin A in coffee, dried grapes and grape pekmez samples in Burdur, Turkey. *Journal of Research in Veterinary Medicine*, *38*(1), 46–51.

Zahrnt, V. (2009). For a new classification system of domestic support in the WTO agreement on agriculture. *Journal of World Trade*, *43*(6), 1325–1343.

Zappile, T. M. (2011). Nonreciprocal trade agreements and trade: Does the African Growth and Opportunity Act (AGOA) increase trade? *International Studies Perspectives*, *12*(1), 46–67.

Zieman, G. A. (2012). Participant observation. In Klein, S. (Ed.) *Action Research Methods: Plain and Simple* (pp. 49–67). Palgrave Macmillan US.

Index

Note: Tables, figures, and boxes are indicated by an italic *t*, *f*, and *b* following the page number.

For the benefit of digital users, indexed terms that span two pages (e.g., 52–53) may, on occasion, appear on only one of those pages.